MW01068264

Atlantic Bridges

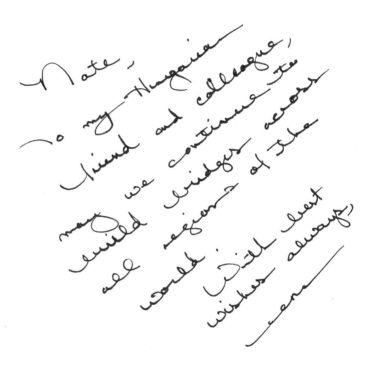

Atlantic Bridges

America's New European Allies

Janusz Bugajski
and
Ilona Teleki

Published in cooperation with the
Center for Strategic & International Studies

ROWMAN & LITTLEFIELD PUBLISHERS, INC.
Lanham • Boulder • New York • Toronto • Plymouth, United Kindom

This book is dedicated to my European brother Tadeusz.

This book is dedicated to my parents and their success at bridging the Atlantic.

ROWMAN & LITTLEFIELD PUBLISHERS, INC.

Published in the United States of America
by Rowman & Littlefield Publishers, Inc.
A wholly owned subsidiary of The Rowman & Littlefield Publishing Group, Inc.
4501 Forbes Boulevard, Suite 200, Lanham, Maryland 20706
www.rowmanlittlefield.com

Estover Road
Plymouth PL6 7PY
United Kingdom

Published in cooperation with the Center for Strategic
International Studies

Copyright © 2007 by Center for Strategic & International Studies

All rights reserved. No part of this publication may be reproduced, stored
in a retrieval system, or transmitted in any form or by any means, electronic,
mechanical, photocopying, recording, or otherwise, without the prior permission
of the publisher.

British Library Cataloguing in Publication Information Available

Library of Congress Cataloging-in-Publication Data

Bugajski, Janusz, 1954-
    Atlantic bridges : America's new European allies / Janusz Bugajski and Ilona Teleki.
    p. cm.
    Includes bibliographical references and index.
    ISBN-13: 978-0-7425-4910-4 (cloth : alk. paper)
    ISBN-13: 978-0-7425-4911-1 (pbk. : alk. paper)
    ISBN-10: 0-7425-4910-0 (cloth : alk. paper)
    ISBN-10: 0-7425-4911-9 (pbk. : alk. paper)
    1. United States—Foreign relations—Europe, Central. 2. Europe, Central—Foreign
relations—United States. 3. United States—Foreign relations—Europe, Eastern. 4.
Europe, Eastern—Foreign relations—United States. 5. United States—Foreign
relations—Former communist countries. 6. Former communist countries—Foreign
relations—United States. 7. European Union—Former communist countries. 8.
European Union—United States. 9. United States—Foreign relations—European
Union countries. I. Teleki, Ilona. II. Title.
JZ1480.A54.B84 2006
327.730437—dc22   2006019775

Printed in the United States of America

♾TM The paper used in this publication meets the minimum requirements of American
National Standard for Information Sciences—Permanence of Paper for Printed Library
Materials, ANSI/NISO Z39.48-1992.

Contents

Acknowledgments

This book is the product of a project entitled "America's New Allies," conducted by the New European Democracies Project, formerly the East European Project, at the Center for Strategic and International Studies. The authors would like to thank their team of associates and researchers comprising Besian Bocka, Rebecca Gilbert, Michael Hendley, Julie Jaffarian, William Spencer Jones, Zsofia Lukacs, Eszter Pall, David Plotz, Marta Selinger, Jane Sklenar, Natalia Soczo, Milena Staneva, William Sullivan, Nolan Theisen, Maria Toshkova, Natalie Zajicova, Dragomira Zhecheva, and Jonathan Zuk.

Abbreviations

AFD	Alliance of Free Democrats, Hungary
AFOR	Albania Force (NATO Mission)
ANC	Alliance of a New Citizen / New Citizen's Alliance, Slovakia
ASPA	American Service-Members' Protection Act
BALTBAT	Baltic Battalion
BALTDEFCOL	Baltic Defense College
BALTNET	Baltic Airspace Surveillance System
BALTRON	Baltic Naval Squadron
BALTSEA	Baltic Security Assistance Group
BMD	Ballistic Missile Defense
BPU	Bulgarian Popular Union, Bulgaria
BSP	Bulgarian Socialist Party, Bulgaria
CAP	Common Agricultural Policy
CCP	Czech Communist Party, Czech Republic
CDM	Christian Democratic Movement, Slovakia
CDP	Civic Democratic Party, Czech Republic
CDU-CPP	Christian Democratic Union–Czechoslovak People's Party, Czech Republic
CEE	Central and Eastern Europe
CENTCOM	United States Central Command
CFSP	Common Foreign and Security Policy
CIS	Commonwealth of Independent States
COMECON	Council for Mutual Economic Assistance
CP	Civic Platform, Poland
CSAT	Romanian Supreme Defense Council

CSDP	Czech Social Democratic Party, Czech Republic
DLA	Democratic Left Alliance, Poland
DP	Democratic Party, Poland
DSB	Democrats for a Strong Bulgaria, Bulgaria
DTI	Defense Transformation Initiative
EAPC	Euro-Atlantic Partnership Council
EC	European Community
EDA	European Defense Agency
EETAF	East European Task Force
ENP	European Neighborhood Policy
EOD	explosive ordnance disposal
EP	European Parliament
e-PINE	Enhanced Partnership in Northern Europe
ESDP	European Security and Defense Policy
ESS	European Security Strategy
ESTPLA	Estonian Platoon
EU	European Union
EUFOR	European Union Force
EU Force	see EUFOR
FDI	Foreign Direct Investment
FFF	For Fatherland and Freedom, Latvia
Fidesz	The Alliance of Young Democrats—Hungarian Civic Party/Union
FPL	First Party of Latvia, Latvia
FU	Freedom Union, Poland
GDP	Gross Domestic Product
GFU	Greens and Farmers' Union, Latria
GRP	Greater Romania Party, Romania
HDF	Hungarian Democratic Forum, Hungary
HDFR	Hungarian Democratic Federation of Romania, Romania
HJLP	Hungarian Justice and Life Party, Hungary
HRUL	For Human Rights in a United Latvia, Latvia
HSP	Hungarian Socialist Party, Hungary
ICC	International Criminal Court
ICJ	International Court of Justice
IFOR	Implementation Force (NATO in Bosnia-Herzegovina)
ISAF	International Security Assistance Force
KFOR	Kosova Force (NATO)
LITCON	Lithuanian Contingent
LITDET	Lithuanian Detachment

LITPOLBAT	Lithuanian–Polish Battalion
LitPo'Ukrbat	Lithuanian–Polish–Ukrainian Battalion
LJ	Law and Justice, Poland
LPF	League of Polish Families, Poland
LU	Labor Union, Poland
MCN	Multinational Corps Northeast
MDS	Movement for a Democratic Slovakia, Slovakia
MFN	Most Favored Nation
MoD	Ministry of Defense
MP	Member of Parliament
MRF	Movement for Rights and Freedom, Bulgaria
NACC	North-Atlantic Cooperation Council
NAMSA	NATO Maintenance and Supply Agency
NATO	North Atlantic Treaty Organization
NBC	anti-nuclear, biological, and chemical unit
NC3A	NATO Consultation, Command and Control Agency
NEGP	North European gas pipeline
NEI	Northern European Initiative
NGO	Nongovernmental Organization
NHP	National Harmony Party, Latvia
NMS	National Movement Simeon II, Bulgaria
NRF	NATO Response Force
OIF	Operation Iraqi Freedom
OSCE	Organization for Security and Cooperation in Europe
PCC	Prague Capabilities Commitment
PfP	Partnership for Peace
PHC	Party of the Hungarian Coalition / Hungarian Coalition, Slovakia
POLUKRBAT	Polish-Ukrainian Battalion
PP	People's Party, Latvia
PPA	Polish Popular Alliance
PPP	Polish Peasants Party, Poland
PRT	Provincial Reconstruction Team
PSDP	Polish Social Democratic Party, Poland
PSDR	Party of Social Democracy of Romania, Romania
RFE	Radio Free Europe
RHP	Romanian Humanist Party, Romania
RIS	Romanian Intelligence Service
RRF	Rapid Reaction Force
SCP	Slovak Communist Party, Slovakia
SD	Self-Defense, Poland

SD-CU	Slovak Democratic and Christian Union, Slovakia
SDP	Social Democratic Party, Romania
SDR	Strategic Defense Review
SEDM	South East Europe Defense Ministerial
SEEBRIG	Southeastern Europe Brigade
SFOR	Stabilization Force (NATO in Bosnia-Herzegovina)
SNP	Slovak National Party, Slovakia
UDF	United Democratic Forces/Union of Democratic Forces, Bulgaria
UF-DU	Union of Freedom-Democratic Union, Czech Republic
UK	United Kingdom
UN	United Nations
UNAMI	UN Assistance Mission for Iraq
UNMIK	United Nations Interim Administration Mission in Kosova
UNSC	United Nations Security Council
VOA	Voice of America
WE	West European
WEU	Western European Union
WMD	Weapons of Mass Destruction
WTO	World Trade Organization

Introduction

New Allies, New Challenges

America's new allies in central and eastern Europe (CEE) will contribute to the shaping of relations between the European Union and the United States over the coming years. The CEE states[1] confront significant challenges because they are members of both the North Atlantic Treaty Organization (NATO) and the European Union, and thus play rapidly evolving security and foreign policy roles in today's shifting transatlantic relations. Although CEE countries show many similarities, each has a distinct historical experience, foreign policy, security capability, regional position, political constellation, and domestic public perception. Moreover, the major political parties, the incumbent governments, and political opposition groups in these new European democracies offer disparate policy prescriptions for foreign policy vis-à-vis the EU and the United States.

All of the new allies in central and eastern Europe emerged after decades of communism, and they shared important domestic and foreign policy priorities as they sought to join the major international institutions. In general terms, most of the CEE states continue to view the United States as their predominant ally and most important security partner, and they are committed to further NATO and EU enlargement. Each country, however, has also developed distinct strategic interests and national priorities. The CEE region does not form a compact and unified bloc of states. Instead, a dividing line may be emerging between the wider Baltic region (including Poland) and the central European region, a line that is most evident in perceptions of instability along the eastern borders of central and eastern Europe and a sense of a growing threat from Russia. This emerging divider may be reflected in each country's intensity of commitment to active Atlanticism.[2]

Each new ally increasingly weighs its specific national interests on a range of political, security, and economic issues against the interests of its neighbors, its regional partners, the western European capitals, broader or common EU interests, and transatlantic relations. Countries that see more immediate security threats in their neighborhoods or calculate that the older EU capitals will not sufficiently defend new member states' interests tend to be more Atlanticist. They view the United States as more capable of providing political and security assistance. In some countries, similar foreign policy priorities are shared across the mainstream political spectrum. In others, a greater degree of differentiation is evident among political parties in their support of or resistance to U.S. policy. Opposition parties in particular have tried to benefit from a public mood that is not well disposed toward foreign military engagements or the perceived loss of national sovereignty.

Each of the CEE countries, much like the rest of Europe, faces novel security threats and intricate foreign policy challenges, especially given the difficulties of maintaining the cohesion of both European and transatlantic institutions. These threats range from ethnic tensions and mass migration to organized crime, international terrorism, and weapons proliferation. Some states also view the lack of political stability and international integration among their neighbors as a latent security threat whether the threat is to their own national independence, territorial integrity, diaspora rights, social stability, economic development, or investment opportunities.

In many respects, the most serious security challenge for the Atlantic Alliance is the ongoing rift between the United States and the European Union, a transatlantic relationship that is commonly depicted as competitive and conflictive. Some analysts have characterized the disparity in power between the two sides as tantamount to an unbridgeable chasm.[3] The "power gap" between the United States and the EU is a consequence of numerous factors, including military capabilities, national interests, regional priorities, differing threat perceptions, and security strategies.[4]

Since the terrorist attacks on September 11, 2001, the United States has focused more intensively on overcoming global threats and grappling with regional insecurities; during this same period the EU has been preoccupied with its own institutional enlargement and integration. Although Washington views international Islamist terrorism as the most critical national security challenge, many European states consider a spillover of Middle Eastern instability to be potentially more threatening. The United States is focused on preemptive and even preventive military action against real and potential threats while the EU has been more concerned about state sovereignty; "soft" security strategies such as peacekeeping, humanitarian operations, crisis response, and reconstruction work; and preserving the legitimacy of multinational institutions.[5]

In addition to their policy differences, both the European Union and the United States are suffering from persistent and growing weaknesses that could further divide the alliance. The EU has a capability gap with regard to its potential military dispositions while the United States has a credibility gap in terms of its potential political influence. Moreover, the EU's economic slowdown—growth of gross domestic product (GDP) for 2005 was at a mere 1.6 percent—will have long-term ramifications for its expenditure on both "hard" and "soft" security.[6]

These differences between the United States and the EU do not signal that the alliance should be discarded. Several fundamental U.S. and European interests are reconcilable, including dealing with the proliferation of weapons of mass destruction (WMD), international terrorism, regional conflict, failed states, ethnic instability, mass migration, cross-border crime, and assuring vital energy supplies. In many cases, the United States requires EU political support, military assistance, and complementarity in a host of softer security components such as law enforcement, intelligence sharing, and peacekeeping. The EU itself is eager to better coordinate foreign policy with Washington on questions that the Europeans consider central to their interests or in which they have made military and economic investments.

Beyond the tangible threats themselves, one of the major transatlantic security challenges will be to maintain sufficient alliance cohesion in tackling these threats. Although Americans and Europeans usually have similar perceptions about the most threatening security challenges, they differ markedly on how best to deal with real and potential threats.[7] In extensive public opinion surveys, it seems clear that EU citizens are less willing to support military force without the seal of multilateral institutional approval.[8] The EU countries also tend to be ambivalent concerning their global role and the costs they are willing to bear. At the same time, according to various public opinion surveys, support for strong U.S. leadership in world affairs has significantly declined since 2002.[9]

Surveys and analyses also demonstrate the EU's split personality: many Europeans would like the EU to develop into a major power fully independent of the United States, but very few would be willing to spend more on defense in order to realize such ambitions. The CEE countries have generally exhibited a more pro-United States approach than many of their western European neighbors; however, public opinion and political positions are shifting, and in several states opinions are converging with opinions in the older EU countries.

At the same time, the military imbalance between the United States and the European Union continues to grow.[10] Although defense spending among the fifteen EU members in the early 1990s stood at approximately 60 percent of the U.S. figure, by 2004 it had dipped to less than 50 percent. The annual EU defense budget amounted to $175 billion in 2004 while that of the United

States stood at $500 billion. While the United States has approximately 1.4 million soldiers, with about 400,000 available for foreign operations and capable of being deployed quickly, the twenty-five EU countries have 1.9 million personnel in the armed forces, with only around 50,000 who can be sent abroad rapidly.

The gap between the United States and the European Union in military technology has also grown precipitously in recent years. The recent inclusion of ten new EU members will not improve these disparities. Although the United Kingdom and France have embarked on their own programs of military modernization and the EU as a whole is planning to upgrade its air fleet, precision weaponry, and satellite reconnaissance, most of the EU members have not seriously or systematically modernized their armed forces.

The political and security role of the new allies can be better understood by examining current relations between the CEE states, the United States, and the major EU countries and how these have developed during the Bush presidency. Hence, one needs to ascertain whether support for U.S. foreign policy is genuinely based on shared values and long-term interests or is contingent and conditional on short-term opportunities, incentives, and pressures.

During the Iraq crisis, the CEE countries together with several western European allies in effect created an alternative EU grouping to challenge the notion that the Paris-Berlin axis speaks for Europe. Looking toward the United Kingdom as a role model, several CEE countries have sought to emulate London's position by avoiding stark choices between the United States and Europe and by successfully combining both orientations in their foreign policies.

There are five sets of questions about CEE relations with the United States in the aftermath of their EU accession that are pertinent and important.

CEE SUPPORT FOR THE UNITED STATES

How dependable is CEE political support for U.S. foreign policy in critical security arenas, whether in the campaign against international terrorism or for specific political and military missions outside the European area? Is support for the United States motivated principally by the foreign policy aims of current governments, and what is the position of the most significant parliamentary opposition? Is pro-U.S. support genuinely based on shared values and long-term interests, or is it contingent and conditional on tactical opportunities and pressures? One also needs to assess the most influential media outlets and nongovernmental organizations (NGOs) and their impact on public opinion and political debate. In the future, political leaders may be more reticent about backing of U.S. policy if their support would cause a loss of domestic popularity and legitimacy.

EFFECT OF EU MEMBERSHIP ON BILATERAL RELATIONSHIPS

Will CEE support for and solidarity with the United States endure in light of the region's inclusion in the European Union and the prospective emergence of a more coherent EU foreign and security policy? Will the new allies become "Brussified," or will Brussels become more Atlanticist as a result of EU enlargement eastward? Does support for the United States strengthen or weaken any country's regional role or position within the European Union? In the event of a slowdown in EU enlargement and possible reversals in the construction of a coherent EU foreign and security policy following the failure of the EU constitutional treaty, will the new allies focus more on their national interests than either their broader European or transatlantic interests?

EFFECT OF ANTI-AMERICANISM ON U.S. RELATIONSHIPS WITH CEE COUNTRIES

How deeply does governmental support among the new allies for either the United States or the European Union extend into public attitudes and expectations, and what is the extent and potential impact of anti-Americanism in the CEE countries? How is public opposition to foreign military missions linked with rising trends of anti-Americanism in the broader Europe? Urgently needed are more comprehensive assessments of public support for government policies that back Washington. Moreover, anti-Americanism may become a reaction to widespread perceptions in both western and eastern Europe that the CEE states have become mere vassals of Washington. In an act of apparent independence or in a demonstration of Europeanness, several CEE capitals could increase their neutrality or even opposition to U.S. policy.

FISSURES IN POLICY SOLIDARITY AMONG CEE COUNTRIES

What major differences in approach toward the transatlantic relationship are likely to emerge in the CEE capitals? What are the policy positions of the two EU aspirants—Bulgaria and Romania—now scheduled to accede to the EU in 2007? Will the foreign policy gap already evident between Poland and the Baltic region on the one side and the central European capitals on the other side widen in the coming years given the slowdown in EU integration and enlargement?

ATTEMPTS BY WASHINGTON TO MAINTAIN POLICY SOLIDARITY

How can Washington ensure that it will have dependable partners within the European Union and sufficient areas of commonality with the new allies to avoid strategic divergence on essential security questions in the years ahead? In sum, how can Washington forestall the EU from developing into a potentially competitive and even hostile international bloc?

*   *   *

Policy makers in the United States can view the European Union's ongoing internal crisis following the failure of the constitutional treaty in France and the Netherlands as either an obstacle or an opportunity. They may conclude that the Europeans proved incapable of acting together and calculate that Washington can work better bilaterally with individual European allies in a variant of divide and rule, which could prove ultimately damaging to U.S. interests by weakening the multinational alliance. Alternatively, a more sober assessment would recognize the perils of a disunited Europe for an effective U.S. policy. Indeed, the United States should look to its new and largely loyal allies in central and eastern Europe for a realistic picture of the EU's predicament.

The CEE capitals contend that disunity inside the European Union could undermine economic development and foster populism, protectionism, extremism, and nationalism across Europe and thereby make Washington's closest allies less effective and predictable partners. Euro-skepticism, or opposition to more intensive EU integration, especially in the security and foreign policy arena, does not necessarily equate with pro-Atlanticism. In addition, nationalist separatism and isolationism evident in several EU capitals may also fracture and undermine the NATO alliance and further endanger the transatlantic link. Resistance to a common EU foreign policy or limited contributions to the EU's security missions may also be mirrored in an unwillingness to participate in NATO operations. This could contribute to estranging several CEE countries from Washington, especially if nationalist or protectionist governments were to gain power.

Without a firm U.S. commitment to the wider European project, U.S. security and its global reach will also be negatively affected. The EU's failings are abundantly evident, especially in its lack of clear vision and leadership, the weakness of European identity, the embryonic nature of continental patriotism, the democratic deficit in EU decision making, including a marked distance between leaders and voters, and the limited military capabilities and power projection linked with a propensity for risk aversion in international affairs. An uncertain and disunited Europe, distracted and alienated by its internal differences, could become even more problematic for Washington.

The U.S. administration needs to ensure that it has dependable and durable partners among the CEE states in order to have more predictable and productive relations with the EU as a whole. To accomplish this strategic objective, Washington needs to focus on long-term political investments by refocusing the NATO alliance, ensuring U.S.-EU complementarity, jointly pursuing the expansion of democratic systems, rewarding its new allies, intensifying economic and social interchanges, promoting military rebasing, improving public diplomacy, defusing any current or latent controversies, and more effectively engaging emerging allies throughout central and eastern Europe. Recommendations in each of these areas are developed in the concluding chapter.

NOTES

1. In this book, the CEE states comprise Bulgaria, the Czech Republic, Estonia, Hungary, Latvia, Lithuania, Poland, Romania, Slovenia, and Slovakia.

2. David Král, "Enlarging EU Foreign Policy: The Role of New EU Member States and Candidate Countries," *Enlarged European Union and Its Foreign Policy: Issues, Challenges, Perspectives* (Prague: EUROPEUM Institute for European Policy, 2005).

3. Robert Kagan, "Power and Weakness: Why the United States and Europe See the World Differently," *Policy Review*, no. 113 (June/July 2002).

4. See Philip H. Gordon, "Bridging the Atlantic Divide: From Solidarity to Recrimination," *Foreign Affairs* 82, no. 1 (January/February 2003). Despite the political rifts, economic relations between the United States and the European Union continue to boom. For example, Europe provides 75 percent of all investment in the United States and is the biggest foreign source of U.S. jobs. U.S. business in CEE is also expanding, and by 2004 U.S. businesses had invested 60 percent more in the region ($16.6 billion) than in China ($10.3 billion); see William Drozdiak, "The North Atlantic Drift," *Foreign Affairs* 84, no. 1 (January/February 2005).

5. John Lewis Gaddis, "Grand Strategy in the Second Term," *Foreign Affairs* 84, no. 1 (January/February 2005).

6. EUROSTAT, "Real GDP Growth," epp.eurostat.cec.eu.int (accessed February 24, 2006).

7. *Transatlantic Trends 2004 Partners* (Washington, D.C.: German Marshall Fund of the United States, 2004), 3, www.transatlantictrends.org/doc/2004_english_key .pdf.

8. American Character Gets Mixed Review; U.S. Image Up Slightly, but Still Negative, 16-Nation Pew Global Attitudes Survey (Washington D.C.: Pew Research Center, Pew Global Attitudes Project, June 23, 2005).

9. *Transatlantic Trends 2005* (Washington, D.C.: German Marshall Fund of the United States, 2005), www.transatlantictrends.org/doc/TTKeyFindings2005.pdf.

10. See Alberto Alesina and Francesco Giorazzi, "More Military Spending in Europe is Needed," May 2002, http://post.economics.harvard.edu/faculty/alesina/columns/military_spending.pdf. For more details, see *Report on Allied Contributions to the Common Defense: A Report to the U.S. Congress by the Secretary of Defense*, March 2000, www.defenselink.mil/pubs/allied_contrib2000/allied2000.pdf, and *Report on Allied Contributions to the Common Defense: A Report to the U.S. Congress by the Secretary of Defense*, July 2003, www.defenselink.mil/pubs/allied_contrib2003/allied2003.pdf.

Chapter One

Strategic Choices
NATO and EU Membership

This chapter provides an assessment of the strategic dilemmas and policy choices faced by America's new allies in central and eastern Europe as they seek to balance their relations with the United States, NATO, and the European Union. It examines in detail the "inclusionist" and "exclusionist" arguments pertaining to EU integration and considers what role the new allies can play in the EU and what influences the EU and some of its older states can exert on the security and foreign policies of the CEE capitals. This chapter also explores relations between old and new allies within the EU in the context of a rapidly changing transatlantic relationship. The evolution of NATO as a credible political and security institution will also be evaluated in the context of the enlargement of the alliance, changing security priorities in the United States, and the development of a fledgling EU foreign and security policy.

The transatlantic relationship has been severely tested since the launch of the U.S.-led campaign against global terrorist networks in the fall of 2001. Major differences between the responses of Washington and the responses of some of the major western European capitals to the terrorist challenge and the subsequent Iraq crisis have revealed a more profound divergence over not only strategies and tactics for combating international terrorism and dealing with weapons of mass destruction (WMD) proliferation and rogue-state actors but also the projection of U.S. military power and the role of major international institutions.

Although Washington views much of the EU as lacking both military capability and political will, Paris and Berlin consider the United States to be a unilateralist power whose actions may actually fan the flames of international conflict. If the transatlantic relationship is allowed to drift from one crisis to another without greater diplomatic, political, and security cohesiveness, the EU might detach from U.S. policy as well as hinder Washington in its quest for global security objectives. Thus, the enlargement of the EU, if it is handled wisely by the U.S. administration, can deliver opportunities for rebuilding and strengthening the transatlantic alliance and enable the alliance to more effectively address a plethora of international threats.

With the attainment of NATO and EU membership, Europe's newest democracies in central and eastern Europe achieved the targets they set for themselves when communism collapsed and the Soviet bloc disintegrated. However, the CEE countries' redefinition of their strategic objectives for the next phase of development is only gradually emerging. The rupture in transatlantic relations has led to CEE countries envisaging themselves as bridge repairers and alliance facilitators in the coming years. Despite the rift between Washington and several western European capitals, the close CEE ties with the United States places them in a potentially valuable position. Questions remain, however, whether the CEE capitals are equipped to handle such a task, whether they will become minor players between the bigger powers, or whether they will actually exacerbate the existing divisions in the NATO alliance.

Finding answers to these questions is of particular importance for U.S. policy makers, who should avoid oversimplifying Europe's common predicament as they work to reach a fuller understanding of evolving policy perspectives toward the United States, NATO, and the European Union among Europe's restored democracies. Significant questions are looming for the U.S. administration in its ongoing global campaign against unconventional insecurities. For example: What is the depth and breadth of support for Washington among countries that entered the EU in May 2004 or that are scheduled to accede in 2007? What will be the impact of EU membership on the foreign policies and transatlantic relations of the new member countries? How, in turn, will the new members affect the EU's evolving foreign and security policies?

THE NATO ANCHOR

Throughout central and eastern Europe, NATO is still perceived as the most important guarantor of European security. Although NATO is viewed as the world's most effective military and political alliance, all CEE capitals believe that the alliance must adapt more effectively to the new global challenges with U.S. leadership. There has been a growing realization in the region that NATO cohesion is at risk and that the organization is becoming less capable, functional, and relevant to both U.S. and European strategy. Increasing doubts about NATO's efficacy and the progress of an autonomous EU security component have troubled the CEE states for two main reasons: the potential evacuation of the United States from Europe, and the potential renationalization of European security that could leave central and eastern Europe prone to new vulnerabilities and insecurities.

Since the disappearance of the Soviet military threat in the early 1990s, U.S. troop strength in Europe has declined from approximately 350,000 to approximately 100,000 while the NATO allies reduced their ground forces by some 500,000 soldiers and their assets by about 40 percent. Washington plans to scale back its presence in Europe further to approximately 50,000 to 60,000 military personnel while it expands its forces near emerging crisis zones.[1] Despite these trends, most of the CEE states have resisted any undermining of NATO by the emerging EU structure, especially in the foreign policy and security arenas. They are wary of being pulled into a conflict between Europe and the United States and having to make uncomfortable choices between NATO and the European Union. The new democracies do not want to see the development of two alliance systems or an enhanced role for Russia in its relations with the European Union. CEE governments seek instead a renewed and revived role for NATO during the next decade.

Public support for NATO membership was overwhelming in most of the CEE states, especially in those countries with a history of Russian military intervention or with a vision of permanent security through integration with the West.[2] Moscow's opposition to their NATO accession further stiffened the determination of CEE capitals to join the organization. NATO is viewed in its traditional and modern roles as ensuring the security of Europe and, in the post-9/11 setting, promoting security beyond Europe's borders. Washington itself has pushed through many of the initiatives that have transformed NATO's strategic mission from a purely defensive one into that of a security provider increasingly involved in missions outside NATO's traditional area, including the western Balkans, Afghanistan, and Iraq.[3]

Despite NATO's partial evolution, analysts concur that it has lost much of its relevance as both a military and a political institution as a result of increasing U.S. unilateralism and a U.S. focus since 9/11 on more reliable and compact "coalitions of the willing." Neoconservative influence in U.S. policy making depicted both the United Nations and NATO as insufficient instruments for decisive action, as demonstrated by their limited successes in the Balkans in the 1990s. U.S. neoconservatives viewed the EU as an obstacle to U.S. power projection, as lacking in military capacity, and with divergent policies toward international terrorists and rogue states.[4] NATO itself became a source of frustration for Washington because of its decision-making stipulations as well as its slow transformation from a territorial defense force to an alliance with usable forces overseas. Estimates made during 2004 indicate that only between 3 percent and 5 percent of NATO's 2.5 million available troops were actually deployable.[5]

CEE states concur with U.S. complaints that the European allies have failed to sufficiently restructure and re-equip their military forces to confront the new security threats effectively. At present, the EU countries possess a combined force of approximately 1.8 million troops, but only a fraction of this total can be deployed to crisis zones. The bulk of EU defense investment is devoted to personnel and infrastructure, not new equipment and research, and there is substantial duplication in efforts by member states because each capital maintains its own command structure, headquarters, logistics, training, and procurement agencies. Moreover, analysts calculate that the United States has surged ahead in the revolution in military affairs, with its increasing use of modern information and communication technologies, which has created problems in interoperability, complicated decision making in defense issues, and weakened transatlantic military cooperation.[6]

It is generally understood in central and eastern Europe that NATO needs to match its political objectives with its military capabilities while it works closely with other international institutions, including the EU. CEE states dispute the opinions of some U.S. and European commentators that NATO has outlived its purpose and should be disbanded while Europe gains its full security independence.[7] They do not see NATO as an instrument of U.S. pressure to split the EU, as an impediment to Europe developing its own security structures, or as a competitor for the EU's emerging security pillar. At the same time, they seek a more assertive vision of transatlantic security in which NATO undertakes a leading role and the North Atlantic allies act in unison.

Most of the CEE capitals would agree with the proposition that to be more effective NATO must project itself toward neighboring regions by offering close ties and eventual membership to all countries in the Balkans and the European part of the former Soviet Union. Some analysts would argue that, as the indispensable pillar of the democratic "Western project" in an increasingly interdependent world, the security and cohesion of the Atlantic community will depend on the capacity of its members to cooperate as they address problems that stem from issues outside the current NATO member area.[8]

Following the deep political rifts over Iraq, it remains doubtful whether both sides of the Atlantic are fully "ready and willing to overcome their differences and reaffirm their basic common interests in security and other relations: the essence of the NATO alliance."[9] If NATO cannot reconstitute its cohesion and the EU pursues a separate security track, NATO itself may either become superfluous or shrink into a smaller alliance with a mini-NATO emerging between the United States and its core supporters in Europe. Indeed, despite efforts to revive the organization in the war against international terrorist networks, NATO is now viewed as a marginal or supplementary player in U.S. military strategy.

The Prague summit in November 2002 proposed the creation of the NATO Response Force (NRF) to give the alliance the capability of applying force rapidly in emergency situations.[10] The NRF is planned to consist of up to 21,000 personnel drawn from the pool of European high-readiness forces capable of fighting anywhere in the world at seven to thirty days' notice. The NRF was to be launched by 2006, but its actual deployment will remain contingent on political consensus within the alliance. The troops themselves are to be drawn from the same limited pool of deployable forces as the EU's Rapid Reaction Force (RRF),[11] an arrangement that may give rise to disputes over the organization responsible for running a specific military operation. NATO needs to review its force generation and funding mechanisms and assess how these relate to long-term defense planning.[12] Some analysts are also uncertain whether NATO can be successful in the task of national and civil reconstruction or in a range of soft-security provisions. CEE officials doubt whether NATO and the EU can simultaneously develop such capabilities without undermining the effectiveness of both organizations.

In conditions of modern warfare, CEE states and the European Union as a whole need rapidly deployable forces with independent logistics and a well-trained cadre for effective involvement in peacemaking, peacekeeping, and other contemporary multinational operations.[13] Some analysts point out that many of the CEE countries are smaller but better prepared to meet the demands of new missions by either NATO or the EU because they have conducted a deep restructuring and downsizing of their militaries away from static defense postures. Moreover, the participation of most CEE countries in U.S.-led missions during the past decade has given them direct on-ground experience and enhanced their interoperability with U.S. forces. Their engagement in such operations has catalyzed necessary defense reforms, whether in terms of creating an all-volunteer and professional force, assembling constabulary-like units, and acquiring appropriate hardware for rapid deployment and self-sustainability. Nevertheless, military restructuring has proved difficult for many new NATO members because of steep budgetary costs and negative social consequences associated with military downsizing.

Although the CEE states supported Washington in its military campaigns in Afghanistan and Iraq, they were apprehensive that NATO was being tasked in a secondary role after the two combat missions were largely accomplished. Some capitals were concerned that the alliance was disregarded when Washington decided to deploy in the Middle East as the White House wanted to avoid delay and obstruction. CEE leaders expressed reservations about President Bush's "coalition of the willing" as a viable long-term mechanism for expanding the zone of security. The conditionality of this arrangement and the inherent unilateralism that it implied also risked creating countervailing coalitions that would split the Western project and undermine long-term strategic objectives of both Europe and the United States. The toolbox concept of NATO coalition building has been sharply criticized in the region because it seemed to relegate NATO and the new allies to the status of a mere technical instrument of U.S. foreign policy.

A number of other outstanding questions about NATO remain open, including changes in the command structure and the redistribution of senior command positions as the United States scales down its military presence in Europe in line with long-term Pentagon plans. Above all, however, the CEE capitals are concerned about a potential reversal in the internationalization of defense policy in Europe—NATO's major achievement—without anything effective to replace it.[14] NATO would then become another Western European Union, a European arrangement that proved ineffective and was eventually disbanded. Hence, the new allies are supportive of providing NATO with a permanent liaison office at the EU's military headquarters in Brussels. This would place some brakes on an independent EU security structure that could challenge NATO's competence and existence.

EU FOREIGN AND SECURITY POLICY

A fundamental requirement for an emerging and expanding international entity such as the European Union is its capability to develop and uphold a unified foreign policy based on a collective identity around which common interests can be defined. Title 1, Article B of the 1992 Treaty on the European Union declared an intention to assert the EU's "identity on the international scene, in particular through the implementation of a common foreign and security policy." During the 1990s the EU did develop an effective common policy of inclusion toward eight CEE aspirants. At that time, there was overall consensus that EU enlargement would generate CEE stability and prosperity and thus bring security benefits to the union as a whole.[15] A timetable was determined for the entry in 2007 of two further states, Bulgaria and Romania, in order to keep their reformist endeavors on track. Indeed, the gravitational pull of the European Union and the conditions that need to be met by each country to secure membership has been the most successful aspect of EU foreign policy for more than a decade.

Following the failure to adopt the EU's constitutional treaty, however, the debate over the EU's internal structure and ultimate spatial contours has preoccupied all member states, while the crafting of a coherent and unified external policy remains problematic and elusive. European Union members exhibit diverse positions on numerous issues; and the institution as a whole does not possess the instruments, particularly military instruments, to conduct an effective and coherent foreign and security policy. Moreover, an economic downturn within the union and the slowing down of EU enlargement as a result of internal resistance could not only make the EU less attractive for neighboring states but also undermine its ability to exercise meaningful international influence.

With the entry of eight CEE countries in May 2004 and the expectation of two more in 2007, the EU will comprise twenty-seven states with a combined population of approximately 480 million people and one-quarter of the world's GDP. However, sheer population size and economic weight in themselves do not ensure that the EU will automatically develop into an important political player on the international stage. Most analysts in fact concur that the union is underperforming despite its significant potential by remaining distracted by diverse national interests and that it is unable to convert its substantial economic power into effective political influence.

The EU's substantial enlargement eastward has added additional challenges in both its internal functioning and its external relations. New members have injected differing foreign policy perspectives into an already complex institutional and decision-making process, and it will take time to assimilate differing national priorities into union policy. In addition, any decisions on further enlargement will need to weigh the positions of the new members and the political and economic condition of new aspirants. During 2005–2006 the EU initiated accession talks with Croatia, recognized Macedonia as a candidate for membership, and launched or recommended stabilization and association agreements with several other west Balkan states, including Albania, Serbia, Montenegro, and Bosnia-Herzegovina. Without a realistic prospect and timetable for inclusion in the union, EU influence could significantly diminish in countries along its eastern and southern borders.

Two core elements of EU foreign policy decision making—process and agenda—need to be scrutinized to determine whether their impact on policy is substantive or merely symbolic. Although the EU has a number of common institutions, it does not currently possess clear-cut and authoritative executive and legislative branches. The Council of the European Union is the main decision-making body, but its responsibilities and operations in the field of foreign and security policy are still evolving. Representatives of member states meet within the council and each country is represented only by ministers responsible for specific issues agreed upon in a common agenda, whether foreign affairs, finance, social affairs, transport, or agriculture. The presidency of the council is held for six months by each EU member state on a rotational basis, thus complicating consensus building and decision making.

The European Commission consists of nationals from every member state but they are not elected. The commission's president chooses the commissioners from lists of three nominees per member state, and the list is subsequently approved by the European Parliament. The commission proposes legislation on which the European Parliament and the Council of the European Union can decide. It was created to represent interests common to all member states. Although the commission has the right to take any initiative it considers appropriate in order to attain the objectives of the various EU treaties, most proposals are responses to legal obligations, technical requirements, or to a specific request for action from another institution, a member state, or from interested parties.

The European Parliament, which is directly elected, cannot initiate laws and does not control significant resources, although several member states would like to see its authority enhanced.[16] Although the EU's constitutional treaty was intended to reinforce the union's democratic basis by giving more powers to the European Parliament, as well as to national parliaments, it has remained unclear whether this would actually enhance or undermine the development of a common foreign policy. Any consolidation of EU foreign policy in Brussels could in practice lead to conflicts with those member states that are strong advocates of an independent posture by national governments in the arena of external affairs.

Disputes are ongoing whether the European Council (heads of state of the member countries who gather four times a year at EU Summits), the Council of Ministers, the European Commission, or the European Parliament should be strengthened in determining foreign policy.[17] The larger states generally favor a stronger European Council and Council of Ministers in which state sovereignty is upheld, while many of the smaller members prefer a more effective European Commission and European Parliament. During the debate on the constitutional treaty, the CEE capitals were opposed to western European proposals for creating an EU avant-garde in the area of security and defense. The new allies helped to push through important amendments in the final draft of the mutual defense clause of the treaty that made it less competitive with NATO's Article 5 and more compatible and interconnected with NATO stipulations.[18]

The failure of the EU's constitutional treaty after its rejection in referenda by French and Dutch voters in May and June 2005 generated confusion on the future of the union's foreign and security policy. Among the constitutional stipulations that will presumably be abandoned was a longer term in office for the president of the Council of the European Union, a change generally opposed by the smaller states that calculated this would concentrate power among the larger countries and weaken the prerogatives of the European Commission and European Parliament in external affairs.

The EU's emerging foreign policy and security apparatus has exercised limited influence over the policies of individual governments. Although the European Council makes pronouncements on external affairs reflecting the consensus of the member states and provides a general framework for action by the Council of Ministers and the European Commission, member states are not bound to follow its policy directions. This relatively weak position in foreign policy is gradually changing, especially since the adoption in December 2003 of the EU's security strategy. The new CEE members were not deeply involved in its creation, however, nor in the creation of the Common Foreign and Security Policy (CFSP) that emerged from the European Political Cooperation in 1991, nor in the endorsement of the European Security and Defense Policy (ESDP) in December 2002. The ESDP basically covered civilian and military crisis management, known as the Petersburg tasks, enshrined in Article 17 of the Treaty on the European Union.[19]

CEE capitals are also debating whether to support the growth of a European foreign affairs service. Such a diplomatic corps could be beneficial to small countries and new members by increasing their representation in a unified service since they possess only limited resources to develop their own diplomatic corps. The larger and more ambitious CEE states such as Poland face a dilemma as they fear a diminution of their own sovereignty and independent foreign policy through the creation of an EU foreign ministry and a single foreign service. The smaller CEE states anticipate that a stronger CFSP with an EU foreign minister and diplomatic service might provide them with more influence than they would have as separate international actors. They would also like to see these offices attached to the European Commission rather than the Council of the European Union, within which the larger member states tend to dominate. An EU foreign service could enable the smaller capitals to cut down on their diplomatic expenditures and make better use of their most experienced diplomats.

Ultimately, if the European Union intends to play a more coherent and effective role in world affairs, its member states will need to delegate greater responsibilities to a central authority and place stricter restrictions on the rules of consensus in decision making. For the EU to operate authoritatively on the world stage, member states will need to raise defense budgets, conduct institutional reform, and establish more effective mechanisms. EU members may also need to create a defense pact among themselves, much like NATO, with mutual security guarantees, a unified command structure with streamlined decision making, and more modernized military forces:

> Without these reforms, and despite its high degree of civilian/economic cooperation, EU foreign policy may amount to little more than "social work" in the

eyes of the international community. Enhanced cooperation may not be enough
to provide a true joint operational capability for issues with a crisis/security defense dimension, especially after the next series of enlargements.[20]

The inclusion and participation of CEE countries in all EU institutions has
intensified debate about institutional arrangements, the decision-making
process, and, even more, about the EU's foreign policy agenda.[21] Although
analysts have argued that the CFSP is intended to promote a common European identity and a coordinated foreign policy, the EU's expansion may make
this objective even more difficult to attain. Given the EU's institutional and
procedural complexity, each of the new members will need to develop an effective strategy for consensus building and deal making within the EU in order to promote its own foreign policy priorities and gain support from the EU
as a whole. Simply pushing for one capital's interests without seeking agreement and consensus with other countries could invariably lead to conflict and
isolation. Success will also require reciprocal support for the distinct foreign
policy priorities of each country's closest EU partners.

To function within a coherent international entity, the EU member states
will need to agree on a concrete agenda and an implementable set of common
policies. However, while the EU foreign agenda has expanded, differences
among member states in their priorities and approaches have also widened
significantly. In particular, some of the CEE states have injected a more robust eastern dimension into all EU institutions and have pushed for more far-
reaching engagement with countries such as Ukraine, Belarus, Moldova, and
Georgia. Poland, in particular, sees itself as a bridge between the EU and the
"wider Europe" beyond the European Union's current eastern borders.

By contrast, some of the older EU countries have developed a more expansive agenda toward the Mediterranean region, are reluctant to enlarge the
EU further eastward, and are pursuing a closer engagement with Russia regardless of Moscow's restorationist domestic and foreign policies. In some
instances, this has provoked disputes between the western European and eastern European states. For example, Warsaw, Vilnius, and Riga have complained about German energy transportation arrangements with Russia that
evidently disregard and undermine the security of the CEE states.

Periodic meetings of a self-styled EU core group, essentially comprising
Germany, France, Belgium, Holland, and Luxembourg, to discuss security issues have excluded the CEE states and have been heavily criticized in central
and eastern Europe. Proposals for the creation of an EU directorate or a small
European security council have been attacked by the CEE capitals because
this would exclude their input and undermine the legitimacy of the CFSP.[22]

Many of the EU's new members contend that they are seemingly more committed than France and Germany to a joint EU foreign policy, especially toward the non-EU eastern European countries. This has raised important questions over what mechanisms and policies can be developed collectively by the EU that would enable effective decision making in dealing with longer-term foreign and security challenges.

The dispute over the precise identity of America's European partner will preoccupy experts within both NATO and the EU in the coming years. The debate could continue to divide Europe into Atlanticist and Europeanist proponents and alienate NATO states, such as Turkey and Norway that are not part of the European Union. Such internal fractures will also dent the EU's credibility as a coherent force and emerging global power and will make the European Union a less attractive partner for Washington. Some analysts have concluded that for the next decade the enlarged Europe will be engaged in a great debate between "the forces of Euro-Gaullism and Euroatlanticism. On its outcome will depend the future of the West."[23]

A major point of dispute between the United States and the EU concerns the balance between hard power and soft power. Military soft power is defined in the EU's Petersburg tasks in terms of peacekeeping, humanitarian operations, crisis response, and reconstruction work. The use of EU soft power is constrained by collective decision making and the need for member consensus and international legitimacy. Hence, the EU process itself imposes significant limitations on the projection of military power by the union.[24]

Some EU governments do not want NATO to take aboard soft-power functions as this could duplicate or undermine the EU's own efforts. Although some policy makers and analysts evidently favor a transatlantic division of labor, in reality hard and soft methods are increasingly interconnected. Although Washington needs assistance in such fields as intelligence gathering, law enforcement, peacekeeping, and economic reconstruction, the EU is dependent on U.S. military prowess in crisis situations and war fighting. Some analysts have also proposed a division of security responsibilities by regions instead of by functions, whereby the EU would focus primarily on the greater European region and the United States would have priority throughout the Middle East and Asia.[25]

CEE officials were initially suspicious after the issuing of the Saint Malo document in December 1998. This was a joint British-French initiative designed to outline the concept of an EU defense capability that could function "within or outside" the NATO framework through a separate EU chain of command. Central and eastern Europe generally supported the U.S. position that Europe's defense identity should develop within NATO and should meet the standards of the "three Ds" as outlined by U.S. secretary of state

Madeleine Albright—no duplication of NATO institutions, no decoupling of NATO from Europe, and no discrimination against non-EU members. This approach was incorporated in NATO's Washington summit communiqué in April 1999.

In practical terms, for the EU to achieve genuine independence in its security policy and fully terminate its position as a U.S.-protected region, it would need to create separate and distinct institutional and defense capabilities. This would include an all-EU chain of command and military staff and a capable all-EU military force. CEE capitals held serious doubts that such a common and effective security policy could emerge because too many deep divergences exist among the EU capitals. Furthermore, implementing such a policy would be a costly operation at a time when EU defense budgets were already allocated, overstretched, and unlikely to be raised.

None of the CEE capitals wanted to see the ESDP develop into a European defense union within the EU that would somehow "balance" the United States or NATO. Having accepted the ESDP on condition that it did not conflict with NATO's viability, CEE states pursued an arrangement that would evolve into an effective complementary structure alongside NATO and the United States.[26] Any duplication or competition between NATO and the EU in the area of security has been generally perceived negatively in the CEE region. Likewise, any moves toward a two-speed ESDP, in which a smaller group of EU members participate in deepening and separating their security structures, would be seen as the renationalization of foreign and defense policy. In this context, deep suspicions exist throughout central and eastern Europe that France in particular was intent on weakening the transatlantic link even at the cost of European unity.

Some Western analysts have warned that NATO and the U.S. connection is threatened by accelerating EU integration and an evolving EU security policy.[27] They have alerted Washington and its closest European allies to the fact that the EU constitution and other agreements explicitly create a federal national security structure superior to that of any member state and that the principle of unanimous consent may be watered down by qualified majorities in the coming years, giving France and Germany a preeminent role in foreign policy. Such developments will be closely monitored by the CEE countries, which want to avoid a major rupture within NATO, any reduction of NATO's role, domination by any single power or group of states, and any diminution of their own influence inside the European Union.

To counter the emergence of an alternative to NATO or a severely diminished alliance, the CEE capitals have also supported the construction of a European Security and Defense Identity (ESDI) within the NATO structure. This initiative was launched at the NATO Berlin ministerial meeting in June 1996, which also decided to plan for the deployment of combined joint task forces by member states within NATO's structures. The CEE capitals supported the position of Prime Minister Tony Blair of Great Britain that Europe's foreign and security policy should be shaped in close cooperation with Washington and should actually enhance U.S.-EU ties.

Each of the CEE countries seeks to preserve NATO solidarity and effectiveness and to maintain common planning and implementation. Hence, they stress the indivisibility of NATO and the EU in their security roles. They also want to be consistent in their policies in order to maintain credibility in the international arena. From their perspective, European unity is severely weakened without a strong transatlantic link, while transatlantic relations become fractured with a divided and weak EU. Above all, the CEE newcomers are seeking a stronger and more unified Europe that complements NATO and the United States and does not compete with or undermine the transatlantic connection in handling international security challenges. As members of both NATO and the EU, they want to participate constructively in the decision-making process on vital strategic issues in both institutions.

Membership in the EU, whether current or prospective, also places some obligations on members and aspiring states. For example, during negotiations within the EU on the development of the CFSP, each state committed itself to abide by the obligations stemming from Chapter V of the Treaty on the European Union, including the fulfillment of Article 11 on CFSP objectives in active support of the EU's foreign and security policy in the "spirit of loyalty and mutual solidarity." Members pledged to refrain from undertaking any actions that were deemed contrary to the interests of the European Union or likely to impair its effectiveness as a cohesive force in international relations. The EU's constitutional treaty also contains a provision for mutual defense in case of attack, similar to Article 5 of NATO's Washington Treaty.

Although most of these EU commitments are primarily declarations, do not envisage concrete actions, lack a concerted and common foreign policy toward areas such as the Middle East, and represent a compromise among member states, difficulties arise when relations with the United States are directly affected. This has on several occasions placed America's new allies in delicate and sometimes conflictive situations, as has been the case with the International Criminal Court (ICC). The EU disagreed with Washington's objective of concluding as many bilateral agreements as possible with European capitals with the aim of excluding U.S. soldiers from the jurisdiction of the court. When a country such as Bulgaria eventually acceded to the common EU position on the ICC after heated internal discussions, one negative consequence was the reported blocking of U.S. military assistance to Sofia.

An even more poignant example of disputes among allies was the position of the new allies toward the Iraq crisis in early 2003, particularly over whether a clear United Nations Security Council mandate was necessary for military action by NATO or any looser coalition. The CEE capitals were particularly concerned about Russia's veto power in the Security Council that could constrain Washington and NATO action; they were also concerned about a potential rupture with France if Paris also blocked a UN mandate. Several EU members from western Europe also resisted any out-of-area operations by NATO, while the CEE states generally supported a broader definition of alliance missions as agreed in the new Strategic Concept finalized at NATO's Washington summit in April 1999. NATO was viewed as defending allied interests and not simply allied territory.[28]

Although the EU did not reach a common stance toward Iraq vis-à-vis the United States, those CEE countries that did take a clear pro-U.S. position were sharply criticized by the French and German governments. In January 2003, three prospective EU members—Poland, Hungary, and the Czech Republic—signed an open letter together with Britain, Spain, Denmark, Italy, and Portugal supporting U.S. policy toward Iraq. In February 2003, the Vilnius 10—Albania, Bulgaria, Croatia, Estonia, Latvia, Lithuania, Macedonia, Romania, Slovakia, and Slovenia—signed a similar letter of support for U.S. military action against Baghdad.

President Jacques Chirac of France subsequently lambasted all of the CEE states for their alleged immaturity and disloyalty. Chirac called their declarations "childish" and "dangerous" and added that the CEE states "missed a great opportunity to shut up" on the subject of Iraq. Chirac specifically warned Bulgaria and Romania—the two countries scheduled to join the EU in 2007—that their signatures on the Vilnius 10 letter may have been the ultimate mistake that could cost them their future membership in the European Union. In response to the French assault, the CEE capitals grew markedly suspicious of the Franco-German position and feared a neo-Gaullist plot aimed at pushing the United States out of European affairs.[29] The controversies and mutual charges surrounding the Iraq issue led most of the CEE governments to conclude that finding compromises within the EU and between the EU and the United States was of vital importance for their long-term national security interests.

The 1999 NATO-Serbian war over Kosova had demonstrated in practice that in joint combat operations the European militaries remain hugely dependent on U.S. intelligence, planning, and air power. Although the European Security Strategy (ESS) approved by the Council of the European Union in December 2003 underscored Europe's responsibility for global security where internal and external spheres of security were believed to be indissolubly linked, the interpretation of the ESS and the broader ESDP has varied—the British view them as complementing NATO while the French emphasize the creation of separate European political and military institutions. Washington has supported ESDP where it has meant the modernization of EU capabilities but has remained wary about the potential emergence of an autonomous structure outside NATO that could deplete the alliance and push the United States out of Europe.

ESDP, as an integral part of the CFSP, has gained more tangible structures in recent years.[30] Although it was initially focused primarily on crisis management operations, ESDP acquired a political committee, a military staff, and a planning unit, and preparations were undertaken for a European corps or Rapid Reaction Force (RRF) of approximately 60,000 troops that would give the EU some military credibility. In practice, however, developing a distinct European force has proved slow and resources have been inadequate to enable the EU to conduct high-intensity and low-casualty wars.[31] Meanwhile, unlike most CEE governments, several western European EU governments have been reluctant to support the U.S.-sponsored and NATO-centered NRF because they see it as essentially a U.S. surrogate unit.

The EU's foreign policy posture has gained some institutional coherence with the nomination of Javier Solana to the post of high representative for CFSP; the creation in January 2001 of the Political and Security Committee, a body consisting of ambassadors from each EU member state; and the establishment of the European Union Military Committee, responsible for providing recommendations to the Council of the European Union. Plans have also been drawn up for the creation of a European Intelligence Agency. The sharing of civilian and military intelligence remains inadequate yet essential for developing a common threat assessment and joint security policies to combat emerging threats

All the new allies pledged their support for the ESDP's Headline Goals, the most recent of which were adopted in May 2004 by the EU defense ministers. The Headline Goals focus on an integrated EU approach, involving military and civilian capabilities, to conduct peacekeeping, crisis management, and humanitarian operations. A parallel EU Civilian Capabilities Commitments Conference, held in November 2004, elicited commitments in the areas of policing, rule of law, civilian administration, and civil protection. A civilian Headline Goal was announced to secure the interoperability and deployment of EU member state civilian resources by 2008. The Headline Goals also initiated the creation of rapidly deployable multinational battle groups based on battalion-sized forces with various support elements but without a permanent chain of command that would have duplicated the NATO structure. Several CEE capitals agreed to commit units to the battle groups, which are due to reach full operational capability after 2007.[32] Subsequently, most CEE states participated in Bosnia-Herzegovina in the EU's largest peacekeeping mission, which took over from NATO in December 2004 with 7,000 personnel.

Despite its procedural and operational progress, the EU remains distant from attaining a coherent political and military identity with a single external and security policy. It has limited ability to project common military power involving the use of force. It remains largely an assemblage of sovereign nations with wide differences in foreign policies, strategies, priorities, and capabilities. Questions continue to be raised about how the needs of equality in formulating EU decisions can be reconciled with wide disparities in the resources necessary for implementing these decisions. Burden sharing will not only remain a transatlantic issue but could also develop into an intra-European one as the EU enlarges. Disputes have also arisen over such issues as the creation of an independent European military headquarters and the degree of accountability by the ESDP to national parliaments. In the purely military realm, the EU has major structural weaknesses caused by years of neglect and underinvestment.

Most EU member states are at the end of a defense planning cycle that reflects decisions taken in 1991 and 1992 in the immediate aftermath of the Cold War. At that time defense budgets were cut between 25 percent and 35 percent while only limited reforms of force structures and capabilities were undertaken. Consequently, too many EU militaries remain based on conscription and, because they also remain committed to territorial defense, they are too static for contemporary security and defense needs. It will take a significant period of time before these countries generate a robust, projectable capability.[33]

The position of several CEE capitals has shifted on the question of CFSP and ESDP in that the new EU members see these structures as potential vehicles for defending their common interests and for preventing some of the western European capitals from acting on their narrower national objectives, as has been evident in the western European countries' cordial relations with Vladimir Putin's Russia. Much depends on how the CFSP and ESDP will operate, whether the CEE capitals are included or outvoted, and whether the national interests of the western European countries regularly gain the upper hand. Such a negative scenario could create fresh strains and conflicts within the European Union. Relations between NATO and the EU have also not been clearly defined, in both their military and political components, despite efforts to coordinate security operations under the December 2002 Berlin Plus agreement and other arrangements. Lack of clarity in this evolving relationship will continue to preoccupy both sides of the Atlantic.

In April 2003, in the wake of the Iraq War, the governments of France, Germany, Belgium, and Luxembourg proposed the creation of an autonomous military headquarters in Tuvren, Belgium, for planning and conducting EU operations without recourse to NATO assets. Some EU members harshly criticized this proposal because they felt it unnecessarily duplicated NATO military capabilities. After prolonged debate, a compromise was reached during 2003 and endorsed by the Council of the European Union whereby a small EU cell was established at NATO headquarters to improve preparations for EU operations with recourse to NATO assets. The main locus of independent EU military operations would be the national headquarters of member states. At the same time, the debate over the circumstances in which NATO as a whole would have a right of first refusal and not engage in a specific military operation was not resolved. In sum, the long-term relationship between NATO and the EU remains uncertain and unspecified.

It is too early to gauge the full impact of the second George W. Bush administration on the NATO alliance and the U.S.-EU link. The notion appears remote that President Bush, because of his alleged unilateralist approach, could become a handmaiden to the building a European superpower. After the shock of Bush's reelection in November 2004, some of the western European elites took comfort in the new cliché that the second Bush administration could be an enormous boost to European federalism. Most polls across Europe showed strong support in the U.S. presidential election for Senator John Kerry, with Poland the only European country to back Bush. With the bogeyman back with a stronger mandate, those Europeans arguing for a declaration of independence from the United States also received a boost.[34] Such sentiments were soon dissipated following two relatively successful visits by the U.S. president to Europe in February 2005 and May 2005, during which he reasserted the importance of Euro-Atlantic solidarity. Failure to approve the EU constitutional treaty during national referenda in France and Holland in May and June of 2005 further diminished the notion of Europe's emerging superpower status and counterbalance to the United States.

VIEWS OF THE EUROPEAN UNION

In public referenda the CEE countries overwhelmingly approved the EU accession treaties, even though in many states the electoral turnout was relatively low. Both before and after gaining entry into the European Union, the CEE region has shown consistent political and public support for membership, while active opposition has proved limited.[35] Slovakia registered the highest backing in May 2003, with 92 percent, and votes in several other countries approached that percentage (see table 1.1). Public opinion polls in Bulgaria and Romania—the upcoming accession countries—also

Table 1.1.   CEE Countries' Votes to Join the European Union

Country	Percentage approving accession to EU	Date of approval
Slovakia	92	May 2003
Lithuania	90	May 2003
Slovenia	90	March 2003
Hungary	84	April 2003
Czech Republic	77	June 2003
Poland	77	June 2003
Latvia	67	September 2003
Estonia	67	September 2003

Source: Eurobarometer 2003.2: Public Opinion in the Candidate Countries (European Union, July 2003), http://europa.eu.int/comm/public_opinion/archives/cceb/2003/CCEB2003.2_Full_Report_Final.pdf.

indicate strong support for the EU at 69 percent and 70 percent, respectively.[36]

One overriding question is whether support for Washington in the CEE capitals will endure in the context of EU integration, especially if a more coherent EU foreign and security policy were to develop. Will the new allies become "Brussified" or will Brussels become more Atlanticist as a result of the EU's enlargement eastward? In addition, what are the policy positions of the next two EU entrants, scheduled to accede to the EU in 2007? Broadly speaking, in the region there are two contrary views about what impact EU accession and the transatlantic divide will have on the international loyalties and security postures of the CEE states. These perceptions and prescriptions can be categorized as inclusionist and exclusionist.

Inclusionism

The inclusionist viewpoint supposes that as these consolidated new democracies move into the EU, fully adopt all EU standards, become more economically compatible, and are blended into the pan-European mainstream, their distance from the United States will accelerate. Moreover, because these states are generally demographically small and economically weak, their potential pro-U.S. influence within the EU will remain limited. In time, attitudes that oppose the United States or are neutral to the United states will probably become more prevalent among the younger generation and the new political elites who will have little memory of the importance of the United States in their country's liberation from communism and Sovietism.

In such a scenario, the CEE states will strive for an equal footing in the development of the CFSP while they uphold certain distinct foreign policy priorities. Poland and other CEE countries supported the creation of an EU foreign affairs minister in order to enhance Europe's capacity to speak with one voice on important policy issues. However, that voice may not be the one desired by Warsaw or its neighbors; instead it may be a compromise distilled among twenty-five capitals that could weaken the connection with Washington.

Although it is too early to specify the full impact of EU accession on the CEE capitals, particularly as the European Union itself is undergoing substantial changes, an emerging EU security and foreign policy could become more popular or less resistible among the new allies. This may be especially true if the CFSP calls for reduced spending on defense and little or no involvement in out-of-Europe combat operations and only occasional engagement in peacekeeping or postconflict reconstruction missions.

Many citizens in the CEE countries also aspire to extensive welfare provisions and are opposed to more substantial defense spending that could eat into their expectations for attaining higher living standards. Some fear that long-term CEE reliance on the EU's structural funds could transform these societies into aid-dependent ones and undermine the liberal economic model that has been so rigorously pursued over the past decade. Enhanced welfare provisions could also make these states more inward looking and loyal to the EU institutions rather than outward looking, entrepreneurial, and innovative in their approach.

Reinforcing this inclusionist argument is the growing frustration in central and eastern Europe with the U.S. administration because, despite its welcome words of gratitude, Washington has not reciprocated sufficiently in material and political terms for the substantial support provided by a number of CEE capitals for U.S. policy in the Middle East and elsewhere. As a consequence, some of the new members may either become loyal but minor players in the EU or contribute in a more significant way to an emerging Euro-focused and less Atlanticist security structure.

Issues such as continuing U.S. visa requirements, the unfulfilled promise of assistance with unpaid Iraqi debts, the provision of only limited contracts in Iraqi reconstruction, and limited U.S. business investment and security assistance remain sore points in much of the CEE region. Indications or perceptions that the United States will take CEE support on controversial foreign policy questions for granted may also become a political factor emboldening proponents of anti-U.S. and pro-EU sentiments and positions in the years ahead.

U.S. policy makers should be fully aware that public support in central and eastern Europe for the military mission in Iraq has been lukewarm at best throughout the Iraq operation. Even though most governments backed

Washington publicly, they closely monitored the public mood and the stance of the political opposition and the major parliamentary parties. In practice, CEE governments sometimes issued contradictory statements to placate both Washington and their own citizens, but they may find such a split stance increasingly untenable in the future and may adopt a more consensual or neutral position under a convenient EU cover.

If military operations such as the Iraq mission are considered too costly politically and as failing to bring expected tangible economic benefits, commitment and support for the United States may become increasingly strained. The conditionality of support for U.S. operations could then come to the forefront. Moreover, with regular election cycles and a more assertive public opinion that generally opposes foreign military engagements, the reliability of several new allies may come into question. Indeed, public opinion polls in a number of CEE countries have demonstrated declining support for not only the Iraq mission but also the United States in general. Although anti-war movements and public demonstrations in CEE countries have been small and marginal in comparison with western Europe, trends in public attitudes must be monitored as these countries merge more closely with their western neighbors and social expectations are increasingly reflected in government policy.

For example, with regard to support for military involvement in Iraq, fewer than 40 percent of Poles backed such a deployment in early 2005, and a majority of citizens were strongly opposed, which placed additional pressure on the already weak government in Poland.[37] Similar data have been registered in other coalition states. For example, in the Czech Republic, public opposition registered at 70 percent in April 2003 as coalition troops entered Iraq and held fairly steady so that, by March 2005, 64 percent opposed intervention in Iraq.[38] In Hungary, 54 percent of the public wanted the country's troops to return from Iraq at the end of 2004, when parliament denied an extension of the troop mandate.[39] Even in Romania, one of the staunchest allies of the United States in its Middle East policy, public support fell steadily throughout 2004 and 2005. Only 41 percent of Romanians cited in an October 2005 survey agreed with the presence of Romanian troops in Iraq.[40]

Thus, favorable views of the United States among the new allies have been diminishing during the past few years, related to what has been widely perceived as a faltering mission in Iraq and insufficient reciprocity from the United States in assisting the new democracies. For example, in Poland in 2000, 86 percent of those surveyed held a positive opinion about the United States; however, this figure dropped to 79 percent in 2002 and continued to decline to just over 50 percent in March 2003 and to less than 50 percent at the end of 2004.[41]

It will be instructive to observe how these sentiments might be exploited to their political advantage not only by ultranationalists, radical leftists, and anti-globalists but also by more mainstream political formations as the debate on the transatlantic relationship intensifies. Inclusionists may increasingly believe that support for U.S. policy contributes to European disunity and damages the interests of the new EU entrants. One important long-term debate could be whether declining support for Washington in the CEE states, if that materializes, comes about primarily as a reaction to a particular military mission or a specific U.S. presidency or as an indicator of broader and deeper political trends throughout the region.

Exclusionism

With regard to the future strategic choices of America's new allies, the counterview to inclusionism is exclusionism. Exclusionists believe that membership in the EU will serve to sharpen political disputes, economic conflicts, and social protests within the union. They believe it will become easier and more commonplace to blame Brussels for unmet aspirations and restrictive regulations and to claim that the smaller countries are drowning in the European mainstream. Some political leaders in the CEE states may maintain high popularity ratings by distancing themselves from specific EU policies. This may stall or even significantly reverse the European Union's integrationist trends.

The conflict between Poland and the European Commission over the adjustment in voting rights between the Treaty of Nice and the formulation of the EU constitution may be indicative of future disputes that could turn public opinion and political leaders against Brussels and the larger EU states. More recent frictions have included French threats to withhold EU regional funds from CEE countries that allegedly threaten French businesses by offering potential investors low tax rates. An additional complication will be the transformation of foreign policy making in central and eastern Europe, in which various domestic actors, including government ministries and agencies, will be closely engaged in the EU integration process. This may complicate decision making and lead to conflicts among member states and within various EU institutions.

Deepening EU integration may actually increase an anti-EU or an anti-Brussels mood among some new entrants and even strengthen their U.S. connection. In particular, if the European Union moves toward a more federalized or centralized structure dominated by the larger states, most CEE capitals will be staunch in their opposition. For example, President Vaclav Klaus of the Czech Republic has consistently warned against EU political harmonization and centralization that could eliminate the sovereignty of individual countries.[42] However, it is evident that most Euro-skeptics are not necessarily staunch Atlanticists. Populists, nationalists, and protectionists tend to be suspicious of both international arrangements, and they express fear of domination by both Brussels and Washington.

Apprehension about foreign control and loss of sovereignty is common-place in small states, even when xenophobia and isolationism are not pro-nounced. Countries such as Slovenia, Slovakia, and the Czech Republic that do not feel especially vulnerable to pressures from the former "Soviet space" may increasingly adopt the positions of some of their western European neigh-bors regarding the EU's eastern dimension and other foreign policy issues and could favor soft-security approaches to global threats. However, if political forces that come to the fore stress the alleged loss of national identity and state independence to EU institutions, some small CEE states may increasingly choose a form of foreign policy neutrality that will not promote either EU or U.S. interests.[43] A nationalist resurgence in several CEE countries and among western European states also cannot be discounted, whether it is based on a protectionist economic agenda, majority-minority disputes, an anti-Islamic backlash, an anti-immigrant platform, or an intrusive cross-border orientation to protect people of the same ethnicity in neighboring states.[44]

In the exclusionist variant, the impact of the CEE countries on EU deci-sions regarding external security policy may remain restricted while the larger western European states maintain their preponderant influence. Some CEE officials complain that they have only limited influence within lower levels of the bureaucratic hierarchy where more entrenched interests are at play and can delay or block inputs and decisions.[45] The smaller states, in-cluding the newcomers, seek access to the higher reaches of the EU leader-ship and fear being marginalized by the bigger powers. In their representation in EU institutions they accepted a certain degree of proportionality in, for ex-ample, the double-majority system that supplements the one country–one vote stipulation by altering the voting power of states in the Council of the European Union according to their population size. However, any long-term estrangement from the EU's emerging foreign and security policy that con-sistently neglects the inputs of the new democracies could be a major cause of rupture within the union and could stimulate pro-U.S. positions.

Instead of a blanket acceptance or rejection of EU policy, CEE interests and impact in the union are more likely to be issue specific. For example, if Russia maintains its assertiveness while the EU's security and foreign policy is per-ceived as inadequate or based on the narrower national interests of individual western European capitals that ignore the concerns of the three Baltic countries, the pro-Washington position will be fortified in Tallinn, Riga, and Vilnius. In-deed, these capitals may favor a more pronounced U.S. role in regional security and in return may even support controversial U.S. foreign policy decisions.

Poland is seeking to inject a more active eastern dimension into EU policy by supporting the political, economic, and social transformation of its eastern neighbors and extending the zone of security through NATO membership to Belarus, Ukraine, and Moldova. EU resistance to such initiatives could increasingly estrange Warsaw and enhance Poland's ties with Washington. Tight EU border controls could stand in the way of Poland's economic and trade relations with its nonaccession neighbors, and reductions in cross-border trade could bankrupt numerous small businesses in the poorer eastern regions of the CEE states.

The domestic impact of EU membership is likely to vary considerably among the countries of the region. Where economic expectations among aggrieved social sectors are unmet, isolationist and anti-EU currents may grow as disillusioned voters cast their support for populist and nationalist parties. Some longtime members of the EU have implemented measures to restrict the movement of laborers and other migrants from the new EU entrants for two years after the date of accession, with the possibility of an additional five-year transition period. Many of the new CEE member states infer that such measures signify their second-class status. When the remaining unprofitable industries are closed down in central and eastern Europe because of EU requirements, unemployment will rise, welfare benefits will diminish, and a resentful working class stratum without immediate employment prospects may increase.[46] In sum, if the new members conclude that they are receiving an unfair deal in such questions as structural funds, investment and employment opportunities, or voting rights, their Euro-skepticism may heighten.[47]

If the agricultural sector in central and eastern Europe declines as a result of EU requirements, competition, and limited subsidies, populism and protectionism could register a greater impact. If CEE entrepreneurs feel hamstrung by EU regulations, support among the emerging business class for EU deepening is likely to decline. If Brussels takes a soft position toward Moscow or disregards the positions of front-line states, diplomatic opposition could also expand. If immigration becomes a significant issue in the region, especially where it exacerbates disputes over welfare, crime, or cultural and religious assimilation, xenophobic anti-foreigner sentiments could be mobilized. Some rightist formations may increasingly mirror the policies of popular anti-immigrant counterparts in western Europe, including the Danish People's Party, Austria's Freedom Party, the Flemish Bloc in Belgium, and the National Front in France. None of the CEE states is adequately prepared, either economically or socially, for any large inflow of immigrants.

Free-market Euro-skeptics in central and eastern Europe as elsewhere complain about the EU's bureaucracy and its evident socialist tendencies that thwart market competition and stifle democratic principles. They also point to the negative impact of joining the Euro zone, which allegedly undermines national sovereignty and can restrict economic development. Socially conservative populists in central and eastern Europe believe the EU fosters immorality, anti-religiosity, anti-traditionalism, cultural corruption, and a loss of national independence.[48]

Euro-skeptics of various political stripes are deeply suspicious of the EU's ultimate objective of purportedly seeking to establish a highly centralized European superstate or a United States of Europe. Hence, almost every initiative, from the European RRF to the EU constitutional treaty, has been perceived as a step in this direction. While some Euro-skeptics seek a complete restructuring of the EU, with more powers given to national parliaments, the more radical voices call for their country's complete withdrawal from the union.

The idea of a differentiated EU—with the various EU members progressing toward integration at varying speeds—may appeal to some new members but not to others. In fact, EU members can currently adhere to or remain uninvolved in the European Monetary Union, the Schengen Agreement, and various foreign policy and defense policies. Indeed, mechanisms do exist for enhanced cooperation between a smaller number of EU states.

Nevertheless, a more concrete dual-track or two-speed Europe, with members having differing inputs in decision making, could stir political resentment and opposition in the CEE capitals. If France continues to be viewed as using the European institutions to preserve and expand its influence, this could precipitate a backlash among several states. Moreover, if Paris or Berlin pursues a supranational or federal model for the EU, a number of capitals in both western Europe and central and eastern Europe could be estranged. It would be difficult, however, for France or any other country to direct EU policy among twenty-five or more member states. Even France and Germany working in tandem will meet with problems if they seek to determine EU foreign policy; they may need to include some of the other large states such as the United Kingdom, Italy, Spain, and Poland in the process.

The failure of the EU to pass the constitutional treaty weakened France's position and created uncertainty over further EU integration and enlargement. The EU appears to lack leadership and direction, which could slow down the process of enlargement. A hiatus in further EU expansion could also alienate those CEE members that are seeking to draw their eastern and southeast European neighbors into the union in order to stabilize the wider region. If the EU is increasingly led by a combination of larger powers and behaves as a counterweight to the United States, it will also alienate many of the CEE governments that oppose a competitive transatlantic agenda. Some analysts argue that attempts in 2002–2003 by President Chirac to unite Europe around a policy of rivaling U.S. policy resulted in splitting Europe rather than simply splitting the transatlantic alliance, and it ultimately demonstrated French weakness.[49]

One cannot assume that all countries will be equally mature in handling all the stresses and strains of the EU's convulsions. In some CEE states, lingering questions remain over the permanent contours of the political system, with latent prospects for populism, nationalism, and other forms of extremism. Some ambitious politicians may swing in a nationalist or anti-minority direction if they see clear political advantage. The political culture of tolerance and compromise will continue to be tested by EU and U.S. policies and by the strains and contradictions among the allies as well as by the domestic impact of international institutional integration.

FOREIGN AND SECURITY POLICIES OF CEE COUNTRIES

The evolving foreign and security policies of the CEE countries have a western dimension in dealing with the European Union and its older member states as well as an eastern dimension involving the transitioning countries that emerged from the former Soviet Union.

Impact on the EU

Failure to approve the EU's constitutional treaty in mid-2005 foreshadowed a period of uncertainty over the future of the European Union itself. The outcome of the constitutional crisis will depend on the objectives and strategies of specific international players and their ability to operate according to coherent interstate interests. Constitutional failure and growing confusion in the EU may also generate long-term problems for any U.S. administration seeking an effective global agenda with a consistent European partner. If the ultimate objective is a united Europe with a singular foreign and security policy, such a goal has become more distant and elusive after the French and Dutch referenda in May and June 2005 that rejected the constitutional treaty. The document itself is likely to be abandoned because the consensus of all twenty-five states cannot be met, and it is highly doubtful whether any politician will be able to convince French and Dutch voters to change their views in a second plebiscite.

The defunct constitutional treaty was intended to provide more structure and impetus to EU decision making, especially in external affairs. After initial reservations about the thrust and impact of the document, the new EU members were eager to make the innovative system work. The United

Kingdom, the three Nordic states, the central Europeans, and the three Baltic countries in particular hoped the constitutional treaty would limit French pretensions to European leadership and even bolster transatlanticism in a larger union. In the future, if Paris and Berlin decide to focus on creating a smaller and tighter mini–European Union, this could marginalize and alienate many of the CEE states. The prospect of a two-speed or a two-directional Europe causes fear and insecurity among the new members because they are not closely linked with the Franco-German core and do not possess the economic power or political influence to join such an arrangement. Although some political strategists in Warsaw, Prague, and Budapest may harbor such long-term aspirations, Paris and Berlin are unlikely to accept them into their inner sanctum.

The nature and future of a "core Europe" remain uncertain. Rather than a distinct and separate political and economic unit, core Europe is more likely to remain a political axis with aspirations to a joint foreign and security policy but still largely dependent on the political identity of the governments of individual member states. For instance, a Christian Democrat government in Germany is less likely to invest political energy in developing a narrow EU axis with France and other smaller neighbors and instead may redirect Berlin's foreign policy on a more Atlanticist trajectory.

Many among the French, Dutch, and German electorates perceive the central European newcomers as contributors to the EU's problems. Central Europeans are widely depicted as threatening several basic continental comforts, including the protectionist welfare states and an EU sheltered from global insecurities and economic competitiveness. Central Europeans are also seen as the thin end of a wedge of enlargement that some predict will destroy the national identities of continental western Europeans by bringing in Turkey and Ukraine with a combined population of almost 120 million. Such perceptions have raised phobias over enlargement and even increased Euro-skepticism in western Europe. Simultaneous French opposition to enlargement and CEE influences in the European Union may in turn heighten anti-French feelings and be manifest in growing Euro-skepticism among the EU's new members.

The failed EU treaty may increase the danger of CEE exclusion from important economic and political decisions and could result in slowing CEE economic integration within the union by postponing their entry into the Schengen border agreement and the EU's monetary union. The problems of CEE countries are compounded by a shortage of trained diplomats and only limited experience in pursuing informal contacts outside of the official EU format, which is important for alliance building.

French resistance coupled with German collusion could bring the EU's enlargement project to a screeching halt. If the remaining European states—

including Albania, Belarus, Bosnia-Herzegovina, Croatia, Kosova, Macedonia, Moldova, Montenegro, Serbia, Turkey, and Ukraine—are unable to ensure their prospects for joining the western democracies in an institutional format, the EU's current borders could destabilize. In addition, if there develops a core Europe that disengages from further enlargement or seeks to insulate itself from the rest of the continent at the same time that Russia becomes more regionally assertive, much of central and eastern Europe could experience a new period of instability, disinvestment, and economic decline.

The majority of EU newcomers favor both a wider and a stronger EU that can project its influence rather than remain embroiled in its own internal problems. Many also seek an economically more liberal EU with a more open market in all arenas, including the service industry in which the new members are especially competitive, as well as limited EU interference in domestic fiscal and tax policies. After receiving lectures for more than a decade by officials in several EU capitals to open up their societies and economies, the new members are now directing this same advice at the more protectionist and isolationist westerners.

For many central Europeans, a strong EU actually means an economically liberal union committed to low taxes, minimal state interference, tight budgets, and strong economic growth. Most CEE capitals seek economic intergovernmentalism, not economic integrationism. Hence, for them the EU's constitutional failure could be a major setback if a new formula for international consensus cannot be found easily. The failure of the constitution could impede Europe-wide reforms toward a freer market and potentially terminate any unified foreign policy on matters of critical concern to CEE capitals. At the same time, CEE officials are cautious about any potential renegotiation of the EU's constitutional treaty that would move the EU closer to a statist economic model.

Thus, decisions on the EU's 2007–2013 budget were urgently needed. The current six-year budget was due to expire in 2006, and any solution required major concessions from the United Kingdom, France, and Germany. A realistic budget remained essential for further EU enlargement and for satisfying new members and major budget beneficiaries such as Poland. However, the UK's six-month presidency of the union, from July to December 2005, seemed unable to reinvigorate the EU around its economic base. Indeed, divisions were evident over Prime Minister Tony Blair's proposal for a complete overhaul of the EU budget and a renegotiation of the Common Agricultural Policy (CAP). Eventually, a compromise formula was reached whereby the United Kingdom conceded to a reduction in its annual rebate, France agreed to a review of all EU spending in 2008, and the new member states negotiated reduced aid, although higher than earlier British proposals, with relaxed rules for accessing funds.[50]

Countries with large agricultural sectors such as Poland have become increasingly dependent on CAP subsidies for their farming sectors and on structural funds for important infrastructure projects, which constrained them from fully supporting the British position on the EU budget. Warsaw tried to position itself as a mediator between the French and British positions because it supported London's stress on economic liberalization while simultaneously backing a strong cohesion policy because it benefited from the EU's agricultural and infrastructural subsidies. In this dispute, Poland also visualized itself as a natural spokesperson for the new EU members from central and eastern Europe and sought to stem a potential rise of Euro-skepticism as a consequence of the failed French and Dutch referenda and the constitutional disputes in the summer of 2005.

Several western European states have welcomed EU expansion to encompass the CEE states because enlargement could buttress their own position within the union and move the EU in a desired direction. The United Kingdom in particular has supported countries that will shift the center of gravity in the EU toward a more Atlanticist position strategically, a nonfederalist and noncentralized direction politically, and a more liberal direction economically.[51] Meanwhile, some of the smaller EU members also welcome small and medium-sized CEE states with which they can cooperate more closely in order to balance the influence of the larger powers. And countries with markets that are more open also welcomed those CEE capitals that have demonstrated their commitment to a liberal economic agenda against the corporatist and statist policies evident in Berlin and Paris. As a result of these common aspirations, the CEE capitals have developed productive bilateral relations with a number of older EU members, especially with the United Kingdom and the Nordic countries. The CEE newcomers are also supportive of further EU enlargement because they see enlargement as a practical method for securing their own borders, increasing economic opportunities, and enhancing their influence within the EU structures by bringing in closely allied states.

It would be difficult to envisage a joint grand strategy by all the CEE countries in their policies within the union. Although each CEE state will have some impact on decision making within the EU, they are likely to develop and uphold differing national interests and priorities and are unlikely to agree on all objectives. Instead of taking the measure of CEE states by their blanket impact on EU foreign and security policy, the influence of CEE capitals will need to be assessed on a case by case basis, whether the issue is EU policy toward Russia, the Balkans, the Middle East, or the Mediterranean region or concerns over EU functional policies regarding borders, security, migration, or taxation. For example, several CEE countries have been campaigning to bring Turkey and eventually Ukraine and other eastern European states into the EU fold, but they have encountered stubborn resistance from the larger western European members.

Interest groups within the EU—both western European and CEE member states—will sometimes form to push for a particular policy approach. For example, in their assertive policy toward Ukraine during the Orange Revolution at the close of 2004, several CEE capitals acted in concert and had some impact in Brussels. Other crises are likely to materialize that will give the CEE countries opportunities to work in unison. The CEE countries can also act together more effectively in longer-range coordination by convincing the EU to adopt an enhanced European Neighborhood Policy (ENP) toward the remaining eastern European states. However, the internal constitutional controversy has caused CEE capitals to fear that the EU may turn increasingly inward by focusing on its institutional capacity and become less flexible and creative in its eastern dimension.

Before the long-term impact of central and eastern Europe on EU policy can be assessed, questions need to be raised regarding CEE countries' relations with the United States. Will close ties with Washington strengthen or weaken any country's regional role or position within the European Union? The CEE states will not simply follow the U.S. lead, especially if this conflicts with their national interests inside the European Union or estranges them from Brussels and other major member states. Moreover, it does not serve U.S. interests to have compliant partners inside the EU that have little constructive input into U.S. or EU policy and little lasting influence in Brussels.

Increasing institutional complexity resulting from enlargement may in itself affect the internal cohesion, functioning, and policy consensus of the EU and have an impact on its reliability as a U.S. partner.[52] The addition of new members with diverse interests may lead to more intense struggles within the European Union and may affect EU policy in areas of particular interest to Washington, including trade, business, environment, monetary policy, and security issues.[53] For example, substantial resistance exists within the EU to the expansion of NATO's mandate beyond the European theater. France, preferring to work through the EU, has been opposed to extending the NATO role in Iraq, the Middle East more generally, and in counterterrorism operations.[54] By contrast, the CEE states tend to prefer NATO operations as this keeps the organization active and the United States engaged with its European allies.

In the security arena, some U.S. policy makers may prefer a less coherent and effective European Union that is less likely to consistently oppose U.S. foreign policy. A weak EU could serve to strengthen bilateral links with individual EU countries and enable Washington to bypass the complex EU decision-making process. The United States could thereby build more effective coalitions and supportive alliances and even play individual member states off each other to achieve its objectives. Such a position is generally opposed in the CEE capitals, which resist the nationalization of foreign and security policy and seek a strong and capable leadership in Brussels that includes CEE countries in decision making. Hence, CEE states tend to be more integrationist than intergovernmental, and they view the intergovernmental approach as more beneficial for the larger western European states. CEE leaders have calculated that it would better serve both U.S. and European interests to have a coherent and Atlanticist CFSP than a fractured EU approach that will be exploited by capitals seeking to lessen U.S. involvement in European affairs.

One vexing challenge will remain for the foreseeable future: the degree of U.S.-EU cooperation and coordination as the EU's security and foreign policy institutions continue to evolve. Despite the possibility of greater centralization in decision making, the EU lacks a sufficient capacity and a clear-cut mandate from its members to conduct a bilateral strategic relationship with the United States. This will require at the very least a tighter consensus on foreign policy and security issues among the major EU states.

Impact on Other Eastern European Countries

The CEE countries have sought to prevent any lasting divisions between themselves and the rest of eastern Europe. Barriers to political, economic, and security integration would evidently damage interstate relations, encourage Russian revanchism, and potentially destabilize a wider region. Each CEE country has supported the further eastern enlargement of both NATO and the EU in order to promote the reform process among neighbors, build productive market economies, and ensure security in countries that remain prone to instability.

Although the CEE states have attempted to construct a common EU foreign policy toward Russia, the Vladimir Putin government complains that the CEE states have infected the EU with Russophobia, thereby making it more difficult for Moscow to influence Brussels to its strategic advantage. According to Russian officials, European parliamentarians from central and eastern Europe have injected a "spirit of confrontation and intolerance toward our country" into this pan-European body.[55] The Kremlin, claiming that Baltic representatives are purposely "complicating" Russia's dialogue with the EU, has singled them out for particular criticism. At the same time, Russian officials are seeking to promote fractures in the EU by appealing to traditional partners in Paris and Berlin and complaining about the alleged dangers posed to the EU-Russia relationship by the CEE states.

In reality, the new members of the EU, especially those countries that are most prone to negative Russian influences, have contributed a dose of realism about Russia and Putin's expansionist and restorationist ambitions in eastern Europe.[56] Although these countries have been pushing for the EU to respond appropriately, in unison, and with strict conditionality to a concerted Kremlin-directed threat to redivide Europe, their approach is resisted by most of the larger western European members. For Germany and France in particular, commercial pragmatism prevails over geostrategic calculation and long-term political impact. CEE capitals, wary of any compromises with the Kremlin that will weaken the U.S. role and endanger their own security interests, have a more distrustful view of Moscow's intentions and are determined to keep contentious issues on the EU radar screen. For the CEE countries, Washington is the only credible guarantee against Russian aspirations toward Europe, whatever form these may take.

The majority of the CEE states have been firm supporters of both NATO and EU expansion eastward not only to Belarus, Ukraine, and Moldova but also to all of the Black Sea states, including those in the south Caucasus, and a greater openness to the central Asian countries. The United Kingdom and the Nordic states generally support this position. By contrast, France and Germany believe that the EU has reached its maximum practical extent, and some even contend that it has expanded too far and too fast already. CEE capitals argue that the EU's European Neighborhood Policy has been inadequate in providing the struggling democracies of eastern Europe with a sufficient incentive to reform. Some of the older EU members contend that the European Union has only limited funds available to pursue a wider Europe strategy and to offer entry to countries such as Ukraine.

CEE capitals view Russia as a priority in the EU's security policy and have watched with increasing trepidation as President Vladimir Putin has concentrated power in the Kremlin and pursued a more assertive and dominating policy toward neighboring countries. They see themselves as frontier states facing complex and growing security challenges to their east—the biggest challenge being Russia itself. CEE capitals do not support Russia's membership in the EU and NATO because they fear Russia could turn both the union and the alliance into mere political organizations devoid of meaningful defense capabilities.

The European Security Strategy (ESS), issued by the EU in December 2003, states that "the integration of acceding states increases our security but also brings the EU closer to troubled areas."[57] Moreover, the union is called upon to "promote well governed countries to the east of the EU with whom we can enjoy close and cooperative relations." Such a strategy can bring the EU into collision with Russia over its CIS neighbors especially, according to the ESS, if the EU insists on "tackling political problems" to its east because "the best protection for our security is a world of well-governed democratic states." Some EU officials also continue to press Russia to agree to crisis management rules for possible future EU-led missions in the Caucasus and Moldova and to end its border disputes with Estonia and Latvia in order to stabilize the region.

In its policy toward Russia, the EU exhibits divisions between pragmatists and realists. Pragmatists led by France and Germany are seemingly willing to overlook negative trends in Russian politics and the Kremlin's attempts to rebuild its sphere of dominance in the CIS and a zone of influence throughout central and eastern Europe. Pragmatists view Russia strategically as a growing economic partner and even as a useful counterbalance to the United States. Moscow for its part has traditionally used its direct bilateral ties with Paris and Berlin to bypass central European capitals, avoid censure by a united EU, and attempt to divide the Atlantic Alliance.

Close relations among the French, German, Italian, and Russian presidents have raised concerns in the CEE capitals over the reliability and solidarity of some EU member states. For example, President Aleksander Kwaśniewski of Poland expressed concern over the planned construction of the North European gas pipeline (NEGP) running beneath the Baltic Sea from Russia to Germany. Russian government–owned Gazprom, the world's largest gas exporter, planned to commence construction of the pipeline in 2006. Kwaśniewski has criticized the lack of involvement of all EU member states in the planning of NEGP. The governments of Poland, Belarus, Ukraine, and the three Baltic states stand to lose millions of dollars in transit fees after the pipeline is completed in 2010 and Russian gas is able to bypass their countries en route to western Europe. Although CEE leaders support diversifying energy supplies and transit routes, they fear that the NEGP project may provide opportunities for political blackmail by Moscow as the CEE states remain highly dependent on Russian energy supplies.

Russian officials are intent on deflating EU capabilities in their neighborhood. They were buoyed by the failure of the EU's constitutional treaty, and critics claimed that the EU's enlargement strategy was the cause of the problem because Brussels supposedly overestimated its absorption capacity during the accession of the CEE countries.[58] Moscow felt uneasy about the EU's eastward expansion for several reasons: Russia was excluded from the process of a united Europe, the EU brought into the union allegedly Russophobic states, and the EU encouraged Russia's Near Abroad to canvass for EU membership. Kremlin officials were likely to use the constitutional failure to encourage a halt to further enlargement, demand the EU's acknowledgement of Russia's primary responsibility in the post-Soviet states, and push for a closer link between two unions—the EU and Russia's zone of interest as Moscow defines it.

Central European realists remain suspicious of Putin's policies because of sober calculations based on contemporary policies rooted in historical experience. For them, the May 9, 2005, World War II Victory Day celebrations in Moscow were a pertinent example of Russia's approach. For the Russian elites, Victory Day was intended to display Russia's historic stature as a great power as well as raise the country's position in the current global struggle against tyranny and terrorism. In stark contrast, central Europeans believe that basing a country's stature on a soiled Soviet past will only increase suspicion and distrust over Russia's current policies and future objectives. Unless Moscow openly acknowledges the role that Soviet leaders played in Europe's destruction and division in the past, CEE countries will find it difficult to envisage how Russia can contribute to Europe's reconstruction and unification in the future.

Pragmatists in western Europe have criticized the new CEE members for their alleged Russophobia and for seeking to shift EU foreign policy toward Russia in a more assertive and aggressive manner. CEE representatives and their publics often perceive western European members of the EU as appeasers of Russia, while western Europeans view CEE members as too hostile toward Moscow.[59] CEE capitals may increasingly challenge and even confront the western European states to take a tougher stance in defense of their interests vis-à-vis Moscow and not engage in narrow national agendas and limited self-interest at the expense of the EU as a whole. On the other hand, perceptions in the EU of alleged CEE Russophobia could isolate CEE countries from some of the older EU members and may become an additional challenge to constructing a common EU foreign and security policy.

The new members and other realists remain concerned that the EU has no common or effective foreign policy toward Ukraine, Belarus, Moldova, Georgia, and Russia and that such disunity and lack of clarity can be manipulated by Moscow to its advantage. Germany, France, and Italy in particular seek to maintain strong bilateral ties with Russia; if it comes to a more serious confrontation, they may not wish to jeopardize these relations for the sake of Ukraine or any other regional issue. Indeed, several CEE capitals complain that the EU as a whole has failed to condemn persistent Russian pressures against the three Baltic states despite the fact that they are now part of the European Union. Moscow refuses to accept the Baltic countries as fully sovereign, and the EU acts as if they are unimportant peripheries. None of these countries wants to be perceived as a zone of any neighboring state.

In March 2003, the European Commission issued its communication on a wider Europe that laid the foundations for the EU's ENP toward nearby countries.[60] The EU has treated the CIS countries differently from the western Balkan states, which were given the prospect of joining the EU through stabilization and association agreements provided they fulfilled the membership criteria stipulated by the Copenhagen European Council in 1993. The ENP did not offer the prospect of EU membership to the remaining East European states; instead, these countries other than Russia would be involved in ENP action plans.[61] Each was required to make commitments that could be monitored; if reforms were successfully completed, the EU would engage them in its networks and programs and negotiate closer agreements. The ENP also lacked a strong regional or multilateral component that could strengthen regional security.[62] Without more effective incentives, such as the prospect of eventual EU membership, the ENP is in danger of losing its momentum as a mechanism for promoting economic and structural reform.

CEE capitals have argued that the EU needs to provide Ukraine, Belarus, Moldova, and Georgia with a clearer and more hopeful message that the European Union would remain open to new members. If the EU neglects this, CEE countries have argued, commitment to reform will gradually dissipate in the three countries and they will either remain in an unstable gray area or succumb to overwhelming Russian influence and reenter Moscow's orbit. CEE countries point out that, in contrast, NATO membership has remained open to these capitals provided that they fulfill various criteria for reform through which they could graduate from the Partnership for Peace (PfP) programs to Membership Action Plans (MAPs) over a number of years.

To CEE leaders it often appears that close personal relations between several EU heads of state and President Putin drive EU policy toward Russia. The persistence of close bilateral links between a number of western European capitals and Moscow at the expense of the CEE countries could raise the level of Euro-skepticism among the new allies and generate rifts in other areas of EU policy. CEE officials seek to discourage a passive EU approach toward Russia and any EU neglect of the democratic aspirations of residents in neighboring countries. In stark contrast, the larger EU capitals seem hesitant to offer any realistic prospect of EU membership to the East European states as they evidently consider them as lying within the zone of Russian strategic interests and fear that a policy of inclusion would lead to a deterioration of relations with Moscow.

Russian authorities certainly do not welcome an assertive eastern policy by Brussels and have sought to weaken any common front by exploiting Russia's bilateral ties with individual EU capitals. Division among EU members in their policies toward Moscow has been evident. Some of the traditional members call for a strategic partnership with Russia, but many of the new entrants view this as a strategic error that would gain the Kremlin unwarranted influence in EU policymaking, especially in the foreign and security dimension, and diminish their own national interests.

Poland, the largest country to join the EU in 2004, has tried to pursue a distinct foreign policy agenda in Brussels, especially its goal of achieving a special status in the EU for Ukraine, Belarus, and Moldova, with the prospect of future membership.[63] The Polish government considers itself a spokesperson for Ukraine's integration into the EU and NATO because it believes that only such a policy can bring stability to Europe's eastern flank.

The upheaval in Ukraine at the close of 2004 highlighted the concerns of CEE neighbors and the evident inadequacy of the EU's good-neighbor policy toward the nearby eastern European states. A Polish member of the European Parliament, Jerzy Buzek, and other CEE delegates led calls in the parliament for the EU to dispatch a high-level delegation to Ukraine during the election crisis in November–December 2004. The European Parliament's resolution against the manipulation of elections by the Leonid Kuchma regime in November 2004 was initiated and pushed through by the new member states. Poland's Foreign Minister Włodzimierz Cimoszewicz of Poland in late 2004 acknowledged that the EU's relatively fast decision making helped defuse the election standoff and attributed this effectiveness to the role of the new CEE members.[64]

The Polish first deputy foreign minister, Jan Truszczynski, stated that Warsaw would use its influence in the EU to push Brussels toward deeper engagement with Moldova on the Transnistria standoff and to resolve the dispute over the separatist area under the auspices of the action plan signed by Brussels and Chisinau in April 2005. Truszczynski also asserted that deploying international monitors on the Transnistrian part of the Moldova-Ukraine border could pave the way toward a lasting settlement of the conflict in the breakaway region.[65]

Polish analysts continue to express anxiety that, while Russia intensifies its efforts at reimperialization, Warsaw's EU partners will be seeking to convince the Poles that there is nothing to worry about.[66] Brussels has placed Ukraine on a par with other neighbor states in the eastern Mediterranean and North Africa and has thereby frustrated both Warsaw and Kyiv. Poland believes that if Ukraine was convinced of the prospect of EU inclusion, its domestic reform process would be significantly stimulated. Without such a prospect, Ukraine's pursuit of structural reform could be jeopardized. Indeed, the enduring commitment to EU and NATO accession of the new coalition government will be a litmus test for the effectiveness of both international organizations.

In the meantime, Poland has also tried to pull Germany into a more forthright policy toward Ukraine, and Poland's support for Germany's permanent membership of the UN Security Council may depend on Germany's support for a more coherent eastern policy by the EU. Poland sees Ukrainian independence and democracy as a critical counterbalance to Russian neoimperialism and authoritarianism. The Polish view is not shared wholeheartedly by

Berlin, which wants to see the EU's eastern border more tightly sealed and does not envisage an early prospect of Ukrainian membership.[67] Polish campaigning on the Ukrainian predicament caused Warsaw and Berlin in October 2004 to finally issue a joint declaration confirming "Ukraine's European aspirations" and the "huge role it plays in European security" while calling upon the EU as a whole to recognize the country as a "key neighbor" with a market economy and to establish a free trade zone with Kyiv.[68] Despite its assertiveness, Warsaw needs to be careful lest it is perceived as neglecting the foreign policy priorities of its major EU partners in western Europe, and some reciprocation and compromises will be necessary. Warsaw will need to offer support to the older EU members in return for their backing for Poland's eastern dimension.

In addition, the various CEE countries have taken divergent approaches toward their eastern neighbors. Although the Baltic states took a prominent stance regarding Kyiv during the election crisis in November–December 2004—President Valdas Adamkus of Lithuania involved himself directly in mediation efforts in Kyiv and Foreign Minister Artis Pabriks of Latvia called for a common CEE approach that could pressure the EU to take a more active eastern role—in Hungary and the Czech Republic the official position toward the Ukrainian crisis was more circumspect. CEE countries, through various EU institutions and initiatives, will have further opportunities to become more intensively involved with their eastern neighbors. For example, the prospect of an EU foreign service raises the possibility of diplomatic posts in Moscow, Kyiv, and Minsk in which the CEE countries will be keenly interested.

NOTES

1. Vince Crawley, "European Command Eyes Shifts to Bulgaria, Azerbaijan, Uganda," *Army Times*, November 22, 2004; see also Mike Allen and Thomas E. Ricks, "U.S. to Cut Forces in Europe, Asia," *Washington Post*, August 14, 2004.

2. Tatiana Kostadinova, "East European Public Support for NATO Membership Fears and Aspirations," *Journal of Peace Research* 37, no. 2 (2000): 235–49.

3. R. Nicholas Burns, "The War on Terror is NATO's New Focus," *International Herald Tribune*, October 6, 2004. Burns was the U.S. ambassador to NATO when this article was published.

4. Stefan Halper and Jonathan Clarke, *America Alone: The Neo-Conservatives and the Global Order* (New York: Cambridge University Press, 2004), 94–98.

5. Because only 3 to 5 percent of NATO's 2.5 million available troops were deployable in 2004, U.S. frustration has been rising with the slow transformation of NATO's Cold War territorial defense forces to usable forces; see Jeffrey Simon,

NATO Expeditionary Operations: Impacts upon New Members and Partners, Occasional Paper no. 1 (Washington, D.C.: National Defense University Press, 2005), 39. Also available online at www.ndu.edu/inss/Occassional_Papers/ SIMON_OP_032005.pdf.

6. Burkard Schmitt, "European Capabilities: How Many Divisions?" in *EU Security and Defence Policy: The First Five Years (1999–2004)*, ed. Nicole Gnesotto (Paris: European Union, Institute for Security Studies, 2004), 89–110.

7. Among the anti-NATO commentaries, see Jonathan Steele, "NATO is a Threat to Europe and Must Be Disbanded," *The Guardian*, November 8, 2004.

8. Edward A. Kolodziej, "Introduction: NATO and the Longue Duree," in *Almost NATO: Partners and Players in Central and Eastern European Security*, ed. Charles Krupnick (Lanham, MD: Rowman & Littlefield, 2003), 4.

9. Robert E. Hunter, "A Forward-Looking Partnership: NATO and the Future of Alliances," *Foreign Affairs* 85, no. 5 (September/October 2004): 14.

10. "Prague Summit Declaration," NATO, November 2002, www.nato.int/docu/ pr/2002/p02-127e.htm; "The Future of the NATO Response Force" (text of video teleconference, NATO, January 22, 2004), www.nato.int/docu/speech/2004/s040122a .htm.

11. The European Union has also set up a Rapid Reaction Mechanism, an emergency fund for quick response to crisis anywhere in the world, comprising technical teams for mine clearing, mediation, police training, election monitoring, and strengthening civilian administrations.

12. Mark Joyce, "NATO Must Decide How to Use Its Response Force," *Financial Times*, April 21, 2005.

13. Jeffrey Simon, *NATO Expeditionary Operations*, 1.

14. Janusz Onyszkiewicz, "The Central Issue for NATO," *Baltic Defence Review* 1, no. 11 (2004): 94.

15. For a valuable analysis of the EU's positive impact on domestic political developments in the CEE states through "active leverage" after the decision had been made to bring them into the union, see Milada Anna Vachudova, *Europe Undivided: Democracy, Leverage, and Integration after Communism* (Oxford: Oxford University Press, 2005). A similar case can be made for NATO membership.

16. Kalypso Nicolaidis, "We, the Peoples of Europe...," *Foreign Affairs* 83, no. 6 (November/December 2004).

17. A thorough overview of EU institutions can be found in John Van Oudenaren, *Uniting Europe: An Introduction to the European Union*, 2nd ed. (Lanham, MD: Rowman & Littlefield, 2005).

18. David Král, "Enlarging EU Foreign Policy," 7.

19. "Common Foreign and Security Policy: An Introduction," European Union, February 2002, www.europa.eu.int/scadplus/leg/en/lvb/r00001.htm#a19004.

20. Michael E. Smith, *Europe's Foreign and Security Policy: The Institutionalization of Cooperation* (Cambridge: Cambridge University Press, 2004), 253.

21. For a detailed analysis of CEE accession to the European Union, see Karen E. Smith, *The Making of EU Foreign Policy: The Case of Eastern Europe*, 2nd ed. (New York: Palgrave Macmillan, 2004).

22. Simon Duke, "The Enlarged EU and the CFSP," Reports and Analyses no. 2/04/A (2004), Center for International Relations, Warsaw, 5–6, www.csm.org.pl/en/files/raports/2004/rap_i_an_0204a.pdf.

23. Timothy Garton Ash, *Free World: America, Europe, and the Surprising Future of the West* (New York: Random House, 2004), 50.

24. Hanns W. Maull, "Europe and the New Balance of Global Order," *International Affairs* 81, no. 4 (July 2005): 781.

25. Dominique Moisi, "Whither the West?" *Foreign Affairs* 82, no. 6 (November/December 2003).

26. Antonio Missiroli, "Central Europe between the EU and NATO," *Survival* 46, no. 4 (Winter 2004–2005): 121–36.

27. Jeffrey L. Cimbalo, "Saving NATO From Europe," *Foreign Affairs* 83, no. 6 (November/December 2004).

28. Peter W. Rodman, "Drifting Apart? Trends in US-European Relations," (Program Brief, vol. 5, no. 21, Nixon Center, Washington, D.C., June 1999), 42, www.nixoncenter.org/publications/Program%20Briefs/vol5no21drift.htm.

29. Jiri Sedivy and Marcin Zaborowski, "Old Europe, New Europe and Transatlantic Relations," *European Security* 13, no. 3 (Autumn 2004): 207.

30. For details see Nicole Gnesotto, "Introduction, ESDP: Results and Prospects," in *EU Security and Defence Policy: The First Five Years (1999–2004)* (Paris: European Union, Institute for Security Studies, 2004), 11–31. Also available online at http://ue.eu.int/uedocs/cmsUpload/EU%20Security%20and%20Defence-the%20first%20five%20years.pdf.

31. Andrew Moravcsik, "Striking a New Transatlantic Bargain: Back on Track," *Foreign Affairs* 82, no. 4 (July/August 2004).

32. Niels Aadal Rasmussen, "The EU Enlargement Eastwards and the ESDP," DIIS Report no. 2005:7 (Copenhagen: Danish Institute for International Studies, April 2005), 24–25, www.diis.dk/graphics/Publications/Reports2005/nra_eu_eastwards_web.pdf. In addition, at the Military Capabilities Commitments Conference in November 2004, the Czech Republic committed to form a battle group with Germany and Austria, Hungary committed to form one with Italy and Slovenia, and Poland and Slovakia committed to form one with Germany, Lithuania, and Latvia.

33. Julian Lindley-French and Franco Algieri, *A European Defence Strategy* (Gütersloh, Germany: Bertelsmann Foundation, May 2004), 34, www.cap.lmu.de/download/2004/2004_Venusberg_Report.pdf. The authors also point out that the European Union lacks a single strategic concept and has failed to establish a fully functioning European RRF consisting of 60,000 troops, which was due to be ready by 2003. The EU's fundamental problem is the usability of its forces: of the 1.7 million people in uniform, only 170,000 (10 percent) are militarily usable and fewer than 50,000 can be deployed for peacekeeping missions and combat operations.

34. *Economist*, November 11, 2004.

35. Eurobarometer 2003.2: Public Opinion in the Candidate Countries (European Union, July 2003), europa.eu.int/comm/public_opinion/archives/cceb/2003/CCEB2003.2_Full_Report_Final.pdf.

36. For public opinion data on Romania, see Sever Voinescu and Gabriela Dobre, *Public Perceptions on Foreign Affairs in Romania* (Bucharest: Institute for Public Policy, October 2005), www.ipp.ro/altemateriale/IPP%20foreign%20policy%20poll.pdf. For Bulgaria, see "Poll Shows Nearly 70 Percent of Bulgarians Support EU Entry," *BTA Sofia*, March 31, 2005 (access via BBC Monitoring, International Newswire).

37. "Skutki Zaangazowania Polski W Iraku" [Effects of Polish Involvement in Iraq], Komunikat z Badan (Warsaw: Centrum Badania Opinii Spolecznej [Public Opinion Research Center], January 2005), www.cbos.pl.

38. John Springford, "'Old' and 'New' Europeans United: Public Attitudes towards the Iraq War and U.S. Foreign Policy," (Background Brief, London: Centre for European Reform London, 2003), 3, www.cer.org.uk/pdf/back_brief_springford_dec03.pdf, references a poll conducted by the Public Opinion Research Center of the Institute of Sociology of the Czech Academy of Sciences (CVVM); "Two-Thirds of Czechs Disapprove of Iraq War—Poll," Czech News Agency, March 18, 2005.

39. "Hungarian Troops to Leave Iraq," *New York Times*, November 16, 2004.

40. Voinescu and Dobre, *Public Perceptions on Foreign Affairs in Romania*, 26.

41. "The Poles about the U.S. Presidential Election" (Warsaw: Centrum Badania Opinii Spolecznej [Public Opinion Research Center], September 2004), www.cbos.pl.

42. Vaclav Klaus, "Why Europe Must Reject Centralisation," *Financial Times* (Europe), August 30, 2005.

43. A useful discussion of the fear of EU absorption, the preservation of ethnic identity, and the dynamism of multiple identities in Slovenia can be found in Ales Debeljak, *The Hidden Handshake: National Identity and Europe in the Post-Communist World* (Lanham, MD: Rowman & Littlefield, 2004).

44. For a valuable analysis of new manifestations of nationalism in the European Union, see Zsuzsa Csergő and James M. Goldgeier, "Nationalist Strategies and European Integration," *Perspectives on Politics* 2, no. 1 (March 2004): 1–17.

45. Lithuanian officials from the Ministry of Foreign Affairs and the Ministry of Defense, interviewed by the authors, Vilnius, May 2005. See also Tomas Valašek, "New EU Members in Europe's Security Policy," *Cambridge Review of International Affairs* 18, no. 2 (July 2005): 217–28.

46. John P. Hardt, "European Union Accession, May 2004: A Mixed Blessing," *Newsnet* 44, no. 5 (October 2004): 3.

47. Attila Ágh, "Smaller and Bigger States in the EU25: The Eastern Enlargement and Decision-Making in the EU," *Perspectives* 21 (Winter 2003/2004): 5–26.

48. For a valuable study of central European political populism, see Kai-Olaf Lang "Populism in Central and Eastern Europe: A Threat to Democracy or Just Political Folklore?" *Slovak Foreign Policy Affairs* 6, no. 1 (Spring 2005).

49. Ash, *Free World*, 82.

50. Ahto Lobjakas, "EU: Budget Deal Allows Consolidation of Enlargement," Radio Free Europe/Radio Liberty, December 17, 2005. The new member states are due to receive more than €100 billion in aid. Out of that sum, Poland alone will receive nearly €60 billion. See also *BBC News*, "Key Points of the EU Budget Deal," December 17, 2005, news.bbc.co.uk/2/hi/europe/4537912.stm.

51. Officials of the British Foreign and Commonwealth Office, interviewed by the authors, London, March 2005.

52. Michael J. Baun, "EU Enlargement and the Acquis Communautaire: Consequences for Transatlantic Relations," AICGS/DAAD Working Paper Series (Washington, D.C.: Johns Hopkins University, American Institute for Contemporary German Studies, 2002), www.aicgs.org/Publications/PDF/baun_daad.pdf.

53. U.S. companies will seek sufficient protection from any adverse effects on tariffs and trade from EU enlargement. Enlargement may also create new opportunities for U.S. investors because of the creation of a more unified European market that could eliminate regulations that disadvantage U.S. businesses in comparison with their EU competitors operating in the CEE candidate states.

54. William Drozdiak, Geoffrey Kemp, Flynt L. Leverett, Christopher J. Makins, and Bruce Stokes, "Partners in Frustration: Europe, the United States and the Broader Middle East," Policy Paper (Washington, D.C.: Atlantic Council of the United States, September 2004): 24.

55. See the interview with Sergey Yastrzembsky, President Putin's special representative for relations with the European Union, by Natalya Melikova, "These People Have Brought a Spirit of Primitive Russophobia to the EU," *Nezavisimaya Gazeta*, November 17, 2004.

56. Janusz Bugajski, *Cold Peace: Russia's New Imperialism* (Westport, CT: Praeger/CSIS, 2004).

57. A Secure Europe in a Better World (Paris: European Union, Institute for Security Studies, December 2003).

58. Igor Torbakov, "Russian Political Thinkers Join the Debate on Europe," *Eurasia Daily Monitor*, no. 123 (June 24, 2005), http://www.jamestown.org/edm/article.php?article_id=2369936.

59. Toomas Hendrik Ilves, "The Pleiades Join the Stars: Transatlanticism and Eastern Enlargement," *Cambridge Review of International Affairs* 18, no. 2 (July 2005): 191–202. Ilves is a former Estonian foreign minister and a member of the Foreign Affairs Committee of the European Parliament.

60. "Wider Europe—Neighbourhood: A Framework for Relations with Our Eastern and Southern Neighbours" (Brussels: Commission of the European Communities, 2003), europa.eu.int/comm/world/enp/pdf/com03_104_en.pdf.

61. Dzintra Bungs, "The EU and NATO, Their Policies toward Neighbouring Countries, Especially Countries of Central Europe, the South Caucasus, and the Russian Federation," in *An Enlarged Europe and Its Neighborhood Policy: The Eastern Dimension*, ed. Atis Lejins (Riga: Latvian Institute of International Affairs, 2004), 6–28, www.lai.lv/Kopaa_ANG.html. In 2004, Ukraine and Moldova received action plans within the ENP framework, but Belarus was not involved in the process because of its authoritarian regime.

62. Karen E. Smith, "The Outsiders: The European Neighborhood Policy," *International Affairs* 81, no. 4 (July 2005): 757–73.

63. Judy Dempsey, "EU Urged to Devise New Track; Neighbors See Need for Kiev Incentives," *International Herald Tribune*, November 23, 2004.

64. Breffni O'Rourke, "Poland Says Ukraine Crisis Proves Merit of EU's New Eastern Members," Radio Free Europe/Radio Liberty, December 10, 2004.

65. *RFE/RL Newsline* 9, no. 81, part 2, April 29, 2005.

66. "Empire Strikes Back: Top Analysts Discuss West's and Poland's Policy toward Ukraine and Russia," *Rzeczpospolita*, November 6, 2004.

67. "Daily Views Polish-German Differences over 'Initiative for Ukraine,'" *Rzeczpospolita*, November 12, 2004.

68. "Poland, Germany Seek EU Recognition for Ukraine as 'Key Neighbor,'" *Rzeczpospolita*, October 12, 2004.

Chapter Two

Transatlantic Connections

The end of superpower bipolarity between the United States and the Soviet Union ensured that during the 1990s the United States became the sole preeminent military power and security provider on the international stage. Its new status enabled Washington to act unilaterally in any military mission in almost any part of the globe. At the same time, since the end of the Cold War the European Union has emerged as a distinct international entity and a political organism that has consolidated its economic cohesiveness. Moreover, because the EU no longer needed Washington to provide a security umbrella against a conventional danger, the United States could increasingly focus on other regions where its political and economic interests were deemed to be most threatened. These developments, coupled with the emergence of a global unconventional radical Islamist terrorist threat, the danger of weapons of mass destruction (WMD) proliferation to authoritarian or unstable states or to nonstate aggressors, and differing perspectives on how to respond effectively to these challenges, have generated disputes within NATO. Although the Central and East European (CEE) states were the beneficiaries of the end of bipolarity, after freeing themselves from Moscow's control they soon became entangled in a growing transatlantic rift.

AMERICAN TIES

CEE views of the United States have been shaped primarily by the Cold War and its immediate aftermath. The United States was seen throughout the region as the bulwark against communism and Soviet expansionism and as the beacon of freedom, democracy, and national independence.[1] Washington was perceived as instrumental in the collapse of Communist Party rule and the unraveling of the Soviet bloc. The United States has also been viewed as providing critical political, economic, and security support during the process of post-Communist democratization and ensuring that most of the CEE states were integrated in the NATO alliance.

In most of the CEE countries, the United States is recognized as the leader of the democratic community that has invested more than any other allied capital in the region's transformation and remains essential for ensuring security in the eastern part of Europe. The United States is also widely viewed as the key force for moving the boundaries of NATO and the transatlantic alliance further eastward. The EU as an institution and its western European member states are not considered in the CEE countries to have sufficient military power, international prestige, and political will to ensure further NATO enlargement eastward. As a result, each CEE capital has sought to develop a special relationship or a strategic partnership with the United States and to maintain a close bond in an uncertain international environment.

CEE capitals consider the United States to be a strong balancer and to possess a policy toward Russia that is more realistic, clear-cut, and consistent than the policy of the EU. The United States is the primary western power that Moscow clearly respects, and CEE countries have calculated that a close alliance with the United States will help protect them against present and future Russian pressures. Washington is considered vital in several CEE capitals as Vladimir Putin's Russia tries to be more regionally assertive in order to create a "neighborhood of client states."[2] By contrast, EU policy is perceived among many CEE officials as inconsistent and inadequate while the EU as a whole is not fully respected by the Kremlin as a major global power. Moscow has been able to exploit its bilateral relations with countries such as France and Germany to try to divide the European Union, sideline the CEE capitals, and undermine the transatlantic link.

For its part, the United States has been supportive of the CEE states for several reasons. U.S. military protection of Western Europe and the political liberation of Eastern Europe are an important legacy of the Cold War and the U.S. investment in European security. The successful construction of democratic polities and market systems has been seen as a major achievement of U.S. foreign policy and a culmination of decades of intensive diplomatic engagement and material investment. CEE countries also became valuable role models for political and economic transition, and their experiences could evidently be applied to other systems emerging from dictatorships. The commitment of the George W. Bush administration to promoting democracy in other regions heightened the prominence of the CEE states as pertinent examples of success, not only for the eastern neighborhood but also for the Caucasus, Central Asia, and the Middle East.

CEE relations with the United States also need to be seen in a broader transatlantic context after the end of the Cold War. Transatlantic links have weakened in recent years for several reasons. First, the end of bipolarity was precipitated by the disappearance of a clear Soviet enemy that, by threatening European security, had cemented the NATO alliance. Second, the evolving European entity was more than just an economic project; instead, it was a grouping that had political and security aspirations. Third, EU developments raised the ambitions of some western European capitals that at the end of the Cold War saw an opportunity to reduce U.S. presence and influence in Europe and create a more Eurocentric structure. Fourth, the United States has been reluctant to use NATO as the military organization of first resort when U.S. national interests have been directly challenged. Fifth, any power that becomes as dominant and predominant as the United States automatically and invariably breeds resentment and opposition, even among traditional allies.

Anti-Americanism—a sixth point—has a long tradition in western Europe and has intensified in recent years. It consists of a fusion of resentments against U.S. military predominance, economic omnipresence, and mass cultural influence. Many Europeans now also equate globalization with Americanization, and this has accentuated fears of U.S. economic and cultural imperialism.

Seventh, a series of U.S. policies added fuel to the flames of anti-Americanism during the first presidential term of George W. Bush. Policy disputes include those over the Comprehensive Test Ban Treaty and national missile defense, the U.S. reluctance to join the global ban on land mines, Washington's nonacceptance of the International Criminal Court (ICC), and the slighting by the United States of the Kyoto Protocol on climate change.

An eighth reason for the weakening transatlantic links is that some nationalist politicians in Europe foresee a future EU that will compete with the United States. Such postures have contributed to disputes between the CEE capitals and those western European governments that are willing to build European identity around opposition to U.S. policy. Hence, EU resistance to military action in Iraq in 2003 was not viewed in most CEE countries as motivated primarily by moral beliefs or legal precedent but, instead, by a mixture of pacifist convenience and a cynical intent to widen the transatlantic rift.

During President Bush's first term, relations between the United States and many of the EU member states deteriorated, and the role of the NATO alliance, which keeps the United States closely engaged with and in Europe, came under severe strain. Among the most disputed issues between the United States and its EU allies were the lingering questions of U.S.-European burden sharing, Europe's emerging defense pillar, NATO's new missions, and the U.S.-led campaigns against terrorists and rogue states. CEE governments became seriously concerned that after September 11, 2001, the U.S. war against international terrorists would sideline both Europe and NATO as U.S. strategic priorities and negatively affect the security of the CEE countries.

Policy makers in the United States drew some specific lessons from the 1999 NATO military campaign over Kosova, during which the inadequacies of European defense capabilities were glaringly exposed. Pressing questions about burden sharing and power sharing in the U.S.-European relationship continue to be raised, and Washington remains critical of the glaring inadequacies in EU defense spending in the age of global terrorism and regional instabilities. Although some EU states accuse the United States of being a unilateralist bully, Europe is often accused of dependence, complacency, and—most recently—obstruction. Some U.S. officials have concluded that EU unwillingness or incapability to contribute militarily, as well as the EU's frequent criticisms of U.S. policy, may lead to NATO becoming increasingly irrelevant to future security challenges. Thus, the United States will have no alternative but to act alone or with dependable partners, whether in Europe or elsewhere, when combat is considered necessary.

Officials in Washington remain dubious about the feasibility and applicability of the embryonic European defense pillar. Questions continue to be raised about European contributions to its own defense and the interface between traditional alliance structures and the emerging CFSP in terms of decision making, use of resources, and troop deployments. In addition, reports of Iran and other states developing nuclear weapons capabilities that can be targeted at Europe cause Washington to feel that European states should make a greater contribution to developing anti-missile systems. The question of costs and capabilities is uppermost, and there is profound skepticism in Washington about the commitment of the European allies.

Allied leaders have assessed the successes and shortcomings of peace enforcement missions in Bosnia-Herzegovina and Kosova and the practicality and efficacy of NATO's new Strategic Concept. This will have major ramifications not only for the two international "dependencies" in southeastern Europe but also any future peacekeeping and state-building missions, especially as the Bush administration is seeking more substantial U.S. troop reductions in Europe. Washington is determined not to undertake any new missions in Europe; hence, any renewed conflicts on the continent or in countries not viewed as crucial for U.S. national interests will necessitate an all-European force if future peace-enforcement operations are indeed undertaken.

The United States continues to monitor the progress of the allied contribution to the campaign against international terrorist groups. Policy makers and defense planners have been critical of allied participation in the military aspects of the ongoing campaign. The offensive in Afghanistan was essentially an Anglo-U.S. operation at the outset, and other conflict zones such as Iraq have not elicited any significant military assistance from the European allies other than United Kingdom, Poland, Italy, and Spain as well as smaller military or specialist units from other CEE states. NATO's planned NRF is to consist of 21,000 rapidly deployable troops by the fall of 2006.[3] It seems unlikely, however, that NATO can rapidly adapt to fight the new kinds of wars without greater defense spending, force modernization, and specialization in expeditionary as opposed to defensive missions.

Washington, with several of its European allies, has also encouraged NATO to transform itself accordingly and adapt the NRF for a range of contemporary security challenges. NATO's growing role in Afghanistan through its provisional reconstruction teams is intended to prepare the alliance for future similar operations.[4] By contrast, a bloc of EU states led by France prefers to operate through EU security instruments and maintain NATO's focus on conventional warfare. Such an approach could have two deleterious consequences: it could make NATO superfluous, and it could reinforce a division of labor between U.S. war fighting and European peacekeeping. While NATO would become redundant in this scenario, Europe would still remain a security dependency of the United States.

In sum, the prospects of a declining NATO, a deteriorating U.S.-European relationship, an incapable EU defense policy, and an emboldened Russia amid escalating terrorist threats and radical regimes developing WMD are a nightmare scenario for many policy analysts on both sides of the Atlantic Ocean. The EU's newcomers calculate that they can help prevent such a scenario by strengthening the U.S.-NATO relationship, contributing to NATO's new missions, and demonstrating that the strategic choice is not between Washington and Brussels but that both capitals are essential for ensuring transatlantic security.

REVIVING U.S.-EU RELATIONS

The onset of the second Bush presidency in early 2005 precipitated a period of rebuilding U.S.-EU relations as Washington appeared to step back from a unilateralist approach in dealing with emerging international challenges. U.S. officials sought to rebuild their relations with several western European states. President Bush's European trip in February 2005, at the start of his second term in office, was an important gesture of reconciliation after several years of tension. Meetings in both the NATO and EU formats at summits in Brussels indicated that Washington continued to place high value on both institutions and viewed Europe as an important partner for the United States.

Nevertheless, it remained unclear whether the rifts visible during the first Bush term were simply temporary disputes or whether moves toward reconciliation were short-term efforts in a steadily declining relationship. A statement by Chancellor Gerhard Schröeder of Germany on the eve of the Bush trip to Europe in February 2005 seemed to undermine the notion that NATO was the primary platform of transatlantic dialogue.[5] Schröeder's idea that the EU should play the principal partnership role with the United States elicited only limited backing among delegates at an annual security conference in Munich. The notion did receive an endorsement from President Jacques Chirac, thus reviving the specter of a Franco-German security axis. However, any sustained attempts to base the European project on the principle of distinctiveness from or opposition to the United States is unlikely to be successful and indeed may simply serve to divide the European Union.

Washington understood that with its military forces and economic capabilities thinly stretched following the Afghan and Iraq interventions, it needed allies and partners to assist in vital reconstruction work as well as EU diplomatic and economic support to deal with other crisis points. This approach was welcomed among mainstream voices in both the Republican and Democratic parties in the United States. Since the onset of European integration, U.S. administrations have largely supported the process although occasional fears have been voiced about an emerging European Union that projects itself as a counterweight to the United States and challenges or directly opposes U.S. strategic interests. Such fears have been exaggerated during the Iraq crisis; neither France nor Germany were capable of mobilizing or sustaining European unity on the basis of an anti-U.S. policy, and neither possessed the capabilities to project serious military power. However, the EU could play an obstructionist diplomatic role and undermine the United States at a political level. In such circumstances, outright opposition by Washington to an integrated EU approach could backfire against U.S. interests by alienating other allies and stiffening anti-U.S. sentiments throughout Europe.

The U.S. secretary of state, Condoleezza Rice, instead of promoting confrontation, stated in Paris in February 2005 that the United States welcomed growing European unity as this could presage the emergence of a stronger Europe that would act as a partner in building a more secure world.[6] President Bush also supported European integration during his visit to the headquarters of the Council of the European Union in Brussels in February 2005. He asserted that integration could enable the development of a close partnership in the "hard work of advancing freedom in the world."[7] Nevertheless, the Bush administration's support for a united and strong EU remained conditional and contingent on a workable alliance to effectively confront various international crises. Such support could be muted or withdrawn if the EU seeks to play the role of a neutral or acts in opposition to the United States. In addition, Washington calculated that the CEE states would help to fortify the transatlantic stream inside the EU and prevent the EU from moving in an anti-U.S. direction. At the same time, the United States would uphold its policy of seeking to develop strong bilateral ties with its closest European allies.

It seems improbable that the United States would welcome the EU as an equal global force and establish joint institutions through which it would make joint decisions on vital strategic issues.[8] Hence, the idea of a U.S.-EU treaty or the creation of permanent EU-U.S. institutions such as a transatlantic council seems improbable. Instead, Washington will continue to view the EU as a potentially effective regional organization that can exert substantial influence in a wider Europe largely through its economic and diplomatic instruments and primarily through the incentive of membership in the EU itself.

The relationship between the United States and the European Union will remain asymmetrical because Washington possesses global interests and unmatched military power. In many instances, however, the United States needs the EU as a diplomatic and economic player, a generator of stability within an expanding Europe, and a supplementary security contributor outside the European zone.[9] Hence, the second George W. Bush administration has focused on rebuilding a partnership with the EU to aid in dealing with the threat of nuclear proliferation in Iran, advancing the Israeli-Palestinian peace process, and upholding the embargo on sensitive military exports to China.

In this wider transatlantic context, where the U.S.-EU relationship has been marked by disputes and conflicts, the CEE countries have aimed to uphold a viable U.S.-European partnership by maintaining the U.S. presence in Europe and raising U.S. interests in CEE developments. An important reason for active CEE involvement in U.S. military missions following September 11, 2001, has been to show political solidarity with Washington. The new democracies avoided adopting positions contrary to those of the White House, and they wanted to be seen as reliable long-term allies.

Policy makers in the United States should be concerned, however, that national memories of U.S. assistance in helping to eradicate communism and building democratic systems are gradually receding in the CEE region. Future relations are more likely to be based on starker pragmatic choices and state interests rather than on historical links and national gratitude. For example, moral debts to the United States are likely to lose out to practical requirements such as gaining EU funding, especially during an election year, and maintaining good relations with the larger and richer western European neighbors.

Although the CEE countries are not economically or militarily powerful, many have made it a national priority to contribute to NATO and U.S. missions, thereby demonstrating that they have graduated from consumers to producers of security. In addition to participation in NATO missions in Bosnia-Herzegovina (1995–2004) and Kosova (1999–present) and in the Italian-led Operation Alba in Albania after the 1997 crisis, several CEE states have made contributions to the U.S.-led coalition missions in Iraq and Afghanistan.

It is useful to determine the contributions of America's new allies to NATO's various missions, to U.S. anti-terrorist coalitions, as well as to other foreign security operations and to assess the extent of likely future contributions. The first major NATO operation began in 1995 in Bosnia-Herzegovina—the Implementation Force (I-FOR) and Stabilization Force (S-FOR) missions—and lasted until the end of 2004 when the EU took over the operation. Poland, among the new NATO members, made the largest contribution and was followed by Romania, the Czech Republic, Hungary, Bulgaria, and Slovakia. In the NATO mission in Kosova that began in June 1999, Estonia, Latvia, and Lithuania in addition to other NATO newcomers contributed troops. Participation in NATO missions has led to greater role specialization, given the scarce financial resources of all new allies. For example, the Czechs have focused on developing nuclear, biological, and chemical decontamination units; the Hungarians, on engineering squads; and the Romanians, on mountain light infantry units.

Several CEE states have made direct military contributions to the U.S.-led mission in Afghanistan since 2002, despite their limited military budgets. After August 2003, NATO assumed greater security responsibility for Afghanistan under the International Security Assistance Force (ISAF) mandate and encouraged NATO aspirants to dispatch small units in peacekeeping and reconstruction efforts. NATO subsequently stated its responsibilities in the wider Black Sea region at the June 2004 Istanbul summit, thus confirming its growing out-of-area mission.

Poland contributed combat troops during the U.S.-led invasion of Iraq in April 2003 and later led a sizable contingent of multinational forces in a sector of Iraq under its control. Warsaw dispatched an elite commando unit during the Iraq War and then emplaced approximately 2,400 troops to control a sector of central Iraq. The total contingent in the Polish-led Multinational Division Center-South zone has comprised approximately 5,670 soldiers, including units from Bulgaria, Hungary, Latvia, Lithuania, Romania, Slovakia, and Ukraine. Troops from Albania, the Czech Republic, Estonia, Macedonia, and Moldova have also participated in U.S.- and British-controlled zones. Postwar stabilization efforts under Operation Iraqi Freedom have involved combat operations, peacekeeping, and civic reconstruction.

By the fall of 2003, the CEE states made up approximately half of the non-U.S. peacekeeping troops in Iraq.[10] Almost all the central Europeans granted some form of overflight and ground transport rights to coalition forces en route to the Persian Gulf. Bulgaria and Romania allowed the United States to use their air bases as, respectively, logistics and refueling centers, and Hungary made available its Taszar air base for U.S. operations. In fact, the new allies offered their facilities to U.S. and allied forces even before they became NATO members. Since the mid-1990s, the U.S. military has held periodic exercises in several CEE states. A number of CEE countries have also participated in NATO missions in Bosnia and Kosova under U.S. command, and every CEE state except Belarus engages in a partner program with at least one U.S. state national guard.

Several of the new allies have developed niche capabilities—including expertise in demining and in chemical, bacteriological, and radiological decontamination—that are valuable for Washington. In addition, in March 2003 Budapest allowed an air base in southern Hungary to be used by the Pentagon for training up to 3,000 Iraqi volunteers who would serve as guides and liaison personnel for coalition forces. Some CEE states have also hosted exercises for the U.S. military, and several CEE capitals have volunteered to conduct officer-training programs to prepare Iraqi security forces for eventual independent operations.

Despite their contributions to recent U.S.-led missions, the CEE capitals remain hamstrung by limited capabilities and costly military programs. The annual defense budget of the new NATO members totals less than $10 billion and their restricted manpower permits only small military contributions.[11] Because of both financial and political factors, several CEE states planned to withdraw their forces from Iraq by the close of 2005. Polish and other officials admitted that Poland's ambitions were bigger than its material base and that they could not participate in the mission in Iraq without more substantial U.S. assistance. Warsaw and other capitals wanted to avoid the creation of a two-tiered military comprising a small, modernized, and mobile elite force in addition to a larger conventional outfit that lacks resources for restructuring.

Of the new NATO allies, Hungary evacuated its troops in January 2005. Poland, Bulgaria, and Lithuania planned to withdraw their forces from Iraq by the end of 2005, although each country pledged to continue its involvement in Iraq in some other role. In December 2005, the newly elected Polish center-right government announced that Polish forces would stay in Iraq for several more months and participate in training Iraqi forces. The Czech Republic and Estonia decided in early 2005 to extend their troop presence until the end of 2005, with the possibility for smaller units to uphold their mission. For Slovakia, continuing military support remained contingent on a United Nations Security Council resolution. Only Romania and Latvia seemed officially committed to staying alongside U.S. forces indefinitely.

The White House appreciates that many of the CEE capitals delivered when it was most needed in Afghanistan and Iraq. It was not simply a question of troop numbers, which remained restricted, but of political commitment based on shared principles and common goals. The Bush administration could thereby underscore that it was not alone in its preemptive missions, despite the reluctance of several major NATO members to make contributions. The new allies also gained benefits from participating in international anti-terrorism operations and other military tasks, including a faster track to NATO entry, U.S. security guarantees, closer military-to-military contacts, the encouragement of U.S. investment, and the likelihood of gaining U.S. military bases in the coming years. However, mounting casualties among coalition members and terrorist threats directed against several CEE countries have tested the durability of the ad hoc military coalitions.

In terms of potential security threats, the CEE states continue to trust Washington as a security provider more than they trust any European capital or the EU as a collectivity. The U.S. connection as well as NATO's Article 5 security guarantee were the main reasons why they all petitioned for NATO membership. Their stance has been reinforced by the specter of a more assertive and expansive Kremlin and by the potential for instability emanating from countries along the eastern borders of central and eastern Europe.

As an important element of their U.S. security guarantee, the CEE states have welcomed the prospect of U.S. military bases on their territories. By the close of 2005, after several years of discussion and review, Poland, Romania, and Bulgaria were poised to host U.S. troops and logistics in compact staging areas. According to several reports, a self-contained and rotational brigade combat team will deploy in and out of various CEE locations.[12] Central and eastern Europe will also receive some command and control components, training facilities, prepositioned stocks of heavy equipment, and power projection infrastructure. This would provide the United States with greater military capability and strategic flexibility while it enables a more rapid deployment of U.S. forces and equipment to crisis points in the Middle East, the Caucasus, and Central Asia. It is hoped that the infusion of the U.S. military and the prospect of civic works and infrastructure projects near base locations will raise pro-U.S. sentiments in these countries. In December 2005 Secretary of State Condoleezza Rice signed a landmark agreement with Romania to establish U.S. military bases in the country, and a similar accord was arranged with Bulgaria in 2006.

One troubling question that confronts all the new allies is whether the U.S. security connection is genuinely based on long-term interests or has become contingent on tactical opportunities and conditioned on short-term objectives. Policy analysts need to ascertain whether the United States and the CEE countries can become long-range strategic allies and not just short-term instrumental partners. To answer these questions, the policies of current CEE governments need to be weighed against the postures of major opposition parties, trends in public opinion, and the impact of EU membership.

Two developments in particular must be carefully monitored: the staunchly pro-EU position of the mainstream CEE center-left parties and the growing Euro-skepticism, anti-federalism, and even nationalism among some CEE center-right formations. Center-left parties such as the Hungarian Socialists, the Czech Social Democrats, and the Polish post-Communist left may increasingly adopt the Euro-focused positions of their western European counterparts, while center-right neoliberal formations such as the Civic Democratic Party in the Czech Republic and the Hungarian Civic Party may take more Euro-skeptical positions but without a strong and countervailing Atlanticism because of their concern about defending national sovereignty and limiting their international military involvement. Both tendencies could weaken the pro-U.S. stance of the new allies.

Such political trends are compounded by concerns among CEE leaders that their countries have not received sufficient reciprocal benefits from the United States in return for their participation in military coalitions. They argue that they have withstood staunch opposition from several EU partners and have not succumbed to terrorist threats and domestic public opinion opposing military action alongside the United States. For example, CEE officials complain about the strict U.S. visa regime their citizens encounter, and they have been disappointed by the level of U.S. business investment, the limited contracts offered in Iraq's material reconstruction, and Washington's pressure for the CEE countries to write off the substantial financial debts owed them by Baghdad. A growing number of citizens and politicians in the CEE region complain that the Bush administration has simply used the CEE states as political cover and that Washington will forget their sacrifices when it becomes convenient. Cynicism and even resentment have permeated public debate throughout the region, and the U.S. administration should be listening closely.

Economic trends between the United States and central and eastern Europe are also troubling from the perspective of building a strong and durable alliance. At the turn of the twenty-first century, the new allies were conducting between half and three-quarters of their trade with the EU countries and less than 5 percent of their trade with the United States.[13] U.S. business investment has also been limited. Among the CEE countries that receive the largest share of U.S. foreign direct investment, Hungary has recorded about a quarter of its total foreign direct investment from the United States; Poland, 15 percent; and the Czech Republic, 6 percent. These figures for the CEE countries have remained low in comparison with U.S. foreign direct investment in western Europe and other regions of the world. Indeed, in the period 2003–2004, of the total amount invested by U.S. companies in Europe as a whole, less than 10 percent reached the CEE economies.[14]

Support remains shallow among the CEE countries for Washington's military missions in the Middle East and elsewhere. Even though most government leaders have backed the U.S. position, they closely track the public mood in their countries as well as the stance and impact of the political opposition. If public opinion were to be transformed into political action, support for future U.S.-led missions that are not approved by the UN Security Council or by NATO acting in unison seems less likely in the region.

The security and foreign policy approaches of CEE countries will also need to be more closely synchronized with the European Union if Brussels develops a more coherent and unified policy. Moreover, the military capabilities of all CEE capitals remain restricted and overstretched amid budgetary cutbacks and the growing primacy of social and economic priorities. Thus, the durability and dependability of the CEE capitals in their support for Washington cannot be guaranteed. Indications or perceptions that the United States will take CEE support on controversial foreign policy issues for granted may in itself also become a political factor emboldening anti-U.S., pro-EU, or neutral positions in the years ahead.

Soon after the reelection of President George W. Bush in November 2004, Poland and other CEE states signaled their convictions that Washington needed to adopt a more consensual approach toward its European allies.[15] At the same time, the CEE states called on Paris and Berlin to become more active in healing transatlantic rifts by contributing more significantly to Iraq's reconstruction. It was clear that the United States needed additional partners in its Middle Eastern policy, and the new allies wanted to use this opportunity to reinvigorate the NATO alliance.

NEW ALLIES' BALANCING ACTS

Central European countries understand they have entered the European Union at a time of transatlantic troubles, and they are working to maintain good relations with both the United States and the EU member countries despite U.S.-EU disagreements. Public opinion in the CEE states is in flux, however, and generational change combined with unilateralist U.S. policies could tilt public sentiment away from Washington.

Delicate Balancing Act

Although political divisions between the United States and the EU have widened, the entry into the EU of new U.S. allies from central and eastern Europe in 2004 has presented both opportunities and difficulties for Washington. With their attainment of NATO and EU membership, the new democracies have achieved the targets they set for themselves when communism and the

Soviet bloc disintegrated in the early 1990s, but a redefinition of their strategic objectives for the next decade or more is only gradually emerging. A primary goal envisaged by the CEE states will be as Atlantic bridge repairers and alliance facilitators. For the new allies, being good Europeans means being good transatlanticists. However, questions remain whether CEE states are capable of fulfilling such a task, whether they will become minor players caught between the larger powers, and whether they will actually exacerbate the persistent conflicts within the alliance.

The transatlantic relationship continues to be strained over a number of issues, including the handling of the U.S.-led campaign against international Islamist terrorists, the war in Iraq, and appropriate methods of eliminating the threat of the proliferation of WMD. Secretary of Defense Donald Rumsfeld's depiction of a Europe divided into "old" and "new" members, designed to chide France and Germany for their opposition to the war against the Iraqi regime of Saddam Hussein, was widely viewed as serving U.S. interests by trying to divide Europe into loyal and unreliable allies.

The CEE countries, the eastern part of the Rumsfeld's "new" Europe, have displayed solidarity with the United States despite concerns that this could jeopardize their entry into the EU. Regardless of their actions over Iraq, the Czech Republic, Estonia, Hungary, Latvia, Lithuania, Poland, Slovakia, and Slovenia did enter the EU on May 1, 2004. The Czech Republic, Hungary, and Poland have been NATO members since 1999; the other states were invited to join in November 2002 together with two EU candidates, Bulgaria and Romania. Each of these countries has had to perform a precarious balancing act between Washington and several major EU capitals, an endeavor that could prove equally challenging during the second Bush term.

The terrorist attacks on the United States on September 11, 2001, presented an opportunity for the CEE states to demonstrate their commitment to the transatlantic relationship and to U.S. global engagement against new security threats. As a result, most CEE countries responded quickly and positively in support of Washington's global anti-terrorist campaign, including the overthrow of the Taliban regime in Afghanistan. The mission in Iraq was more problematic, not only because combat troops were required for an international coalition but also because involvement placed the CEE capitals in direct conflict with France and Germany, two pivotal EU states. Thus, whether through action or inaction, the CEE countries were inadvertently forced to choose between the United States and Europe, a choice they would not wish to repeat in the future.

Maintaining a workable equilibrium between the United States and the EU has proved difficult in practice. Should relations between the United States on one hand and France and Germany on the other continue to be strained, particularly in the event of a crisis over Iran, North Korea, Israel, or some other regional trouble spot, the CEE capitals may be pressured to make unwanted choices between their loyalty to the EU and their commitment to the United States. The reasonably united CEE position on display over Iraq could begin to fracture, much as it did in western Europe when some capitals adopted positions contrary to U.S. strategy. Unattractive U.S. policies could contribute to altering political currents within each country, and specific political parties may seek to benefit from a public mood that generally opposes military involvement overseas. Indeed, such issues are likely to come to a head following the elections of new governments in 2006 that may prove better attuned to the public mood.

Should the Bush administration fail to pay sufficient attention to political developments across the CEE region, it could undermine the support base for the United States in Europe and even enhance anti-Atlanticist currents within the EU. Conversely, a political malaise resulting from the failed EU constitutional treaty, disputes over the allocation of EU regional funds and the overhaul of the CAP, and growing differences over the EU's emerging CFSP could serve to strengthen CEE links with Washington in the years ahead.

Policy makers in the United States should avoid oversimplifying Europe's internal contours while they gain a better understanding of issues that will determine CEE policies toward the United States, NATO, and the European Union. Substantive questions are looming for the White House in the global campaign against unconventional insecurities and how these should be handled. It is important for Washington to ascertain the depth and breadth of support for the United States among countries that entered the EU in May 2004 or that are scheduled to accede in 2007. Moreover, U.S. policy makers need to scrutinize carefully the impact of EU enlargement on transatlantic relations and the effect new members will have on the EU's embryonic foreign and security policies.

Every CEE government seeks to preserve NATO solidarity and effectiveness because Europe's security is believed to hinge on the U.S. connection. The CEE states also want to be consistent and effective in their policies in order to maintain credibility in the international arena. From the vantage point of the CEE states, European unity may become further fractured without a close transatlantic link, and relations with the United States could further deteriorate if the EU is deeply divided in its foreign policies. The new allies favor a stronger and more unified Europe that complements NATO and the United States and does not compete with or undermine NATO in resolving pressing security challenges. As members of both NATO and the EU, CEE capitals want to participate individually in the decision-making process on critical strategic issues without having to choose between Washington and Brussels.

EU membership places certain obligations on members and aspirants according to the three "pillars of the union." During negotiations with the European Union to develop the CFSP, each state committed itself to abide by obligations stemming from Chapter 5 of the Treaty on the European Union, including the fulfillment of Article 11 on CFSP objectives in active support of the EU's foreign and security policy in the "spirit of loyalty and mutual solidarity." Members pledged to refrain from undertaking any actions contrary to the interests of the EU or likely to impair its effectiveness as a cohesive force in international relations.

Although most of these EU commitments are primarily declarations and do not envisage concrete actions, difficulties arise when relations with the United States are affected. This has on several occasions placed America's new allies in delicate and even conflictive situations, as has been the case with controversies surrounding the creation of the ICC, which began its work in July 2002.[16] Most CEE capitals initialed the ICC agreement in 1998–1999 and subsequently ratified it in compliance with EU requirements. Washington sought permanent immunity from the prosecution of U.S. citizens through the use of bilateral agreements with ICC signatory countries; these are known as Article 98 exemption agreements. The EU adopted a common position in 2002 in support of the ICC and lobbied against Washington's efforts to conclude as many bilateral agreements as possible with European capitals with the aim of excluding U.S. soldiers from the jurisdiction of the ICC.

The U.S. administration warned that it would cut off military aid to countries that refused to sign the immunity agreement under the provisions of the American Service-Members' Protection Act (ASPA) passed by the U.S. Congress in 2002. In July 2003, Washington severed military aid to thirty-five countries; among them were six future EU members. When several countries—Bulgaria and Croatia, for example—eventually acceded to the common EU position on the ICC, one negative consequence they suffered was that the United States, citing ASPA, cut off military assistance. Conversely, when Romania signed the Article 98 agreement exempting U.S. service personnel from prosecution in Romanian courts, the EU expressed deep regret for the candidate country's independent action and Romania's qualifications for EU membership came under question.

Another significant area of transatlantic balancing has involved defense procurements and the central and eastern Europe's purchase of modern weaponry. Although traditional EU states expected the candidate countries to purchase western European manufactures, some of the new allies chose to buy U.S. hardware, partly for political reasons. For example, Warsaw decided to purchase U.S. F-16 fighter aircraft rather than Swedish-British Gripen jets;

Warsaw calculated that this would consolidate relations with Washington and bring other military and economic benefits.

An even more poignant example of the minefields obstructing transatlantic navigation was the position of America's new allies toward the Iraq crisis in early 2003. Although the EU as a whole did not reach a common stance over Iraq, those CEE countries that adopted a clear pro-U.S. position were sharply criticized by France and Germany. In January 2003, three prospective EU members—Poland, Hungary, and the Czech Republic—joined with the United Kingdom, Spain, Denmark, Italy, and Portugal in signing an open letter, known as the "Letter of the Eight," in support of U.S. strategy toward Iraq. In February 2003, the Vilnius 10 initialed a similar letter of support for U.S. military action in Iraq. CEE leaders calculated that Franco-German opposition to the United States was primarily intended to split NATO and push the United States out of European affairs, which reinforced CEE support for Washington.

President Jacques Chirac subsequently lambasted all the CEE states for their alleged immaturity, disloyalty, and recklessness, and he threatened that they risked being excluded from the EU. In addition to criticisms pointed at the largest EU newcomer, Poland, Chirac warned Bulgaria and Romania, the two countries slated to join the EU in 2007, that their signatures on the Vilnius 10 letter may have cost them their future EU membership. CEE support for Washington evidently demonstrated to French leaders that the new EU entrants were more concerned about their relations with the United States than their support for European integration.[17] The events surrounding the Iraq conflict convinced most CEE governments that finding compromises within the EU and between the EU and the United States was of vital importance for their long-term national security interests.

For most CEE states, the U.S. connection is the key security relationship in the post-Soviet world. Indeed, NATO itself has traditionally been viewed as an alliance that guarantees U.S. involvement in ensuring the security of individual European states. The EU is perceived as primarily an economic alliance although one that is gaining increasing political coherence that may either complement or challenge the United States on a range of foreign policy issues. Greater EU self-assertion in the security realm, led by the larger member states, could also undermine the overall political consensus within each CEE state and fracture the relative international cohesion they displayed at the onset of the Iraq War.

A joint grand strategy agreed on by all the CEE countries in the European Union seems doubtful. Although all CEE states will have some impact on decision making, each capital is likely to uphold differing national interests and priorities, and they are unlikely to agree on all fronts. Rather than having a singular impact on EU foreign and security policy, CEE influence will need to be measured case by case, whether in dealing with EU policy toward Ukraine, Russia, the western Balkans, or the Black Sea region or EU functional policy regarding borders, security, migration, and taxation.

In some instances, interest groups within the EU will form to push for a particular policy approach, and these may include both western European and CEE member states as was the case when the EU countries considered the issue of the U.S. invasion of Iraq. Other potential crises are likely to materialize; these crises may give the CEE countries opportunities to work in unison or they may contribute to diversifying their approaches. Diversity in central and eastern Europe has been evident already on a range of internal and external issues, whether the constitutional treaty, voting rights, or further EU enlargement. If political forces stress the alleged loss of national identity and state independence to EU institutions, some capitals may increasingly choose a form of foreign policy neutrality that will promote neither EU nor U.S. interests. A nationalist resurgence in several CEE and western European states cannot be discounted, whether based on a protectionist agenda, social conservatism, majority-minority disputes, or an intrusive cross-border orientation to protect kindred in neighboring states.

Although all the CEE countries share a commitment to the Atlantic connection, location and comparative size have generated some differences in approach. Smaller states such as Slovenia, Slovakia, Hungary, and the Czech Republic feel less vulnerable to pressures from the "post-Soviet" region and may be more inclined to follow Brussels or Germany and France and favor soft-security approaches toward emerging regional threats. By contrast, the Baltic states, because of their size, location, and history, have placed more emphasis on strong relations with the United States as long as Brussels and the key western European capitals continue with their compromising stance toward Moscow.

Poland views the U.S. link not only as a guarantee of national security but also as a means to raise its regional, European, and even global stature. Warsaw's prominent role in Iraq alongside the Americans and the Britons has been a consequence of both calculations. Nevertheless, in the longer term, uncritical support for the United States may prove politically damaging, as it seemingly places the supportive country in the role of a supplicant or even a satellite, harms transatlantic relations by fostering simplistic divisions between supporters and opponents, and polarizes political discourse and national decision making.

The Iraq imbroglio has demonstrated the dilemmas of the CEE countries. If the CEE capitals conclude that involvement in U.S.-led military operations costs too much politically and fails to deliver the expected economic benefits, support for the United States may erode and the legitimacy of the government's policy will be undermined. Moreover, regular election cycles and a growing public mood that opposes foreign military engagements may call into question the reliability of some new allies. Indeed, public opinion polls in several CEE countries indicate declining support for not only the Iraq mission but also the United States in general. Although anti-war movements and public demonstrations in CEE countries have been small and rare compared with those in western Europe, trends in public attitudes and motivations must be closely monitored.

Support for CEE military involvement in Iraq has been steadily declining since the beginning of the operation in early 2003. By September 2004, fewer than 25 percent of Poles backed their troops' deployment, which placed additional pressure on the already weak center-left government.[18] Similarly, between 65 and 75 percent of citizens in the Czech Republic opposed their country's involvement in the U.S.-led coalition despite the pro-U.S. position of the incumbent Czech administration.[19] In November 2004, Hungary's parliament lacked a two-thirds majority needed to extend the service of Hungarian troops in Iraq by three months. A November 2004 poll showed that 54 percent of Hungarians supported the return of the troops and 37 percent approved an extension.[20] In Bulgaria, only 12.1 percent of the population in 2005 favored the presence of Bulgarian troops in Iraq.[21]

Favorable views of the United States among the new allies have also been diminishing in recent years, a development that should trouble Washington. The evolving views are related to the perception of a faltering mission in Iraq and insufficient U.S. reciprocity for the new allies for their involvement in the "coalition of the willing." In Poland, 86 percent of those surveyed in 2000 held a positive opinion about the United States, but this figure dropped to 79 percent in 2002, and to just over 50 percent in March 2003.[22] One opinion poll in Poland on the eve of the U.S. presidential election in November 2004 indicated that President Bush's foreign policy had worsened the view of United States for 40 percent of respondents. A March 2005 survey showed that 43 percent of Czechs agreed with the statement: "U.S. foreign policy is threatening the current world."[23] In Slovakia, support for the United States was low (54.3 percent) at the start of the Iraq War in March 2003 and hovered at this level until September 2005.[24] In addition, although young people have traditionally viewed the United States positively, support among youth could decline as their exposure to EU influences intensifies.

Negative sentiments toward the United States can be exploited not only by ultranationalists, radical leftists, anti-globalists, and assorted populists but also by more mainstream political formations during decisions on transatlantic relations. Indeed, support for U.S. policy may be seen as contributing to European disunity and damaging the interests of the new EU entrants by undermining their relations with Brussels and with individual western European capitals. For instance, at the close of 2005, the controversy over secret U.S. Central Intelligence Agency prisons in Poland and Romania, where terrorist suspects were purportedly held and tortured, undermined the reputation of both countries in western Europe and even led to calls for an EU censure if the allegations were confirmed following appropriate investigations.

One overriding question is whether falling support for the United States in CEE countries is a reaction to a particular military mission or a specific U.S. presidency that will sooner or later undergo a reversal, or whether it is indicative of longer-term trends in the CEE region. If the new allies feel less secure in the wake of the Iraq War and if terrorist threats against their territories were to materialize, support for Washington could plummet, with a slimmer likelihood that commitments would be forthcoming for any future military operations.

Official reactions to Bush's reelection were formally congratulatory across the CEE region, but the general feeling in CEE capitals was that they must continue to tread carefully between Washington and Brussels and that this could become increasingly difficult and precipitate further divisions within both the EU and individual states. Since the Bush reelection, the strategic approach of the new allies has taken on a duality: to promote greater cohesion within the EU in its relations with the United States, and to rebuild damaged ties with France and Germany. The likelihood of developing a coherent EU transatlantic policy that successfully incorporates both of these priorities depends largely on the willingness of Paris and Berlin to synchronize their foreign policies and forge compromises with the EU novices and with the staunchly pro-Atlanticist west European capitals.

With twenty-five members now in the EU, its new diversity could make decision making even more difficult, especially over legitimate conditions for the use of military force and the implementation of the European Security Strategy (ESS). The unity displayed by the CEE states over the Iraq mission may also prove transient. Differences of approach have already emerged over a number of foreign policy and EU-related issues. For example, Poland did not receive support from its neighbors when it demanded the implementation of the Nice provisions that gave Warsaw substantial voting rights in the EU Parliament. In fact, several central European states remain skeptical of an ambitious Poland that could pull their foreign policies in an undesired direction. Dissatisfaction has also been voiced with Warsaw for seeking to resolve the EU budget crisis in 2005 by suggesting reduced structural fund payments to CEE states and claiming to speak for all EU newcomers without sufficient regional consultation. Moreover, each CEE capital is likely to develop close relations with specific counterparts in western Europe, thus further diversifying their foreign policies.

Policy makers need to carefully consider, case by case, what specific foreign and security policy issues are likely to further push apart the United States and an enlarged EU, including the CEE countries, over the coming years. It may not be simply a matter of differing priorities; it might also involve differing approaches toward managing or resolving any particular crisis. Perceptions of the United States and the style and substance of U.S. leadership will play an important role.

Evolving Perceptions of the United States

The CEE states have continued to support U.S. leadership in transatlantic relations as this prevents the possibility of domination by any one EU country as well as the formation of narrow coalitions inside Europe that could exclude the newcomers. A worrying trend in recent years has been the growth within the EU of an anti-Americanism that may increasingly infect the CEE countries, and within the United States a corresponding Europhobia or Euroneutralism that could further divide the NATO alliance. In recent years, the United States has become less Eurocentric because of Washington's foreign policy priorities after 9/11 as well as internal demographic changes, including the numerical growth and influence of East Asian and Latin American constituencies, changes that have increased resonance in policy-making circles in Washington.

There are many varieties of anti-Americanism, a phenomenon that may be linked with anti-Westernism, antiglobalism, anticapitalism, cultural conservatism, and nationalist isolationism. However, most of these trends are either marginal or have limited political impact at the present time. A more worrying form of anti-Americanism is linked with an emerging European nationalism that is based on the supposed cultural, political, social, and moral superiority of the EU model and the alleged progressiveness of the supranational European identity in contrast with a U.S. identity.[25]

Any power that becomes as dominant and predominant as the United States automatically breeds a degree of resentment and opposition among even traditional allies. Several western European capitals have criticized the CEE countries for being easily manipulated by Washington although they have few concrete benefits in return for their support. Poland in particular is believed to have learned the hard lesson that the United States will not be helpful in Warsaw's relations with its western European partners and will not provide expected benefits to Poland such as visa waivers and financial windfalls from the Iraq operation.[26] Some western European capitals remain suspicious about the new CEE members, especially when they are perceived as attempting to leverage their relations with the United States in order to undermine the

Franco-German tandem or inject their pronounced Atlanticist orientations into EU foreign policy.

A key question within the CEE countries states concerns shifting public attitudes toward the United States and the possible link between public opposition to foreign military missions and rising trends of anti-Americanism throughout Europe. Anti-Americanism has a long tradition in western Europe, where it has been principally based on a mixture of rightist nationalism and leftist elitism. It consists of a fusion of resentments against U.S. military predominance, economic omnipresence, and mass cultural influence. Many Europeans now also equate globalization with Americanization, and this has accentuated fears of corporate and cultural imperialism. U.S. actions have fueled the flames of anti-Americanism during the George W. Bush presidency, including disputes over the Comprehensive Test Ban Treaty and national missile defense, U.S. reluctance to join the global ban on land mines, the U.S. refusal to join the ICC, and the U.S. snub of the Kyoto Protocol on climate change.

CEE governments have looked on in dismay as leading French and German politicians have flaunted their latent anti-American prejudices and used them as political and electoral tools. Some social democratic and Euro-nationalist politicians even foresee a future EU that will compete with and confront the global reach of the United States. Such postures have contributed to disputes between the CEE states and several western European capitals. Many analysts in central and eastern Europe believe the French elite, in particular, harbor a long-term agenda to forge a European identity built around anti-Americanism or in stark opposition to U.S. policy. CEE analysts view French attacks on "anti-hegemonism" and French calls for "European self-identification" as barely camouflaged anti-Americanism.[27] Hence, CEE states concluded that French opposition to military action in Iraq in 2003 was not motivated primarily by moral arguments or legal tenets but by a deliberate attempt to widen the transatlantic rift.

In the post–Cold War era, and especially in the post-9/11 period, anti-Americanism has regenerated in western Europe among political and cultural elites, disaffected publics, and younger activists in search of a demonstrable cause. There is a danger that anti-Americanism could become one of the defining elements of European identity in an expanding EU. Anti-Americanism will also have an impact on the rising elites in the CEE area who may be increasingly influenced by the western European capitals and estranged from the United States. Some CEE analysts believe that anti-Americanism has become a more coherent "all-purpose ideology" and a "catchall platform for protest-vote politics" that transcends traditional left-right divisions.[28] After the collapse of the Soviet Union, the United States became the sole superpower and the main scapegoat for all global ills. Many western European intellectuals claim that the EU's opposition to U.S. interests and ambitions is simply an act of self-defense.[29]

Leaders and policy makers in central and eastern Europe are concerned that EU countries such as France, believing that Europe should be a political, economic, and cultural rival of the United States, will not desist from their anti-U.S. agenda regardless of the specifics of U.S. policy. In this vein, some EU officials have expressed skepticism about genuine U.S. support for European integration; they claim a "values gap" across the Atlantic and contend that Washington is willing to pursue divisions within the EU to serve its own interests.[30] This could become a self-fulfilling prophecy as U.S. officials will increasingly question the rationale of European integration if this is seen to be a growing force of opposition to U.S. national interests. However, the United States may also face a fractured Europe that becomes an even more unpredictable and unreliable partner and a further source of international discord.

Numerous issues have increasingly portrayed and projected a Europe-against-America framework. Although Europe believes the United States fixates on military resolution to world crises and consistently devalues nonmilitary approaches to security, Europe is said to be overly enthralled with soft-security issues that have little deterrence value and do not win real wars. Moreover, the EU itself is seen to be deeply divided and devoid of a common foreign policy. The EU's CFSP has been criticized for squandering time, energy, and resources because no deployable military force underpins it as well as for its inability to respond quickly to a crisis and resolve pressing international problems as its decisions are based on consensus between a growing number of member states. Some U.S. Republican Party legislators have dismissed the EU approach toward terrorism and rogue states as one of pacifism, appeasement, and even submission.

Many western Europeans have concluded that the United States is evidently unwilling and unprepared to act in a multilateral framework, does not wish to share leadership during a crisis, and disregards international organizations such as the United Nations. Western Europeans resent that the United States focuses on great power politics and, because of the EU's limited military capabilities, relegates or sidelines the EU to the role of a minor player on important international issues. Washington is seen as pursuing a narrow, self-serving agenda and as unwilling to consider the views and concerns of its allies.

Many in the United States expect the EU will not act at all unless it receives an appropriate UN mandate. For example, the U.S.-sponsored NRF, intended for expeditionary warfare, has been restricted by French leadership to use only in the European theater, is not to be used in a preemptive manner, and can become operational only after obtaining a UN mandate.[31]

Although Washington concluded during the NATO war over Kosova in 1999 that obstructive European political meddling in the military campaign and regular political interference with targeting compromised operational security, some EU states believed that the United States excessively dominated the air campaign and diplomacy received insufficient attention.[32] Although Washington is charged with disregarding questions of human rights, the EU is accused of sacrificing security and allowing radical states and substate actors to manipulate the human rights issue to prevent decisive action to eliminate security threats.

The Bush Doctrine of preemptive military action against terrorist bases and states believed to be harboring terrorist cells has come under severe criticism in European policy circles. In CEE countries, preemptive or preventive military action tends to be viewed more sympathetically, partly because of their own history with aggressive neighbors.[33] To many western Europeans, however, U.S. preemption disregarded international norms, undermined state sovereignty, and set a disturbing precedent for aggressive action against independent states couched as defensive measures. Western Europeans criticized the United States for relying during any crisis on a military response, and many EU elites looked upon the resort to war as a failure of diplomacy and international politics. In addition, the George W. Bush administration was widely viewed in Europe as arrogant, impatient, insensitive to its allies, unwilling to engage in prolonged consultation, and disdainful of international law and institutions.

U.S. policy makers counter that many European states have proved to be irresponsible and complacent in the face of serious and imminent threats.[34] They point out that the policy of preemption is an act of self-defense of last resort if other means fail to dissuade and deter attacks against U.S. interests. Without the possibility of preemption, the United States purportedly leaves itself vulnerable to indiscriminate terrorist attacks against civilians.[35] U.S. officials also point out that Europeans have failed to develop any realistic policy to tackle arms proliferation or transnational terrorism. They argue that diplomacy and negotiations simply do not work with an amorphous and vehemently anti-Western movement such as Al Qaeda and with regimes that do not recognize or follow international norms.

A fundamental point of friction and suspicion between Washington and several EU capitals concerns alleged White House attempts to "divide and rule" the European Union by promoting a policy of "disaggregation" between member states.[36] The supposed objective is to weaken attempts at integration, whether by supporting the dilution of EU unity through calls for open-ended enlargement or by playing off different European states against each other. U.S. policy makers dispute such accusations and assert that, as the United States seeks partners and supporters in the absence of a coherent and uniform EU foreign and security policy, it will continue to deal with individual EU states.

The U.S. search for supporters within the EU does not necessarily constitute a strategic attempt to undermine or weaken the union, especially as such a policy could ultimately backfire and serve to bring the EU states closer together. A successful U.S. policy of fragmenting Europe would undercut U.S. interests because it could also generate instability within the EU and along its borders as well as disable the union from being a helpful diplomatic or military partner in various global issues. A number of CEE policy analysts favor a change of U.S. outlook on the future of the EU that would incorporate a more direct acceptance of a united Europe with a distinct foreign policy.[37]

Some U.S. analysts also argue that anti-Atlanticist forces exist within the EU that relish conflict with the United States because this promotes the notion of European distinctiveness and an EU counterweight to U.S. hegemony. EU nationalists allegedly develop conspiracy theories to demonize the United States and to stimulate anti-Americanism. Hence, theories of U.S. domination or disaggregation are widely propounded in order to foster unity built on a distinct European identity in opposition to U.S. policy.

Intensive global public opinion polling since the onset of the war in Iraq has demonstrated that support for and solidarity with the United States have steadily declined throughout Europe. Favorable opinions by Britons of the United States dropped from 75 percent in 2002 to 55 percent in 2005.[38] In France, the equivalent drop was from 63 percent to 43 percent.[39] Even in Poland, a staunch U.S. ally, positive views of the United States declined from 79 percent in 2002 to 62 percent in 2005.[40] Although most of the negative views were focused on the Bush presidency, respondents also expressed broader problems with the U.S. role in the world. A great deal of resentment has been generated by the perception that the United States acts unilaterally and pays scant attention to the interests of other countries when it makes policy decisions.

Equally worrisome for Washington is the fact that polling results indicate that Euro-skepticism among European publics and reservations about the EU have not corresponded with a desire for closer transatlantic ties. Although a clear majority of Americans favor a close partnership with the EU, a majority of western Europeans prefer a more independent EU posture, and CEE citizens may increasingly share this perspective in the years ahead. In 2004 one authoritative international survey reported that, for the first time, 55 percent of Europeans found U.S. leadership in the world undesirable and sought more independence from Washington.[41] This trend was not limited to a few countries in Secretary Rumsfeld's "old" Europe but was increasingly common across the continent, including in the CEE countries.

Despite these negative perceptions, the second Bush administration has provided opportunities for redefining the NATO alliance and enabling the United States and EU to act in concert on specific issues of common concern. The White House evidently calculated that it would be preferable to have the EU engaged in a looming crisis over Iran or in the Israeli-Palestinian conflict rather than have the EU stand in opposition to the United States. Moreover, the renewed Bush focus on an agenda of "expanding freedom and democracy" provides greater opportunities for the EU to work in tandem with Washington, whether through its economic incentives or its soft-power capabilities.

Nevertheless, by mid-2006 the warming U.S.-EU relationship had still not been adequately tested by a major new international conflict, and it remained uncertain how both sides would respond to an escalating crisis in the Middle East or the Far East. In particular, it has been difficult to ascertain whether U.S. global objectives had remained constant while its strategy was being adapted or whether the objectives themselves had been diluted or diverted, largely because of the costly Iraq imbroglio, thus necessitating a change of strategy to bring aboard the majority of Europeans.

The transatlantic divide was only partly bridged at the EU and NATO summits in February 2005, which President Bush attended. All sides agreed that they needed to work together to resolve the numerous insecurities confronting both sides of the Atlantic Ocean. However, while the EU focused primarily on soft-power strategies, Washington reserved the right to use force where necessary. EU suspicions that the Bush administration will act unilaterally and even provocatively where it sees U.S. interests directly endangered have not been fully allayed. Meanwhile, the White House continues to view with apprehension the EU's embryonic security and foreign policy, and it seeks to ascertain whether the new EU policy will complement or challenge the NATO alliance and U.S. global interests.

NOTES

1. For a background analysis, see Ronald D. Asmus and Alexandr Vondra, "The Origins of Atlanticism in Central and Eastern Europe," *Cambridge Review of International Affairs* 18, no. 2 (July 2005): 203–16.

2. Latvian representatives of nongovernmental organizations, including the Latvian Institute for International Affairs, in conversations with the authors, Riga, June 2005.

3. Thomas Harding, "NATO Offers Reaction Force to Aid Airlift," *Daily Telegraph*, October 14, 2005.

4. Mark Joyce, "NATO's Incremental Transformation," *International Herald Tribune*, October 8–9, 2005.

5. David Král, "Bush's Trip to Europe 2005—The Ball is in Europe's Court," Policy Brief (Prague: EUROPEUM Institute for European Policy, February 2005), 2, www.europeum.org/doc/arch_eur/Bush_ETrip_2005.pdf.

6. Condoleezza Rice, "Remarks at the Institut d'Etudes Politiques de Paris—Sciences Po," Paris, February 8, 2005, http://www.state.gov/secretary/rm/2005/41973.htm.

7. George W. Bush, "President Discusses American and European Alliance in Belgium" (remarks in Brussels, February 21, 2005), www.whitehouse.gov/news/releases/2005/02/print/20050221.html.

8. Walter Russell Mead, "Goodbye to Berlin? Germany Looks Askance at Red State America," *National Interest* Spring 2004: 19–28.

9. For a cogent argument about U.S.-EU complementarity, see Zbigniew Brzezinski, *The Choice: Global Domination or Global Leadership* (New York: Basic Books, 2004).

10. Matthew Rhodes, "Central Europe and Iraq: Balance, Bandwagon, or Bridge?" *Orbis* 48, no. 3 (Summer 2004): 423–36.

11. Tomasz Szayna, *NATO Enlargement 2000–2015, Determinants and Implications for Defense Planning and Shaping* (Santa Monica, CA: RAND, 2003): 52–59.

12. Michael P. Noonan, "When Less is More: The Transformation of American Expeditionary Land Power in Europe," E-Note, Foreign Policy Research Institute, Philadelphia, May 24, 2005, www.fpri.org/enotes/20050524.military.noonan.redeploymenteurope.html.

13. Matthew Rhodes, "Whose Trojan Horses?" *International Affairs* 57, no. 4 (Autumn 2002): 631.

14. Jennifer L. Koncz and Daniel R. Yorgason, "Direct Investment Positions for 2004," *Survey of Current Business* 85, no. 7 (July 2005): 40–53, www.bea.gov/bea/ARTICLES/2005/07July/0705_DIP_WEB.pdf.

15. "Allies in Iraq Urge Consensus on EU and Bush," *Financial Times*, November 5, 2004.

16. Other issues of transatlantic dispute include the Kyoto Protocol, the Comprehensive Test Ban Treaty, and the Chemical and Biological Weapons Convention, all of which the United States has refused to ratify.

17. Stanisław Parzymies and Sylwia Kanarek, "Poland's Relations with France," in *Yearbook of Polish Foreign Policy*, 2004, ed. Barbara Wizimirska (Warsaw: Polish Ministry of Foreign Affairs, 2005): 199.

18. "Skutki Zaangażowania Polski W Iraku" [Effects of Polish Involvement in Iraq].

19. See CVVM poll referenced in John Springford, "'Old' and 'New' Europeans United," 5; and "Two-Thirds of Czechs Disapprove of Iraq War—Poll," *Czech News Agency*, March 18, 2005.

20. "Hungarian Troops to Leave Iraq," *New York Times*, November 16, 2004.

21. "Poll Shows Majority of Bulgarians Oppose Mission in Iraq, Foreign Bases," *Bulgarian News Agency (BTA)*, March 17, 2005 (access via BBC Monitoring, International Newswire).

22. "The Poles about the U.S. Presidential Election."

23. "Over Half of Czechs Critical of U.S. Policy," *Czech News Agency*, March 24, 2005.

24. "Iraq-USA-Korea—'Axis of Evil' for Slovaks—Poll," *CTK News Agency*, Bratislava, March 14, 2003 (access via BBC Monitoring, International Newswire); and "Key Findings 2005," 17.

25. For a useful discussion see Ash, *Free World*, 48.

26. German representatives of the German Marshall Fund of the United States and the Center for Applied Policy Research, conversations with the authors, Berlin and Munich, June 2005; and British officials from the Foreign and Commonwealth Office, conversations with the authors, London, March 2005.

27. Jaroslaw Bratkiewicz, "Poland's Engagement in the War and Stabilisation in Iraq," in *Yearbook of Polish Foreign Policy*, 2004, ed. Barbara Wizimirska (Warsaw: Polish Ministry of Foreign Affairs, 2005): 25–26.

28. A valuable overview can be found in Ivan Krastev, "The Anti-American Century?" *Journal of Democracy* 15, no. 2 (April 2004): 5–16.

29. For an excellent analysis of anti-Americanism since the creation of the republic, see Barry Rubin and Judith Colp Rubin, *Hating America: A History* (Oxford: Oxford University Press, 2004).

30. Anthony Blinken, "The False Crisis Over the Atlantic," *Foreign Affairs* 80, no. 3 (May/June 2001).

31. Michael Mihalka, "NATO Response Force: Rapid? Responsive? A Force?" Connections: *The Quarterly Journal* 4, no. 2 (Summer 2005): 69, www.pfpconsortium .org/PRODUCTS/publications/journals/pfpc_qj4_no2_en.pdf.

32. Philip H. Gordon, "NATO after 11 September," *Survival* 43, no. 4 (Winter 2001): 4.

33. Gordon R. Hammock, "Iraq, Preemption, and the Views of Poland, the Czech Republic, and Hungary," *Air and Space Power Journal* 17, no. 3 (Fall 2003): 84–92, www.airpower.maxwell.af.mil/airchronicles/apj/apj03/fal03/hammock.html.

34. Adrian Hyde-Price, "Continental Drift? Transatlantic Relations in the Twenty-First Century," *Defense Studies* 2, no. 2 (Summer 2002): 6.

35. National Security Strategy of the United States of America (Washington, D.C.: White House, September 2002), www.whitehouse.gov/nsc/nss.pdf.

36. A useful overview can be found in John Van Oudenaren, "Containing Europe," *National Interest* (Summer 2005): 57–64.

37. Based on discussions with foreign policy officials in Bucharest, Romania, October 2005.

38. American Character Gets Mixed Review; U.S. Image Up Slightly, but Still Negative, 16-Nation Pew Global Attitudes Survey.

39. Ibid.

40. Ibid.

41. Ronald Asmus, Philip P. Everts, and Pierangelo Isernia, "Across the Atlantic and the Political Aisle: The Double Divide in U.S.-European Relations" (Washington, D.C.: German Marshall Fund of the United States, August 2004), www.gmfus.org/doc/across%20atlantic.pdf.

Chapter Three

Poland

The Key to Central Europe

Although Poland does not possess significant economic strength, the country's size and strategic location have enabled Warsaw to play an increasingly prominent role within the European Union. Poland has been the most assertive New Ally in its security and foreign policy agenda and has emerged as America's key partner in Central Europe. It views itself as the leader of the enlarged EU's Atlanticist current and actively seeks to bridge the transatlantic divide. Since the fall of communism, Poland has benefited from a pronounced foreign policy consensus across the political spectrum. However, the country's longer-term political development may not be so easily predicted with the emergence of factors that could work against the American link, including political opposition, public disenchantment, EU enticements, and economic pressures.

Through its political and economic transformation and rapid integration into NATO and the EU, Poland has emerged as the newest substantial presence in European politics. With a population approaching forty million, in a key strategic location, with a growing economy, and a strong national consciousness, Poland is a medium-sized power whose voice cannot be neglected in EU decision making. Warsaw consistently looks upon the United States as its chief ally, patron, and partner, and because of its staunchly pro-American agenda, Poland forms the Atlantic "core" in Central-Eastern Europe (CEE). Its position has provoked some consternation and criticism in several West European capitals. As a result, Warsaw will have to navigate some stormy intra-European and transatlantic waters in the years ahead.

All Polish governments since 1989, regardless of their political origins and platforms, have proved equally committed to structural transformation and to Western institutional integration. Differences over budgetary priorities, welfare

79

spending, and social programs were not serious enough to endanger the pace and direction of reform. Such consistency successfully propelled the country on the road to both NATO and EU membership, while helping to attract substantial foreign investment. Political competition has taken place within certain democratic parameters, while populist, nationalist, and other extremist elements were largely marginalized.

Poland has also avoided domestic ethno-nationalist conflicts or any major ruptures with its neighbors, despite the fact that seven new states appeared on the country's borders—a united Germany, Czech Republic, Slovakia, Russia, Lithuania, Belarus, and Ukraine. Moreover, Poland is a fairly homogenous society and all governments have tried to be inclusive of the largest minorities especially as they do not challenge the administrative or territorial cohesion of the state. Furthermore, productive relations have developed between Poland and most of its new neighbors.

Early on during the democratic changes, Warsaw set for itself a number of distinct security and foreign policy priorities, and most of these have been achieved. Poland left the Moscow imposed Warsaw Pact and COMECON (Council of Mutual Economic Assistance) in the early 1990s, which were promptly dissolved. It joined various international financial institutions, including the World Bank and the International Monetary Fund, and a number of pan-European bodies, including the Council of Europe. Poland's most important success was gaining membership in NATO, an alliance to which it aspired after freeing itself from Soviet overlordship. Although the prospect seemed unrealistic at the outset, by the time of the 1996 NATO Summit membership became guaranteed. Poland has since contributed to the Alliance in terms of peacekeeping duties, joint planning, intelligence sharing, and various specialized operations. Warsaw has been praised ahead of other new members for taking its NATO responsibilities seriously and meeting most of the requirement and pledges that it made when it petitioned for inclusion.

Under communism, Poland saw itself as a bastion of resistance and solidarity against international dictatorship. In a democratic setting, Warsaw perceives itself as the key Euro-Atlantic link in Central Europe. Such a strategic position has implications in several directions. Toward the East, and its neighbors in Russia, Belarus, and Ukraine, Poland acts as a model and a magnet for democratic reform, market development, social progress, foreign investment, technological innovation, industrial modernization, and European integration. Toward its north and south, Poland forms the core of a new democratic chain that stretches from Estonia to Slovenia and Bulgaria. Although this is not a formal structure, the constituent countries can act in concert when their interests are at stake. This was most visible during the Vilnius 10 process intended to substantially enlarge NATO throughout CEE.

And toward the West, Poland seeks to promote balance in relations between Brussels and Washington and to maintain the American presence in Europe. Poland, together with its Central European and Baltic neighbors, operates according to two basic principles: to keep NATO united and effective, and to maintain U.S. engagement in Europe. In Warsaw's estimation, even if the former endeavor fails, the latter must succeed to help ensure the country's security. In order to demonstrate its commitment to NATO, during the 1990s Warsaw conducted deep reforms within its armed forces to bring them in line with Alliance standards. Troop numbers were reduced from 400,000 to 150,000, the defense budget was raised to nearly 2 percent of GDP annually, conscription was cut, with the aim of creating a fully professional army—by 2003, half of the military was staffed by professionals—while the number of units involved in territorial defense was reduced and the number deployable for out-of-area missions was increased.

Ultimately, none of the new European democracies display much trust in an EU defense pillar or a NATO security guarantee without the U.S. presence. In the wake of the Iraqi crisis, the overriding fear has been that if France or Germany or any other power can block Alliance planning for military assistance to a long-standing NATO ally, such as Turkey, and thereby disregard NATO's Article 5 guarantee, then an Alliance reaction to a potential Russian threat could prove even more timid. Poland remains concerned about the resurgent Gaullist strategy in Paris, which promotes a strong Europe in closer partnership with Russia in opposition to purported Anglo-Saxon hegemony. Warsaw and its CEE neighbors are likely to resist any vehemently anti-American policies promulgated by political circles in some West European capitals.

Officials in Warsaw view the United States as the preeminent guarantor of Poland's security and national independence. They remain skeptical about West Europe's security capabilities and deliveries, however glossy these may look on paper. Moreover, they are fearful lest some new French-German-Russian axis undermines America's engagement in Europe and diminishes their own sense of security. Poland's objective is not to choose between Europe and America but to help protect Europe by keeping America engaged on the "old continent."

Poland is an important strategic partner for the United States for several reasons. First, the country helps to maintain and consolidate its influence and presence in a key part of CEE. Second, it counters French attempts, whether real, planned, or perceived, to push Washington out of European affairs by developing a distinct and detached EU foreign and defense policy. And third, Poland provides the core of a new informal alliance that has been willing to collaborate with Washington militarily against terrorist movements, rogue states, and other security threats outside of the European continent.

As Washington has encountered obstruction and uncooperativeness in Paris and Berlin, it has redirected its resources and refocused its interests on more willing allies elsewhere in Europe. Washington plans to reposition some of its military bases to CEE, including Poland. As U.S. forces need to become more flexible, specialized, and easily deployable to the new arc of conflict that spans the Middle East, the Caucasus, and Central Asia, the New Allies located closer to these regions can act as military hubs for American forces. American troops are likely to be welcomed in countries such as Poland, Romania, and Bulgaria because their presence will demonstrate Washington's commitment to CEE security.

NATO expansion to eastern and southeastern Europe has contributed to enhancing the shift in America's security focus to the Black Sea–Caspian–East Mediterranean triangle. Romania and Bulgaria offer more direct routes to the Middle East, across the Black Sea to the Caucasus, or through Turkey. Meanwhile, Poland can also provide a central transit point, base, and hub facing regions adjoining the Black Sea and the Caspian Sea. The strategic and economic significance of these regions is increasing, especially with the development of oil and gas lines from Russia and Central Asia and with ongoing regional conflicts that challenge the security interests of the United States and its NATO allies.

NATO enlargement has been viewed as a practical method for reinvigorating the transatlantic link and creating a larger pool of interoperable countries with which the United States can construct coalitions for future security operations. NATO expansion may also constitute a valuable means for buttressing the American position vis-à-vis the European allies. It has given Washington additional voices of support within NATO's decision-making process and broadened diplomatic and political assistance in various international organizations. Nevertheless, the American-European relationship remains troubled and the New Allies, especially Poland, have found themselves caught between American expectations and EU requirements as they moved into the Union.

Some European commentators contend that Washington has deliberately played the Polish card against the European Union. Indeed, a pro-American Poland, together with other dependable neighbors has provided a counterbalance against those European states that vehemently oppose much of U.S. policy. Although Warsaw may not currently possess substantial economic or military weight, over the next decade the situation could alter to its advantage if Poland's economy continues to grow and if the United States can divert a greater volume of resources and investment into the country to help solidify its political support and military capabilities.

Poland's high prestige in Washington is not merely a consequence of an effective Polish lobbying effort, but is measured by the assistance that the country has consistently offered to the United States since the end of the Cold War. Warsaw has received various rewards as a result. For instance, Poland was the first country among the new Alliance members to command an important NATO exercise in May 2003 in the port city of Szczecin. It commanded one of the four stabilization zones in post-Saddam Iraq and former Polish finance minister Marek Belka served as deputy chief of the U.S. Office of Reconstruction and Humanitarian Assistance for Iraq. Poland has thereby gained substantial political capital in Washington for its stellar support throughout the Iraqi campaign even while it has come under criticism from some of its West European (WE) partners.

For the major EU member states, Poland was too big a country to be excluded from the process of enlargement. On the other hand, Poland's political and strategic proximity to the United States created some frictions and concerns in Brussels about Poland's loyalty and dependability. Some EU diplomats have even dubbed Poland as an American client, vassal, and mercenary or Washington's "Trojan horse" in Europe, indicating a fear that through Warsaw and other Central European capitals the White House will acquire substantial influence over EU policy and European affairs.

The Polish authorities do not fully relish the role of mediators between Europe and America as this could rebound negatively on them and generate blame for further transatlantic ruptures. Polish analysts contend that one should not undertake a task that could easily end in failure and leave the party susceptible to blame. However, the role of a power broker and facilitator may have some appeal if Poland can thereby raise its stature among the West European states while maintaining a strong American connection. Such a balancing act will prove difficult to perform given that French and German policy makers have treated Warsaw with reservation if not distrust as an upstart ingratiating itself with the sole superpower. Ultimately, it is Poland's firmness rather than deference to the United States that could transform the country into a more influential EU member. While its relations with Washington remain sound and durable, by asserting its own specific national interests Warsaw is more likely to amass credibility on both sides of the Atlantic.

THE EUROPEAN UNION

Poland is the sixth largest state in the European Union, with a population of approximately thirty-eight million. A critical debate in Poland has revolved around the future of EU integration and the contours and content of the Union's emerging foreign and security policy. Various political leaders from a spectrum of political parties expressed doubts about the EU Constitution.

Warsaw planned to hold a public referendum on the document until the French and Dutch no votes in June 2005 postponed Poland's decision. All the major political parties remain suspicious of steps toward a federal Europe in which national foreign and security policies are subsumed under centralized decision making in Brussels and become susceptible to the primary influence of the large member states. President Aleksander Kwaśniewski and other Polish leaders expressed their reservations that such developments were premature and will need to take another generation.[1]

Since it entered the Union in May 2004, Warsaw has also proven to be a tough negotiator on such internal EU questions as the constitutional treaty, voting rights, and EU budgets. Some of the Polish elites also view the country as a vanguard of more liberal economic policies that challenges the traditional European state welfare systems. The Polish authorities complained that the older EU members were trying to shield their countries against competition from Polish labor, products, and services.[2] Warsaw has also prided itself on successfully implementing all EU regulations and abiding by its commitments to the Union.

However, Warsaw needs to be careful not to persistently antagonize the larger West European capitals and thereby lose its influence and stature in the Union.[3] Warsaw has feared that its interests would be ignored by the larger WE states and this has contributed to its strident and sometimes confrontational position on several issues. Poland's leaders continue to learn the value of compromise and diplomacy that may trim the country's immediate goals in order to improve its longer-term influence.

Warsaw initially opposed the EU's constitutional provisions that retracted some of the benefits it gained under the 2001 Nice Treaty, including the weighted voting system in the Council of Ministers. Poland was heavily criticized by Paris and Berlin, in particular, for its inflexibility in reaching a compromise. The Nice arrangement defined a new system of voting giving Poland only two less votes than Germany even though its population constitutes only half that of Germany's.[4] Berlin is also the largest contributor to the EU budget, allocating about 25 percent of the total and almost sixteen times more than Poland. The Germans objected that Poland would be almost equal to Germany in the decision making process while being one of the largest beneficiaries of the EU budget. Ultimately, the German position prevailed and Poland obtained fewer votes in the EU Council of Ministers.

Under strong pressure from the larger EU members and following the withdrawal of Spanish support, Poland was eventually persuaded to make compromises over the Nice arrangements in the draft EU Constitution. Warsaw seemed to be gradually learning to act more pragmatically within the Union. Madrid, for example, was willing to sacrifice its increased voting rights for more substantial EU funds. There were fears that Berlin could more tightly control the 2007–2013 budget and deny resources to Poland if Warsaw insisted on preserving the Nice treaty arrangements. On the other hand, it was not to Germany advantage to have an economically weakened Poland potentially susceptible to populist pressures and mass out-migration. Poland and its CEE neighbors also complained that financial support from the EU budget has been less than expected during the latter stages of accession talks. Hence, the calculation was that it would need greater voting rights in the Union for its voice to be heard and its interests defended.

Although some Polish analysts assert that Polish and EU interests are identical, in reality there are significant divergences between member states on various issues, especially in the security arena. Warsaw governments feared deeper integration between Germany, France, and the Benelux countries that would exclude Poland and other CEE countries. Some analysts believe that the specter of an EU "hard core" with a "European Directorate" and a "two-speed" integration process is a means for Berlin and Paris to apply pressure on the smaller states and EU newcomers to fall in line with their policies.[5] Deeper integration around issues such as defense, foreign policy, immigration, and tax policies would effectively isolate those left outside the process. For instance, a focus on immigration could create new barriers for workers and immigrants from the CEE states, while uniform taxation in the EU could discourage foreign investors from countries such as Poland.

Polish officials initially warned that rejection of the Constitutional Treaty in a public referendum would doom the country to self-isolation and help to revive the notion of a "two-speed" Europe or a two-tiered EU "hard core" and periphery. However, the French and Dutch "no" votes removed much of the spotlight from Poland and its stance toward the Constitution. Nevertheless, the anxieties expressed by Polish leaders indicated that Warsaw did not want the country to be perceived as a pariah within the Union.

Fruitful Polish-German relations are a major key to bridging divisions between WE and CEE and Warsaw often refers to its ties to Berlin as a "strategic partnership." Germany has become Poland's most important trading partner (accounting for a third of Polish exports and just under a quarter of imports in 2003) and has promoted Poland's membership in all Western organizations. However, political relations have been marred by differing approaches to the Iraqi war and festering bilateral issues, such as the planned creation of a Center Against Expulsions in Berlin focusing on ethnic German expulsions from Poland at the close of World War Two. For its part, Germany does not want to be placed in a role of balancing an Atlanticist "East" and a Europeanist "West" and it maintains reservations over Warsaw's suspicions toward Russia and its aspirations in bringing its eastern neighbors into the European Union.[6]

Poor Polish-German relations play into the hands of anti-enlargers favoring a "core Europe" who claim that the inclusion of CEE states will foster gridlock in the Union. Sensible voices in the Polish administration and legislature play down disputes over such issues as history, labor rights, or aid funds in order to focus on building closer ties with Berlin that could be enormously beneficial in gaining support for Warsaw's foreign policy priorities, especially its Eastern Dimension. This is also economically beneficial since any perceived threats to EU cohesiveness will rebound negatively on the newer members as investors may withdraw their capital to more stable and predictable locations.

Polish authorities remain suspicious of any German-French axis and its underlying anti-American and anti-Atlanticist slant. To counter such a trend, Polish strategists have favored the reinforcement of the Weimar Triangle between Poland, Germany, and France by including the United Kingdom.[7] Such a grouping could become a valuable forum for discussing and coordinating issues of EU foreign and security policy in general and the EU's Eastern policy in particular.

Poland has maintained a close relationship with the United Kingdom and calculated that London could most effectively counter the development of a French-German axis by establishing close ties with all major EU powers and not excluding itself from "inner core" decision making.[8] However, Warsaw's intention to transform the informal Weimar Triangle into a more durable and institutionalized regional initiative involving both old and new EU members have been resisted by its two western partners, especially by the French. The Polish authorities calculated that such an informal grouping could be particularly useful during crisis situations such as the Iraqi war and it could also focus on social, economic, cultural, humanitarian, and environmental issues.[9]

Polish-French relations have been tense on many occasions during the past fifteen years.[10] Paris opposed Polish entry into NATO and in the early 1990s French president Francois Mitterrand sought to weaken Polish links with the United States and was one of the few Western leaders who did not visit Warsaw. Paris was opposed to NATO and EU enlargement and seemed to have minimal concern for the security priorities of the CEE capitals. In fact, French public opinion has been consistently negative about EU enlargement and opposed the accession of countries such as Poland.

During preparations for the war in Iraq in 2003, President Jacques Chirac's diatribe against the CEE capitals and his dismissal of Poland as a newcomer in world politics that should not take part in serious debates led to serious doubts about the sincerity of Paris in accepting the Central and East Europeans as equals in the European Union.[11] Indeed, on several occasions Polish officials have underscored that they rejected being lectured by others on how to be good Europeans and envisaged a "Europe of equals."[12]

Despite these political disputes, in recent years France has become the largest foreign investor in Poland as well as one of the biggest exporters. By the end of 2003, the total stock of French capital invested in Poland exceeded $13 billion. With Polish accession to the EU, French manufacturers gained more significant opportunities to expand into a sizeable new market, thus contributing to creating jobs in France. The French public will need to be more effectively informed about such beneficial developments because doing so would help to limit fears of CEE citizens flooding the country. Nevertheless, Paris was angered by Warsaw's decision in 2002 to purchase American F-16 fighter jets rather than their French equivalent. The relocation of a Peugeot-Citroen car manufacturing plant from Poland to Slovakia was widely viewed as a political rather than an economic decision.

In the security arena, Warsaw has expressed concern that several WE states sought to bypass NATO and duplicate its military structures by developing autonomous military forces. Instead of focusing on creating viable rapid response units within the Alliance to meet new security challenges, the EU was evidently distracted in devising a purely European security structure. Polish officials argued that EU defense capabilities should be developed primarily within NATO's European Security and Defense Identity (ESDI) so as not to duplicate and weaken NATO. Nevertheless, Poland has contributed to the EU's "civilian instruments for crisis management" through its involvement in the first EU police mission in Bosnia-Herzegovina, which took over from the UN in January 2003. Warsaw was also prepared to assign units to serve under the EU flag within the ESDP framework, including a minesweeper, salvage vessels, and troops. In this way, leaders in Warsaw have backed the development of a single EU foreign and security policy, but one that supplements NATO and does not compete with it.

Because Poland was not a EU member at the time that ESDP was evolving, Warsaw was critical over the creation of a EU rapid reaction force as agreed in Helsinki in December 1999. France's support for a planning capacity independent of NATO heightened Warsaw's concerns that ESDP would duplicate the Alliance framework. Poland also feared that ESDP could become a vehicle for growing Russian influence in European security in league with the larger EU powers in which Poland would be marginalized. Concerns about exclusion from security decision making in the EU and any EU pressure on Warsaw to distance itself from Washington actually buttressed Poland's pro-Atlanticism as a means for national defense based on negative historical experiences with West European protection of its national interests.

Polish voters overwhelmingly backed EU accession in a referendum in June 2003, with over 77 percent approving from a turnout of 58 percent. After

Poland joined the EU in May 2004, policy makers increasingly viewed the ESDP, which they initially treated with marked skepticism, as an opportunity to create a credible European pillar and prevent the renationalization of European security policy.[13] The emerging EU defense structure has been supported in Poland as a means for creating a more effective partner for the United States. This position has been encouraged by Warsaw's increasing sense of influence within the European Union. In operational terms, Poland is in the process of preparing a battalion of gendarmeries for EU foreign operations.

Poland seeks a strong, united, and internationally active EU and not a Union that is either ruptured by internal and transatlantic disputes or dominated by an "inner core" or "directorate." Warsaw seeks a workable system of checks and balances by member states especially with regard to the EU's foreign and security policy. On the other hand, some officials realized that as Poland asserted its position in the EU, it too could become part of the "inner sanctum" or a "leading group" in the Union. From this perspective, it will be instructive to see how Poland's progress within the EU impacts on its foreign and security policies and affects its currently strong Atlanticism.

Contrary to many WE suppositions that Poland would become a Euroskeptic and exclusively Atlanticist element within the Union, Warsaw transformed itself into a consistent advocate of a unified EU foreign and security policy in which it seeks to play an influential role. It believes that the EU should acquire greater military power and cohesion in order to be able to cooperate more effectively with the U.S. president. Kwaśniewski argued that Poland's national foreign policy will not disappear as a result of closer EU integration but, on the contrary, some of its objectives may be more effectively achieved through a common European foreign policy.[14]

Warsaw has supported the development of a strong EU Commission and EU Parliament that would help open the Union to further expansion. It backed the creation of the post of EU foreign minister and an EU diplomatic service while endorsing the development of the Union's security strategy.[15] It became more open to the idea of enhancing the EU's autonomous planning capacities, supported creating a European planning cell at NATO headquarters in Belgium, and backed language in the European Security Strategy (ESS) document that confirmed the transatlantic link. Officials did not see these initiatives as necessarily duplicating NATO but as a form of complementarity, in which the EU was more suited to perform low-intensity peacekeeping operations.

The arms industry has become a significant point of contention that places Poland and its CEE neighbors between the EU and the United States. In recent years, Warsaw has promoted closer ties between its own arms industry and that of other EU members, while denying that this was related to any disappointment with its cooperation with Washington.[16] The newly created European Defense Agency (EDA) is supposed to specify the types of weapons the EU requires and to determine whether their manufacture can be coordinated in several member countries. Polish Defense Minister Jerzy Szmajdzinski asserted that Poland would purchase weapons from European manufacturers if they were cost effective and met Warsaw's defense requirements. Poland viewed the EDA as a mechanism for military integration but feared that the CEE's smaller military industries may not be able to withstand the growing monopolization of the larger WE enterprises.

Poland may participate in EDA projects for building modern command and communications systems to supplement its military collaboration with the United States where there are greater legal restrictions on sharing new technologies. Warsaw has also voiced complaints that it did not receive adequate compensation from the United States in offset deals for the purchase of American F-16 planes. The Polish authorities are seeking closer cooperation with Britain, France, and Germany, which account for about 80 percent of the EU's armaments potential.

INVOLVEMENT IN NATO

Warsaw and its CEE neighbors have expressed concern that some West European states are seeking to develop an independent EU counterweight or counterpart to NATO, which in effect may push countries such as Poland even closer to the United States. Polish leaders therefore remained cautious in developing an autonomous EU force and the formation of a European Defense Union. Such a structure is perceived as a potential competitor with NATO and the United States, as well as being prohibitively costly. In order to reinforce the Alliance and maintain its role as the principal security organization, Warsaw has supported such initiatives as the Prague Capabilities Commitment, the NATO Response Force, and joint international projects against WMD proliferation. It also proposed establishing a NATO Allied Forces Training Center in Poland.

Poland views NATO as both a vital defense alliance and a multinational security institution within which a European pillar can be developed. With the EU only slowly evolving a security and foreign policy dimension, Warsaw wants NATO to remain as the main deterrent against external aggression while it develops a more active eastern policy. Polish officials have also supported the "selective globalization of NATO's stabilization activity" by expanding NATO's "out of area" operations, whereby Poland remains a close partner of the United States in confronting global threats.[17] Warsaw also calculated that an expanded NATO would effectively protect the security of new democracies.

The reduced role of NATO in U.S. strategy since 9/11 has been received with concern in Warsaw, which fears that the organization may wither away without American resolve and new Allied missions. As a consequence, U.S. interests in Europe could become more tenuous. It was evident during the military operations in Afghanistan and Iraq that Washington was attaching little value to collective Alliance decision making and combat actions. Polish officials and analysts warn against turning NATO into a mere "tool box" for the United States in its various security missions, as this would diminish the Alliance into a reserve force for Washington and eliminate it as a serious security player.[18]

Both the Polish leadership and the general public appear committed to maintaining the country's military role and indeed Poland has the highest percentage of the population who favor increased defense spending; the figure stood at 41 percent in 2004, even ahead of the United Kingdom at 28 percent.[19] Poland has a respectable record of participation in NATO operations and other multinational missions. Indeed, between 1993 and 2000, 42,000 Polish soldiers participated in forty-six peacekeeping missions led either by NATO, the UN, the OSCE, or the EU.[20] For example, from 1996 onward, Polish soldiers and civil personnel took part in the IFOR and SFOR missions in Bosnia-Herzegovina within the Nordic-Polish Combat Group. In 1999, Polish troops also took part in the humanitarian mission in Albania within the multinational NATO AFOR operation.

Poland performed more prominently in the war over Kosova than several of its neighbors. Warsaw even offered its ground troops to NATO in the event that a ground operation was deemed necessary in the wake of the bombing of Serbia in the spring of 1999. Poland also dispatched approximately five hundred troops to Kosova under NATO's K-FOR (Kosova Stabilization Force) mandate within the Polish-Ukrainian Battalion; this unit also included Lithuanian forces. It actively participated in peacefully pacifying conflicts in the divided city of Mitrovica and performed numerous functions including protecting civil organizations, supporting humanitarian aid, and assisting the local police forces.

U.S. RELATIONS

Poland and the United States have developed close relations since the unraveling of communist rule in 1989. Every post-1989 Polish government has proved to be a vehement supporter of a strong American link both bilaterally and through NATO; a priority backed by leaders of the nearly ten million Polish-Americans. The two capitals have cooperated on a range of issues, including nuclear proliferation, counterterrorism, intelligence sharing, law enforcement, human rights, regional cooperation, United Nations reform, and military missions.

Polish leaders want to see America's global primacy preserved as they have little trust in other global actors, are generally skeptical toward multinational institutions and place an emphasis on "effective multilateralism," and are willing to support the proactive use of military force where they deem it necessary.[21] This is based partly on negative historical experiences with multinational bodies and partly on support for American foreign policy, which Warsaw has viewed as being protective of the country's national interests. Poland's relative weakness based on its geopolitical location, especially when it stood outside of NATO and the EU, consolidated Poland's support for the American superpower. Given that the European Union has not developed an effective military umbrella and the Polish economy is too weak to finance a sufficient modernization of the military to defend the country alone, the United States continues to be viewed as a vital protector.

By contrast, several West European states are perceived in Poland as dangerously pacifist or willing to make bilateral agreements with Russia. The latter was evident in the Paris-Berlin-Moscow axis formed against the U.S.-led military operation in Iraq. The United Nations is criticized in Poland for being unable to prevent conflict or to provide security for states threatened by neighbors. The veto powers of selected states in the UN Security Council demonstrates that the world body relegates the national interests of smaller countries. According to the Security Strategy developed by the Ministry of Defense, although Poland considers the use of force on the international arena should be limited to self-defense, this can also include "operations carried out on the basis of an international community mandate" which does not necessarily involve the United Nations.

Warsaw has been willing to "strongly oppose all those who show aggression and break human rights."[22] Although supportive of international law and international institutions, officials in Warsaw have often seen these as inadequate and inefficient in dealing with new global threats. Even within the European Union, Poland sought to strengthen references to the legitimate use of force and for decoupling this principle from the mandate of the UN Security Council. The UN is widely perceived among Polish decision makers as a method for promoting or legitimizing the interests of larger powers such as Russia and China rather than defending the rights of their neighbors. The history of the UN during the Cold War, in legitimizing Soviet control over half of Europe, underscores the limited credibility of the world body among former Moscow satellites.

Ingrained skepticism toward the United Nations and international laws that encourage inaction was on display during the Kosova crisis in 1999.[23] There was little debate in Warsaw about the ultimate legality of the NATO operation against Serbia although the mission did not have a UN mandate and was questioned by several allies, including France and Germany. Warsaw calculated that noninvolvement would have placed constraints on NATO and set a potentially negative precedent. It also endeavored to demonstrate solidarity with Washington and favored a strong U.S.-led alliance forged in joint operations.

The Polish authorities have noted with pride two core elements of their foreign policy: that they stood with the United States during its moment of need vis-à-vis Afghanistan and Iraq, and that Poland's actions overseas were in accordance with its liberating traditions and in defense of international security.[24] Moreover, Warsaw calculated that support for Washington at such a critical time constituted an important political investment if at a future date Poland found itself in need of U.S. assistance to protect its own security. Hence, sending troops to Afghanistan and Iraq was also a calculated insurance policy. Above all, Polish officials feared any abandonment by Washington of its coresponsibility for European security.

The Polish position was evident in the staunch political support that Warsaw afforded the United States in the military operation "Enduring Freedom" in Afghanistan and in the run up to the Iraqi mission in 2003. A small contingent served in Afghanistan in the framework of the 6,500-strong International Security Assistance Force (ISAF) under U.S. control that was transferred to NATO in late 2003. Warsaw also declared that it was willing to reposition some of its force in Afghanistan as the mission in Iraq was reduced and where it had demonstrated its ability to perform serious military tasks.[25]

With regard to Iraq, as far back as 1990, Polish intelligence officials had offered assistance to Washington during the Gulf War and the Polish embassy in Baghdad represented U.S. interests during the Saddam Hussein regime. Warsaw signed the "letter of eight" in January 2003 expressing support for American policy in overthrowing the Saddam regime in Baghdad even though public opinion was lukewarm. Other signatories included Hungary, the Czech Republic, Britain, Spain, Italy, Portugal, and Denmark. In January 2003, the European Parliament passed a non-binding resolution opposing unilateral military action against Iraq by the United States, claiming that a preemptive strike would not be in accordance with international law and the UN Charter. Poland's Prime Minister Leszek Miller was subsequently criticized by Berlin for failing to notify German Chancellor Gerhard Schroeder about his pro-Washington stance even though the two leaders maintained good relations. Poland joined the "coalition of the willing," consisting of forty-nine countries who were in favor of forcibly removing Saddam Hussein from power.

Poland's military contribution in Iraq included the dispatch of a *Grom* special operations unit, consisting of fifty-four elite troops, the Xavery Czernicki logistics support vessel with a *Formoza* navy commando unit, and seventy-four anti-chemical contamination troops to the Persian Gulf during the U.S.-led invasion in March-April 2003.[26] *Grom* was the only unit from CEE involved in ground operations in "Operation Iraqi Freedom," alongside tens of thousands of U.S. and UK forces. After the occupation was secured, Warsaw was allocated the administration of one of four "stabilization zones." The sector encompassed predominantly Shiite territory in central-southern Iraq and the mission was to restore and maintain public order. Warsaw dispatched approximately 2,500 troops to the area where Polish forces constituted the core of a multinational division of nearly 10,000 soldiers from two dozen countries, including Spain, Ukraine, Bulgaria, Hungary, Slovakia, Latvia, and Lithuania, in addition to forces from outside CEE.

Having contributed the third largest allied force in Iraq, after the United States and Britain, and displaying substantial professionalism in managing a diverse multinational division, the Polish authorities initially declared that they would only pull out their troops from Iraq after the stabilization mission was successfully completed. They based their decision not on perceptions of direct threat from the Middle East or because of concern over the presence of weapons of mass distruction (WMD) in Iraq. Some observers have labeled Polish policy as one of "bandwagoning," in which a weaker country seeks benefits from a strong and hegemonic power by supporting its foreign policy. Other concepts can also be applied to this relationship, but Warsaw's overriding objective was to demonstrate its solidarity with the United States and illustrate that Poland was America's "model ally."[27] This would help concretize the relationship of "reciprocal obligation" so that the Iraqi mission would become an "insurance policy" for long-term Polish security.

Warsaw also calculated that it would secure more privileged access for Polish companies in Iraqi reconstruction and the rearmament of the Iraqi military. In reality, only a handful of Polish companies have been involved in these programs and some officials have complained about the nontransparent nature of bidding for Iraqi projects in which American corporations have prevailed. Additionally, the Iraqi deployment has exceeded Warsaw's defense budgeting and may therefore have impeded planned reform and modernization in Poland's armed forces.

As a consequence of the lessons learned from its Middle Eastern deployments, Warsaw has sought to develop a new Strategic Defense Review (SDR). By 2004, Poland had a total military force of some 150,000 troops and maintained approximately 4,700 troops in expeditionary expeditions abroad, or 6.2 percent of its total professional force.[28] By the close of 2004, Warsaw had about 1,000 troops allocated to UN peacekeeping operations in Lebanon and Syria, 350 troops in SFOR in Bosnia-Herzegovina, 800 troops in KFOR in Kosova, and 2,500 troops in Iraq.

During 2002, Warsaw finalized a contract to purchase forty-eight American F-16 multipurpose warplanes for a price tag of $3.5 billion in order to upgrade its air force to NATO standards, despite strong competition from French and Anglo-Swedish manufacturers.[29] The deal also included pledges of $6 billion in U.S. investments in the Polish economy and promises to increase the purchase of Polish goods. This deal provoked disputes with several of Poland's future EU partners, while there were also disagreements with Washington over the execution of offset obligations associated with the F-16 contract. This involved U.S. corporate investments in new technologies and Poland's defense industry. By mid-2005, U.S. and NATO investments in Poland totaled some 121 projects and included the modernization of several military airports.[30] Further economic issues that could impact negatively on Warsaw's relations with its EU partners included Polish plans to purchase U.S. Boeing planes rather than EU Airbuses for its civilian fleet.

Warsaw's adherence to U.S. foreign policy goals indicated that political leaders were intent on joining America's "inner circle" of dependable allies. However, Poland's value to the United States remains contingent on several factors, including its contribution to American missions, its continuing political support for Washington, its effectiveness as an influential regional power, its prominence within the European Union, and its pursuit of defense sector reform to modernize Poland's armed forces. Officials in Warsaw are intent on convincing Washington that it is in America's direct national interest to protect and enhance Poland's security.[31] However, they also stress that the U.S. administration will need to more clearly define why its relations with Poland are important and durable. Polish officials are also seeking longer-term forms of cooperation with the United States, particularly in the area of economic investment.

Polish authorities may also increasingly recognize that they can criticize U.S. policy when this is deemed necessary without joining the anti-American camp. Indeed, after it became clear that stocks of WMD could not be found in Iraq, President Kwaśniewski expressed "discomfort" that Poland may have been "misguided" by information from Washington prior to the Iraqi intervention.[32] Disappointment with the results of U.S. strategy in Iraq has been growing in official circles, as the country remains unstable despite general elections and the large-scale military presence and its future is uncertain. In October 2004, Defense Minister Jerzy Szmajdzinski stated that the entire Polish contingent should be withdrawn from Iraq by the end of 2005, regardless of the security situation.[33] Although government spokesmen claimed that Szmajdzinski had not consulted with the prime minister before issuing the statement, it was evident that a potential pullout had been deliberated in government circles.

Most Polish politicians believe that the country will carry more weight within the European Union if it is viewed as a strong U.S. ally rather than a neutral power.[34] However, Warsaw must remain watchful that its close relationship with Washington does not alienate it from the EU and distance it from Germany and France in particular. In a brewing scandal at the close of 2005, Poland and Romania became prime suspects in allegations that they hosted secret CIA prisons where terrorist suspects were held and tortured.[35] Both capitals denied the reports and declared that they would cooperate in investigations launched by the Council of Europe. If the charges were proven, Poland could face some form of censure by the EU, including a possible suspension of voting rights, and would lose a great deal of credibility among its West European partners.

Some WE commentators contend that Polish foreign policy has assumed a triumphalist tone in recent years and accuse Poland of being a "Trojan horse" for expanding American influence in European affairs. Some French commentators have gone even further to claim that the aim of U.S. policy is to use Poland and other new CEE members to gradually undermine EU policy making and eliminate Franco-German leadership in the Union.[36] Polish officials counter that such views are fabrications and indicate the lingering prejudices of some WE capitals toward the CEE states and toward the United States. They also underscore the differing visions of Paris and Warsaw regarding the future of European security, with France seeking a more autonomous structure and Poland opposed to the creation of an alternative to NATO.

Poland has benefited from its close ties with the United States and its engagement in military operations. Polish servicemen have gained direct combat and postwar peacekeeping experience and collaborated closely with U.S. and other NATO forces. According to Polish Prime Minister Marek Belka, the experience in Iraq has enabled Polish military units to "measure up to the standards of the best European armies."[37] Washington also plans to relocate some of its troops to Poland as part of its global repositioning of forces. Warsaw has welcomed the creation of small U.S. bases as have several other CEE countries, especially as this could attract American investments as well as closer military ties. Polish officials, especially in the Defense Ministry, have also welcomed Polish participation in the U.S. (National) Ballistic Missile Defense (BMD) system and seemed willing to host some elements of the BMD "shield" such as radar systems, launch pads, and other facilities.[38] Defense Ministry officials contend that the deployment would strengthen Poland's importance for the United States, for NATO, and for the European Union since the country did not currently possess any NATO military installations or command structures.

Despite these initiatives, Polish officials, including President Kwaśniewski's national security adviser Marek Siwiec, warned that relations with the United States were in danger of stagnating as a result of limited benefits from the

American side and anger over visa requirements for Polish citizens.[39] Foreign Ministry spokesperson Bogusław Majewski claimed that new U.S. entry procedures, introduced in January 2004, requiring biometric identification for aliens, was a potential public relations disaster with Poland.[40] Officials and analysts point out that Poland unilaterally waived visas for Americans and scrapped fees for U.S. citizens traveling to Poland. Despite such measures, Polish citizens were not only required to have visas to enter the United States, but also needed to pay for them even if their applications were rejected. To counter Polish disquiet over visa requirements, in February 2005 the White House announced a new "road map" that would lead to a liberalization of visa regulations and eventually to Polish citizens not requiring U.S. visas. The move did little to assuage skepticism among the Polish public as the process would be long and arduous. In May 2006, the U.S. Senate approved measures enabling Polish citizens to visit the United States without visas, but the provision faced numerous hurdles before it could become law.

Concern and even resentment has been expressed over limited Polish economic opportunities in postwar Iraq, with investment awards favoring American and British companies. Officials contend that Polish companies have had substantial experience in Iraq during the 1970s and 1980s, many Iraqis have studied in Poland, while the Polish embassy in Baghdad represented U.S. interests in Iraq for more than ten years after the 1991 Gulf War. Poland's reconstruction reward from the Iraqi operation have been dismissed by many critics as dismal. By the end of 2004, Polish firms only gained contracts worth about $130 million, and most of this sum went to one company, PHZ Bumar, which gained two arms contracts.[41] This was a fraction of the figure Warsaw had been hoping for.

Poland planned to gain several other benefits from its prominent participation in the "coalition of the willing," including substantial U.S. financial and technological assistance in modernizing Poland's armed forces and greater American investments in the Polish economy, especially in modern technologies. However, the gap between the promise and the reality of U.S. assistance has been widening. Although in February 2005 President Bush reportedly pledged to President Kwasniewski during the latter's visit to Washington that U.S. aid for the modernization of Poland's armed forces would be increased to $100 million, in the following month the U.S. House of Representatives significantly lowered this amount. Poland intended to use these resources to purchase modern equipment, including reconnaissance systems from the United States. Some Polish commentators complained that once again Poland had been cheated and was acting as a submissive partner to America.[42] Moreover, officials pointed out that Warsaw was footing a huge bill for its troops in Iraq, estimated at around $90 million for 2004 alone. Washington had only offset some $27 million of this sum, a figure comparable to sums afforded to countries with only a few dozen troops in Iraq.

By the beginning of 2005, even members of the ruling Democratic Left Alliance (DLA) were voicing their opposition to Polish military involvement in Iraq and proposed introducing amendments to legislation dealing with dispatching troops abroad. A DLA draft amendment envisaged that military units could only be sent abroad in future either under a UN mandate or as a result of a separate international agreement, and with parliamentary consent.[43] In April 2005, the authorities announced that Poland aimed to withdraw its forces from Iraq at the beginning of 2006.[44] While the government claimed the move was driven by limited military resources, it was also a response to negative public opinion over the government's performance during an election year and partly a reaction to disappointment at Washington's policies toward Poland. Defense Minister Szmajdzinski added the proviso that the mission could be extended if the UN Security Council voted a new mandate for 2006 or if the Iraqi government specifically asked Poland to retain its troops in the country.[45]

Despite the tensions that crept into the U.S.-Polish relationship, institutional cooperation between the two capitals continued to expand. The 2002 Defense Transformation Initiative (DTI), designed to transfer American experience in military transformation to Poland, has been renewed annually, and a program for modernizing Poland's armed forces between 2003 and 2008 was launched. In March 2005, Washington and Warsaw prepared the first joint counterterrorism working group involving the United States and a Central European country.[46] The group planned to issue recommendations for improving collaboration in such areas as intelligence sharing, training of experts, and legal measures.

In the economic and business arena, Warsaw remains concerned that transactions with the United States are anemic as compared to growing commerce and investment with Poland's EU partners. For instance, in 2004, Polish exports to the United States amounted to only 2.7 percent of the country's total, as compared to 32 percent with the EU. Similarly, a mere 3 percent of Polish imports originated in the United States, compared with 23 percent from Germany alone.[47]

Public support for Washington will be measured partly by the long-term success of the stabilization mission in Iraq. It will also be raised by a clearer American position in support of democracy in Russia and backing for NATO enlargement to include Ukraine. Polish officials and analysts have been suspicious of an American-Russian relationship that gives Moscow a free hand to reverse the democratization process at home and engage in a neoimperialist policy toward its neighbors. Washington's approach to Putin has often been confusing and potentially destabilizing for Poland, especially as Warsaw continues to see the United States as the only credible guarantor against Russian aggression. On the other hand, any future Polish support for U.S. military missions will be more carefully weighed against domestic public opinion, available state resources, the stance of EU partners, and Poland's long-term national interests.

Poland is likely to develop into an ally that is more critical of the United States and more discerning in supporting Washington's policies. This will be beneficial to both Poland and the United States as Warsaw's loyalty and solidarity cannot be doubted among American policy makers. Poland will benefit by having more political inputs into its foreign policy decision making and it will be viewed by other EU members as a more impartial European power. The United States could thereby gain an ally that will have more influence in the European Union because of its independent stance and Poland would be able to discard its negative image as an American stooge in Paris and Berlin.

REGIONAL RELATIONS

Poland is the largest and most populous state in Central Europe, it has played a historically important role in the region, and it retains the largest economy and military potential in CEE. Since the collapse of the Soviet bloc, Warsaw has sought to play an active regional role through both bilateral and multinational linkages. Indeed, the country's importance in the European Union could largely hinge on its regional importance both in Central Europe and in relation to the "eastern sphere." In this context, Warsaw has sought to revive the Visegrad Group, consisting of Poland, the Czech Republic, Hungary, and Slovakia, established in the early 1990s to help coordinate approaches toward NATO and the European Union. It has supported joint Visegrad positions in the framework of the EU. Poland has also sought to enhance the role of the Council of Baltic Sea States and established an interparliamentary group with Lithuania. It consistently backed further NATO and EU enlargement to include Romania, Bulgaria, and other Balkan and Black Sea states.

In the security realm, Warsaw has developed various forms of military cooperation with its immediate neighbors. A Polish-Ukrainian battalion (POLUKRBAT) has operated in Kosova, a Polish-Lithuanian battalion (LITPOLBAT) was also formed for peace missions, and in 1999, together with Germany and Denmark, Poland formed the trilateral Multinational Corps Northeast (MCN) and proposed to expand this corps to include the three Baltic states. The Chief Command of the MSN was located in the Polish port of Szczecin. Warsaw also strongly supported NATO enlargement and canvassed vigorously for the inclusion of its neighbor Slovakia and the three Baltic states.[48]

Despite Poland's efforts, the Visegrad group has not been a united entity on all foreign policy issues, and even with regard to the Iraqi intervention differences emerged between the four states.[49] Divisions have also been evident over the draft EU Constitutional Treaty and the Nice voting model, in which Poland found itself isolated in the region. Some Czech and Slovak commentators even accused Warsaw of weakening the entire group by entangling it in needless controversies within the EU. Prague in particular has remained reticent in supporting the Visegrad initiative and has been suspicious of excessive Polish influence.

Some Polish analysts have proposed a wider consultative mechanism within the European Union, comprised of Visegrad, the Baltic states, and future East Balkan members. Such a grouping could evidently push for common positions in the Union, particularly with regard to the "Eastern Question."[50] Many of the problems faced by CEE in dealing with Russia could thereby be demonstrated to be a common EU problem, while the "Europeanization" of Ukraine, Moldova, Belarus, and Georgia can be prioritized as a common EU challenge. This would help prevent the EU from juxtaposing a choice between support for Poland's eastern policy or a strategic partnership with Russia while buttressing Poland's voice and influence within the European Union.

Attempts have been made to revitalize the Visegrad Group after all of its members had entered both NATO and the European Union. In April 2005, ministers of the four states responsible for regional policy signed a declaration to initiate joint measures to revive territorial cooperation through the development of transportation corridors and local infrastructure. The objective was to help shape EU policy in supporting and funding these regional endeavors.[51]

In practice, rather than becoming an effective and united interest group within the EU, the Visegrad initiative is unlikely to evolve much beyond sponsoring various regional projects. Several CEE capitals have been reluctant if not resentful toward Poland's attempt to position itself as a regional power or even a regional leader. This has been demonstrated in practical issues such as the debate over the Nice Treaty where only the Euro-skeptic Czech President Vaclav Klaus supported the Polish position on advantageous voting rights. Poland failed to coordinate its approach with Visegrad neighbors in negotiating over the EU's structural funds for accession states, whereas the four countries may have been more successful in working together. Warsaw was also disappointed in its failure to mobilize its neighbors in any significant common projects through the "Riga Initiative" launched by President Kwaśniewski in March 2003.[52]

The scope of Visegrad has been a source of contention. For example, Polish officials disagreed with Hungary's proposal to include Austria and Slovenia in the Visegrad format, arguing that this would dilute its distinct identity. Some level of economic competition between the New Allies was also evident in terms of their attractiveness for foreign direct investment, whether because of lower labor costs, smaller corporate taxes, better infrastructure, and a more favorable investment climate.

Polish analysts contend that while the country is simply too big a player not to be ambitious, it is also too weak at present to be a major player.[53] Such a situation creates tensions between Poland's aspirations and capabilities. On occasion, tensions are also evident with some CEE neighbors, which are perceived in Warsaw as cooling off in their Atlanticism and gradually becoming "Brussified" as small EU states. Officials in Warsaw remain suspicious that several CEE neighbors prefer to be linked with the larger EU member states and are willing to sacrifice their distinct CEE identity and interests within the Union.

THE EASTERN DIMENSION

Warsaw's underlying strategic rationale contends that political, economic, and social instability along its eastern borders impacts negatively on Polish and European security.[54] The long-term goal of all postcommunist Polish administrations has been to free the region from Russia's neoimperial influence and establish a "democratic cordon" of states along its eastern frontier.[55] In Warsaw's calculations, the most effective mechanisms for achieving such an objective is to propel its eastern neighbors toward both NATO and EU membership as such concrete prospects will help consolidate democracy, the rule of law, market economies, and security sector reforms.

Poland's National Security Strategy underscores that NATO remains the key platform of international security cooperation and the main pillar of political and military stability on the continent. Hence, Warsaw has consistently advocated an open door policy for NATO for all European countries that meet the criteria for membership. Poland also sees itself as a pioneer of reform in postcommunist Europe and a major player in the region in advocating its neighbors' membership in Western institutions, promoting democratic governance and civil society, and helping to build competitive capitalist economies.

Warsaw has understood the potential value of the EU's CFSP as a method for involving the Union in resolving the "eastern question."[56] Polish authorities have been pushing the EU Council, the EU Commission, and the EU Parliament to pursue a more activist policy toward its eastern neighbors while complaining that the Union has been characterized by inertia, accommodation, and exaggerated concern about Russia's negative reaction to reform along its western borders. Polish officials also point out that the EU has avoided criticizing Moscow for its declining democratic practices and deteriorating human rights record, thus encouraging further Russian regression.

In 1998 Poland proposed the creation of an EU Eastern Dimension through a "European space of political and economic cooperation within a wider Europe" at a time when it was initiating its own membership negotiations with the Union.[57] It canvassed for EU Association Agreements, or "Partnerships for Association," with Ukraine, Belarus, and Moldova, together with roadmaps for their eventual EU inclusion.[58] In 2002, the EU launched its Wider Europe–New Neighborhood initiative, which was renamed as the European Neighborhood Policy (ENP). In November 2003, the European Parliament adopted a resolution on "Wider Europe" that was largely in line with Polish proposals.

Since it entered the Union, Warsaw has sought to play a central role in shaping the EU's eastern policy and in developing closer ties with its eastern neighbors. Indeed, Polish officials view these countries as a separate and special category for more intensive EU involvement. Warsaw's proposals were not fully endorsed by its West European partners who were primarily concerned about Poland's assertive approach and its repercussions for EU-Russia relations. They considered the ENP, which did not specify future accession for the participating states, as a sufficient incentive. Germany in particular intended to maintain a "strategic partnership" with Russia and develop sectoral ties with the Russian economy. It did not want to undermine these relations by pushing for EU expansion eastward. France also pursued a Russia first policy and ignored the standpoint of Poland and other CEE states which it viewed as too confrontational toward Moscow.

From Poland's perspective, Ukraine is the pivotal country in the region that must be drawn into the Western fold and prized away from Russian influence. Warsaw played an important role during the election crisis in Ukraine in November–December 2004 as President Kwaśniewski intervened directly as a mediator between the two Ukrainian presidential candidates with U.S. support and EU acquiescence. Polish officials have unambiguously backed the further enlargement of the European Union eastward and pushed for EU Action Plans and Partnership and Cooperation Agreements with Ukraine, Belarus, and Moldova.[59]

These proposals were amplified following Ukraine's Orange Revolution. Poland's foreign policy goals for 2005, approved by parliament in February 2005, specified support for the democratic transformation of Ukraine. Warsaw viewed itself as a bridge between the EU and the "wider Europe" in the east.[60] However, Warsaw has also been careful not to push itself forward too strongly lest it be attacked by its EU partners as being too regionally ambitious and provocative toward Moscow.

In January 2005, President Kwaśniewski formally backed Ukraine's application to join the EU after his Ukrainian counterpart, President Viktor Yushchenko, announced Kyiv's ambition to enter the Union.[61] Kwaśniewski declared that Brussels should put forward a "more daring plan of action" toward Ukraine and set a date for the start of accession negotiations. Meanwhile, Poland's parliamentary speaker Włodzimierz Cimoszewicz warmed that some EU members will object to further Union expansion as they still remain unconvinced that the entry of ten CEE countries was ultimately beneficial.[62]

Poland has been campaigning vigorously in support of Ukraine's membership in both NATO and the EU.[63] It has tried to inject a singular approach into the EU's Eastern policy and consistently supported Ukraine's entry into NATO—for which President Bush gave conditional backing during President Yushchenko's visit to Washington in April 2005. The authorities in Warsaw proposed in January 2005 that the Union's relations with Ukraine should be raised to the level of "strategic partnership" thus opening the door to future integration.[64] Poland wants the EU to have a more distinct foreign and security policy, but one that is backed by strategic vision, political will, and military muscle. Although the Polish authorities have tried to establish a more influential role for itself within the EU and within its neighborhood, it remains doubtful whether Warsaw will be able to muster sufficient support in the Union, beyond Central Europe, the Baltics, and Scandinavia, to ensure Ukraine's future EU membership. Close relations between Berlin, Paris, and Moscow indicate that this will remain an uphill struggle.

In January 2005, Polish parliamentary speaker Cimoszewicz approved the idea of establishing a tripartite Interparliamentary Assembly between Poland, Lithuania, and Ukraine after a meeting with his Lithuanian counterpart Arturas Paulauskas.[65] The assembly would exchange contacts and information on European issues. The three countries already shared bilateral parliamentary assemblies and the tripartite format was approved in both Vilnius and Kyiv. Its primary purpose was to advance Ukraine's aspirations to join NATO and the EU by imparting Poland's and Lithuania's reform experiences to the Ukrainian parliament. In May 2005, the three capitals also decided to field a tripartite peacekeeping battalion (LitPolUkrbat) in order to develop the existing bilateral Polish-Ukrainian and Polish-Lithuanian battalions. The unit, consisting of 640 troops, was dispatched to Kosova at the end of 2005 and could in future be deployed for peacekeeping missions in Moldova and Georgia.[66]

Poland has also positioned itself to play a constructive role in fostering democratic changes in neighboring Belarus and has come under bitter attack by the authoritarian regime of President Alyaksandr Lukashenka. All of Belarus's Central European neighbors were concerned about the outcome of the presidential elections in March 2006 and the prolongation of the Lukashenka regime, which could have a negative impact on their own security. Poland and the three Baltic states, in particular, have been pushing the United States and the EU to become more directly and comprehensively engaged with Belarus in order to promote democratization and eventual European and transatlantic integration for this estranged and isolated republic. The Europeanization of Belarus would help stabilize a wider Europe and promote U.S. national interests by reinforcing transatlantic relations.

Warsaw makes a clear distinction between Russia on the one hand and Ukraine, Belarus, and Moldova on the other. It underscores that Russia has no prospect of joining the European Union and does not itself seek membership. Hence, the EU and Russia should remain as two sovereign partners but not entitled to block the other party's interests.[67] A struggle has developed within the EU regarding the appropriate approach toward Russia, and Poland is at the forefront of those states that seek a more assertive policy toward Moscow. Polish spokesmen believe that the Union should show greater concern over anti-democratic tendencies in Russian politics and demonstrate that the West does not approve of the authoritarian system being established by President Putin. Polish officials criticize the inconsistencies of their WE Union partners who condemn extrajudicial killings in Israel and elsewhere but fail to criticize Russia for a much more brutal policy toward civilians in Chechnya.

Warsaw has been particularly concerned that Russia is seeking to create fractures in the EU by pursuing differing approaches toward the WE and the CEE countries and using its ties with the former to undermine the latter. According to President Kwaśniewski, Russian policy toward the EU creates the danger of manipulation and abuse and Poland wants the EU's relations with Moscow to be decided and implemented by consensual agreement in Brussels. There have been several examples of how Moscow has dealt with Paris and Berlin over the heads of the CEE capitals. During the late 1990s, as Poland prepared itself for EU membership it reintroduced visas for Russian citizens and Moscow strongly objected to such visa requirements for citizens crossing into the Russian exclave of Kaliningrad. France lobbied on Russia's behalf to the dismay of Polish officials who strongly criticized French President Francois Mitterand.[68]

In April 2005, Germany and Russia agreed to construct a new gas pipeline through the Baltic Sea that would bypasses Poland. Such an arrangement with Russian energy directly concerns the entire EU, particularly those states that are almost fully dependent on Russian supplies. The proposed pipeline has the potential of undermining Polish and CEE security.[69] Hence, Warsaw asserted that this project needed to be discussed within the Union and not simply on a bilateral basis. Chancellor Gerhard Schröeder's comments that

German-Russian relations are better than they have been for a hundred years were poorly received in Warsaw.[70] While Poland views Russia as a power to be contained, Germany sees Russia as its principal partner in the east. Such a position could exacerbate existing rifts in Polish-German relations.

As a result of the unreliability of several WE states, Warsaw has sought to convince Washington to have a more realistic policy toward Russia and its eastern neighbors. Officials were heartened by unflinching U.S. support for the pro-democracy upsurge during Ukraine's Orange Revolution in November–December 2005, and by President Bush's visits to Riga (Latvia) and Tbilisi (Georgia) during his trip to Europe in May 2005. His backing for the popular revolutions in Georgia and Ukraine indicated that Washington wanted to maintain its active support for democratic forces throughout the former Soviet Union, while upholding its relations with Russia.[71] Poland believes that the development of a joint and effective U.S.-EU policy toward Russia and the East European states outside the EU would strengthen opportunities for democratic development in the region and enhance Poland's security as well as that of its allies.

Since the collapse of the Soviet bloc, Russian leaders envisaged postcommunist Central Europe as consisting of a string of neutral and weak states regardless of their internal political and economic makeup. A primary Kremlin objective was to deter or prevent these countries from moving into NATO and further diminishing Moscow's strategic maneuverability. The Kremlin sought the region's demilitarization and neutralization so that it would form a buffer between NATO and the CIS (Commonwealth of Independent States). This would have enabled Moscow to once again act unilaterally throughout the region as it depicted its own security as paramount and its national interests as more important than that of its neighbors.

Once NATO invitations had been issued to the Central Europeans, the Russian authorities seemed resigned to the loss of Poland as a buffer state and a neutral neighbor. Nonetheless, Russian strategists still perceived the country's full integration into the Western system and especially Poland's accession to NATO as an obstacle and challenge to Kremlin influences over the three Baltic republics, Ukraine, and Belarus. Hence, the democratic Polish governments were treated with suspicion and hostility throughout the 1990s.

Following the collapse of the Soviet empire, a historic struggle reemerged between Poland and Russia. This has centered on their competition over a region that formed part of the Polish-Lithuanian Commonwealth from the fifteenth to the eighteenth centuries and then fell under Muscovite control until the demise of communism. Ukraine, Belarus, and Moldova form the modern battleground between an Atlanticist and European Poland and a Eurasian Russia. The Russian elite is deeply suspicious of Polish motives and believes

Poland was a major culprit in the breakup of the Soviet imperium and now seeks to fracture Russia and its "Eurasian" allies.

The neutralization of Polish influences eastward is deemed essential by the Russian regime and President Vladimir Putin has intensified and implemented such an approach. Moscow remains keenly watchful of close cooperation between Warsaw and its eastern neighbors, fearful of Polish and Western influences that could permanently tear Ukraine and Belarus away from the Russian orbit. Hence, Polish political, cultural, and economic influences have been attacked and opposed by Moscow and its various interest groups in the region.

At the outset of Putin's tenure in 2000, Moscow appeared to inject more pragmatism into its relations with the four Visegrad states. Political relations with Russia seemed to improve as the Kremlin evidently calculated that it needed to adapt to an enlarging and developing EU in which Poland would soon be a member. However, as Putin endeavored to raise Russia's stature through economic and political instruments, relations soured precipitously. From 2003 onward, a mini "cold war" unfolded between Moscow and Warsaw over a number of disputed issues. The tug-of-war over Ukraine in late 2004 convinced the Kremlin that Poland was its chief regional adversary, while Putin's real ambitions were confirmed for the Polish elites.

Moscow remains deeply troubled that the CEE states serve as attractive models for the neighboring CIS countries, undermine their continuing dependence on Russia, and could even pull some of Russia's federal regions away from Moscow's control. Poland is at the center of this unwelcome "Eastern policy" which among Russian elites is perceived as a revival of "Polish imperialism." Hence, Poland eastern neighborhood is precisely where "Euramerica" clashes most directly with "Eurasia" and the outcome along this tectonic plate remains uncertain.

Warsaw pursues a common EU policy and a complementary EU-U.S. policy toward Russia, and both could prove a major challenge over the coming decade. Some critics contend that an effective "grand strategy" will not be possible to implement and attempts to do so could create new fractures within the EU and NATO. Poland will try to leverage its close ties with Washington and its growing influence within the EU to have a constructive impact on its eastern neighbors and even on Russia itself—constructive in the sense that Polish officials seek to expand European institutions eastward and to curtail Moscow's ability to block this process.

While some American and European policy makers have argued that Putin had rejected the doctrine of "multipolarity" in his dealings with the United States, such premature hopes were dashed when Moscow sided with France and Germany during the Iraq crisis. Putin again publicly elevated "multipolarity" as a strategic objective, meaning the pursuit of multiple power centers in order to diminish American dominance. Such a position is vehemently opposed by Poland, as Russian policy is designed not so much to strengthen Europe as to weaken America and its role on the old continent.

Although Moscow adopted a relatively mild approach toward NATO's second substantial enlargement in 2003, Putin declared that his objective was to create structures that facilitated the "unification of Europe" together with Russia. This would evidently constitute one strong "pole" to balance the United States. At a time when Washington has been preoccupied with Iraq and global terrorist networks, the Kremlin calculates that it can take the steam out of NATO expansion, enlist European support for its security proposals, diminish the position of CEE states, and exacerbate any latent transatlantic divisions.

Putin has repeatedly stressed his yearnings for NATO to become a "political organization" and not a security alliance. This has serious repercussions for new members such as Poland where Russian cooperation with the Alliance becomes another means for undercutting NATO's rationale as an effective military structure that can operate outside the zone of member states. It is also a blatant attempt to weaken the American-European security relationship and to expose former Soviet satellites, including Poland, to renewed and unwelcome Russian influences.

The Russian leadership seeks two strategic long-term objectives: access to NATO and EU decision making and major political influence from the Balkans to Central Asia. Putin understands that Russia is too weak to prevent further NATO enlargement. Instead, the Kremlin aims to minimize the impact of NATO's growth by obtaining a role in Alliance decision making. Putin also realizes that NATO has weakened as a coherent institution because the United States increasingly acts with willing partners during international crises. Hence, the Russian president fortifies his ties with Washington when it benefits Moscow and forges alternative coalitions in order to exploit America's strategic weaknesses. Any transatlantic conflicts are a strong temptation for the Kremlin to revive its "divide and conquer" strategies.

Poland was apprehensive when French and German leaders, in opposition to U.S. policy in Iraq during 2003, courted Moscow in a counterweight axis to Washington's coalition. Such a strategy indicated a unilateralist approach by several large EU members that ignored the views of EU newcomers such as Poland. Moscow has also pushed in the EU capitals for a freer hand in its regional policies. For example, the Kremlin is canvassing for an international seal of approval as the primary peacekeeper or conflict manager in Central Asia, the Caucasus, and other former Soviet territories. This would entail significant leeway for Moscow in dealing with independence movements within the Russian Federation, enhance political and economic influence among neighbors, and even enable military operations in nearby regions on the pretext of protecting its strategic interests and assets regardless of the opposition of indigenous governments.

During the past decade, Moscow has expanded its peacekeeping operations in the CIS with little regard for a UN or OSCE (Organization for Security and Cooperation in Europe) mandate. The Kremlin claims that "Muslim radicalism" constitutes a threat to Russia and its neighbors and seeks to camouflage its own expansionism as a struggle against "fundamentalism and terrorism." Putin calculates that the West will accede to Russia's increasing pressures and economic and security influences in its "near abroad" while the United States remains preoccupied on other fronts. This would effectively neutralize all the former East European satellites, including Poland, with Moscow pushing itself forward as an indispensable center of power alongside Washington and Brussels.

In this challenging strategic environment, Warsaw seeks to enhance its own position and prestige while upholding American engagement throughout CEE. To successfully navigate such a strategy the authorities need to achieve three overriding objectives: to consolidate Poland's position as a reliable NATO ally; to gain an important role in EU decision making especially with regard to the Union's foreign and security policy; and to maintain its close relationship with the United States.

POLITICAL OPTIONS

Several Polish policy analysts have described a fracture in the country's political consensus on key foreign policy issues, although it is difficult to ascertain how much of this is genuine and how much a question of tactics.[72] Although the basic tenets of Polish foreign policy remain unchanged, including the U.S. alliance and EU and NATO membership, some analysts believe that a new formula needs to be established for Poland's place in the world based on a multiparty consensus. This would include a clear approach toward international institutions, toward the role of force in international relations, and toward Poland's "strategic partnerships." While in the past there has been greater consensus on relations with the United States than the European Union, specific policy approaches toward both may become increasingly diversified and divisive.

During the tenure of the center-left Democratic Left Alliance (DLA) between 2001 and 2005 Polish commentators from the center-right opposition asserted that the strong support shown to the United States by the DLA government and President Kwasniewski personally were indicative of former communists purposively demonstrating that they had shaken off their Soviet past. Indeed, the center-right formations have talked about their allegedly more authentic pro-American policy based on "Atlantic solidarity" and traditional bilateral links.[73]

Rather than criticizing the direction of Polish policy or the U.S. administration, the main opposition parties, Law and Justice (LJ) and Civic Platform (CP) assailed the center-left government for ineptitude. It allegedly squandered opportunities to enhance Warsaw's position vis-à-vis Washington regarding issues such as visa waivers for Polish citizens, reconstruction contracts in Iraq for Polish companies, and the execution of offset contracts in return for Warsaw's purchase of American F-16 aircraft.[74] The more radical Polish parties accused the administration of servility and corruption.

EU criticisms of the Polish government position toward the Iraqi war were vehemently attacked by several opposition parties, whereas government officials felt more constrained. In particular, there were strident condemnations of Paris, which spilled over into attacks on the French position toward Poland's EU accession negotiations. President Chirac's provocative statements on the eve of the Iraqi intervention in April 2003 reinforced fears that Poland would become a second-class EU member, thus heightening Euroskepticism among the opposition.

The center-left government, formed around the DLA and the smaller centrist formations such as the Freedom Union (FU), the Polish Peasants Party (PPP), and the Democratic Party (DP) proved generally supportive of EU membership, although differing on their approaches to EU integration and the Constitutional Treaty. Leftist formations, including the Labor Union (LU) and the Polish Social Democratic Party (PSDP), have been more outspoken against the American link and favored a stronger and federated EU with a distinct security structure. However, they held limited public backing and are unlikely to have any significant influence on Polish foreign policy in the near future.

Euro-skeptics favoring a more distinct "Polish way" could be grouped into two broad categories: the liberal free-marketeers and the conservative protectionists. The CP and LJ, both with significant parliamentary representation, encompassed these two political strands and comfortably won the October 2005 parliamentary elections, although they proved unable to establish a coalition government. The LJ subsequently formed a minority government that became reliant on parliamentary support from two of the smaller and more radical parties.

While in opposition, both center-right parties were highly critical of EU bureaucratism, statism, and centralism. CP leader Jan Rokita strongly criticized what was widely perceived in Poland as discrimination against Polish political and economic interests in the enlarged Union. Nevertheless, the CP backed a more pronounced Polish role in the Union together with an effective common EU foreign and security policy, an enlarged Eurozone, an expanded Schengen area, and further EU enlargement eastward.[75] The LJ supported

Poland's accession into the EU, but was generally more skeptical about the Union and its impact on Polish sovereignty and society than the CP.

During preparations for Poland's referendum on EU accession, held in June 2003, the political climate in Poland heated up as opponents of Union entry charged that the government was surrendering too much Polish sovereignty. While center-right free marketeers claimed that the EU was too statist and centralized, the rightist protectionists asserted that the European free market would destroy Polish agriculture, strip the country of its most important assets, and undermine Poland's "national identity."[76]

In terms of the EU's economic policy, CP leader Rokita noted the irony that the EU had repeatedly berated Poland to open itself up to market competition and free trade, but was now being offered the same advice by Warsaw. CP spokesmen contended that the EU needed greater economic competition and liberalization in order to be economically strong and complained about the socialist and welfarist model that prevailed in France. Neither the CP nor the LJ were enamored of the EU's Constitutional Treaty, but they also claimed that its failure could delay the CEE countries in catching up economically with the WE as the older EU member states would deliberately slow down the process of economic integration.

LJ leaders have strongly criticized Paris and Berlin for seeking to establish a European super state and a "multipolar" system that would counteract American influence. They also accused both capitals of pandering to Russian strategic and economic interests. This evidently necessitated a stronger Polish-American partnership, which they pledged to develop in the event of election victory. LJ has also been highly critical of Berlin and warned about the alleged rise of German nationalism either in league with France or Russia, or with both.

Warsaw's initial tough stance toward certain internal EU reforms, such as the revision of the Nice Treaty that gave Poland substantial voting rights, has been partly driven by pressures exerted by the center-right opposition. Indeed, CP leader Rokita coined the phrase "Nice or death" to gain public support against the EU constitution and the center-left administration. Warsaw was caught in a difficult position because it did not want to lose even more popularity by being perceived as wavering or as sacrificing Polish national interests. Leaders of both CP and LJ were initially opposed to ratifying the EU's Constitutional Treaty on the grounds that it undermined Polish voting rights as specified in the Nice Treaty. They attacked the government for agreeing to a compromise solution on the voting based on a double majority system. At the same time, they did not consider that the failure of the constitution would necessarily signal a long-term crisis for the Union. The center-right parties also pledged to push more forcefully for the WE states to open up their service market to competition from new members.

In terms of foreign and security policy, the center-right formations, including the CP and LJ, asserted that they sought a strong EU together with a firm transatlantic connection and the continuing presence of U.S. forces in Europe.[77] But for them, as for the center-left, a strong and united Europe did not mean a federal Europe in terms of its internal structure. Indeed, there is a lack of clarity among all parties as to what the final structural contours of the EU should look like. By backing a "united Europe" they evidently envisaged a Union in which Poland could exert a strong influence. The CP favored the creation of an EU foreign ministry, a common defense and equipment policy, and a joint rapid reaction military force that could interact more effectively with the United States. The LJ has been more cautious about all aspects of EU integration and stressed that any EU structures dealing with foreign and security policy must be closely tied to the United States. Hence, LJ leaders have been fully supportive of locating U.S. bases on Polish territory, with LJ leader Jarosław Kaczyński describing them as a guarantee of Poland's independence.[78]

Nevertheless, once in office, the LJ did not exhibit a radical anti-EU and pro-American posture but sought to balance these relationships. It proved to be a hard bargainer within the EU, as evidenced in the Union's budget debate. However, it also shared some of the welfarist economic positions of states such as France and Germany even while differing in the security realm on the future of NATO and the American connection.[79] Warsaw largely concurred with French resistance to deep reform of the EU budgetary system and the reduction of agricultural and regional subsidies as these continued to benefit the most deprived areas of the Polish countryside. Paradoxically, despite differing approaches toward foreign and security policy, shared economic positions could move the LJ administration closer to both Paris and Berlin and distance it from London.

While in opposition, center-right leaders voiced vehement criticisms of the French role in the EU and in allegedly fostering transatlantic divisions. However, as a potential referendum approached, the CP and LJ became less critical of the EU's Constitutional Treaty. Andrzej Olechowski, the CP founder, believed that despite its shortcomings the Constitution would streamline the Union's operations, establish a more coherent foreign policy, and enhance the role of parliament.[80] He asserted that Warsaw had to be closely involved in the EU integration process, even with flawed compromises, as this would serve national interests and increase Polish influence in the future shape and structure of the Union. Other center-rightists were less sanguine about the Constitution and argued that by amending the Nice voting system Poland would be at a disadvantage in gaining equal treatment in the allocation of EU structural funds.

In center-right estimations, Poland maintains a strong element of trust in America's political and military responses to crisis whereas doubts remain about the effectiveness of any EU security guarantees to Poland. For CP leader Rokita, attempts to build a European Union in order to rival the United States or efforts aimed at undermining European unity in order to improve relations with the United States were both unacceptable options as they did not enhance the cohesion of the transatlantic alliance.

Center-right leaders also complained that some of the larger WE members were attempting to sideline Poland in discussions and decisions on a common EU foreign and security policy. They pointed to "summit meetings" between Paris, Berlin, Madrid, Rome, and Moscow, which failed to include representatives from Warsaw or any neighboring CEE states. As a consequence, they called for closer coordination between the smaller countries and a much closer relationship with the UK because of the convergence of positions on such issues as security and the American relationship.

Nonetheless, several opposition commentators have also warned that Poland risked losing any influence in the EU if it did not construct better relations with both Germany and France and stopped blindly following U.S. policy.[81] They felt that constant Polish support for Washington on various issues damaged the country's reputation among the WE public and its political elites. Some critics went even further and charged that by consistently and uncritically supporting U.S. policy, Warsaw was actually undermining Allied unity and European solidarity, marginalizing itself within the EU, and undercutting the effectiveness of its own Eastern policy.[82] Such commentators believed that Poland was being induced by the United States to divide Europe, from which only Washington benefited. At the same time, Warsaw was allegedly duped by the Bush administration in being told that it would gain tangible benefits from its military involvement in Iraq.

Several populist-nationalist formations in Poland are more overtly anti-EU. They include the leftist Self-Defense (SD) and the rightist League of Polish Families (LPF). Both tried to capitalize on Euro-skeptic and anti-French or anti-German sentiments during parliamentary debates by asserting that Poland must not become a "client state" of Germany and allow itself to be "exploited" by the EU. Both parties claimed that EU membership would lead to a loss of national identity and allow for renewed German irredentism toward Polish territory. The inclusion of both parties in a new coalition government with the ruling LJ in May 2006 raised concerns that Polish foreign policy could become increasingly confrontational.[83]

Poland has a relatively weak isolationist stream and membership in NATO has been viewed across the political spectrum as essential for the country's long-term security. Only the small ultra-right and ultra-left groupings opposed any foreign commitments by Warsaw and urged Poland's absolute neutrality and absence from NATO. The SD accused the government of servility toward the West, particularly in its relations with the United States and urged an independent Polish stance, while the LPF was more neutral toward America and hostile to the European Union. Both streams were staunchly opposed to Poland's inclusion in the EU or any other supranational body that purportedly restricted the country's sovereignty.

All Polish governments will be faced with the task of trying to reconcile the European and Atlantic directions in Warsaw's national policy and defining the future of NATO as a system of mutual defense and international security. The two major center-right parties, the CP and LJ, supported the previous government's decision to send troops to Iraq, even though public opinion was largely against the military mission. Only the more extreme parties, such as SD and the LPF, voiced strong objections with the latter calling for the immediate evacuation of Polish troops. In April 2005, SD leader Andrzej Lepper claimed that the government was not serious about withdrawing troops but was simply changing the name of the operation from stabilization to a training mission.[84]

Opposition criticism of Polish participation in the Iraqi conflict has focused primarily on the dangers faced by Polish troops, on the legality of such participation under the Polish constitution, and on the costs of the Iraqi mission from a relatively scarce defense budget. There have been fewer concerns about Poland bypassing the United Nations Security Council in its support of Washington. Although the issue of gaining UN approval was raised by several major parties prior to the Iraqi war, the most outspoken were the small populist nationalist SD and the LPF, led by Roman Giertych, which opposed U.S. actions in general and Polish military involvement in Iraq under any conditions. Both of these radical groupings essentially promoted Poland's isolationism but with limited public resonance.

The center-right LJ strongly supported U.S. intervention in Iraq even without any explicit UN backing. The larger opposition parties did not challenge Warsaw's support for the United States, which was considered as the ultimate guarantor of Polish security. While some of the centrist and leftist formations feared that Warsaw's unwavering support for Washington could undermine its relations with France and Germany, the center-right displayed fewer apprehensions as they viewed the United States as an essential counterbalance to French, German, and Russian ambitions on the European mainland.

With Poland's general elections approaching in the fall of 2005, several opposition parties indicated that they would use the Iraqi issue in the election campaign against the ruling party and called for a referendum on withdrawing Polish troops. In particular, the Polish Popular Alliance (PPA) and the Labor

Union (LU) made the question of a Polish pullout from Iraq a central feature of their campaigns. They argued that the government had failed to convince the public that staying in Iraq was in Poland's national interest. Meanwhile, the center-rightist CP and LJ continued to criticize the administration for failing to secure any tangible benefits for Poland from its involvement in Iraq.

However, the center-right leader Lech Kaczyński, who won the presidential elections in October 2005, asserted that Polish forces could stay in Iraq beyond the end of 2005 if Washington promised more financial assistance and other benefits. In December 2005, the new government announced that Poland would maintain a scaled-down troop presence of 900 combatants in Iraq until the end of 2006 and could further extend the mission. At the same time, Warsaw proposed various reforms in planning for future operations by creating a central fund that would benefit economically weaker partners who were willing to participate in military actions alongside their NATO allies.

The center-right government formed at the close of 2005 is likely to maintain Poland's Atlanticist direction and may prove even more challenging within the EU in asserting the country's national interests. This does not mean that Poland will be less European-oriented. On the contrary, Warsaw may push for both an expanded and stronger European Union in a "strategic alliance" with the United States, and try to more effectively leverage its ties with both entities.

The majority of parties have been supportive of a prominent regional role for Poland even where they are suspicious of deepening EU integration. Moreover, some center-right leaders have called for a more activist regional policy with the Visegrad neighbors in pursuit of EU and NATO membership for Ukraine, Belarus, Moldova, and Georgia. Before the September 2005 general elections, Rokita, chairman of CP, called for a "common European neighborhood policy towards the East" that would be more active than the efforts of the center-left government.[85]

Policy differences between government and opposition were also reflected in Poland's Eastern options. The major center-right opposition wanted Warsaw to be more assertive toward Moscow than the center-left government. The victory of the LJ and CP and the emergence of a center-right government led to vehement condemnations from Moscow where some commentators claimed that "Russophobic nationalists" had come to power in Poland who would allegedly play the "anti-Russian card" in the European Union and the United States.[86] The new administration in Warsaw will need to be careful and not succumb to potential provocations and political traps laid by Moscow that could undermine Poland's position in the EU and its credibility with the United States.

A handful of smaller Euro-skeptic parties also displayed some pro-Russian sentiments not because they necessarily supported Putin but because some ultranationalist groups view Russia as a useful counterbalance to the EU, to "Western domination," and even to the United States. These include Self-Defense (SD) and the League of Polish Families (LPF); the latter emanates from the prewar "endecja" or national-democrat tradition and has been vehemently anti-German with pan-Slavic leanings.[87] Both groups gained parliamentary seats following the October 2005 elections and could gain influence in foreign policy following their inclusion in the LJ administration. They may estrange several WE capitals from Warsaw because of their combination of social conservatism, political religiosity, and economic protectionism.

PUBLIC OPINION

Recent years have witnessed growing public interest in foreign policy issues, especially as citizens realized that with NATO and EU membership domestic and external affairs were increasingly interlinked. In general, the Polish public views the country's active engagement in international affairs as more beneficial for the state than remaining passive.[88] Public support for EU membership has remained high. However, the Union is not perceived as a security or political organization but mostly in economic, legal, and social terms. There is limited public understanding about the purposes or development of CFSP or ESDP and other EU security dimensions. Instead, respondents generally hold the view that EU entry helps ensure free trade, travel, and employment, while the EU will benefit from Poland's relatively cheaper labor force.[89] However, on the negative side, a sizeable minority views the EU as potentially threatening to Poland's sovereignty and as providing an opportunity for the buyout of Polish land and national assets. Such opinions prevail among the least educated and poorest sectors of society who also tended to oppose Poland's NATO membership.

The level of public support for EU entry dropped somewhat prior to Poland's accession, because of fears and uncertainties stoked by Euro-skeptic political voices. In a poll conducted on the eve of membership in April 2004, 47 percent of people expressed reservations as to what EU accession would mean for them, while one-fifth voiced outright fear. Only 35 percent of respondents felt hope, pride, or a sense of joy, while 44 percent agreed that EU membership was favorable for the Polish economy and 30 percent disagreed.[90] Almost 89 percent were convinced that the EU would mean higher consumer prices even though most acknowledged that living standards were superior inside the European Union. A quarter of respondents were positive that Poland would catch up with its EU partners within ten years, 18 percent believed it will take fifteen years, and 21 percent forecast twenty years. Thirty-two percent expected their personal financial situation to worsen after Poland's accession, with only 20 percent convinced it would improve.

Despite these fears, on the eve of Poland's entry 53 percent of respondents supported closer political integration with the EU although a third would prefer that the Union remain primarily a free trade area rather than a political or security organization. However, backing for closer political integration was evident among 70 percent of people under fifty years of age. In sum, 40 percent of respondents considered that accession was a good option, while 28 percent thought it was a bad choice but still the best one available. The majority of Poles calculated that without EU membership their country would become poorer and more isolated. Only 18 percent claimed that accession was the wrong choice and better alternatives were available. The poll indicated that only 24 percent of respondents thought that the EU would threaten Polish culture and traditions, while 22 percent believed it would have a favorable impact.

Since Warsaw joined the EU in May 2004, a reasonably high level of public support has been maintained. In August 2004, 70 percent of respondents expressed such views while only 21 percent opposed.[91] Within this figure, 39 percent believed that EU membership brings more benefits than costs and the rest were willing to remain patient or saw no viable alternatives. By February 2005, support for Poland's EU membership increased to 77 percent, with only 14 percent against.[92] The Polish public also supported a more coherent EU foreign policy. According to a Eurobarometer survey in October–November 2004, 78 percent of those polled would favor a more active CFSP, well above the EU average, and a similar number supported an effective ESDP.[93] Despite this trend, following the failure to approve the EU Constitution in France and Holland, Polish support for the document also plummeted from 60 percent in May 2005 to 40 percent in early June 2005, with a quarter undecided.[94]

Opinion pollsters have also analyzed responses by social sectors and found that support for EU integration was initially lowest among the farming lobby but visibly improved when the feared negative impact on Polish farming did not materialize. During the first year after EU accession, direct subsidies from the EU budget supplemented by Polish government funds reached over 1.3 million Polish farmers, or over 85 percent of all registered agricultural producers.[95] Farmers were thus able to invest in and modernize their farms, to combine plots in order to benefit from EU aid, to increase exports to the EU market, and to raise their living standards. They also received 60 percent of the direct subsidy rate in force in the old European Union in 2005—up from 55 percent in 2004.

The business sector has also benefited from EU accession as Polish companies, although weak in terms of capital, seemed well prepared to compete on the European market. Some WE leaders complained about the low corporate taxes in Poland and other CEE states but eventually had to adjust their own tax rates when it became clear that countries such Germany would be increasingly exposed to more open competition.

Additionally, the younger, higher educated, and better paid social sectors are more likely to back the EU, seeing the organization as an avenue for personal opportunity and career advancement. This included supporters of the major center-left and center-right parties. The prospect of market opportunities has reportedly spurred public initiative, boosted Polish exports especially in the food, chemical, furniture, and clothing industries, increased the competitiveness of Polish business, and improved labor efficiency. Rather than focusing on EU funding, Polish politicians are seeking to extol the structural benefits of membership as the Polish economy grows by attracting foreign investment.

The majority of opinion poll respondents have consistently stated that Polish foreign policy should aim at maintaining good relations with all EU member states. According to a poll conducted in June 2003, two thirds believed that Poland would play an important political role in the European Union.[96] In polls taken between July and October 2003 on the question of what should be most important in Polish foreign policy, 54 percent of respondents favored "good relations with the EU" and only 34 percent stated that Warsaw should focus on "good relations with the United States." Opinions of specific EU countries have varied considerably. Over the last decade, France has become one of the least popular WE nations. From 61 percent expressing positive sympathies toward France in 1993, the figure declined to 45 percent by 2004. Over this same time period, positive attitudes toward Germany have remained under 40 percent.[97]

Public support for NATO entry has remained consistently high in Poland, initially peaking at 73 percent in 1998. This figure has remained steady and in September 2004, two-thirds of respondents supported Poland's membership with only 8 percent opposed.[98] The totals reached 81 percent for and 8 percent against in April 2005.[99] The Alliance was viewed as the only viable security option for Poland that would finally end the country's historical vulnerability to dominant neighboring powers.[100] NATO's security guarantees for each member state, underpinned by the United States, were the key factor in the pursuit of accession. During 1999, 42 percent of respondents believed that NATO membership would be another form of subordination to a foreign power or organization; nevertheless, even one-third of this number still supported Poland's entry.[101] However, only 40 percent of those polled during 2004 favored stationing troops from other NATO states on Polish territory.

Poles also expected NATO membership to strengthen the country's international and regional position and to solidify the partnership with the United States. However, once Poland and two other CEE states were invited to join at the Madrid summit in 1998, interest in membership decreased. Further decline in support was recorded when NATO undertook offensive action against

Serbia in the spring of 1999, with only weak approval for the engagement of Polish troops in military operations abroad. However, support for NATO increased after its successful operation against Belgrade and a narrow majority backed dispatching troops to Kosova as part of NATO's KFOR peacekeeping mission. NATO membership was clearly a learning process for the Polish public, as they began to understand the new responsibilities that members were required to bear.

Soon after the September 11, 2001, attacks on the United States, an overwhelming number of Poles were united in support of almost any kind of anti-terrorist offensive and 77 percent declared that Poland should be prepared to fulfill its obligations as a NATO member and close ally of the United States.[102] Subsequently, public opinion was in favor of the United States overthrowing the Taliban regime in Afghanistan and of Polish participation in the postwar mission. Although this support subsided somewhat prior to the deployment of 300 Polish soldiers in Afghanistan, it increased again as the mission developed and stood at some three-quarters in April 2002.[103]

Public opinion polls have consistently indicated strong pro-American sentiments in Poland. However, long-term trends demonstrate that opinions are invariably linked with particular aspects of U.S. policy. Although anti-Americanism is unlikely to mushroom, pro-Americanism could be gradually transformed into public indifference. While between 1993 and 2003, pro-American sentiments averaged at about 60 percent, by the close of 2004 this figure had reportedly slipped to 45 percent, evidently tied to popular opposition to Polish military engagement in Iraq and other questions linked with this operation.[104]

In February and March 2003, 62 percent of respondents supported proposals to relocate American military bases from Germany to Poland and only 38 percent opposed, but the findings were more nuanced.[105] By the close of 2004, three out of five respondents favored stationing specialized radar facilities to better protect Polish airspace, 52 percent supported small U.S. bases with the potential to bring in additional American troops at a time of crisis, and only 35 percent backed the creation of large-scale American bases.[106]

President Bush has maintained fairly high approval ratings in Poland, especially by overall European standards. For instance, according to polls conducted in July 2002, 73 percent of respondents had a positive view of the U.S. president and only 8 percent negative, thus placing him as the most liked foreign leader in Poland.[107] Even regular Bush critics such as the prominent political activist and a key former advisor to Solidarity, Adam Michnik, stated that it was not the Bush administration that led to the "destruction of humanitarian principles," as charged by some Western intellectuals but the "tolerance of totalitarian regimes and the cowardly silence about the crimes of the dictatorships in Iraq, North Korea, Libya, and

Cuba."[108] Paradoxically, even though the Iraqi mission has not proved popular among Poles, the majority of respondents admired President Bush's high ethical standards and his clarity on the issue of good vs. evil.[109]

Public opinion polling results during and after the Iraqi war proved to be mixed. By May 2004, 74 percent of those surveyed reportedly opposed military involvement in the Iraqi stabilization mission, while only 22 percent supported it.[110] This was the widest disparity since the onset of the Iraqi operation. Between June 2004 and January 2005, opposition to Polish engagement in Iraq varied between 66 percent and 74 percent, while support spanned a narrow range between 23 percent and 28 percent.[111] By January 2005, 51 percent of respondents believed that Polish involvement in Iraq would result in more financial costs than benefits, and only 16 percent believed the opposite, indicating disillusionment with prospects of an economic boost for Poland from the war in Iraq.[112] Moreover, only 17 percent thought that Polish engagement in Iraq would bring the country political benefits, 39 percent considered that it would result in political losses, and 32 percent believed it would change little for Poland on the international arena.

In early 2005, 63 percent of respondents believed that Polish troops stationed in Iraq should return home as quickly as possible. This represented an increase of 13 percent since the previous month's polling, while 32 percent thought they should stay. About 86 percent of respondents also feared that as a result of its involvement in Iraq, Poland could become a prime target for terrorist attacks. The death of four Polish citizens in Iraq during the course of the opinion survey had a direct impact on negative public perceptions of the mission. Budgetary issues also played a role, in that 85 percent of respondents were convinced that the Iraqi operation was proving too costly for Warsaw.[113] But despite widespread reservations about the Iraqi imbroglio and the policies of President Bush, the United States itself was viewed positively by 62 percent of the Polish public, according to results of a major international survey released in June 2005. However, only 47 percent claimed they had confidence in Bush's leadership in world affairs.[114]

Fewer statistics are available on public opinion according to party affiliation or voting preferences. However, one survey completed in December 2004 on the question of Poland's troop presence in Iraq indicated that 56 percent of DLA voters supported the mission, as did 38 percent of LJ supporters and 35 percent of the CP. By contrast, 72 percent of supporters of the ultra-protectionist SD and 86 percent of the LPF opposed any form of Polish military involvement in Iraq.[115]

Public opposition to the Iraqi deployment has not been matched by public demonstrations, indicating that opposition to Polish involvement in the U.S. coalition is neither organized nor passionate. Only a few dozen protesters gathered outside the U.S. embassy in Warsaw and in a handful of other Polish cities during the course of the war. Polish anti-U.S. and anti-globalization movements are poorly developed and have little public resonance.[116] Observers point out that unlike in many WE countries there is little or no tradition of either pacifism or anti-Americanism in Polish society. Nonetheless, some analysts suggest that anti-Americanism could become a factor in the future as in other EU states, especially where it successfully combines a wide assortment of ideologies, including nationalist, leftist, and anti-globalist, and preys on resentments that could be heightened through contacts with West European anti-Americanism.[117]

Public support for NATO has remained constant in Poland, regardless of the progress of the Iraqi war. Approximately two-thirds of Poles remain committed to membership in the Alliance and understand its value as a capable organization for defense, while less than 10 percent have been openly opposed to NATO membership.

The upcoming generation in Poland may not feel as closely linked with the United States and may increasingly gravitate toward WE not only in terms of work, entertainment, education, leisure, mores, fashion, and other pursuits but may do so even in terms of their politics and perceptions of America. A growing number of Polish students are attending WE universities rather than U.S. ones and bilateral exchange programs are declining. Such a trend may have long-term consequences for views of America and the alliance among an educated public.

Since the Iraqi war distrust of America seems to have grown as well as disappointment that Washington appeared to take Poland for granted as a loyal and reliable ally. Such views, which some Polish commentators have described as a more realistic and sober appraisal of world affairs, could become part of the political climate and result in an increasing distance from the United States. The visa waiver issue remains extremely sensitive in Poland. Parliament has been unanimous in calling for a visa waiver for Polish nationals and the fulfillment of a U.S. temporary worker program for Polish citizens. Complaints about Washington's treatment of Poland have reportedly resulted in a fall in support for U.S. policy. For instance, in September 2004, 40 percent of opinion poll respondents reported that the foreign policy of the Bush administration had worsened their stance toward the United States, while only 15 percent said that it had improved their views of the United States.[118]

At the same time, Russia continues to be perceived by Polish public opinion as the gravest potential threat to Poland's independence and to the security of the wider CEE region. This was evident during the 1990s when President Boris Yeltsin sought to threaten and dissuade Warsaw from joining

NATO. Russian policy in the Balkans in support of Serbia against the NATO airwar increased Polish resentment against Moscow.[119] Negative opinions about Russia steadily declined after the Kosova war. Nevertheless, the majority of Poles believe that Russia under President Putin has become an assertive and aggressive power determined to reestablish its dominance in CEE.[120] Russia is no longer an outright enemy, but neither is it a friendly neighbor. Cautious Polish attitudes toward the Russian regime

> originate from a more general conviction based on historical experience that Russian political declarations should never be fully trusted: consequently, the post-11 September American-Russian rapprochement is also seen in Poland as only a passing phenomenon.[121]

NOTES

1. "Our Europe: Now Kwaśniewski Speaks on EU Enlargement, European Constitution, U.S. Relations, and Iraq," *Gazeta Wyborcza* (Warsaw), April 30, 2004, pp.11–13.

2. "Europe 'Surprised' at Poland's 'Unexpected Success' with EU Debut," *Rzeczpospolita* website, Warsaw, April 30, 2005, www.rzeczpospolita.pl.

3. Heather Grabbe, "Poland: The EU's New Awkward Partner," *CER Bulletin* (London, Center for European Reform) no. 34 (February/March 2004).

4. Robert Soltyk, "How Much Power, How Much Money," *Gazeta Wyborcza* (Warsaw), September 22, 2003.

5. Bartosz Jałowiecki, "Poland Should Keep Away from the Franco-German EU Integrating Machine," *Wprost* (Warsaw), January 11, 2004.

6. Kai-Olaf Lang, "The German-Polish Security Partnership Within the Transatlantic Context—Convergence or Divergence?" *Defense Studies* 2, no. 2 (2002): 105–22.

7. Heather Grabbe and Marcin Zaborowski, "Czy Rodzi się Nowa Wspólnota Interesow?" [The Birth of New Common Interests?] *Rzeczpospolita*, July 12, 2004.

8. Jadwiga Stachura, "Poland in Transatlantic Relations," in *Yearbook of Polish Foreign Policy, 2004*, ed. Barbara Wizimirska (Warsaw: Polish Ministry of Foreign Affairs, 2005), 125.

9. Stanislaw Michałowski, "Poland's Relations With Germany," in *Yearbook of Polish Foreign Policy, 2004*, ed. Barbara Wizimirska (Warsaw: Polish Ministry of Foreign Affairs, 2005), 189–97.

10. Vanda Knowles, "Security and Defence in the New Europe: Franco-Polish Relations—Victim of Neglect?" *Defence Studies* 2, no. 2 (2002): 87–104.

11. *Le Monde*, online at www.lemonde.fr/article/0,5987,3218-309684-000.html.

12. According to Polish Foreign Minister Włodzimierz Cimoszewicz, quoted in "EU/Iraq: Chirac Blasts Candidate Countries For Pro-U.S. Stance," *European Report* 19 (February 2003).

13. Tomasz Paszewski, "Przyszłość CFSP/ESDP A Stosunki Transatlantyckie: Punkt Widzenia Polski i Francji," [The Future of the CSFD/ESDP and Transatlantic Relations: The Point of View of Poland and France] (Warsaw: Center For International Relations, April 24, 2004).

14. "Polish President Interviewed on EU Constitution Referendums, EU Foreign Policy: Interview with Polish President Aleksander Kwaśniewski, by Marek Ostrowski: "Europe Will Ask for a Pause?" *Polityka* (Warsaw), June 9, 2005.

15. For a valuable analysis of the evolution of Polish security policy see Marcin Zaborowski, *From America's Protégé to Constructive European: Poland's Security Policy in the 21st Century*, Occasional Paper no. 56 (European Union: Institute for Security Studies, December 2004): 20.

16. Jędrzej Bielecki and Zbigniew Lentowicz, "America Is Not Enough; Poland wants Closer Cooperation with Europe's Arms Industry," *Rzeczpospolita*, February 1, 2005.

17. Polish Minister of Foreign Affairs, Adam Daniel Rotfeld, at the session of the Sejm on January 21, 2005, Ministry of Foreign Affairs.

18. Janusz Onyszkiewicz, "Sojusze Jak Róże?" [Alliances are like Roses?] *Polska Zbrojna* (Warsaw), no. 11 (2004), www.csm.org.pl/pl/files/Sojusze.

19. The German Marshall Fund of the United States, *Transatlantic Trends, 2004* (Washington, D.C., 2004).

20. Czesław Piątas, "Poland's Military Contribution to Transatlantic Security Policy," *Military Technology* (Bonn, Germany: Monch Publishing Group) 24, no. 8 (August 2000): 91–96.

21. Marcin Zaborowski, "Between Power and Weakness: Poland—A New Actor in the Transatlantic Security," *Reports & Analyses* (Center for International Relations, Warsaw) September 2003, 4/03/A: 4.

22. Ministry of Defense, see website at www.wp.mil.pl.

23. Zaborowski, *Between Power and Weakness: Poland*, 6–7.

24. As during the "Polish President's Address in the Presence of the U.S. President at Wawel Castle," TV Polonia, Warsaw, May 31, 2003.

25. For a valuable analysis of the Polish experience in Iraq see Maria Wągrowska, "Polish Participation in the Armed Intervention and Stabilization Mission in Iraq," *Reports & Analyses* (Center for International Relations, Warsaw) May 2005, 08/04: 1–31.

26. "War in Iraq: Showing Our Support," *The Warsaw Voice*, April 4, 2003. There was some disquiet in Warsaw when news of the GROM operations leaked out to the press from official U.S. sources. Polish Defense Minister Jerzy Szmajdzinski asserted that top-secret activities involving Polish special forces should not be used for public relations purposes by the White House. See "Poland Requests USA not to Give Away Special Units Operations–Minister," Polish Radio 1, Warsaw, March 27, 2003.

27. Zaborowski, *Between Power and Weakness: Poland*, 12.

28. Jeffrey Simon, *NATO Expeditionary Operations: Impacts Upon New Members and Partners*, Occasional Paper no. 1 (Washington, D.C.: Institute for National Strategic Studies, March 2005), 22.

29. Dariusz Wisniewski, "Relations Between Poland and the United States," in *Yearbook of Polish Foreign Policy, 2004*, ed. Barbara Wizimirska (Warsaw: Polish Ministry of Foreign Affairs, 2005), 183. The deal was to be primarily financed by a long-term loan of $3.8 billion granted to Warsaw by the U.S. government.

30. Polish News Agency (PAP), "Training, construction work under way at future F-16 jets air bases in Poland," Warsaw, June 9, 2005.

31. Based on interviews with Polish government officials in Warsaw in March 2005.

32. Witold Żygulski, "From Madrid to Iraq and Nice," *The Warsaw Voice* (Warsaw), March 24, 2004.

33. Interview with Szmajdzinski in *Gazeta Wyborcza* (Warsaw), October 4, 2004.

34. Dawid Warszawski, "Why the Poles are in Iraq," *The Walrus Magazine*, (2003), http://walrusmagazine.com/article.pl?sid=03/11/17/2210203.

35. William Kole, "Romania, Poland Scrutinized Over Prisons," Associated Press, December 6, 2005.

36. Alix Chambris, "Czy Polska Jest Koniem Trojańskim Ameryki w Europie? Uwagi o Francuskich Stereotypach Na Temat Stosunków Polsko-Amerykańskich" [Is Poland America's Trojan Horse in Europe? Observations about French Stereotypes of Polish-American Relations], *Polska W Europie* 2, no. 46 (2004): 89–93.

37. Global News Wire—Asia-Africa Intelligence Wire, "Iraq Mission Changed Poland's Position in the World—PM," July 19, 2004.

38. Olaf Osica, "Poland: A New European Atlanticist at a Crossroads?" *European Security* 13, no. 4 (2004): 313–14.

39. Jan Repa, "Poland Seeks Iraq Reward," *BBC News On Line*, Europe, 27 January 2004, http://news.bbc.co.uk/2/hi/europe/3433087.stm.

40. Bruce Konviser, "Kwasniewski to Press Bush on Visa Rules," *The Washington Times*, January 27, 2004, A13.

41. Jakub Jedras, "Republican, But Also Disappointed," *Transitions-On-Line*, November 10, 2004.

42. "'Submissive' Poland Unlikely to Get Pledged U.S. Military Aid," *Trybuna* (Warsaw), April 11, 2005.

43. Polish Radio, Warsaw, April 15, 2005.

44. Associated Press, "Kwaśniewski: Poland Remains a Staunch Ally in Iraq," Warsaw, April 13, 2005.

45. Monika Ścisłowska, "Polish Defense Minister Says Country's Forces Should Leave Iraq by Early 2006," Associated Press, April 12, 2005.

46. Agence France Presse, "US, Poland Launch First U.S.-Central Europe Counter-Terror Working Group," March 31, 2005.

47. Marek Ostrowski and Jacek Safuta, "Kwadratura Trójkąta," *Polityka* (Warsaw), no.19 (2003).

48. Juraj Marusiak, "Poland as Regional Power and Polish-Slovak Relations," *Slovak Foreign Policy Affairs* 1/2001: 36–55.

49. Jacek Gajewski, "Visegrad Cooperation," in *Yearbook of Polish Foreign Policy, 2004*, ed. Barbara Wizimirska (Warsaw: Polish Ministry of Foreign Affairs, 2005), 222–32.

50. Piotr Chmielewski and Anton Podolski, eds., "Skazani Na Konflikt?—Stosunki Polsko-Rosyjskie Po Ukraińskiej Pomarańczowej Rewolucji" [Destined for

Conflict?—Russo-Polish Relations Following Ukraine's Orange Revolution], (Center for International Relations, Warsaw, March 2005), 3.

51. Polish News Agency, "Visegrad States Sign Declaration on Cooperation in Regional Policies," April 15, 2005.

52. Roman Kuzniar and Andrzej Szeptycki, "The Role of the United States in the Foreign Policy of the Third Republic of Poland," in *Bridges Across the Atlantic? Attitudes of Poles, Czechs and Slovaks Toward the United States,* edited by Lena Kolarska-Bobinska, Jacek Kucharczyk, and Piotr Maciej Kaczyński (Warsaw: Instytut Spraw Publicznych, 2005), 139.

53. From personal discussions with the authors in a roundtable with NGO representatives organized by the Center for International Relations in Warsaw in March 2005.

54. Antoni Podolski, "Polska Strategia Bezpieczeństwa Narodowego Jako Praktyczna Implementacja Europejskiej Strategii Bezpieczeństwa—Między Teorią a Praktyka" [Poland's National Security Strategy as a Practical Implementation of Europe's Security Strategy—Between Theory and Practice], *Reporty I Analizy* (Warsaw: Center for International Relations, 2005), 1/05: 10. For background see Christopher S. Browning and Pertti Joenniemi, "The European Union's Two Dimensions: The Eastern and the Northern," *Security Dialogue* 34, no. 4 (December 2003): 463–78.

55. Olaf Osica, "In Search of a New Role: Poland in Euro-Atlantic Relations," *Defense Studies* 2, no. 2 (Summer 2002): 26.

56. Kai-Olaf Lang, "Poland and the East: Poland's Relations With Russia, Belarus, and Ukraine in the Context of European Eastern Policy," (Comments, 23, German Institute for International and Security Affairs, June 2005), 5.

57. Włodzimierz Cimoszewicz, "The Eastern Dimension of the European Union: The Polish View," Warsaw, February 2003, website of the Polish Ministry of Foreign Affairs.

58. Polish officials argued that despite the political situation in Minsk, Belarus should not be left outside the ENP, as the initiative sent an encouraging signal to the public and to political forces that opposed President Alyaksandr Lukashenka's antireformist and isolationist regime. They also sought to extend the ENP to the South Caucasian states of Georgia, Armenia, and Azerbaijan.

59. Włodzimierz Cimoszewicz, "Poland in the European Union: What Foreign Policy?" Public Address Given at the Polish Institute of International Affairs, May 22, 2003, *The Polish Foreign Affairs Digest* 3, no. 3 (8) (2003): 14.

60. Jakub Jędras, "Poland: A Bridge of Sighs," *Transitions-On-Line*, February 24, 2005.

61. Agence France Presse (AFP), "Polish President Backs Ukraine's Move to Apply for EU Membership," January 28, 2005.

62. PAP News Agency, "Poland Supports Ukraine's EU Aspirations," February 23, 2005.

63. See the interview with President Aleksander Kwaśniewski in Judy Dempsey, "Poland's Leader Calls for a Pluralistic, Open, and New Europe.... Including Turkey and Ukraine," *International Herald Tribune*, September 2, 2004.

64. Polish Minister of Foreign Affairs, Adam Daniel Rotfeld, at the session of the Sejm on January 21, 2005, Ministry of Foreign Affairs.

65. Baltic News Service, "Polish Parliamentary Chair Supports Idea of Establishing Tripartite Parliamentary Assembly with Ukraine," Lithuania, January 14, 2005.

66. Vladimir Socor, "Poland, Lithuania, Ukraine Create Inter-Parliamentary Assembly, Joint Battalion," (Jamestown Foundation) *Eurasia Daily Monitor* 2, no. 96 (May 17, 2005).

67. Katarzyna Pełczyńska-Nałęcz, "The Enlarged European Union and its Eastern Neighbors: Problems and Solutions," (Warsaw: Center for Eastern Studies, October 2003).

68. Andrzej Kapiszewski and Chris Davis, "Poland's Security and Transatlantic Relations," in *Old Europe, New Europe, and the U.S.: Renegotiating Transatlantic Security in the Post 9/11 Era,* edited by Tom Lansford and Blagovest Tashev (Aldershot, UK: Ashgate, 2005), p. 200.

69. Die Presse, "Polish President Discusses Polish, EU's Relations with Russia, Ukraine, Belarus," Vienna, Austria, April 23, 2005.

70. Adam Krzeminski, "Misja Dla 'Konja Trojanskiego': Powinnismy Wykorzystac Dobre Stosunki z USA, by Łagodzic Transatlantyckie Swary" [A Mission for the "Trojan Horse": We Should Take Advantage of Good Relations with the U.S. in Order to Calm Transatlantic Tensions], *Polityka*, no. 17 (2003).

71. Tomasz Paszewski, "Ameryka i Europa—Od Zakończeniu Sporu Do Partnerstwa?" [American and Europe—From the End of the Dispute to a Partnership?] *Reports & Analyses* (Warsaw: Center for International Relations, May 2005), 5/05: 13.

72. "Between 'Real Politics' and the 'Weimar Option.' Remaining at the Margins of the Enlarged EU is not in Poland's Interest," *Rzeczpospolita*, March 4, 2004.

73. Piotr Smilowicz, "Europe, Open Up: Civic Platform's Rokita Outlines 'Vision' for Future Polish Foreign Policy," *Rzeczpospolita*, April 18, 2005. See also Aleksander Hall, "Polska-Ameryka: Wspólne Interesy I Własne Zdanie," *Rzeczpospolita*, May 24, 2003.

74. Krzysztof Iszkowski, "Polish-American Relations as Perceived by Polish Political Parties," in *Bridges Across the Atlantic? Attitudes of Poles, Czechs and Slovaks Towards the United States,* edited by Lena Kolarska-Bobinska, Jacek Kucharczyk, and Piotr Maciej Kaczyński (Warsaw: Institute of Public Affairs, 2005), 88.

75. "Predictable and Flexible PO's Jan Rokita Unveils Party's Vision of Poland's Foreign Policy," *Gazeta Wyborcza* (Warsaw), April 16–17, 2005, A2–A3.

76. Barbara Wizimirska, "Foreign Policy in Public Debate," in *Yearbook of Polish Foreign Policy, 2005*, ed. Barbara Wizimirska (Warsaw: Polish Ministry of Foreign Affairs, 2005), 49–50.

77. Jan Rokita, "Polska Polityka Zagraniczna—Ile Kontynuacji, Ile Zmian" [Polish Foreign Policy—How Much Continuity, How Many Changes], (Warsaw: Center for International Relations, April 14, 2005), 15.

78. Polish Sejm records, 4th term of office, session 67, item 10, January 21, 2004.

79. Marek Matraszek, "A Bit of a Shocker," *Poland Monthly*, no. 47 (January 2006): 34.

80. Andrzej Olechowski, "Czy Warto Umierać Za Nicee?" [Is Nice Worth Dying For?], *Rzeczpospolita*, September 12, 2003.

81. Janusz Reiter, "Kontrolowane Trzęsienie Ziemi" [A Controlled Earthquake], *Rzeczpospolita*, March 19, 2003.

82. Zdzisław Najder, "Między USA a Europa: Polskie Obowiązki," [Between the U.S. and Europe: Poland's Responsibilities] *Rzeczpospolita*, Warsaw, February 15–16, 2003, and "Bez Międzynarodowej Solidarności" [Without International Solidarity], *Rzeczpospolita*, September 9, 2003.

83. Other Europhobic populist-nationalist formations included the Catholic National Movement, the Movement for the Reconstruction of Poland, and the Polish Alliance. All three consistently opposed Poland's links with the EU and especially attacked the lack of reference to "Christian foundations" in the EU's Constitutional Treaty.

84. "Radical Agrarian Party Wants Poland's Immediate Pull-Out from Iraq," Polish Radio, Warsaw, April 15, 2005.

85. From a speech by Jan Rokita, Chairman of the Civic Platform at the "Center-Right Parties Visegrad Summit" in Prague, June 5, 2005.

86. See "Poland and Russia: New Government Must Tread Wisely Not to Make Things Easier for Russian Propaganda," *Rzeczpospolita*, September 30, 2005, 10.

87. Tomasz Zarycki, "Uses of Russia: The Role of Russia in the Modern Polish National Identity," *East European Politics and Societies* 18, no. 4 (Fall 2004): 598.

88. Mateusz Fałkowski, "Attitudes of the Poles Towards the United States of America and Transatlantic Relations," in *Bridges Across the Atlantic? Attitudes of Poles, Czechs and Slovaks Toward the United States*, edited by Lena Kolarska-Bobinska, Jacek Kucharczyk, and Piotr Maciej Kaczyński (Warsaw: Instytut Spraw Publicznych, 2005), 42.

89. "Opinie o Skutkach Integracji Polski z Unią Europejską i Przebiegi Negocjacji Akcesyjnych" [Opinions Regarding Poland's Integration into the European Union and the Process of the Accession Negotiations], Komunikat z Badań, Centrum Badania Opinii Społecznej [Study Summary, The Public Opinion Research Center], Warsaw, May 2000.

90. "Fear and Uncertainty Dominate on Eve of Accession," *Rzeczpospolita*, April 26, 2004, p. A.6.

91. "Pierwsze Oceny Skutków Członkostwa Polski w Unii Europejskiej," [Initial Perceptions of the Results of Poland's EU Membership], Komunikat z Badan, Centrum Badania Opinii Spolecznej, Warsaw, September 2004.

92. Polish Public Opinion, Public Opinion Research Center, Warsaw, February 2005.

93. http://europa.eu.int/comm/public_opinion/archives/eb/eb62/eb62firsten.pdf. The results are similar in other CEE countries.

94. Reuters, "Polish Support for EU Charter Drops to 40%," Warsaw, June 8, 2005.

95. Magdalena Kozmana, "Subsidies are Changing the Countryside," *Rzeczpospolita*, May 2, 2005.

96. www.poland.pl/poll/index.htm, March 10, 2005.

97. "Stosunek do Innych Narodów" [Perceptions with Other Nations], Centrum Badania Opinii Społecznej, Warsaw, January 2005.

98. "Bazy NATO Na Terenie Polski" [NATO bases on Polish Territory], Komunikat z Badań, Centrum Badania Opinii Społecznej, Warsaw, January 2005.

99. "Stosunek Polaków, Wegrów, Czechów i Slowaków Do Członkostwa w NATO I EU," [Polish, Hungarian, Czech, and Slovakian Perceptions of NATO and EU Membership], Komunikat z Badań, Centrum Badania Opinii Społecznej, Warsaw, April 2005.

100. "Polska w NATO" [Poland in NATO], Komunikat z Badań, Centrum Badania Opinii Społecznej, Warsaw, March 1999.

101. "W Przeddzień Przystąpienia do NATO" [The Day Before NATO Entry], Komunikat, Centrum Badania Opinii Społecznej, Warsaw, February 1999. Even skeptical Poles preferred "subordination" to NATO and the United States than a "security vacuum" or exposure to Russia.

102. Agnieszka Gogolewska, "Public Images of Security, Defense, and the Military in Poland," in *The Public Image of Defense and the Military in Central and Eastern Europe*, ed. Marie Vlachova (Geneva: Geneva Centre for the Democratic Control of Armed Forces [DCAF], 2003) 95.

103. "O Przynależności Polski do NATO i Obecności Polskich Zołnierzy w Afganistanie" [About Poland's NATO Membership and the Presence of Polish Soldiers in Afghanistan], Komunikat z Badan, Centrum Badania Opinii Społecznej, Warsaw, April 2002.

104. "Stosunek do Innych Narodow" [Perceptions of Other Nations], Komunikat z Badań, Centrum Badania Opinii Społecznej, Warsaw, January 2005.

105. www.poland.pl/poll/index.htm, March 10, 2005.

106. "Bazy NATO Na Terenie Polski" [NATO bases on Polish Territory] Komunikat z Badań, Centrum Badania Opinii Społecznej, Warsaw, January 2005.

107. "Stosunek Polaków do Wybranych Postaci ze Świata Polityki Zagranicznej" [Polish Perceptions of Selected Personas from the World of International Politics], Komuikat z Badań BS/112/2002, Centrum Badań Opinii Sołecznej, www.cbos.pol.

108. Adam Michnik, "In Support of President Bush: We, the Traitors," *Gazeta Wyborcza* (Warsaw), March 28, 2003.

109. Filip Chybalski, "George Bush a Sprawa Polska," www.e-polityka.pl/article/75343_George_Bush_a_sprawa_polska.htm

110. "Spadek Poparcia Dla Obecności Polskich Żołnierzy w Iraku" [A Decline in Support for the Presence of Polish Troops in Iraq], Komunikat z Badań, Centrum Badania Opinii Społecznej, Warsaw, May 2004.

111. "Skutki Zaangażowania Polski W Iraku" [The Results of Poland's Involvement in Iraq], Komunikat z Badań, Centrum Badania Opinii Społecznej, Warsaw, January 2005.

112. Ibid, September 2004.

113. "Opinie o Obecności Polskich Żołnierzy w Iraku" [Opinions about the Presence of Polish Troops in Iraq], Centrum Badania Opinii Społecznej, Komunikat z Badań, Warsaw, September 2004.

114. "16-Country Global Attitudes Report Released June 23, 2005, Poland," The Pew Global Attitudes Project, Washington D.C., also available at http://pewglobal.org/reports/pdf/247poland.pdf

115. "Polacy O Misji Stabilizacyjnej W Iraku" [Poles on the Stabilization Mission in Iraq], Komunikat z Badań, Centrum Badania Opinii Społecznej, Warsaw, December 2004.

116. Robin Shepherd, "A Bigger EU, and not so Anti-American," *The Washington Post*, May 9, 2004.

117. Adam Michnik, "What Europe Means for Poland," *Journal of Democracy* 14, no. 4 (October 4, 2003): 133–34.

118. "Polacy o Wyborach Prezydenckich w USA" [Poles on the U.S. Presidential Elections], Komunikat z Badań, Centrum Badania Opinii Społecznej, Warsaw, September 2004.

119. "Opinie o Sytuacji w Kraju na Arenie Międzynarodowej" [International Opinions about the Domestic Situation], Centrum Badania Opinii Społecznej Komunikat z Badań, Warsaw, April 1999.

120. Gogolewska, "Public Images," 100.

121. Ibid, 101.

Chapter Four

Holding the Center

Hungary, the Czech Republic, and Slovakia

HUNGARY

Hungary is a land-locked country of 10 million persons with approximately 2.5 million more Hungarians forming minority populations in several neighboring states.[1] Hungary's substantial loss of population and territory following both world wars should have conditioned the country to be a more cautious player in foreign affairs. However, Hungary was one of the first Central and East European (CEE) states to stage a mass uprising against the Soviet-imposed regime in 1956, and in 1989, Hungary challenged Soviet hegemony by opening its border. This allowed East German citizens to leave for the West while the Berlin Wall was still standing. This desire for independence is just as strong today as it was in the past and underscores the belief that a stable transatlantic relationship, where the European Union, NATO, and the United States work in harmony, is essential for the country's security. Hungary has acted as a reliable partner in the transatlantic community and has tried to avoid falling into disfavor with the major EU powers.

The stark transatlantic choices that materialized following the eruption of the Iraq war and the creation of the U.S.-led "coalition of the willing" made the Budapest government apprehensive. Hungary offered its support to the U.S.-led mission thereby going against the Franco-German position on the war. When U.S. Secretary of Defense Donald Rumsfeld distinguished between "old" and "new" European states, this exacerbated Hungary's already strained relationship with France and Germany. The major left-leaning daily summarized Budapest's concern over the transatlantic dispute:

> The Iraq crisis is alarming for us because it involves apparently friendly great
> powers competing with each other, suggesting a crisis of institutions that

Hungary counts on for support, and which it will greatly need in the long-term as well.[2]

As Washington envisioned an "us versus them" division within Europe, this added uncertainty to Hungary's EU accession slated for the next year. The situation led both the governing coalition and the opposition to vacillate between adopting U.S. and Franco-German foreign policy positions.

Both the EU and NATO figure prominently in Hungary's security strategy. The government's National Security Strategy of 2004 emphasized that the widening and deepening of the EU as well as the country's membership in NATO are national security priorities. Hungary's political elite therefore does not wish to choose between Washington and Brussels, as transatlantic cooperation is fundamental to the country's security. Any further disruption in EU-U.S. relations is worrisome for Budapest, which may hesitate to take sides as long as a choice can be avoided. Should Hungary be pressured to choose Washington or Brussels, some analysts believe that Budapest would favor the United States, as "the presumed final guarantor of military security."[3] However, as the EU deepens, and the geopolitical landscape changes, this may not always be the case. As illustrated by the Iraq imbroglio, Hungary may try to appease both the United States and the larger EU powers, and its support for either side will be conditioned by the nature and context of any particular crisis.

A strong transatlantic relationship is in Hungary's interest. If there is overwhelming U.S.-EU consensus over a specific military mission, then Hungary is likely to participate. However, issues that are marked by U.S.-EU divisions are likely to generate uncertainty in Budapest as to its own position. Political leaders cite the example of other countries within the EU, such as the United Kingdom, Denmark, and the Netherlands, when looking for a model to emulate in spanning the Atlantic divide.

The European Union

In December 1991, Hungary completed its Association Agreement with the European Community, covering areas of cooperation, such as trade and legality issues, as well as political dialogue. The document went into effect on February 1, 1994, and in March 1994 Hungary became the first CEE country to apply for membership.[4] Negotiations to join the EU were launched on March 30, 1998. Ahead of official entry, Hungary held a public referendum on membership in April 2003. Out of the 45.62 percent of eligible voters who participated in the referendum, 83.76 percent voted in favor of joining the European Union.[5] The low voter turnout was attributed to the criticism voiced by the main opposition party, the Alliance of Young Democrats-Hungarian Civic Party (AYD-HCP or *Fidesz*), which argued that the ruling coalition failed to ensure sufficient benefits for Hungary during the EU negotiation process.[6]

Parliament voted 365-1 in favor of joining the EU in April 2003 and Hungary became a full member on May 1, 2004.[7] The common perception of the EU among Hungarian political elites is that there are two kinds of EU members: those who can vote in the European Parliament (EP) and wave the EU flag, such as Hungary, and those that form the Eurozone, whose economic power, together with the United Kingdom, allows them to decide the foreign and security policies for the European Union as a whole. Evidently, capitals within the Eurozone will continue to determine the EU's economic and political interests, while those remaining on the outside are in effect relegated to second-class status.[8]

Within the European Union, Hungary is likely to be a conservative and cautious member. Its weight and size help shape its role, leading Budapest to be selective in pushing for specific policies. The authorities want the EU to speak with one voice and expect that the Union will support issues of vital interest to Budapest. Hungary will be resolute about questions pertaining to minority rights, contending that EU membership for its neighbors will guarantee language and cultural protection for Hungarian minorities. For this reason, support for the accession of all neighbors, including Romania, Croatia, Ukraine, and Serbia, has been a key priority for Budapest.

The EU Common Foreign and Security Policy (CFSP) is favored by Hungary, much as it is in other CEE states. According to Hungary's National Security Strategy, updated in 2004, increasing the effectiveness of the CFSP, the enhancement of the European Security and Defense Policy (ESDP), and the integration of Hungary in the institutional structure of the EU are considered priorities for the country's national security.[9] Budapest views CFSP as an opportunity to articulate views on specific foreign policy issues. Even prior to membership in 2004, the EU requested Hungary's help in formulating its European Neighborhood Policy (ENP). Political leaders view EU membership as both a benefit and a limitation. As a small country, the ability to participate in formulating EU policies is advantageous; however, there are limits on the number of issues that Hungary can raise on its own within the Union.

Hungarian officials emphasize that they must adapt to and expand the country's interests into broader areas of foreign and security policy such as contributing peacekeeping units and development aid abroad in order to partake in mainstream EU decision making.[10] However, similarly to other new member states, there are uncertainties regarding the direction in which CFSP will evolve and concern that this will not be in Hungary's direct interest. The foreign policy preferences of some older EU member states are often dictated by former colonial arrangements in Africa and elsewhere, while the orientations of new members are largely directed east and south beyond the EU's immediate border. This CEE orientation stems from the desire to stabilize the bordering states and to generate greater security on the European continent. Yet, these differing priority regions within the enlarged EU could become a future dividing line between new and old members.

The general population also backs the formation of common EU defense and foreign policies. The 2005 Eurobarometer showed that 83 percent of Hungarians were in favor of ESDP and that 73 percent supported CFSP. Sixty-two percent favored the creation of a foreign minister post to represent the collective EU in international affairs and an even stronger majority (72 percent) believed in the EU's ability to promote world peace. Additionally, 67 percent of Hungarians support the creation of a EU rapid reaction force for use in international crises.[11]

Parliament ratified the EU Constitutional Treaty in December 2004 with 304 votes in favor and nine against. A Eurobarometer poll held just prior to the ratification showed that a majority of the general public also favored the constitution (60 percent). Local polls at this time indicated that only 34.5 percent favored holding a plebiscite on the treaty, while 47.5 percent were against a public vote.[12] The overwhelming support of Hungarian MPs for this document underscored the county's position as a supportive EU member. MPs from both major political parties also backed the inclusion of a clause on the protection of minority rights.

The French and Dutch "no" votes on the European Constitution in May and June 2005 and the subsequent failure of agreement on the EU budget at the June 2005 EU Summit dismayed many new members, including Hungary. The French "no" reverberated as a protest against enlargement. Symbolized by the Polish plumber, the fear of immigrants taking jobs away from ordinary Frenchmen underscored the second-class status of new members in the European Union. Furthermore, the budgetary battle between France and the United Kingdom in the summer of 2005, in which London refused to give up the rebate negotiated by former Prime Minister Margaret Thatcher and France refused to negotiate any changes to the Common Agricultural Policy (CAP) left the new EU members urging consensus. Poland offered to reduce its payments in order to resolve the crisis, but the smaller countries, such as Hungary and the Czech Republic, were not enthusiastic about such a compromise.[13]

Under the auspices of the Visegrád Four (V-4), Socialist Prime Minister Ferenc Gyurcsány proposed a transitional, three-year budget deal for 2007–2010 called the "Budapest Compromise." France and Britain began to court the new members to gain support for their budgetary standpoints. As most new members share several economic positions with the United Kingdom, France put forward a diplomatic offensive to try to bring the new members to its side. As a result, Gyurcsány's "Compromise" was received cordially by French and British officials, but without enthusiastic support. Eventually, a compromise solution was reached whereby the UK conceded to a reduction in its rebate, France agreed to a review of all EU spending in 2008, and the new member states negotiated reduced aid, although higher than earlier British proposals, with relaxed rules for accessing funds.[14]

Without a resolution on Europe's future, including institutional enlargement and the EU constitution, Euro-skepticism is likely to grow among new member states. General public support in Hungary for the EU began at a low level of 42 percent in 1997, peaked five years later and then dropped in the pre- and post-accession periods.[15] Support dropped from 63 percent in spring 2003 to 49 percent in the fall of 2004 and to 42 percent in the spring of 2005.[16]

More encouraging, however, is that the highest support for the Union has been registered among young people. Sixty-two percent of Hungarians between the ages of fifteen and twenty-four reported feeling more secure since joining the EU, including 71 percent of students, as documented by the spring 2005 Eurobarometer poll.[17] The older generation does not see the EU as an institution that will enrich their lives personally. Rather, they see their grandchildren, as being able to benefit fully from Hungary's EU membership. The EU-skeptic voter in Hungary is "elderly, less educated than the average, perceives him or herself to be a member of a lower social class, and is likely to live in the least developed and urbanized parts of Hungary."[18]

Involvement in NATO

NATO has been viewed in Hungary as the key guarantor of Europe's security above all other international organizations.[19] The first discussions about NATO and the EU took place prior to the collapse of communism. In 1988, Foreign State Secretary Gyula Horn, as a representative of the liberal communist government between 1988 and 1990, was allowed to address a Political Committee meeting of NATO's Parliamentary Assembly.[20] As the first communist politician to visit NATO headquarters, he advocated the reduction of conventional weapons and armed forces to a level that exclusively serves defensive goals and stated that Soviet forces could be withdrawn from Hungary "within the framework of [a] general European agreement."[21] In February 1990, Horn made a speech at the Hungarian Academy of Sciences in which he referred to the possibility of joining NATO's "political organs." The government at the time reacted negatively to such statements. Communism had not officially been displaced at this point and the government did not favor Budapest's approaches to NATO.[22]

In July 1990, after the demise of communism, Prime Minister József Antall became the first premier from CEE to visit NATO headquarters. He subsequently gave a speech in October 1990, where he stated that NATO was the guarantor for European stability.[23] Even though communist rule had ended, threats to Hungary's security were still present whether from an unstable east or a war-torn former Yugoslavia. The Yugoslav wars negatively affected approximately 350,000 ethnic Hungarians, especially in the Yugoslav province of Vojvodina. Not surprisingly, given the UN's and the EU's poor record in peacemaking in Yugoslavia, NATO remained the most trusted security institution.[24]

By April 1993, Hungary's parliament declared entry into NATO and the Western European Union (WEU) as national priorities. All political parties accepted such inclusion as key objectives with the exception of the extremist Hungarian Justice and Life Party (HJLP). NATO's Partnership for Peace (PfP) program was initiated in 1994 and across the political spectrum NATO and the EU have remained at the core of Hungary's security posture.[25]

Prior to its 1997 invitation to join the Alliance, Hungary leased its Taszár airbase to the United States to facilitate NATO's Implementation Force (IFOR) and later NATO's Stabilization Force (SFOR) in Bosnia-Herzegovina. Hungary participated in both IFOR/SFOR and now contributes to the EU-led EU-FOR mission in Bosnia. In 1999, the Taszár base was used by U.S. fighter-bombers to enable NATO air strikes against Serbia over Belgrade's aggression in Kosova. Approximately 100,000 U.S. troops passed through the Taszár facility while it was in operation.[26] Hungary has also been active in NATO's Kosova Force (KFOR).

In March 1999, Hungary became a member of NATO together with the Czech Republic and Poland. On the same day, a parliamentary resolution on the Basic Principles of Hungarian Security and Defense Policy came into force. It stated that Hungary can maintain its security most effectively as a member of NATO and considered transatlantic cooperation a cardinal factor of European security.[27] Membership granted Hungary a seat at the table with the United States, and it ensured protection from any potential Russian threat that no other international organization could provide.

Hungary has striven to fulfill its obligations as a NATO member. In addition to its continued contributions in Bosnia and Kosova, Hungary has contributed to NATO missions in Afghanistan and Iraq. To support U.S. operations in Afghanistan, Prime Minister Viktor Orbán offered to deploy a medical unit. A parliamentary decision passed in February 2003 allocated fifty medical experts to serve in the International Security Assistance Force (ISAF) and they were deployed between March and September 2003.[28] Hungary provided armaments and supplies to three Afghan National Army battalions valued at $3.7 million.[29] Also in 2003, parliament approved sending up to fifty Hungarian troops to Afghanistan, while Budapest delivered $1 million in humanitarian aid.[30] Hungary's subsequent contribution to Iraq put a limit on its efforts in Afghanistan. Additionally, Hungary increased its troop numbers in the Balkans to replace troops from other countries that were heading to Afghanistan.[31]

Budapest initially sent 300 troops to participate in the Iraqi mission. After they served their mandate, parliament rejected an extension of the mission in December 2004. Most of the opposition deputies voted against the extension. As an alternative strategy to continue Hungary's participation, the Socialist-led government authorized the deployment of 150 Hungarian noncombat troops to provide security for a NATO training base outside of Baghdad.[32] The deployment of troops for NATO operations does not require parliamentary approval.

Budapest has been criticized for its slow pace of defense reform, which has been attributed to the lack of a complete break with the communist structure. Dunay has argued that this has contributed to maintaining close ties between the former Communist Party (now Socialist Party) and the military.[33] Prior to the Defense Law of 1993, when the structural underpinnings for balanced civil-military relations were created, Hungary's defense establishment was divided into two parts.[34] There was a small Ministry of Defense (MoD) and a separate Command of the Hungarian Defense Forces, an arrangement that was devised by the last communist government to make it difficult for its successors to directly control the military."[35] *Fidesz*, together with the Hungarian Democratic Forum (HDF), has striven for a stronger civilian component within the MoD. Both major parties, the Socialists and *Fidesz*, have tried to strengthen their preferred linkages, which delayed the country's capability to meet NATO standards.[36]

Hungary has been working to improve its image within NATO and with the U.S. and has contributed to the three trust funds established by the NATO Secretary-General for Iraq. As one of the top five contributors Budapest allocated 100,000 Euros, 150 troops, and 77 T-72 main battle tanks for Iraq in November 2005.[37] Hungary's goal is to keep 1,000 troops serving in EU and NATO missions.[38] NATO maintains a special calculation for country commitments: the percentage of personnel deployed and the percentage of personnel capable of being deployed. Eight percent is the goal of the first calculation and Hungary has reached this target, whereas most states have fallen below. For Budapest, 40 percent is the goal of the second measure, which

Hungary has yet to reach.[39] However, the country does not have any assets that are critical to major NATO military missions and possesses limited capabilities in training and peacekeeping.

Most Hungarian officials advocate that NATO remain the main forum for relations between the United States and Europe.[40] They contend that the structures already in place within NATO must be developed while political dialogue should be improved. Government officials do not want to task a panel of "wise men" outside of NATO to make decisions, as was proposed in February 2005 by Germany's Defense Minister on behalf of Chancellor Gerhard Schröder. Instead they advocate keeping decision making under the purview of NATO's Secretary General. Although Germany's proposal failed to gain support it did generate heated discussions in Budapest.

NATO's significance for Hungary is well-documented in the country's National Security Strategy drafted in March 2004 and adopted in April 2005. The document emphasizes the importance of "the durable preservation of NATO's central role in the Euro-Atlantic security system."[41] Moreover, Hungary views the transformation of NATO in adapting to the evolving security environment as an imperative. The expansion of NATO to include countries on Hungary's southern border is also perceived as a priority.[42]

Notwithstanding these favorable aspects of Hungary's membership in NATO, the general public views participation in military missions overseas less favorably. This has been attributed to Hungary's lack of a military tradition. Dunay believes that "support for the armed forces in Hungarian society tends to be rather volatile."[43] Support was present for the army's role in protecting villagers during the 1999 and 2000 floods and the NATO operation over Kosova. While 61 percent of the population favored NATO membership in 2000, there is currently less interest in and support for military missions outside of Hungary or beyond its neighborhood. By 2002, 44 percent of citizens perceived membership as a new form of submission to a foreign power, while 41 percent viewed it as a means for guaranteeing Hungary's independence.[44]

U.S. Relations

Hungary seeks to facilitate the strengthening of transatlantic relations by promoting dialogue between the United States and the European Union, which it believes to be inadequate. Using history as a lesson, political leaders contend that U.S. engagement must be preserved, both politically and militarily. The European continent has been divided through war over the past century and U.S. military power and democratic ideals have proved to be forces for positive change. Hungarian leaders respect U.S. world leadership as the strongest military power, spending twice as much of its GDP on armament as the European allies.[45]

The United States was also a model of democracy and a beacon of freedom, especially during Communist rule. U.S. president Ronald Reagan is credited for pushing the Soviet Union toward its own dissolution, and Washington was at the forefront in aiding democratic transitions throughout CEE. However, as priorities and alliances shift, memories can often fade. The Cold War vision of the United States as the gravitational center of the West is receding and geography may triumph over history. Out of necessity, the Central Europeans may gravitate more toward the EU.[46]

In the postcommunist context, U.S.-Hungarian relations have taken on renewed importance and have often been at the center of political competition inside Hungary between the two major political parties. *Fidesz* was in power on September 11, 2001 and the government immediately conveyed its solidarity with and sympathy for the United States and the victims of the terrorist attacks. Prime Minister Viktor Orbán stated that Hungary, as a U.S. ally, would assess the 9/11 attack as one directed against the entire free world.[47] Foreign Minister János Martonyi offered Hungary's assistance to the United States, in accordance with NATO's Article V, in the form of diplomatic, informational, political, economic, and military assistance. The U.S. military air base in Taszár was placed on high alert, and a special air defense alert was ordered over the country.[48] In the aftermath of the crisis, Orbán and his ministers commented frequently on the importance of a strong U.S. presence in Europe.

In May 2002 the government changed hands following parliamentary elections. The Hungarian Socialist Party (HSP) and its smaller coalition partner, the Alliance of Free Democrats (AFD), formed a ten-seat majority in parliament.[49] As Washington launched efforts in late 2002 and early 2003 to gather support for its war against Saddam Hussein, the political dialogue in Budapest remained unchanged: support for the United States in the war against terrorists was a foreign policy priority as long as there was significant international backing. The HSP-AFD coalition supported the U.S. position on Iraq but preferred Washington to be backed with a UN resolution. On September 12, 2002, Foreign Minister László Kovács stated:

"Saddam Hussein and the present Iraqi regime pose a threat to peace in the region and in the rest of the world. I share the view that the United Nations Security Council and the UN member states at large have a duty and a responsibility. Hungary will work closely with our partner in the United Nations to pursue the full implementation of the relevant UN Security Council Resolutions. We will also work closely with the United States and other allies in order to form a strong coalition against terrorism and any threat to world peace. Common efforts of

NATO allies and partners are crucial to our success. This would enhance an even broader coalition of nations. We give priority to measures that are supported by a UN resolution."[50]

Kovács calculated that the United States would not request a Hungarian contingent in the Iraqi war. In September 2002, Kovács stated that if the United States decides to take military action and Hungary may offer its air space, it was unlikely to deploy Hungarian fighting units.[51]

Political debates between the ruling coalition and the opposition party centered on the question of dispatching Hungarian troops to fight in Iraq. On November 5, 2002, in parliament, *Fidesz* deputy István Simicskó questioned the foreign minister on the subject. With mounting U.S. pressure to participate in a "coalition of the willing," a July 2002 visit to Washington by Kovács, whereby he secured an official visit for Prime Minister Péter Medgyessy to the White House, was met with suspicion by opposition deputies. *Fidesz* leaders speculated that the upcoming Bush-Medgyessy meeting was arranged because of HSP promises to end Hungarian soldiers to Iraq. Kovács reiterated that military units would only be dispatched with parliamentary approval.[52]

In January 2003 Hungary became one of the signatories of the "Letter of Eight" together with the United Kingdom, the Czech Republic, Denmark, Italy, Poland, Portugal, and Spain. The letter was printed in twelve European newspapers and highlighted the dividing line on the subject of Iraq. Snubbing the French-German position of a measured and incremental response to the crisis, the Letter of Eight countries clearly aligned themselves with the United States and insisted that the U.S.-European relationship "must not become a casualty of the current Iraqi regime's persistent attempts to threaten world security."[53]

Following the Letter of Eight and the subsequent CEE Vilnius 10 letter, French president Jacques Chirac berated the CEE states for their blatant support of the U.S. position. To soften the French reaction, Medgyessy was later quoted in the French paper, *Libération*, as saying that if he had not signed the letter that he would have been reproached for refusing transatlantic solidarity and that the letter was "a trap that could not be avoided."[54] In April 2003, Prime Minister Medgyessy signed a statement on European solidarity with German Chancellor Gerhard Schröder and Swedish Prime Minister Göran Persson. It asserted that, "The idea of solidarity in the European Union does not only mean financial or economic solidarity, but also and above all political solidarity."[55] Analysts speculated that this was Medgyessy's attempt to placate the European Union after siding with the United States in the Letter of Eight.

The transatlantic crisis over Iraq complicated EU relations for the states joining the Union in May 2004. *Fidesz* also assumed positions that were perceived to be both supporting and opposing the war in Iraq. For example, *Fidesz* did not back military involvement in Iraq without international consent. The party also insisted that troops could be involved in peacekeeping, but not in combat. Iraq demonstrated the cracks in the EU facade when no common European position was formulated. Strong support for the United States placed all of the CEE countries in a tenuous position. When Medgyessy signed the Letter of Eight in January 2003, signaling Budapest's solidarity with Washington, some element of fear was generated among the opposition that resisting France and Germany would jeopardize entry into the Union the following year. For Hungary and other CEE states, the Letter was also a reaction to the French-German tendency to express one categorical view simplistically as "European." Some opposition leaders blamed the manner in which the Letter was issued, rather than disagreeing with its content.

In March 2003, Hungary's airbase in Taszár was opened for the training of up to 3,000 Iraqi exiles by U.S. forces to serve as guides, mediators, and translators during the Iraq mission and between 150 and 300 volunteers of the Free Iraqi Forces (FIF) were trained.[56] Although the HSP government opened the airbase where the training would take place, at the same time it denied the U.S. permission to land aircraft anywhere outside of Taszár. Budapest also refused the U.S. request to expel Iraqi diplomats from the country. Foreign Minister Kovács's explanation for the decision was that Hungary was not at war with Iraq although it had taken steps to assist in the successful implementation of this coalition action when it appeared to be inevitable.[57]

In April 2003, Washington asked Budapest to supply three hundred peacekeepers for Iraq. The HSP called for an urgent parliamentary motion to discuss the proposal, but the vote did not yield the required two-thirds majority. Opposition MPs voted either against the call for an urgent debate or abstained. *Fidesz* supported peacekeeping in Iraq, but wanted "international authorization" from the UN, the EU, or NATO prior to giving its approval. *Fidesz* blocked the urgency motion also because the government proposal was not unequivocal that the troops would only be involved in a peacekeeping mission.[58] *Fidesz* and the HDF blocked the debate on sending troops to Iraq in late April and early May 2003.[59] During this time, HSP deputies accused *Fidesz* of double-talk, by quoting speeches where *Fidesz* leaders were in favor of fighting in the war against terrorists, but were against the idea of sending military troops to Iraq. *Fidesz*'s ambiguity can be partly attributed to public opinion, which was steadily against military action in Iraq. A survey carried out in January 2003 indicated that only 18 percent of Hungarians supported U.S. action in Iraq without a UN mandate.[60]

Following the May 2003 UN Security Resolution 1483, guaranteeing humanitarian aid to Iraq, the four parliamentary parties agreed to adopt a motion on sending a 300-member transport and humanitarian contingent to the Iraqi mission.[61] Mostly consisting of logistics experts to help in reconstruction, the troops were deployed in September with a mandate until December 2004. In spite of what appeared to be the HSP's solid support, international authorization of the peacekeeping mission was important for leaders across the political spectrum. In trying to balance between the United States and the European Union, the HSP occupied a difficult position. HSP Foreign Minister Kovács subsequently outlined, in May 2004, the government's proposal for UN supervision of Iraq in letters addressed to the UN Secretary General and to the UN Security Council. In addition, concerns over prisoner abuse at the Abu Ghraib prison in Baghdad were raised by the ruling coalition. Kovács addressed a letter to U.S. Secretary of State Colin Powell in which he asked for information on the torture of prisoners and urged an investigation.[62] In May 2004 the prisoner abuse scandal was condemned by all political parties. The affair dominated television screens across the CEE region, impacting poorly on the U.S. image.

An attack on Hungarian troops in February 2004 wounded ten soldiers. From the four parliamentary parties, only the HDF opposition favored a troop withdrawal. *Fidesz* requested an emergency meeting of the parliamentary defense committee to discuss Hungary's participation in Iraq, but Defense Minister Ferenc Juhász stated that the attack was a "strong incentive" to continue in the mission.[63] On June 17, 2004, one Hungarian soldier was killed and a second wounded. Prime Minister Medgyessy, during a speech in Brussels, stated that the government would enable anyone who wanted to return from Iraq to do so. Meanwhile, Orbán asserted that it was time for the troops to come home as he did not equate the country's military presence in Iraq with the war against international terrorists, which he still believed was necessary.

Medgyessy resigned in August 2004 over tensions with his party's coalition partner, the AFD, following a government reshuffle.[64] In early November 2004, as the troop mandate was expiring, newly appointed Prime Minister Ferenc Gyurcsány stated that an extension of the country's military presence in Iraq was an impossibility.[65] The government asked parliament to extend the mandate by three months in order to remain in place for the Iraqi elections. However, the request failed in a vote of 191 in favor and 159 against.[66] While Gyurcsány stated that it would be irresponsible to bring the soldiers home before the Iraqi election, he also acknowledged the difficulty in convincing a skeptical public and maintaining the cost of the mission.[67] Hungarian troops left Iraq in December 2004. To compensate for the withdrawal, the government authorized the deployment of 150 non-combat troops as part of a NATO mission, as the dispatch of NATO troops did not require parliamentary authorization.

Support for Washington exists within both of the main Hungarian political factions. Nevertheless, the political infighting conveys a different story. Both the HSP and *Fidesz* have publicly questioned their opponent's commitment to strong U.S. relations. For example, in May 2005 an exchange was recorded between the Chair of the Parliamentary Foreign Affairs Committee and *Fidesz* member Zsolt Németh and the Vice-Chair of the Committee József Kozma from the ruling Socialist Party. Kozma credited the Socialists with elevating relations with the U.S. to their highest level.[68] Németh characterized the HSP's relationship with the U.S. as lukewarm and stated that *Fidesz* would develop closer ties with the U.S. following a 2006 election victory.[69] Both groups are in daily arguments about which party has the key to the White House.

Both parties have labored to tarnish the image of their political rival. The HSP has raised suspicions in Washington concerning *Fidesz*'s allegiance to the United States. In March 2005, on an official visit to Washington, HSP Foreign Minister Ferenc Somogyi warned that should *Fidesz* win the 2006 elections then relations with Washington would be in jeopardy.[70] *Fidesz*, on the other hand, has repeatedly dismissed the HSP as former Communists.[71] Analysts attribute Hungary's bitter political divide to the lack of a major break separating communists from democrats at the end of Soviet rule.[72] Hungary's Roundtable in 1989, which terminated communist reign, involved persons who had held power under the Communist regime together with opposition intellectuals. As the new democrats were primarily scholars who lacked experience in running the country, the ex-communists were asked to help with the government and placed in many key institutions. Hungary thereby did not experience any purges of the old guard that some CEE countries conducted.[73] Regardless of the political posturing by both major parties, Washington is unlikely to witness any significant difference in support, as the major parliamentary parties adhere to basic democratic principles and seek a close relationship with the United States.

Despite political support for strong U.S.-Hungarian relations, several episodes have tarnished the U.S. image in Hungary among the general population, as in other CEE states. For example, some political commentators framed the war in Iraq as a war for oil and not a defense of security and human rights, which impacted adversely on public opinion. Such perceptions have undermined U.S. credibility, and could prove difficult to reverse. Additionally, U.S. business investment in Hungary has become marginal compared to that from EU member states. For the cumulative period between 1990 and 2004, German investment took the largest share of investment in Hungary at 30 percent, followed by the Netherlands at 20 percent and Austria at 11 percent.[74] The United States has accounted for only 5 percent of FDI in Hungary. After the privatization of state companies in the 1990s when the majority of

FDI came from the United States, Hungarian labor became too expensive for U.S. companies while EU countries have created stronger financial ties with their new partners.

Travel to the United States has also contributed to negative perceptions. The inability of Hungarians to travel visa-free, while their country has supported unpopular U.S. global policies, and while EU member states that opposed Washington over Iraq participate in the Visa Waiver Program, has been a major source of frustration in Hungary. The 1998–2002 *Fidesz* and the 2002–2004 HSP governments both worked diligently to alter this detrimental U.S. policy. Orbán reported that he told President Bush that "the strengthening of U.S.-Hungarian ties and friendship largely depends on whether the young generation can get a direct impression of America, or whether they can only see it on television."[75] A roadmap for Hungary's entry into the visa waiver program may help to smooth some ridges in U.S.-Hungarian relations.

In general, Hungarian citizens remain concerned about their security and prefer not to participate in U.S. missions that have the potential to increase risks for the country. In this context, creeping anti-Americanism was evident ahead of Hungary's April 2006 general elections with some opposition newspapers featuring anti-U.S. rhetoric. However, such views are not representative of mainstream party positions. Many scholars have pointed to the shallowness of some west European voices employing anti-Americanism as a simplistic and unifying theme.[76] Elections in Hungary will not be won on the issue of anti-Americanism, but rather anti-Americanism can feature in populist rhetoric with calls for the protection of national sovereignty. The average citizen is more concerned with domestic issues, such as agriculture, pensions, jobs, education, and economy, than foreign policy.

Under the leadership of the 2002–2006 HSP government, Hungarian foreign policy was based on a slogan coined by the former Socialist Foreign Minister László Kovács, now Hungary's EU Commissioner: "More Europe does not mean less America."[77] Kovács wanted to reiterate Hungary's support for Washington at a time when the EU was planning its enlargement into Central and Eastern Europe. Regardless of intentions, Hungary's ties with the EU will inevitably deepen through travel, work, and study opportunities, as well as through trade and investment. As long as the United States remains restrictive in these areas, the EU will develop more intensive ties with Hungarian leaders and citizens and "more Europe" could indeed coincide with "less America."

Regional Relations and the Eastern Dimension

The truncation of Hungary dictated by the Treaty of Trianon at the close of World War I resulted in a third of all Hungarians becoming resident in a new neighboring state.[78] This trauma has haunted Hungarian politics in the post-communist era. As a result, Budapest's priorities have been to aid neighbors in their quest for NATO and EU integration, as this would directly benefit all Hungarian minorities and create a united Euro-Atlantic community in which all Hungarians could participate. Visegrád 3 (V-3) was formed in the early 1990s between Poland, Hungary, and (then) Czechoslovakia as a cooperative mechanism to help plan for admission into NATO and the EU. It later changed its name to V-4, after the January 1, 1993, split of Czechoslovakia into two independent states. In reality, Visegrád cooperation has always been utilized for specific purposes, and future cooperation will likely be focused on exerting influence within the EU when dealing with common issues.

Slovakia hosts a Hungarian minority of about 521,000 or 9.7 percent of the total population.[79] Relations with Slovakia were particularly strained under Vladimír Mečiar's nationalist and anti-minority leadership during much of the 1990s. Budapest welcomed the Slovak change of government in 1998 and was highly supportive of the country's bid for both EU and NATO membership. Hungary was the first of the Visegrád 4 whose parliament approved the protocol of Slovakia's NATO accession.[80] Budapest also backed Bratislava's EU accession.

Hungarian-Slovak relations have been reasonably stable although a few sensitive issues have persisted. The long-disputed Gabčíkovo-Nagymaros hydro dam project on the Danube, which was created following a 1977 agreement between Hungary and Czechoslovakia, was taken to the International Court of Justice (ICJ) in The Hague in 1994. In 2004, the two governments agreed to establish an economic commission of experts to resolve the conflict and pledged to follow EU directives. Another issue of contention was Budapest's introduction of a Status Law in 2001, designed to strengthen the identity, culture, and language of Hungarians in neighboring states, which was met with strong criticism from Bratislava and Bucharest. Slovakia saw it as a violation of the country's sovereignty and of international law. The European Commission resolved the issue in 2003 with an agreement on the mutual support of minorities in the spheres of education and culture. Bratislava and Budapest have also differed in their approaches to resolving historical injustices between their two countries, including an apology and compensation for the post–World War II Beneš decrees, when between 75,000 and 90,000 Hungarians were resettled from Slovakia to Hungary and 70,000 to 75,000 Slovaks from Hungary to Czechoslovakia. Over 500,000 Hungarians in Czechoslovakia were accused of participating in war crimes in 1945 and had their property confiscated and citizenship and other rights denied.

Hungary's main political parties strongly support the integration efforts of neighboring countries. Romania hosts the largest Hungarian minority, numbering approximately 1.5 million. The Hungarian parliament ratified Romania's EU Accession Treaty in October 2005 despite concerns that the environmental protection standards for Romania have not been as stringent as those for the 2004 enlargement countries, following three toxic spills into the shared Szamos and Tisza rivers. Although Budapest has provided strong support for Romania's inclusion into both NATO and the EU, relations have been strained by differing views about minority protection. Budapest's Status Law generated harsh criticism from Bucharest with an eventual compromise reached in 2003 whereby Hungarian identification cards could only be used in Hungary, while Romania would acknowledge educational benefits for Hungarians on its territory.

The Balkan states are a priority for Hungary as they flank the country's southern border. To the south, Hungarian minorities are present in the province of Vojvodina in Serbia and in Croatia. Due to proximity and history, the Balkan region is a priority for Budapest's foreign policy. Hungary currently has about 500 to 600 peacekeepers in the Western Balkans and the Visegrád-4 plus two format, with Slovenia and Austria, has proven to be a productive framework for the region.[81] However, Budapest remains skeptical of the EU's Balkan policies and sees these inadequacies as another reason for continued U.S. involvement.

Hungary has supported EU enlargement, as accession promotes and maintains a reform process that is important for minorities in bordering states. Various twinning projects, financed by the Hungarian budget, have raised awareness of the benefits of integration among neighboring states. Budapest has supported small and medium-sized businesses, and conducted training programs for border guards in order to make them compatible with the EU. It has also provided strong support to Croatia's EU bid.

In March 2005, when the EU Council of Ministers decided to suspend accession talks with Croatia due to Zagreb's inability to bring the indicted war crimes suspect General Ante Gotovina to The Hague, Budapest remained in favor of continued talks on Croatia's membership and opposed delaying the opening of negotiations.[82] The spring 2005 Eurobarometer indicated that 73 percent of Hungarians supported Croatia's EU accession, the highest out of all candidate countries. Next in order of support in Hungary for EU entry were: Bulgaria at 59 percent, Romania at 55 percent, Turkey at 51 percent, Macedonia at 38 percent, Serbia and Montenegro at 37 percent, and Albania at 35 percent.[83]

Hungary's political leaders from both major political streams view the strategic partnership between the EU and NATO as essential to facilitating the economic and democratic development of the countries along the EU's border. Budapest's priority countries include Croatia, Serbia, and Ukraine. Budapest supports an EU-NATO partnership to focus on the "eastern questions," despite fears among older EU member states that such a partnership could serve to undermine the EU role and its neighborhood policy (ENP). Similarly to the other CEE states, Hungary sees the ENP as failing to offer sufficient incentives for consolidating the domestic reform processes. In general, Budapest welcomes U.S.-NATO-EU cooperation with strong CEE involvement for engaging Europe's border countries.[84] This could facilitate a stronger response to crises and would help enhance democratic development and ensure lasting security along the EU's eastern border. The status of the CEE countries can be raised within such a format and would serve to steer all international institutions toward joint projects. However, Hungary will avoid maneuvering behind the backs of the larger EU members and will likely try to engage Germany in steering the Union's eastern policies.

Neither *Fidesz* nor the HSP have plans to manage Russia's increasing economic and energy encroachment in the country. *Fidesz* is generally suspicious of Russian neoimperialist ambitions, whereas the HSP has maintained closer ties with Russian elites especially given the fact that many HSP MPs have been educated in Russia. During a February 2005 trip to Moscow, Gyurcsány made a controversial pronouncement by thanking the Soviet Union and the Red Army for "freeing Hungary from fascism 60 years ago."[85] It remains uncertain whether Budapest's careful policy toward Russia would become more assertive under any future center-right government.

Political Options

The main opposition party, *Fidesz*, has lacked political experience, as compared to its Socialist counterpart. Formed in 1988, the party has had to learn how to compete in the political arena. Allegations that the party would become an unpredictable U.S. partner have been exaggerated. The party record demonstrates strong backing for the U.S.-led war against terrorists. Any ambivalence that the party displayed toward the Iraqi crisis was not related to the purpose of the war, but was rather a criticism of the HSP government's handling of the issue. *Fidesz* believed that the ruling Socialists operated with too much secrecy and even the left-leaning daily *Népszabadság* raised the same concern in a commentary on March 26, 2003.[86] The daily also questioned the need for secrecy concerning American use of the Taszár military base.[87]

Fidesz's objections to military action in Iraq surfaced when the war became entangled with issues of human rights. The unfounded claims by the Bush administration that Iraq possessed weapons of mass destruction, compounded by the Abu Ghraib prisoner abuse scandal, raised red flags for *Fidesz* in what it perceived as the HSP's "no questions asked" participation in the "coalition of the willing." It is possible that the HSP government chose secrecy and avoided dialogue with the opposition over Iraq in order to consolidate its own position with Washington. However, excluding the opposition from the debate simply encouraged *Fidesz* to question policy rather than to illustrate that *Fidesz* supported specific positions. When in government between 1998 and 2002, *Fidesz* was labeled by the socialist opposition as volatile and anti-American. Budapest's purchase of Gripen aircraft in the fall of 2001, rather than U.S. fighter planes, and Hungary's ratification of the International Criminal Court Statute in November 2001 were frequently cited to substantiate mistrust in *Fidesz*. The inability of Prime Minister Viktor Orbán to receive an invitation to the White House in early 2002 was also cited by critics as evidence that the party has poor standing in Washington. However, the U.S. embassy in Budapest asserted that *Fidesz* was denied a visit only because the party failed to submit a formal request.

Fidesz has been branded as anti-Semitic, revisionist, and ultranationalist by its most vehement critics on the left. Such allegations have been especially damaging to the party. The anti-U.S. comments made by the chairman of the ultranationalist Hungarian Justice and Life Party (HJLP) István Csurka after 9/11, and the fact that premier Orbán did not publicly refute them, was highlighted by HSP supporters as evidence that *Fidesz* and HJLP not only shared anti-American positions but were also cooperating politically. Others argued in Orbán's defense that commenting on Csurka's rhetoric would have only given international attention to a fringe nationalist. There have also been attempts by the Socialist Party to engender uncertainty in the U.S. administration about *Fidesz*'s reliability as a partner for the United States.[88] In the long term such tactics outweigh the short-term political benefits as they raise doubts about the durability of the U.S.-Hungarian alliance.

Prior to the start of the Iraqi war, the U.S. government requested Hungary's help in staging a military operation from Turkey. On February 19, 2003, the four parliamentary parties did not agree on allowing a NATO shipment to Turkey to cross Hungarian territory, as *Fidesz* initially wanted to ensure that the military hardware supplied to Ankara would be used only for defensive purposes.[89] However, on February 24, 2003, parliament supported sending assistance to Turkey with 335 votes in favor and three against.[90] *Fidesz* gave its consent as NATO formally backed the request. However, when the U.S. asked to use Hungarian airspace in March 2003, *Fidesz* objected during the consultations. Fearing a lack of the two-thirds support necessary in a parliamentary vote, the Socialist government invoked a resolution from 1998 that allowed the administration to act without parliamentary support.[91] *Fidesz* and its coalition partner, the HDF, were outraged by this bypass of parliament on questions of over-flight rights. Party leaders contended that the 1998 resolution was not valid in the current situation, claiming that a decision by the UN, the EU, or NATO was also needed.[92]

Fidesz did not support an extension of Hungary's presence in Iraq past the December 2004 deadline, citing the Abu Ghraib prison abuse scandal as the foremost reason behind their decision. News reports indicated that UK prime minister Tony Blair also made an appeal to Orbán to support the extension of the military mandate. Orbán cited public opposition to the war and that as a representative of the people he could not support Blair's request.[93] Although *Fidesz* took the major blame for blocking an extension, the ruling coalition had actually stopped advocating a prolongation of the mandate calculating that the party would lose public support.[94] Parliament voted 191 in favor and 159 against the extension, short of the needed two-thirds majority.[95]

In the April 2006 parliamentary elections, support for U.S. policy in Iraq did not feature as a campaign issue. Anti-Americanism and anti-Iraq involvement were not used in Hungary as they were in the elections in Spain and Germany. Orbán has been straightforward concerning his position on Iraq. During his visit to Washington in July 2005, he stated that the function of an elected leader is to represent the people. In Hungary, it was difficult to generate support for military participation as "the majority of the people are against U.S. military steps taken outside of NATO."[96] Although there was speculation that *Fidesz* would pursue an anti-Iraq line during the election campaign, this did not happen. While *Fidesz* supported the U.S.- and UK-led efforts in the Iraqi conflict, it did not want to commit Hungarian troops without public support, especially not during an election year. In reality, the *Fidesz* position was no different to that of the Socialist government.

Public Opinion

The war in Iraq was received with general public opposition. The lack of sufficient government communication with the public over Hungary's participation in the war, the abuses in the Abu Ghraib prison, the mistaken or manipulated intelligence over Iraq's possession of weapons of mass destruction, Hungarian casualties, and the general perception that the U.S. unilaterally forced Budapest to give its support, all contributed to a negative public view of U.S. engagement in Iraq. Although the government did not thoroughly explain to the public all of the circumstances relating to Hungary's participation in the mission, it is unlikely that additional information would have altered public opinion. The lack of evidence of weapons of mass destruction, the main pretext for the war, engendered a sense of betrayal by Washington. According to an April 2004 poll, only 15 percent of Hungarians surveyed believed that the war in Iraq was to combat terrorists, 44 percent believed that it was driven solely by U.S. interests, and 22 percent responded that the war was the result of both factors.[97] In general, citizens would prefer Hungary to be a neutral entity, as they feel that alliances are responsible for most of the tragedies of the twentieth century. During the debate on whether or not Hungary would extend its military presence in Iraq past the December 31, 2004, deadline, a November 2004 poll showed that 54 percent of the public supported the evacuation of Hungarian troops.[98]

It is unlikely that the lack of disclosure about Hungarian involvement in Iraq was due to political immaturity, as the HSP is a well-seasoned and professional party. It may have been an attempt to keep the opposition out of the decision-making process. Regardless of the reasons, the result was an increase in anti-American sentiments among the general Hungarian public. Resentment was also visible in political commentaries arguing that the government had done a poor job in presenting itself as a reliable U.S. ally. *Népszabadság*, the leading left-leaning newspaper, chided the government over Hungary's small contribution to the missions in Afghanistan and Iraq. Comparing Hungary to Poland, the anonymous author wrote that Poland was a "poor" but "enthusiastic" ally that would benefit from its strong alignment with Washington during the Iraqi crisis. Unlike the Hungarian Socialist-led government, the paper wrote, "the Poles certainly know what Polish interests are."[99]

There is a lingering sense among many Hungarian citizens that the United States is a bully pushing for others to support its interests. The fight for freedom and democracy that the Bush administration touted as reasons for ridding Iraq of Saddam Hussein did not resonate as strongly as may have been expected from a formerly oppressed country. In 2003, a majority of citizens (56 percent) believed that U.S. went to war for the purpose of obtaining oil in pursuit of its economic interests, while only 31 percent perceived WMD as the impetus.[100]

Concerns over the war in Iraq prompted several protests in Budapest. In February 2003, Civilians for Peace organized a demonstration of 20,000 to 50,000 people. In March 2003, 2,000 demonstrators protested in front of the U.S. and UK embassies and then marched to parliament. In June 2003, Civilians for Peace sent a protest letter to parliament urging legislators not to send Hungarian troops to Iraq. In March 2004, approximately 1,000 people protested at Heroes' Square while the Green movement demanded a pullout from Iraq and protested against the NATO radar station planned to be built in Zengő peak. Analysts claimed that the protest movements were not anti-American, but were opposed to the Bush administration and its "hegemonic policy."[101]

THE CZECH REPUBLIC

Following the end of communist rule in Czechoslovakia, and the official divorce between the Czech Republic and Slovakia on January 1, 1993, the priorities of Czech leaders were to secure membership in both NATO and the European Union, and to maintain U.S. involvement in Europe through strong transatlantic security cooperation.[102] These objectives emanated from a lingering Russian threat felt among the postcommunist leadership that emerged from the Czech dissident movement. The rift in transatlantic relations at the outset of the 2003 Iraq war came at a time when the Czech Republic was trying to develop its identity within both NATO and the EU. The Czech Foreign Policy Strategy, adopted in March 2003, and the country's Security Strategy, updated in December 2003, emphasized the transatlantic relationship as an important pillar of Czech security. Political leaders did not make any provisions for disagreement between the "framework of the European integration process and the Euro-Atlantic alliance."[103] When Jiři Paroubek became Prime Minister in April 2005, he stated that the Czech Republic relied on its membership in both NATO and the EU, "with the understanding that a united Europe and the United States are the decisive driving force of contemporary history."[104] Indeed, Prague does not want to be pressured to choose between the big powers and its position has been characterized as "an instinctive but hesitant Atlanticist."[105]

Czech politics have involved broad coalition building, with key ministerial posts being held by members of different parties with sometimes differing foreign policy positions. For example, the Christian Democrats and Freedom Union have tended to support NATO missions, while the Social Democrats have been hesitant to approve international military involvement. The prospect of divisions within governments relying on slim parliamentary majorities has often steered political discussions toward technical matters rather than broader foreign policy issues. For the political establishment and the general population, domestic interests tend to take precedence over external affairs, which is why Prague has not featured as a major player on the international stage.

The European Union

In October 1993, several months after the peaceful division of Czechoslovakia, the Czech Republic signed an Association Agreement with the European Community. On January 23, 1996, Prime Minister Václav Klaus delivered the country's formal application for EU membership.[106] Accession talks were concluded in December 2002 when the country received an official invitation to join the European Union at the Copenhagen Summit. A Treaty of Accession was signed in April 2003 and in June, 77 percent of the Czech public voted in favor of membership with a 55 percent voter turnout. Support for accession revolved around the assumption that the country should not remain outside of the EU and that membership was the only way to play a role in Europe's future.[107] The country's official entry date was May 1, 2004.

One strain of Czech politics has focused on defending allegedly threatened national interests from outside influences, especially the EU. The most vocal political party holding this line has been the Civic Democratic Party (CDP), and its leader, the current President and former Prime Minister Václav Klaus, has been a vociferous EU-skeptic. Prior to his signature on the Czech application for EU membership, Klaus and the CDP mounted an energetic defense of the national state as a guarantor of national identity and self-determination against the "supranational and sub-national institutions promoted by the EU," both of which they viewed as "inefficient; undemocratic; and irreparably lacking in political, cultural, and historical legitimacy."[108] Nonetheless, a majority of Czech citizens believed that Klaus has unfairly vilified the EU and propagated the wrong image of the Czech nation in the process.[109]

In February 2005, Klaus asked the Constitutional Court to provide a ruling on whether the EU Constitutional Treaty was in harmony with the Czech constitution.[110] One of the most vocal opponents of EU integration, Klaus publicly applauded the failed constitutional referenda of May and June 2005 in France and the Netherlands. Following the unsuccessful votes and the United Kingdom's own postponement of ratification, the Czech government delayed its final decision as to whether a plebiscite should be held. The next government, following the June 2006 election will determine who will make a final decision on the matter, as many political leaders still favor the document's ratification. A majority of the general population is aware of the constitution and the debate surrounding it, but few are familiar with the document's contents.[111] A local poll taken in May 2005 showed that 62 percent of Czechs wanted to hold a public referendum, in which 58 percent indicated that they would vote in favor of the treaty, 26 percent would vote against, and 16 percent were undecided.[112] Consistent with trends found in other new member states, younger people see the EU as offering a greater guarantee of stability for the country than the older generations.

Although there are divisions between Czech politicians regarding the saliency of EU membership, most see the need to participate in the formation of EU policies to ensure that the country's interests are represented. A key example is the development of the European Security and Defense Policy (ESDP) which Czech officials favor as a pillar of NATO and not as a rival. ESDP should evidently share the burden of security with the U.S. and therefore be in a close consultative, if not cooperative, relationship with NATO.[113] This view is shared by all parties across the political spectrum with the exception of the die-hard Communist Party.[114] There is a strong preference for harmonizing the defense planning processes of both the EU and NATO and close coordination between the two organizations was underscored in the country's Conceptual Basis of Foreign Policy for 2003–2006 as a priority.[115]

In addition to EU-NATO cooperation, Prague has welcomed the evolution of the ESDP's crisis management capabilities to prevent or manage conflicts within the European neighborhood. Czech officials see this development as removing the burden previously assumed by the U.S. and NATO. Prague has fully backed EU peacekeeping and humanitarian efforts in Central Europe and the western Balkans and has viewed this dimension of ESDP as a vehicle for strengthening EU ties with the Alliance.[116] At the same time, most officials are weary of attempts to further integrate the country's security structures with the EU. The initial inclusion of a mutual defense clause in the Constitutional Treaty alarmed Prague and prompted calls for maintaining a national veto in all security matters.[117]

Support for deeper EU integration is fractured among Czech political parties. As there is no political European nation, elites and the general population prefer a slow and careful deepening of the EU. Negative perceptions of the EU held by the public stem from concerns that EU decisions affecting the country are made without Czech input. Such views have been propagated by President Klaus who once stated that Czech representatives in the European Parliament (EP) cannot influence anything important.[118] The country's EU integration process has aggravated such sentiments by necessitating the adoption of new laws and regulations that did not generate immediate national benefits.[119] Unable to exert significant influence on EU policies, there has also been a feeling among many Czechs of having obtained only second-class status within the Union.

Involvement in NATO

All postcommunist Czech governments have viewed NATO as the cornerstone of European security. As a dissident leader, Václav Havel initially favored the dissolution of both NATO and the Warsaw Pact. However, once communism fell and Havel became the country's president in December 1989, his attitude toward NATO shifted dramatically. In November 1990 he asserted that NATO was the pillar of European security from which a future European security system will emerge. He thus became one of the most outspoken advocates of the Alliance. In support of ongoing NATO enlargement, Havel argued that, "if Europeans want to take advantage of this chance to create a more just peace than ever before in history, they have to start with reality, and with the expansion of the Alliance as the only functioning defense and security structure."[120]

Events in the early 1990s illustrated for Prague that the end of the Cold War had not eliminated all threats. The Soviet coup attempt in August 1991 where

Communist hard-liners sought to take control of the Soviet Union and reverse President Mikhail Gorbachev's reformist policies, the violent disintegration of Yugoslavia in the early 1990s, and the uncertain development of a newly unified Germany were examples of the security challenges facing Central Europe. A fear of undermining relations with Russia likely led Prague to push hesitantly for NATO membership in the early days of independence. However by 1993, the first Czech strategic defense concept recognized the country's dependence on NATO to manage any threats to its territory.[121] All military reform plans were undertaken with the goal of NATO membership and future Alliance integration became important in forming the "international component of the domestic transition away from communism."[122]

To demonstrate its reliability as an ally, the Czech Republic embarked on defense reform and participated in several humanitarian and peacekeeping missions in order to qualify for NATO entry. In September 1990 the Federal Assembly of the (former) Czech and Slovak Federal Republic passed a resolution allowing for the participation of anti–chemical warfare troops in Operation Desert Shield. Of its 200 troops, one casualty was suffered and four soldiers were wounded. Between 1991 and 1993, 320 troops served in the United Nations Guard Contingent in Iraq following the adoption of UN Resolutions 706/1991 and 712/1991.[123]

Once NATO decided to enlarge eastward in late 1993, Czech officials campaigned for inclusion in the first round.[124] Although eager to accede to the Alliance, parliament did not approve any of the concepts drafted by the Ministry of Defense with the exception of a four-page "National Defense Strategy" that was adopted in March 1997 in order to meet NATO's requirements ahead of the Madrid Summit. Just one month ahead of accession in February 1999, the country's Security Strategy was adopted. The document emphasized the country's readiness to take part in enforcement operations undertaken by the international community aimed at preventing large-scale violation of human rights when there was a strong international mandate for military action.[125] Twelve days after the Czech Republic joined NATO, the Alliance launched a military operation over Kosova. Havel was one of the few officials who supported the NATO action while Prime Minister Klaus vehemently opposed the NATO bombing campaign.[126] Klaus was an early opponent of Czech NATO membership and there were reports that Foreign Minister Josef Zieleniec and President Havel had to push through Prague's NATO policy because of the resistance of the Prime Minister.[127] Despite the largely pro-Serbian sentiments of the Czech citizenry, the government lived up fully to its new responsibilities. The air campaign, which lasted seventy-eight days, halted violence against Kosovar Albanians and the Czech armed forces subsequently contributed a 500-strong military contingent to the NATO-led multinational Kosova Force (KFOR) in June 1999.[128]

After the September 11, 2001 terrorist attacks on the United States, Prague pushed for an immediate NATO declaration under the Article V stipulations concerning mutual military assistance. The government backed Washington's response to the 9/11 attacks after asserting that this was a new type of conflict that threatened every state, including the Czech Republic. It supported Turkey's request for Article V consultations when France and Germany refused. Prague sent an NBC (nuclear, biological, chemical) unit to support Operation Enduring Freedom in Afghanistan and also deployed a field hospital in Afghanistan as part of the International Security Assistance Force (ISAF).[129] Czech special forces were also dispatched to Afghanistan to take part in counterterrorist operations.

During the summer of 2002, Prague sent NBC units to Kuwait and in March 2003 supported Operation Iraqi Freedom, thereby demonstrating that the country was willing to confront criticisms by aligning itself with a U.S. policy that was unpopular among some of the larger EU member states. Prague has made small but important contributions to the war against international terrorists including stationing country representatives at CENTCOM (United States Central Command), providing basing and over-flight rights to U.S. forces, deploying 251 personnel to Kuwait for combating the effects of possible WMD employment, donating military uniforms to the Afghan national army, deploying a 150-man hospital unit, and providing air transport support to NATO for early warning missions.[130] Prague contributed a field hospital in Iraq between the summer of 2003 and early 2004 and later replaced the station with police officer training. In mid-2004, about 100 Czech military police officers traveled to Saiba, in southern Iraq, to train Iraqi police together with British, Danish, and Dutch military personnel. Czech forces are also expected to participate in the new NATO Response Force and Prague has assumed a lead role in NATO's new battalion for defense against biological, chemical, nuclear, and radiological weapons.

Prague's strong commitment to NATO missions stems from a desire to see the Alliance adapt to new security threats and is also underscored by the perception that U.S. engagement is essential for NATO's survival. The former chief of the General Staff of the Czech Republic, Jiří Šedivý, articulated the significance of collective defense under the auspices of NATO, in that "Under U.S. leadership, integrated military commands and defense planning have been established within the Alliance. The result was a gradual assimilation of defense policies and military strategies of European countries, which were previously exclusively national, and consequently, a source of potential conflicts."[131] Maintaining the U.S. political and military commitment in Europe has remained a priority for Prague.

While governmental support for international military and peacekeeping missions, NATO's revival, and continued U.S. engagement has been strong, public backing for NATO itself has been in decline. Although no public referendum was held over NATO membership before admission in 1999, support for the Alliance was recorded at a moderately high figure, between 55 and 61 percent. However, by May 2004 only 49 percent of the population placed its confidence in NATO.[132] In April 2005, only 27 percent of Czechs indicated that they "definitely approve" of the country's membership in the Alliance, whereas 35 percent stated that they "rather approved," 16 percent "rather disapproved," and 12 percent "definitely disapproved."[133] Some analysts have reasoned that Czechs hold passive views on security issues, which is why there is limited support for NATO.[134]

U.S. Relations

The Czech views of the United States contain strains of romanticism, together with overtones of betrayal. The United States has been positively evaluated for its role in 1918 when it supported the creation of an independent Czechoslovak state.[135] In 1945, the United States was seen as having liberated half of Europe from the Nazis. At the same time, Washington was viewed as having betrayed Czechoslovakia to Stalin at the postwar Yalta and Potsdam conferences. However, in 1989 the United States supported the fall of communism and the democratic transition, and the United States was seen as the most important international player during this period. Although the bond with the United States is respected by various elements of the Czech political elite, ties may become increasingly fragile. Differing levels of support for U.S. security policies are evident among Czech officials. Czech backing for U.S.-led missions in Afghanistan and Iraq illustrate this phenomenon. Outgoing President Václav Havel's signature on the January 2003 Letter of Eight in support of the U.S. position toward Iraq conveyed one position; however, his endorsement did not represent the policy of the Czech government.[136] Some government officials paid visits to France and Germany in order to soften Havel's unequivocally pro-U.S. position. Incoming President Klaus was against the international efforts in Afghanistan and was initially opposed to involvement in Iraq, seeking to have the Czech Republic removed from the list of the "coalition of the willing."[137]

All decisions necessitating a choice between the United States and the European Union proved uncomfortable for the Czech leadership and Prague attempted to placate both of its major partners. For instance, the Czech Republic supported the establishment of the International Criminal Court (ICC) through membership of the Like-Minded Group of states at the Rome Diplomatic Conference in 1998. Prague signed the Rome Statute in April 1999 with the intention to ratify the document, which required a constitutional amendment. However, the country remains the only one of the ten new EU members, which has not ratified the Statute. As a result, the country has been subject to criticism from the EU and the Council of Europe. While Prague has claimed that its failure to ratify the Statute stems from the reluctance of parliament to approve various amendments, some analysts view it as an indication of the government's intent not to alienate Washington.[138]

The mixed messages that emanated from the Czech political scene during the early months of the transatlantic crisis over Iraq were indicative of the difficulty the country faced in trying to reach a compromise and then present it as a unified position. The ambivalence did not stem from a simple division between the ruling coalition and the opposition, but rather the greatest "pro- and anti-war division arose within the largest governing party."[139] The senior party of the ruling coalition, the Czech Social Democratic Party (CSDP), was split over Iraq. At its March 2003 party conference the CSDP voted against supporting the U.S. on the grounds that the war had been initiated without UN consent and was therefore a violation of international law. However, Prime Minister Vladimír Špidla chose not to listen to his party.[140] The CSDP, with parliamentary support from its coalition partners, and the opposition Civic Democratic Party (CDP), presented a pro-U.S. position on the war.[141] The two smaller members of the ruling coalition, the Christian Democratic Union–Czechoslovak People's Party (CDU-CPP) and the Union of Freedom–Democratic Union (UF-DU), proved to be more consistent in their positions. The CDU-CPP supported the war based on moral grounds of good versus evil, although it specified its requirement for a UN mandate prior to troop deployment. The UF-DU, on the other hand, unequivocally supported the war in Iraq, including Czech military participation.

Two parliamentary resolutions were passed on the Iraqi question. The first, in January 2003, allowed for the use of Czech air space by U.S. forces. The second, passed in March 2003, set limits on the country's participation in the war. The government acknowledged that it was impossible to resolve the crisis via "peaceful means," yet at the same time indicated that the country would not directly participate in military action, as a mandate from the UN had not been obtained. However, the government did allow for the Czech NBC unit that was already stationed in Kuwait to intervene in Iraq if there were indications that weapons of mass destruction had been used against the Iraqi people or against coalition forces.[142]

The March 2003 parliamentary resolution did not permit Czech troops to enter Iraq without a UN resolution. However, when UN Security Council Resolution No. 1472 was passed on March 28, 2003, allowing for the provision of humanitarian aid in Iraq, the Czech government dispatched its Seventh field hospital to the city of Basra on April 1, 2003, together with a contingent of the NBC unit stationed in Kuwait at the request of the British Army Headquarters in southern Iraq.[143] Prime Minister Špidla was credited with maintaining tangible support for Washington, while Czech politics remained deeply divided on this issue.[144]

The Czech Republic has received praise from the U.S. Department of Defense and the White House for its reliability as an ally and for its contributions in Afghanistan and Iraq. The country has not sent combat troops, but through its niche capabilities it has provided support for U.S. military operations. Parliament approved the deployment of over 100 Czech special forces to serve as reconnaissance experts in the U.S.-led Operation Enduring Freedom in Afghanistan helping to identify remaining Taliban and Al Qaeda forces in the combat zone despite the fact that 75 percent of Czech citizens polled in March 2004 opposed the mission. Even President Klaus supported this deployment.[145] One year later, parliament extended the mission of the Czech unit in Basra, which has trained Iraqi military officers despite substantial public disapproval.[146]

The Iraq engagement has remained unpopular among the Czech public and official explanations as to why the country should participate in the "coalition of the willing" have been insufficiently communicated. It may prove difficult to reverse public opinion with regard to unpopular U.S. policies, as any successes registered by Washington seem unlikely to receive major media coverage. The predominant Czech view of the United States, as a result of the Iraq war, is that of an interest-oriented actor seeking democratic rule in locations where it has direct interests, while neglecting other countries that are in dire need of outside assistance. Such perceptions have been aggravated by the negative publicity surrounding the custody of suspected terrorists at the Guantanamo detention center, together with the Abu Ghraib human rights abuses. At the same time, anti-Americanism does not operate in the Czech Republic as a powerful device to mobilize public opinion. No major political party has used anti-Americanism for political gain and this has not changed since the start of the Iraqi war. If given a choice between being either anti- or pro-American, the Czechs would invariably choose the latter.

Both the average Czech citizen and Czech political officials appreciate the kind words of gratitude from the highest levels of the U.S. government for Czech support of U.S. policies. At the same time, the public and politicians would like to be reciprocated by actions rather than rhetoric. One of the strongest concerns of the country is the costly and difficult visa requirement for travel to the United States. Prague has felt betrayed that despite its support of and participation in the Iraq intervention it has not received any substantial reciprocal benefits from Washington. Citizens feel that there is no reason to treat Germans and Italians more preferably than Czechs and Poles. As a result of this policy, the United States has lost favor among the younger generation overall. To confound the problem, U.S. investment in the Czech Republic has been consistently overshadowed by European investment. Between 1993 and 2002, Germany was the top investor at 31.3 percent, followed by the Netherlands at 18.4 percent, Austria at 10.2 percent, and the United States at 6.9 percent.[147] Foreign direct investment after 2004 demonstrates the Netherlands exceeding Germany, with the United States in fifth position.

Regional Relations and Eastern Dimension

Czechs frequently refer to their country as the filling of a German-Russian sandwich and hold the opinion that history has a tendency to repeat itself. The long-term memory of the West's betrayal before and after World War II, when Czechoslovakia was placed under Soviet control remains cogent. The west European states remained on the free side of the Iron Curtain and were able to rebuild their cities and economies with the help of the U.S.-sponsored Marshall Plan. As a redress for previous wrongs, political and popular belief held that the Czech Republic should assume its rightful place in the Euro-Atlantic community following communism's demise. However, the initial hesitancy by some West European leaders, especially those in France, the Netherlands, Germany, and Austria, to incorporate the renewed democracies into Europe's formal structures, contributed to generating suspicion and mistrust of some western neighbors during the postcommunist period. Czech relations with Austria have been strained due to controversies over the Temelín nuclear power plant and Vienna threatened to block Czech EU accession over this issue. Some German leaders, particularly in Bavaria, wanted Prague to annul the Beneš decrees, which justified the expulsion of Germans from Czechoslovakia after World War II, and threatened Czech EU membership by highlighting this issue. With Czech accession into the European Union, membership has been viewed by Prague as an opportunity to cooperate with former enemies, along the lines of Franco-German reconciliation after the Second World War.[148]

The Czech Republic forms part of the informal Visegrád coalition, formed in 1991 between Czechoslovakia, Hungary, and Poland, to collectively pursue admission into the EU and NATO. However, Visegrád cooperation has not been a priority for the CDP government or for other Czech administrations. President Vaclàv Klaus has been one of the most vehement critics of Visegrád, seeing it as a Western reconstruction of "Eastern Europe" that would not assist with EU accession.[149] Nevertheless, some level of cooperation has been maintained following the admission of all four Visegrád states to the EU in May 2004.

The Czech Republic lacks an activist Eastern policy toward the former Soviet republics. Instead, it has been involved in publicizing grave human rights abuses in repressive states including former Soviet republics such as Belarus. A special unit in the Ministry of Foreign Affairs promotes transformation efforts in dictatorial states complemented by nongovernmental organizations, such as People in Need. Foreign Minister Cyril Svoboda has personally led efforts regarding Cuba, and has publicly condemned the Castro regime. President Havel has used his stature to write widely publicized letters and editorials against oppressive regimes. The Olympic Watch, a small nonprofit organization in Prague, has been admonishing human rights abuses in China in the run-up to the 2008 Olympic games. Prague's strong interest in protecting human rights is worldwide. In addition to engagement overseas, Prague has also been involved in ensuring democratic transformations on the European continent. For example, efforts toward Belarus have involved Czech and U.S. cooperation to fund an independent radio station that will broadcast from Poland into Belarus. And in the Balkans, Prague has focused on developmental assistance to Bosnia-Herzegovina and has backed EU negotiations with Sarajevo for a Stabilization and Association Agreement (SAA). Government initiatives to promote democratization further east have also been appreciated by the general public. According to public opinion surveys, two-thirds of Czechs favor further EU enlargement. The accession of Croatia has registered the greatest support (78 percent), followed by Bulgaria (66 percent) and Romania (48 percent). However, Turkey's plight to join the European Union is not a priority among the Czech population. Only 37 percent of the voting public favors Turkish membership, whereas 51 percent disproved of the country's future accession.[150]

Political Options

The Civic Democratic Party (CDP), the largest center-right party, has been an important political force since its founding in 1991. Its policies initially emphasized Euro-Atlantic priorities including membership in NATO and the European Community.[151] However, following the party's rise to power in June 2002, its support for the EU became more hesitant. Paradoxically, the most Euro-skeptic politician in the Czech Republic, CDP co-founder and current President and former Prime Minister Václav Klaus, signed the country's EU accession treaty in 1996. The CDP was attracted to the economic prosperity associated with membership, but it did not want to relinquish any of the country's sovereignty in the process. CDP criticism of the EU is also a reflection of opposition to entrenched crony politics and clientelism within the Union and is additionally linked to frustration over perceived Franco-German domination. The party's Manifesto of Czech Eurorealism expressed fears over the loss of national identity in a "Fortress Europe" that was seeking to gain superpower status and engendering anti-Americanism to erode the transatlantic link.[152]

CDP leaders were generally satisfied with the failure to ratify the EU constitution in France and the Netherlands. The party is pro-UK in its approach to European affairs and is in favor of Turkey's EU membership, as this would undercut the creation of a European federation.[153] It opposed the 1999 NATO air strikes in Serbia during the Kosova crisis and has been lukewarm toward Visegrád 4 cooperation. Some analysts predict a future shift in CDP policy toward a more pro-EU stance due to an electoral base that consists of many educated and entrepreneurial voters. Hence, CDP Euro-skepticism is likely to change.[154]

The CDP was also opposed to the U.S.-initiated wars in Iraq and Afghanistan. In March 2003 at a meeting with the U.S. ambassador to the Czech Republic, Craig Stapleton, Klaus requested that the Czech Republic be removed from the "list of U.S. faithful."[155] However, Klaus's rhetoric gradually became less consistent on the issue and he began to lean more favorably toward Washington following an April 2003 letter from the White House, in which President Bush stated that he was looking forward to Klaus's leadership.[156] At the same time, Klaus has not become overwhelmingly pro-American.

The Czech Communist Party (CCP) is the only parliamentary grouping that has been consistently anti-American and against European integration. The party received 18.51 percent of the vote in the June 2002 parliamentary elections with 41 seats in the 200-member Chamber of Deputies, becoming the third most popular party.[157] The party has been strongly opposed to Czech NATO membership, describing NATO action against Belgrade in 1999 as an aggressive act. Some leading party members have expressed support for EU membership but the party appears divided on the issue. All other parties represented in parliament have ruled out forming any coalition with the CCP unless the party undergoes major reforms. Its voter base consists primarily of older people who have found it difficult to adapt to the new economic conditions since Czech independence, and also draws support from the heavily industrialized regions.

Public Opinion

Czech citizens see themselves within the mainstream of European and Euro-Atlantic democracy.[158] The general public places high value in a stable neighborhood with a transatlantic guarantee for their security and sovereignty. Concerning general perceptions of the United States, Czechs are almost evenly split in their views. In a March 2005 survey 43 percent agreed with the statement that "U.S. foreign policy is threatening the current world," whereas 40 percent disagreed. Forty-eight percent of Czechs believed that "U.S. foreign policy stands up for the defense of freedom, democracy and human rights," whereas 40 percent rejected this statement.[159] An April 2005 survey showed that 47 percent of Czechs assumed that "the U.S. is striving for stability and peace in the world," whereas 44 percent disagreed.[160] Czechs generally perceived the United States as striving to promote its economic interests through its foreign policy. A March 2005 survey indicated that 76 percent of respondents shared this opinion.[161]

Disapproval of the war in Iraq consistently registered at high levels among the Czech public. Between January and April 2003 opposition to involvement in the conflict stood at 67 percent in January, 71 percent in February, 72 percent in March, and 70 percent in April.[162] An EOS-Gallup Europe poll noted that two-thirds of Czechs did not approve of U.S. unilateral action in Iraq without formal agreement by the UN.[163] A handful of public demonstrations against the war took place in 2003 in front of the U.S. Embassy in Prague, as well as in the cities of Brno and Ostrava with demonstrators numbering between 150 and 1,000. By early 2005, 64 percent of Czechs continued to disapprove of the war.[164] Analysts and politicians alike explained that the high level of public opposition to the war was due to the government's inability to explain its evident necessity and partly because the Czech nation favors pacifism over aggression.[165]

Public support for the EU has been one of the lowest among the new member states. Surveys registered positive sentiments toward the EU at 41 percent in 2005, up from 35 percent in 2004.[166] The relatively high level of Euro-skepticism has been linked with fears of rising prices, the loss of national sovereignty so soon after gaining independence, as well as anxieties over German economic domination. There is also a perception that the EU's "bureaucratic democracy and committee decision making" are not capable of responding to real security threats.[167] However, the political leadership calculates that within a coalition they can have more influence than in isolation, even though there is a lingering perception that foreign policies are already determined by the larger EU powers and that Prague is simply permitted to agree or disagree. Following Czech accession in 2004, greater opportunities opened up for travel and employment throughout Europe thus helping to generate more positive public views of the European Union.

The combination of low support for U.S. action in Iraq and the gradual benefits achieved through EU membership may ensure that Czech citizens become increasingly "European" in their worldview. An April 2005 survey showed that 68 percent of Czechs believed that the EU is "the most reliable protector against possible external threats" whereas only 24 percent put their faith in the U.S.[168] Similar to other CEE countries, support for the EU is highest among the younger generations, or people below the age of forty. At the same time, support for the United States also remains pronounced among young and educated people.

SLOVAKIA

Slovakia is Central Europe's "late bloomer" and still experiences political divisions over the country's foreign policy. After Slovakia gained independence on January 1, 1993, with the breakup up of Czechoslovakia, the country underwent quasi-authoritarian rule during much of the 1990s. Bratislava reached a turning point in 1998, with the election of a determined and united political coalition resolved to reverse the autocratic and anti-western policies of Prime Minister Vladimír Mečiar. Mečiar's government had kept the country out of NATO during the first round of enlargement in 1999. The government disqualified itself by barring the political opposition from any supervisory bodies in parliament, undertaking arbitrary and nontransparent privatization, engaging in the persecution of political opponents and media critics, and promoting the arbitrary and anti-democratic approach of the Slovak intelligence service.[169] Although Mečiar's Movement for a Democratic Slovakia (MDS) received the highest percentage of votes in the October 1998 elections, an eight-party coalition formed in opposition to Mečiar and took office, naming Mikuláš Dzurinda as prime minister.[170] The coalition embarked on an extensive agenda of reform and moved quickly to catch up with its CEE neighbors.

The hard-hitting reforms launched between 1998 and 2002 were praised by the international community, but were less popular at home. With EU and NATO membership pending, the 2002 general elections were viewed by the Western powers as a crucial test for Slovak democracy. Washington, after intense deliberation, stated that if former Prime Minister Mečiar's party returned to power, Slovakia could be excluded from the next round of NATO enlargement. This statement caused consternation in the country, as many Slovaks felt that the U.S. ultimatum was undemocratic.[171] Although Mečiar's MDS again won the largest number of votes, no party was willing to form a coalition with it. Dzurinda was able to establish a government for a second time composed of the Slovak Democratic and Christian Union (SD-CU), the Party of the Hungarian Coalition (PHC), the Christian Democratic Movement (CDM), and the Alliance of a New Citizen (ANC).[172]

The Dzurinda coalition has been distinctly Euro-Atlantic in its focus. The government's Mid-Term Foreign Policy Strategy of the Slovak Republic Until 2015 stated that, "Slovakia will consistently support the policy of developing and strengthening the alliance between the countries of Europe and North America."[173] Bratislava adhered to its pledge. However, the main opposition parties, together with the general population, have been decidedly more Euro-focused than the administration. The parliamentary elections in June 2006 brought to power a nationalist-protectionist coalition whose commitment to Atlanticism will remain suspect.

The European Union

Following the separation of the Czech and Slovak republics, Prime Minister Vladimír Mečiar did not push strongly to join either NATO or the EU, but instead sought to consolidate his own power within the newly independent Slovak state. The Mečiar government was strongly criticized by Washington for its anti-minority policies, the lack of media freedom, official corruption, and cronyism. These policies also isolated Slovakia from potential European partners. Mečiar complained that the European Union failed to distinguish between different types of democracies in the region and argued in domestic political debates that the EU did not understand the country's predicament.[174]

In June 1995, Bratislava submitted its application for EU membership. The European Commission's response listed numerous shortcomings in the applicant, including the lack of an independent judiciary, the political obstruction of public institutions, limits on opposition participation in government oversight, and insufficient rights for minorities.[175] After the election of the Dzurinda coalition, the Commission's Progress Report issued in October 1999 acknowledged Bratislava's accelerated reform program.[176] Slovakia's accession negotiations with the EU opened in March 2000 and on April 16, 2003, Bratislava signed its EU accession agreement, together with nine other candidate countries.

The legacy of Mečiar's authoritarian practices and the wasted years of Slovak isolation made EU membership an even greater priority for the Dzurinda administration. However, the rhetorical attacks by French President Jacques Chirac in early 2003, due to Slovak and CEE support for the U.S. position over Iraq, prompted fears in Bratislava that the older EU members would exclude the new candidates from the Union. Chirac's threats were reminiscent of the region's history of subordination, including the manipulation by larger neighboring powers. In addition to fears of exclusion by the larger EU states, the Slovak government was also concerned that its public referendum on EU entry would fail to obtain sufficient support among Slovak voters as a result of Chirac's derogatory remarks; and indeed, all members of the Visegrád 4 (V-4) group shared these concerns. The V-4 countries, Slovakia, the Czech Republic, Hungary, and Poland, agreed to hold consecutive referendums with the objective of creating a ripple effect of support for EU entry among their citizens. Slovakia's May 2003 referendum narrowly passed the 50 percent turnout threshold necessary for legitimacy, with 92 percent of voters backing accession. Slovakia entered the EU on May 1, 2004.[177]

Among the CEE states, Slovakia has consistently held one of the highest public approval ratings of the EU. Support recorded in 2005, following the country's first year of membership, illustrates these positive sentiments. While the Eurobarometer recorded public support at 54 percent in early 2005, the second highest among the ten new member states, national polling agencies registered this figure at 83 percent support.[178] Political and public backing for the EU has remained pronounced. However, varying degrees of support for specific EU policies have been evident, especially in the areas of foreign policy and defense.

The EU Common Foreign and Security Policy (CFSP) has been viewed positively by Bratislava as a vehicle enabling small states to have a voice in broader foreign policy debates. The country closed the CFSP chapter of the EU *acquis communautaire* without difficulty and aligned itself with the EU's common foreign policy positions. The CFSP has played an influential role in Slovakia's own foreign policy formation leading up to EU accession. However, the EU Security and Defense Policy (ESDP) has been viewed more cautiously. All of the political parties, with the exception of the nationalist Slovak National Party (SNP), saw the development of ESDP as competition to NATO. Only the SNP advocated the expansion of European defense capabilities independent of both NATO and Washington.[179]

In July 2003, the Slovak Foreign Ministry drafted a response paper to the European Security Strategy or "Solana Paper" in which Bratislava confirmed the need for the EU to have a common security strategy that would bolster its efforts to act as a global player. At the same time, the government noted that the United States and the European Union should cooperate as partners due to their shared values and interests, as Bratislava did not want ESDP to develop independently from the United States and NATO.[180] The ministry's response paper tried to strike a balance by acknowledging the EU's desire for a common security strategy, but also emphasized the need for NATO to be reconfirmed as the main pillar of European security. Although popular opinion has favored the development of a separate European security policy, the government has upheld a more pragmatic position. With a distinct European security structure, defense costs would escalate for each EU member and common policies would more likely be decided by larger EU powers rather than by consensus. This could further undermine NATO's security role.[181]

Despite the Slovak public's consistently favorable perceptions of the EU, voter participation in the European Parliamentary elections have been far lower than in West European states. Slovakia registered the lowest voter turnout at 16.7 percent and much of the media attributed this to Slovak apathy toward the European Union. President Ivan Gašparovič and his Czech and Finnish counterparts have favored an overhaul of the European Parliament (EP), arguing that its members should be parliamentarians from the national assemblies in order to strengthen the EP's accountability.

Slovakia has benefited substantially from its EU accession process and its membership. Following years of isolation and exclusion under the Mečiar regime, Slovakia was finally able to pursue EU integration, backed by broad political consensus. Thus, the Dzurinda government was able to adopt an accelerated reform process with only minimal domestic resistance. Within the Dzurinda coalition, only the CDM formally raised concerns regarding the protection of Slovakia's sovereignty against deepening EU integration. One byproduct of the integration process has been Bratislava's cutting-edge flat tax reform, which has generated heated discussion within the EU-15 and has stimulated competition within the Union to attract business investment.

Involvement in NATO

After the 1998 elections, the Dzurinda government engineered an overhaul in defense policy. The governing coalition began a reform of the armed services in order to prepare for NATO membership. During 1999, it supported NATO's Kosova campaign in spite of notable pro-Serb sentiments among Slovak citizens.[182] In 2001, the government enacted numerous legal and structural changes to facilitate the country's integration into the Alliance. For example, Bratislava appointed a state secretary for NATO integration and plans were elaborated for ministerial reforms. Parliament approved a constitutional amendment to facilitate joining collective defense alliances and at the government's initiative, it also approved legislation on national security, defense, and military strategies.[183]

Slovakia was invited to join NATO at the November 2002 Prague Summit. Public opinion polls indicated that more than 60 percent of Slovaks welcomed the invitation, a figure consistent with surveys carried out a year earlier.[184] On March 29, 2004, Slovakia was accepted into the Alliance and membership validated the country's democratic transformation.

Slovakia has participated in numerous peacekeeping missions. Since 1999, Slovak troops took part in the joint Czech-Slovak battalion assigned to the NATO Kosova Force (KFOR). Slovak officers have operated in Bosnia-Herzegovina since 1998, first within the command structures of the

NATO Stabilization Force (SFOR) and subsequently in the European Union Force (EUFOR).[185] Slovak troops have also participated in UN peacekeeping missions in the Golan Heights, Ethiopia, Eritrea, Cyprus, and East Timor.[186] When Slovak soldiers were sent to Kuwait in early 2003, public support for NATO dropped to an all-time low of 34 percent due to the escalating Iraq crisis.[187]

Apprehensions were visible among the Slovak population that Bratislava's participation in the U.S.-led anti-terrorist campaign and in the Iraq war would make Slovakia vulnerable to terrorist attacks. In an interview in October 2004, Dzurinda tried to placate public fears. Defending the government's support for U.S. policies, he noted that the terrorist bombings in Madrid killed citizens of countries other than those fighting in Iraq.[188] However, an April 2005 survey conducted for the Ministry of Defense indicated that half of the public believed that Slovakia's risk of being a terrorist target had increased since the country joined NATO.[189] At the same time, the survey also showed that 56 percent of Slovaks perceived the country's entry into NATO as directly linked to the growth of foreign investment in the country.[190]

Responding to the European Security Strategy, the Slovak Foreign Ministry indicated that NATO was both an important expression of the transatlantic relationship and an essential pillar of European security that should be preserved and expanded.[191] The Mid-Term Foreign Policy Strategy of the Slovak Republic Until 2015 stated that Slovakia considers NATO to be the key instrument for preserving peace and security in the world and that Bratislava would remain active to counter any weakening of Alliance capabilities.[192]

U.S. Relations

U.S.-Slovak relations strengthened substantially following the formation of the Dzurinda government in late 1998. Increased military cooperation, as well as greater volumes of trade and U.S. investment, have been evident. Bratislava publicly sympathized with the United States over the September 11 attacks and approximately 53.4 percent of Slovaks favored U.S. military action against those responsible for 9/11 if clearly proven guilty. At the same time, 46.6 percent were opposed to Slovakia providing support for any retaliatory military action.[193] Shortly after 9/11, the Slovak government approved the usage of its air space and airstrips for the transit of U.S. and coalition military aircraft. A reported 60 percent of the population agreed with the government's commitment to join the global anti-terrorist movement.[194]

Prime Minister Dzurinda did not sign the January 2003 Letter of Eight, authored by the United Kingdom, the Czech Republic, Denmark, Hungary,

Italy, Poland, Portugal, and Spain, in support of the U.S. position on Iraq, although he reportedly supported the statement. He told Prime Minister José
María Aznar of Spain, a signatory of the letter, that the message was composed of "clear words, at the right time."[195] Instead, Slovakia signed the
follow-up Vilnius 10 (V-10) declaration issued by Albania, Bulgaria, Croatia,
Estonia, Latvia, Lithuania, Macedonia, Slovenia, and Romania, on February
5, 2003. The V-10 foreign ministers stated that evidence of WMD in Iraq submitted by the United States to the United Nations was credible and that their
countries would participate in a joint military action should Baghdad not
comply with UN Security Council Resolution No. 1441. Through this support, Slovakia, with the other Vilnius 10 signatories, portrayed itself as a *de
facto* NATO member.

The Slovak cabinet voted in late January 2003 to send a seventy-five-person
NBC contingent to Iraq to be integrated into the Czech NBC unit.[196] Parliament
also gave its consent by passing a resolution on February 6, 2003 allowing the
armed forces to participate in the expected U.S. military campaign. The vote
passed with 81 in favor, 54 against, and 6 abstentions, out of 141 members
present. The approval was conditioned upon a UN mandate to conduct an international military operation.[197] But the decision to deploy soldiers for humanitarian missions was not met with full unanimity within Dzurinda's four-
party coalition. The Slovak Democratic and Christian Union (SD-CU), the
New Citizen's Alliance (ANC), and the Hungarian Coalition (PHC) backed the
government proposal to send troops. However, the Christian Democratic
Movement (CDM) argued that the United States had not presented sufficient
evidence to justify an attack. In the end, the CDM allowed its deputies to make
their own decision whether or not to vote in favor of deployment.[198] Opposition parties charged that government support for the war in Iraq was motivated
by the desire to secure an invitation to NATO.

Public support for the U.S.-led military action in Iraq remained lukewarm.
In a February 2003 poll, 37 percent of the population supported the deployment of Slovak soldiers to Iraq with only 3 percent agreeing to such action
without a UN mandate. Attempting to alter popular sentiments, Prime Minister Dzurinda made numerous public appearances to explain the government's
actions in support of Washington, an unusual practice for CEE leaders. Nevertheless, in April 2003, 74 percent of the public remained against engagement.[199]

A complicating factor during the transatlantic crisis over Iraq was Slovakia's rejection of the Bilateral Immunity Agreement, Article 98, in July 2003.
Bratislava demonstrated support for the general EU position on the International Criminal Court (ICC) and opposition to the U.S. stance.[200] The U.S.
Congress reacted by freezing approximately $10 million in military assistance

to Bratislava, which was restored when Slovakia joined NATO.[201] Bratislava continued its participation in Iraq and renewed its eighty-two-person Slovak military engineering unit deployed in the Polish sector in August 2003.[202] By late November 2003 Washington unblocked the relevant military aid in a sign of gratitude.[203] In January 2004, parliament approved an additional deployment of twenty troops to protect its engineering unit.[204]

Three Slovak military engineers were killed in a mortar attack in Iraq on June 8, 2004. This prompted the CDM to initiate a parliamentary debate on whether or not Slovak troops should remain in Iraq. The CDM and the opposition Direction party (*Smer*) favored an open debate while the opposition Slovak Communist Party (SCP) demanded military withdrawal. President Ivan Gašparovič, commander of the armed forces, stated that it would be impossible to leave Iraq overnight, while parliament called on the cabinet to issue a report on the Iraqi security situation.[205] The report, prepared by Defense Minister Juraj Liška and submitted in July 2004, affirmed that Slovak soldiers would remain in Iraq as the government could not see any credible reason to evacuate them. The soldiers, deployed in mid 2003 with an indefinite mandate, were engaged primarily in de-mining work in southern Iraq.[206] In September 2004, the SCP motioned parliament to withdraw the troops, but only 20 deputies out of 150 supported this proposal.[207]

Although within the governing coalition the Christian Democrats sometimes raised doubts over Bratislava's support for the U.S. Iraq policy, the party contended that its actions were not directed against Washington. At the party's fourteenth congress in April 2003, its leadership issued a statement that their objection to the military operation should not be perceived as anti-American.[208] However, anti-Americanism has been evident in Slovakia and has been considered fashionable among some sectors of youth.[209] Anti-Americans are displeased with the United States as a "world policeman," but do not direct these sentiments against American citizens but against U.S. policies.[210] In a survey conducted in 2002, the United States was most identified by Slovak respondents as economically developed (39 percent), superior, arrogant, and discriminatory (28 percent), and democratic (23 percent).[211] Some analysts attribute this relatively negative perception of America to the absence of a strong historical consciousness with regard to U.S.-Slovak relations. A survey conducted in 2005 demonstrated that 50 percent of Slovak adults were unable to link America to any specific historical event that either favored or harmed their country.[212] Overall, popular sentiment toward the United States among the Slovak public remains lukewarm. According to the German Marshall Fund's Transatlantic Survey for 2005, Slovakia's temperature reading toward the United States registered at 55 degrees in a scale of 0 to 100.[213]

The pro-U.S. policies pursued by the Dzurinda government and the Slovak foreign and defense ministries were prepared by new recruits to the administration, many of whom were educated in the West, including in the United States. Nonetheless, as a result of restrictive U.S. visa requirements and the attractiveness of traveling and working within the EU, fewer Slovak and CEE students are likely to study in the United States in the future. Over time this will result in fewer political and scholarly elites having direct ties to America and will likely impact on Slovakia's Atlantic orientation in the future.

Regional Relations and Eastern Dimension

Visegrád 3 (V-3) was formed in the early 1990s between Poland, Hungary, and Czechoslovakia as a cooperative mechanism to help prepare the three countries for admission into NATO and the EU. The V-3 became Visegrád 4 (V-4) after the January 1993 split of Czechoslovakia. Nevertheless, it has proven difficult for smaller CEE states to maintain a regional alliance. For example, when Poland pressed the European Commission to uphold the voting rights allotted to each new member state under the Nice Treaty, Slovakia initially agreed to back Warsaw's position. In doing so, Bratislava reneged on an earlier agreement made with Germany's Chancellor Gerhard Schröder. The Slovak government tried to resolve its ambiguous position by issuing a public statement indicating that the country "always supports Poland, but at the same time understands the German and French positions."[214]

With EU and NATO membership attained by all V-4 members, Slovakia seeks to play a constructive role within this regional framework. Visegrád cooperation has always been utilized for specific purposes, and future initiatives will likely be vested in exerting influence within the EU on issues such as the development of a common EU energy policy. Working within the V-4, Slovakia has an interest in promoting reform among the EU's neighbors to prepare them for eventual EU membership. Slovakia believes that its own experience overcoming authoritarianism and isolation can aid the transition process in Ukraine, Belarus, and the West Balkan countries. Both Ukraine and Belarus have been designated as foreign policy priorities by the Dzurinda government, which has allocated financial assistance for democratization and civil society projects in both countries.

Ukraine is Slovakia's largest neighbor and bilateral relations have developed in the fields of economy, education, science, culture, and tourism. In October 2005 the Slovak government adopted plans to assist Ukraine in implementing the EU-Ukraine Action Plan within the framework of the EU's European Neighborhood Policy (ENP). The Slovak Ministry of Defense has also provided guidance to Kyiv in the NATO accession process. Bratislava has advocated that the international community give Kyiv clear Euro-Atlantic incentives to help facilitate reforms. In addition to Slovak government support, the well-developed Slovak NGO sector has promoted democratic processes among neighboring states. These initiatives have involved bringing together civil society representatives, media, and democratic activists together with independent experts and representatives of international institutions. Bratislava declared development aid to Serbia a priority in 2002 and established the Bratislava-Belgrade Fund. By 2005 the Fund was implementing sixteen projects in Serbia and Montenegro to promote civil society initiatives, revitalize the social system, renew infrastructure and regional development, and assist in EU and NATO integration efforts. Bratislava has also been a strong supporter of Croatia's bid for EU membership initiating talks at the March 2005 meeting of the European Council after Zagreb failed to qualify for the opening of EU accession negotiations.[215]

Political Options

Several opposition parties, as well as some representatives from the ruling coalition, questioned the legitimacy of the war in Iraq as well as U.S. motives. The *Smer* party, led by Róbert Fico, has questioned Bratislava's backing for Washington and the country's American link. Before its election recess in June 2006, *Smer* was an opposition party with strong popular support. Although *Smer*'s official rhetoric indicates support for both NATO and the EU, the party assumed the Franco-German position over Iraq. *Smer* was critical of the Dzurinda government's unequivocal support for the U.S.-led war calling the coalition "un-European."[216] In a March 2003 interview, Fico stated that he was critical of Dzurinda's foreign policies because of its alleged servility in building "an island of American influence in Europe." According to Fico, Bratislava should cooperate first and foremost with partners in Europe, especially as investments from EU countries far exceed American investments.[217] *Smer* was also critical that the war lacked a UN mandate and refused to lend parliamentary support for the deployment of Slovak military engineers in January 2003. When three Slovak soldiers were killed in Iraq in June 2004, the party demanded an immediate debate on troop withdrawal and assumed a more prominent anti-American profile.[218] Public backing for *Smer* increased from 32 percent in December 2005 to 37 percent in January 2006, the highest figure among all political parties.[219]

The policies of the Movement for a Democratic Slovakia (MDS), led by former Prime Minister Vladimír Mečiar, were responsible for Slovakia's exclusion from the first round of NATO accession. Although Mečiar's government was active in NATO's Partnership for Peace program (PfP) and Bratislava was the first CEE capital to submit its completed discussion documents to NATO,

Mečiar's governing practices were clearly undemocratic.[220] Mečiar, with the help of his coalition partners, the Slovak National Party (SNP) and the ex-Communist Association of Slovak Workers (ASW), transformed Slovakia into a pariah state in the middle of Europe. Prior to the September 2002 general elections, the MDS had toned up its Euro-Atlantic rhetoric, which few NATO or EU leaders viewed as genuine. Both the MDS and the SNP joined the *Smer*-led coalition in July 2006.

The Slovak Communist Party (SCP) that entered parliament for the first time in the 2002 elections, taking 6 percent of the votes, is openly anti-American, against Slovak participation in the U.S.-led war in Iraq, and disapproving of both NATO and the EU. The Communist Party organized two anti-war demonstrations in Bratislava in early 2003 and was the only political party that has maintained a consistent position against U.S. foreign policy.

Public Opinion

Among the CEE states, popular support for the EU has consistently registered at the highest levels in Slovakia, whereas public support for NATO has been among the lowest. The United States only generates lukewarm feelings among the Slovak population. Slovaks positively link the EU to "economic development (high standard of living, low unemployment, social security, prosperity, wealth, welfare protection, trade, satisfaction, jobs, good pay) and democracy (freedom, tolerance, independence, progress, respect for human rights)."[221] The United States is widely viewed more negatively as arrogant and dominant. Images in the Slovak media have been largely unflattering for America and negative perceptions have been accentuated by the Abu Ghraib prison abuse scandal and the cost and difficulty in obtaining U.S. visas.

Slovakia's participation in the war in Iraq prompted a few small protests in Bratislava in early 2003, with participants numbering between one hundred and three hundred persons. The demonstrations, organized by the Communist Party, took place in front of government buildings and the U.S. embassy. Protesters claimed that the war was about oil and was not for promoting democracy. Slovakia's involvement in future military operations is likely to elicit little public and official support under the new coalition government.

NOTES

1. Official statistics indicate that approximately 520,000 Hungarians form a minority in Slovakia, 1.47 million Hungarians live in Romania, and 300,000 Hungarians reside in Serbia and Montenegro. Smaller Hungarian minority populations can be found in the remaining neighboring states, including Croatia, Austria, Slovenia, and Ukraine.

2. BBC Monitoring, Tibor Kis, "Single-Outcome War," *Népszabadság*, March 22, 2003.

3. Tamás Meszerics, "The Security Policy of Hungary," in *'Easternization' of Europe's Security Policy,* edited by Tomáš Valášek and Olga Gyárfášová (Bratislava: Institute for Public Affairs, 2004), 222–31.

4. From the European Commission's Enlargement website: europa.eu.int/comm/enlargement/hungary/ (accessed September 29, 2005).

5. "Hungary: Membership Referendum," *The Robert Schuman Foundation Newsletter* 117 (April 14, 2003).

6. Tamás Meszerics, "The Security Policy of Hungary," 222–31.

7. Associated Press Worldstream, "Hungarian Parliament Backs EU Accession Agreement," April 15, 2003.

8. Interview with Hungarian government officials in Budapest, March 2005.

9. The National Security Strategy of the Republic of Hungary. Entered into force on April 15, 2005. It was adopted as Resolution No. 2073/2004 (iii.31) on March 31, 2004.

10. Interviews with Hungarian Foreign Ministry officials (Budapest, March 2005).

11. Eurobarometer 63.4: Public Opinion in the European Union, Spring 2005. National Report: Hungary, 5.

12. *Népszabadság Online*, "NOL-voks: Nincs Szükség EU-Népszavazásra," [NOL-vote: There Is No Need for an EU Referendum] November 12, 2004, www.nol.hu/cikk_print/339719/ (accessed March 15, 2005).

13. Interviews with Hungarian officials in Budapest, March 2005, Czech officials in Prague, June 2005.

14. Ahto Lobjakas, "EU: Budget Deal Allows Consolidation of Enlargement," *Radio Free Europe/Radio Liberty*, December 17, 2005. The new member states will receive more than 100 billion euros in aid. Out of that sum, Poland alone will receive nearly 60 billion. See also BBC News, "Key Points of the Budget Deal," December 17, 2005, http://news.bbc.co.uk/2/hi/europe/4537912.stm (accessed January 16, 2006).

15. Central and East Eurobarometer (CEEB 8), 1997, 8.

16. Eurobarometer 63.4: Public Opinion in the European Union, Spring 2005. National Report: Hungary, 3.

17. Ibid.

18. Ágnes Bátory, "The Political Context of EU Accession in Hungary," *The Royal Institute of International Affairs* Briefing Paper, November 2002, 7.

19. László Valki, "Hungary," in *Old Europe, New Europe and the U.S.: Renegotiating Transatlantic Security in the Post 9/11 Era*, edited by Tom Landsford and Blagovest Tashev (Burlington, VT: Ashgate Publishing Company, 2005), 240.

20. Valki, "Hungary," 240. The author gives the date of 1998 in his publication, which is incorrect.

21. Reported by the BBC, "Hungarian Foreign Ministry Official Address NATO Assembly," November 19, 1988. Sources cited Budapest Home Service, November 15, 1988 and Hungarian Telegraph Agency, November 15, 1988.

22. Valki, "Hungary," 240–41.

23. Ibid.

24. Ibid.

25. Pál Dunay, "The Half-Hearted Transformation of the Hungarian Military," *European Security* 14, no. 1 (March 2005): 23.

26. Karl Peter Kirk, "U.S. Military Abandons First Outpost in Eastern Europe," *The Associated Press*, June 30, 2004.

27. Quoted in Valki, "Hungary," 244.

28. Ibid. See also, U.S. Department of State, "Patterns of Global Terrorism: Europe Overview," April 29, 2004 www.state.gov/s/ct/rls/pgtrpt/2003/31626.htm (accessed October 24, 2005).

29. United States Central Command, "Hungary in the War on Terror," www.centcom.mil/Operations/Coalition/Coalition_pages/hungary.htm (accessed October 24, 2005) and U.S. Department of State, "Patterns of Global Terrorism: Europe Overview," April 29, 2004, www.state.gov/s/ct/rls/pgtrpt/2003/31626.htm (accessed October 24, 2005).

30. U.S. Department of State, "Patterns of Global Terrorism: Europe Overview."

31. United States Central Command, "Hungary in the War on Terror."

32. Hungarian Kossuth Radio, Budapest, October 17, 2005.

33. Dunay, "The Half-Hearted Transformation of the Hungarian Military," 21–22.

34. Zoltan Barany, "Hungary: An Outpost on the Troubled Periphery," in Andrew A. Michta (ed.), *America's New Allies: Poland, Hungary, and the Czech Republic in NATO* (Seattle: University of Washington Press, 1999): 90–91.

35. Ibid, 90–91.

36. Dunay, "The Half-Hearted Transformation of the Hungarian Military," 21–22.

37. Interviews with defense officials (Budapest, Hungary, March 2005). Agence France Presse, "Iraq Gets Refurbished Tanks from Hungary," November 12, 2005.

38. Interviews with defense officials in Budapest, Hungary, March 2005.

39. Ibid.

40. Ibid.

41. The National Security Strategy of the Republic of Hungary was adopted as Resolution No. 2073/2004 (iii.31) on March 31, 2004, and entered into force on April 15, 2005.

42. Ibid.

43. Dunay, "The Half-Hearted Transformation of the Hungarian Military," 28.

44. Zoltán László Kiss, "Changes in Hungarian Public Opinion on Security, Defence and the Military," in *The Public Image of Defence and the Military in Central and Eastern Europe,* ed. Marie Vlachová (Geneva: Centre for the Democratic Control of the Armed Forces, 2003): 128.

45. Valki, "Hungary," 245.

46. Sara Binzer Hobolt, "Identity and Enlargement," *Journal of European Affairs* 1, no. 1 (August 2003).

47. RFE/RL Newsline, September 12, 2001.

48. RFE/RL Newsline, September 12, 2001 and RFE/RL Newsline, September 14, 2001.

49. The Hungarian Socialist Party (HSP) gained 178 seats; the Alliance of Free Democrats (AFD) 19 seats; a joint HSP-AFD candidate won one seat; and Fidesz-

HDF garnered 188 seats. See *Election Guide* at www.electionguide.org/resultsum/hungary-par-02.htm (accessed September 29, 2005).

50. Comment by Mr. Laszlo Kovacs, Foreign Minister of Hungary, on Iraq, September 12, 2002, www.kum.hu/Archivum/Korabbiszovivoi/2002/KovacsL/0912KLirak.htm (accessed June 4, 2005).

51. BBC Worldwide Monitoring, "Hungarian Minister on EU, Iraq, German and Slovak Elections," *Hungarian TV2 Satellite Service*, September 23, 2002.

52. BBC Worldwide Monitoring, "Hungary Not to Send Fighting Unit to Iraq—Foreign Minister," *Hungarian TV2 Satellite Service*, November 5, 2002.

53. Jitendra Joshi, "Pro-US Letter Exposes Divide at Heart of Europe," Agence France Presse, January 20, 2003.

54. *Libération*, "'Ses Propos Sont Une Erreur'; Irak: Péter Medgyessy, Premier Ministre Hongrois," ('Its matters are an error'; Iraq: Péter Medgyessy, Hungarian Prime Minister) February 19, 2003. Also, *Magyar Hirlap*, quoted in *Radio Free Europe/Radio Liberty Newsline* 7, no. 33, February 20, 2003.

55. IPS-Inter Press Service, "Politics-Hungary: Striving for Balanced Relations with EU and USA," April 19, 2003.

56. Ibid.

57. BBC Monitoring, "Foreign Minister Explains Hungary's Rejecting U.S. Plea to Expel Iraqi Diplomats," *Hungarian TV2 Satellite Service*, March 24, 2003.

58. Agence France Presse, "Hungary Parliament Opens Territory to Iraq Force, But No Ruling on Troops," May 6, 2003. See also BBC Monitoring, "Hungarian Opposition, Government Agree on Amending Proposal for Iraqi Peace Force," *Hungarian Radio*, April 30, 2003.

59. BBC Monitoring, "Hungary: Opposition Again Blocks Peacekeepers to Iraq," *Hungarian Radio*, May 5, 2003.

60. John Springford, "'Old' and 'New' Europeans United: Public Attitudes towards the Iraq War and U.S. Foreign Policy," Background Brief (London: Centre for European Reform, 2003).

61. The parliamentary vote was taken in early June 2003. All 313 deputies present voted in favor of the deployment consisting of "military transport and humanitarian relief personnel." See Agence France Presse, "Hungary Approves Mission of Up to 300 Troops to Iraq," June 2, 2003.

62. Hungarian Ministry of Foreign Affairs press release, "Proposal for UN Security Council Resolution," May 20, 2004.

63. Radio Free Europe/Radio Liberty, "Hungary Vows to Continue Iraq Mission Despite Casualties," 8, no. 32, February 19, 2004.

64. BBC Monitoring, "Hungarian Prime Minister Resigns," August 19, 2004.

65. Judy Dempsey, "Hungary Joins Others in Pulling Troops," *The New York Times*, November 4, 2004.

66. Agence France Presse, "Hungarian MPs Vote to Withdraw Troops by Year-End," November 15, 2004.

67. *New York Times*, "Hungarian Troops to Leave Iraq," November 16, 2004.

68. Hungarian News Agency (MTI), "Relationship between Hungary and U.S. is Focused on Real Issues," *Financial Times Information*, May 1, 2005.

69. Ibid.

70. An example of such remarks was made by Hungarian Foreign Minister Ferenc Somogyi at the Atlantic Council in Washington, D.C., on March 30, 2005.

71. Gábor Horváth, "Orbán Csoportos Reggelin a Fehér Házban" [Orban is at a Group Breakfast at the White House], *Népszabadság Online*, July 20, 2005.

72. Dunay, "The Half-Hearted Transformation of the Hungarian Military," 21–22. Also, interview with Central European analyst in Budapest, June 2005.

73. Interviews with former Hungarian government officials in Budapest, June 2003 and March 2005.

74. National Bank of Hungary, http://itd.hu/itdh/nid/fdi (accessed August 1, 2005).

75. BBC Monitoring, "Hungarian Premier Wants Mutual Visa-Free Agreement with USA," *Hungarian Radio*, October 8, 1998.

76. Ivan Krastev, "The Anti-American Century?" *Journal of Democracy*, April 2004.

77. László Kovács, "More Europe, More America: Hungarian Friendship Bridges the Atlantic Divide," *The Washington Times*, November 5, 2002, A19.

78. Péter Hanák, ed., *The Corvina History of Hungary: From the Earliest Times Until the Present Day* (Budapest: Corvina Books, 1991), 176.

79. See *CIA World Factbook 2005*. www.cia.gov/cia/publications/factbook/geos/lo.html#People (accessed January 17, 2006) and Czech News Agency, "Hungary Would Welcome Gesture in Connection with Beneš Decrees," May 16, 2005.

80. Hungarian News Agency MTI, "Foreign Affairs Spokesman on Hungarian-Slovak Relations," July 14, 2003.

81. Interviews with Hungarian NATO officials in Budapest, Hungary, March 2005.

82. Negotiations with Croatia opened in early October 2005 following the recognition of its cooperation with The Hague.

83. Eurobarometer 63.4: Public Opinion in the European Union, Spring 2005. National Report: Hungary, 7.

84. Interviews with NGO analysts and government representatives in Budapest, Hungary, March 2005.

85. BBC Monitoring, "Certain Things Don't Change in Moscow," text of editorial by Andras Desi: "Exchange of Gestures," *Népszabadság*, February 18, 2005.

86. BBC Monitoring, "Hungarian Daily Slams Government for Poorly Communicating Stand on Iraq War," *Népszabadság*, March 26, 2003.

87. The commentary read: "Why is it necessary to make obscure statements about Taszár, including the citizenship and the identity of the persons receiving training there, even though it is morally adequate and is in complete harmony with our democratic European values to assist the democratization of a dictatorship?" Ibid.

88. Examples can be found in political commentaries in the Hungarian press. See, Népszabadság, "Bush többet várt Orbán Viktortól" [Bush Wants More from Viktor Orbán], October 20, 2005.

89. Radio Free Europe/Radio Liberty Newsline, "Hungarian Parties Fail to Agree on NATO Transit Shipments to Turkey," February 20, 2003.

90. Agence France Presse, "Hungary Permits Transit of U.S. Troops," February 24, 2003.

91. See Valki, "Hungary," 249–50.

92. Ibid. See also, Interfax News Agency, Hungarian Business Report, "Hungarian Government Allows U.S., UK Use of Airspace in Iraq," March 24, 2003.

93. BBC Monitoring, "Hungarian Opposition Chief Turns Down Blair's Request for Iraqi Mandate Extension," November 6, 2004.

94. Zsolt Simon, "Hungarian PM to meet Bush under pressure to withdraw troops from Iraq," Agence France Presse, June 21, 2004.

95. Agence France Presse, "Hungarian MPs Vote to Withdraw Troops from Iraq by Year-End," November 15, 2004.

96. Gábor Horváth, "Orbán Csoportos Reggelin a Fehér Házban" [Orban is at a Group Breakfast at the White House], *Népszabadság*, July 20, 2005.

97. Gallup Poll, Hungary, "Ön szerint mi zajlik Irakban inkább, a terrorizmus elleni nemzetközi küzdelem, vagy Amerika saját érdekeinek védelme?" [What is your opinion, what is going on in Iraq: international fight against terrorism or rather the defense of U.S. interests?] www.gallup.hu/Gallup/release/irak040510.htm (accessed May 3, 2005).

98. Jean-Luc Tesault, "'New Europe's' Support for Bush on Iraq Gradually Falls Away," Agence France Presse, March 19, 2005.

99. BBC Monitoring, "Daily Ambivalent on Hungarian Contribution to USA's Iraq Mission," *Népszabadság*, May 5, 2003.

100. Median Hungary, "Politikai Kutatások: Csökkenőben az Amerika Iránti Rokonszenv" [Political Surveys: Sympathy Toward America is Decreasing], 2003, www.median.hu/kutatasok/Irak_Amerika.htm (accessed July 13, 2004).

101. Hungarian News Agency, "Greenpeace Stages Anti-War Protest in Budapest," February 17, 2003.

102. Petr Vancura, "Czech Republic's Role with Regard to the Trans-Atlantic Security Challenges," in *Old Europe, New Europe and the U.S.: Renegotiating Transatlantic Security in the Post 9/11 Era*, edited by Tom Lansford and Blagovest Tashev (Burlington: Ashgate, 2005), 174.

103. David Král and Lukáš Pachta, "The Czech Republic and the Iraq Crisis: Shaping the Czech Stance," Policy Paper for the Transatlantic Relations Project of the German Marshall Fund of the United States, Europeum Institute for European Policy, January 2005, www.europeum.org/doc/arch_eur/CR_Iraq_crisis.pdf, 40.

104. Cited in *Pravo*, "New Czech Prime Minister Says Europe, U.S. 'Driving Force' of Contemporary History: Statement By Jiri Paroubek," April 27, 2005.

105. See Věra Řiháčková, "Czech Republic: 'Europeanization' of a Hesitant Atlanticist?" (Prague: Europeum, April 2005), 2. See also, Col. Gordon R. Hammock, USAF, "Iraq, Preemption, and the Views of Poland, the Czech Republic, and Hungary," *Air & Space Power Journal* (Fall 2003).

106. BBC Monitoring, "Background: Milestones in Czech-EU Relations Since 1993," June 4, 2003.

107. Radio Praha, "Czechs Give Strong Backing to EU Entry as 77 Percent Vote 'Yes,'" June 14, 2003. Also, interviews with Czech citizens in Prague, June 2003 and June 2005.

108. Sean Hanley, "From Neo-Liberalism to National Interests: Ideology, Strategy, and Party Development in the Euroscepticism of the Czech Right," *East European Politics and Societies* 18, no. 3 (2004), 522.

109. Radio Prague, "Consensus Still Far Away, One Year Into the European Union," April 25, 2005.

110. CTK Czech News Agency, "Review of Major Events in Czech Republic in 2005," *Financial Times Information,* December 5, 2005.

111. A March 2005 Eurobarometer showed that 74 percent of Czechs were aware of the draft treaty, but only 7 percent were very familiar with its overall contents. European Commission, Special Eurobarometer: The Future Constitutional Treaty (March 2005), 4.

112. Associated Press, "Poll: 62 Percent of Czechs Want a Referendum on the European Union Constitution," May 16, 2005.

113. Interviews with defense officials in Prague, June 2005.

114. Zdeněk Kříž, "Comparison of Czech and European Security Strategies," in 'Easternization' of Europe's Security Policy, edited by Tomáš Valášek and Olga Gyárfášová, (Bratislava: Institute for Public Affairs, 2004), 37.

115. Government of the Czech Republic, "Conceptual Basis of the Foreign Policy of the Czech Republic for the 2003-2006 Period," March 3, 2003, www.mzv.cz/ervis/soubor.asp?id=4670 (accessed July 5, 2005), 9.

116. Interviews with Czech defense officials and analysts in Prague, June 2005. See also, Radek Khol, "The Czech Republic and ESDP in 2004," www.cap.lmu.de/transatlantic/download/khol.doc (accessed January 12, 2006).

117. Ibid, 6.

118. Robert Weisman, "EU, From a Skeptic's Point of View," *The Boston Globe,* October 2, 2005.

119. Interviews with Czech officials in Prague, June 2005.

120. Radio Prague, "President Vaclav Havel and NATO," www.radio.cz/en/html/nato_havel.html (accessed December 16, 2005).

121. Thomas S. Szayna, "The Czech Republic: A Small Contributor or a 'Free Rider?'" in *America's New Allies*, ed. Andrew Michta (Seattle and London: University of Washington Press, 1999), 134.

122. Szayna, "The Czech Republic," 121.

123. See Foreign Operations at the Czech Ministry of Defense www.army.cz/scripts/detail.php?id=5807 (accessed January 5, 2006).

124. Szayna, "The Czech Republic," 125.

125. Kříž, "Comparison of Czech and European Security Strategies," 32.

126. Rob Cameron, "Havel Warns of New Balkans War in Montenegro," Radio Praha, July 10, 2000.

127. Vancura, "Czech Republic's Role," 176.

128. Ministry of Defense, Czech Republic, www.army.cz/scripts/detail.php?id=6527 (accessed January 17, 2006).

129. U.S. Department of State, Bureau of European and Eurasian Affairs, "Background Note: Czech Republic," August 2005, www.state.gov/r/pa/ei/bgn/3237.

130. Col. Gordon R. Hammock, USAF, "Iraq, Preemption, and the Views of Poland, the Czech Republic, and Hungary," *Air & Space Power Journal*, Fall 2003.

131. Quoted in FBIS Translated Text, Peter Weiss, "Weekly Argues Strengthening of EU-NATO Ties in Vital Interest of Slovakia," DOMINOFORUM, April 25, 2005.

132. Věra Řiháčková, "Czech Republic: 'Europeanization' of a Hesitant Atlanticist?" (Prague: Europeum, April 2005): 6.

133. CTK, "Czech Poll Shows 72% Support for EU Membership, 62% NATO Membership," April 20, 2005.

134. Věra Řiháčková, "Czech Republic: 'Europeanization' of a Hesitant Atlanticist?" 6. See also Szayna, "The Czech Republic," 131.

135. For an excellent overview of the historical role of the United States in Central and Eastern Europe see Ronald D. Asmus and Alexandr Vondra, "The Origins of Atlanticism in Central and Eastern Europe," *Cambridge Review of International Affairs* 18, no. 2 (July 2005).

136. Many of the Czech Republic's key political personalities represented positions on the Iraqi crisis that were in opposition to the predominant position of their parties. For a detailed review of politicians and their positions, see David Král and Lukáš Pachta, "The Czech Republic and the Iraq Crisis: Shaping the Czech Stance," (Prague: Europeum Institute for European Policy, January 2005).

137. See Vancura, "Czech Republic's Role," 176–77.

138. Czech News Agency, "Xenophobia, Senate Hinders ICC Ratification in Czech Republic," March 11, 2004.

139. Král and Pachta, "The Czech Republic and the Iraq Crisis," 31.

140. Vancura, "Czech Republic's Role," 179.

141. Král and Pachta, "The Czech Republic and the Iraq Crisis," 37–38.

142. Král and Pachta, "The Czech Republic and the Iraq Crisis," 26.

143. Král and Pachta, "The Czech Republic and the Iraq Crisis," 18. See also UN Security Council Resolution 1472 (2003) at daccessdds.un.org/doc/UNDOC/GEN/N03/302/09/PDF/N0330209.pdf1OpenElement (accessed July 14, 2005).

144. Vancura, "Czech Republic's Role," 179.

145. Czech Radio, "Klaus Expresses Support for Czech Soldiers in Afghanistan," March 9, 2004, www.radio.cz/en/news/51513.

146. *CTK*, "Two-Thirds of Czechs Disapprove of Iraq War—Poll," March 18, 2005.

147. Bank Austria Creditanstalt, "Investment Guide/Czech Republic 2004," 11.

148. Martin Ehl, "How Close is Central Europe to the United States?" *Financial Times Information*, July 25, 2003.

149. Hanley, "From Neo-Liberalism to National Interests: Ideology, Strategy, and Party Development in the Euroscepticism of the Czech Right," 518.

150. Czech News Agency, "Czechs Support Multi-Speed Europe Without Constitution—Survey," September 2, 2005.

151. The Civic Democratic Party (CDP) program is quoted in Seán Hanley, "From Neo-Liberalism to National Interests: Ideology, Strategy, and Party Development in the Euroscepticism of the Czech Right," 517.

152. Ibid.

153. Interviews with Czech government officials in Prague, June 2005.

154. See David Král, "The Czech Ratification of the Constitutional Treaty—Victim of the Government Crisis?" Policy Brief, (Prague: EUROPEUM, March 2005).

155. BBC Monitoring, "Czech Daily Says President's Stance on Iraq Sours Ties with USA," April 10, 2003.

156. Ibid.

157. *Election Guide*, www.electionguide.org/resultsum/czechdeputies01.htm (accessed January 15, 2006).

158. Vancura, "Czech Republic's Role," 181–83.

159. Czech News Agency, "Over Half of Czechs Critical of U.S. Policy," March 24, 2005.

160. IPR Strategic Business Information Database, "Majority of Czechs Opposed to U.S. Policy," April 7, 2005.

161. Czech News Agency, "Over Half of Czechs Critical of U.S. Policy," March 24, 2005.

162. CVVM poll referenced in John Springford, "'Old' and 'New' Europeans United: Public Attitudes towards the Iraq War and U.S. Foreign Policy," Background Brief (London: Centre for European Reform, 2003), 5.

163. Ibid.

164. Czech New Agency, "Two-thirds of Czechs Disapprove of Iraq War—Poll," March 18, 2005.

165. Interviews with Czech foreign affairs and defense officials in Prague, June 2005.

166. Czech News Agency, "Half of Czechs Feel Like EU Citizens, But Few Proud of It," June 17, 2005.

167. David Vaughn, "Czechs Can Help Build the New 'European Dream,'" Interview with Jeremy Rifkin, Radio Praha, January 10, 2006.

168. Czech News Agency, "Czechs Most Afraid of Terrorism—Poll in Press," April 11, 2005.

169. CSIS Eastern Europe Project and the Slovak Foreign Policy Association, "Slovakia's Security and Foreign Policy Strategy," (Washington, D.C.: CSIS, June 2001), 4.

170. For data on the September 1998 parliamentary election, see Electionguide .org, www.electionguide.org/resultsum/slovakiares3.htm (accessed December 1, 2005).

171. See Zoltán Mikes, "Slovakia: Meciar Problem Again," *Network of Independent Journalists* 278, June 26, 2002, www.idee.org/nij278.html (accessed July 2, 2005). See also BBC News, "Testing Times for Slovak Politics," June 28, 2002.

172. For the 2002 Parliamentary election results of the Slovak Republic see Election Guide, www.electionguide.org/resultsum/slovakia_par02.htm (accessed September 15, 2005).

173. Mid-Term Foreign Policy Strategy of the Slovak Republic Until 2015, 7.

174. See Heather Grabbe, "A Partnership for Accession? The Implications of EU Conditionality for the Central and East European Applicants," Robert Schuman Centre Working Paper 12/99.

175. European Commission, "Agenda 2000—Commission Opinion on Slovakia's Application for Membership of the European Union," DOC/97/20, July 15, 1997,

europa.eu.int/comm/enlargement/dwn/opinions/slovakia/sk-op-en.pdf (accessed September 10, 2005).

176. European Commission, "1999 Regular Report from the Commission on Slovakia's Progress Towards Accession," http://europa.eu.int/comm/enlargement/report_10_99/pdf/en/slovakia_en.pdf (accessed September 10, 2005).

177. CTK Czech News Agency, "Dzurinda Says Faith, Hard Work Recipe for Referendum Success," May 20, 2003.

178. EU support was highest in Lithuania at 59 percent. Eurobarometer 63.4: Public Opinion in the European Union (Fieldwork May-June 2005, Published September 2005), 94. National Report: Hungary, p. 3. See also UPI, "EU Enjoys Massive Support in Slovakia Poll," April 27, 2005.

179. Vladimir Bilcik, "Slovakia," in *Bigger EU, Wider CFSP, Stronger ESDP? The View From Central Europe*, ed. Antonio Missiroli (Paris: The European Union Institute for Security Studies, Occasional Papers No. 34, April 2002), 31–32.

180. Ivo Samson, "Slovakia," in *Old Europe, New Europe and the US: Renegotiating Transatlantic Security in the Post 9/11 Era*, edited by Tom Lansford and Blagovest Tashev (Burlington: Ashgate, 2005), 233.

181. Ibid.

182. Ibid, 228.

183. Steven Woehrel, Julie Kim, and Carl Ek, "NATO Applicant States: A Status Report," (Washington, D.C.: Congressional Research Service, April 2003), www.fas.org/man/crs/RL30168.pdf (accessed November 20, 2005).

184. CTK, "More Than 60 Percent of Slovaks Welcome NATO Invitation—Poll," *Financial Times Information*, November 21, 2002.

185. Czech News Agency, "Slovak Parliament Approves Redeployment of Afghan Mission," December 15, 2005.

186. U.S. Department of State, "Europe Overview," at www.state.gov/documents/organization/31941.pdf (accessed November 20, 2005).

187. Samson, "Slovakia," 230.

188. FBIS Translated Text, "Dzurinda Defends Slovak Support for Iraq War, Cabinet Record in Mid Term," *Narodna Obroda*, October 18, 2004.

189. FBIS Translated Text, "Poll Shows Most Slovaks Do Not See NATO Entry as Guarantee of Greater Security," *Hospodarske Noviny*, May 10, 2005.

190. Ibid.

191. Samson, "Slovakia," 233.

192. Mid-Term Foreign Policy Strategy of the Slovak Republic Until 2015, 7.

193. Czech News Agency, "Over Half of Slovaks for US Retaliation Over Attacks," *Financial Times Information*, September 18, 2001.

194. Czech News Agency, "Rochel Praises Slovak Stand on Anti-Terrorist Drive," September 22, 2001.

195. Jitendra Joshi, "Pro-U.S. Letter Exposes Divide at Heart of Europe," Agence France Presse, January 20, 2003.

196. Slovak Foreign Ministry Newsletter, www.foreign.gov.sk/En/files/Newsletter-January_2003_en.doc (accessed July 23, 2005).

197. BBC Monitoring, "Slovak Parliament Approves of Sending Troops to Iraq—Details," February 6, 2003.

198. Financial Times Information, "Slovak Party Leaders Divided on Cabinet's Proposal for Sending Troops to Iraq," *Bratislava Pravda*, February 1, 2003.

199. Samson, "Slovakia," 231.

200. Financial Times Information, "Slovak Supports EU Position on International Criminal Court," *TASR*, July 23, 2003.

201. Tibor Ico, "Slovak Daily Sees US Suspension of Military Assistance Over ICC as 'Cold Shower,'" *Hospodarske Noviny*, July 11, 2003.

202. U.S. Department of State, "Europe Overview," www.state.gov/documents/organization/31941.pdf (accessed November 20, 2005).

203. Radio Free Europe, "U.S. Unblocks Aid to ICC Dissenters," November 24, 2003.

204. BBC Monitoring, "Slovakia to Send 20 More Troops to Iraq," Radio Twist Bratislava, January 23, 2004.

205. Czech News Agency, "Gasparovic Opposed to Withdrawing Slovak Troops From Iraq," Financial Times Information, June 22, 2004.

206. Czech News Agency, "Government Supports Slovak Soldiers Further Operation in Iraq," July 14, 2004.

207. Czech News Agency, "Slovak Parliament Rejects Withdrawing Troops from Iraq," September 28, 2004.

208. See Czech News Agency, "CDM's Conference to Set New Party Line," April 5, 2003. See also *BBC Monitoring International Reports*, "Slovak Christian Democrat Head Attacks Anti-Americanism of 'Populist Parties,'" April 5, 2003.

209. Olga Gyárfášová, "The Impact of Anti-Americanism on Democratic Consolidation in 'New Europe,'" *National Endowment for Democracy* (NED), April 21, 2003.

210. Robert Kadlecik, "Slovaks Critical of United States," *Financial Times Information*, *Bratislava Pravda*, June 13, 2003.

211. Olga Gyárfášová, "Perception of the United States in Central Europe—The Slovak Case," in *Bridges Across the Atlantic? Attitudes of Poles, Czechs and Slovaks Towards the United States*, edited by Lena Kolarska-Bobińska, Jacek Kucharczyk, Piotr Maciej Kaczyński (Warsaw: Institute of Public Affairs, 2005), 177.

212. Ibid, 184.

213. *Transatlantic Trends: Key Findings 2005*, 9 www.transatlantictrends.org/doc/TTKeyFindings2005.pdf (accessed December 1, 2005).

214. Ivo Samson, "Foreign Policy in Focus," *The Slovak Spectator*, January 10, 2005.

215. See speech of Slovak Deputy Foreign Minister Magda Vašáryová given at the School of Slavonic and East European Studies (SSEES), University College of London, "Lessons Learned from Building a Civil Society in Slovakia—Spreading Democracy and Stability in Central and Eastern Europe," November 9, 2005.

216. It should be noted that some Smer MPs lent their support in parliament to approving the deployment of Slovak military engineers to Iraq on June 19, 2003. See, Czech News Agency, "Slovak Parliament Approves Sending Military Engineers to Iraq," *Financial Times Information*, June 19, 2003.

217. "Slovak Opposition Leader Fico Sees U.S. Economic Interest Behind Iraq War," Financial Times Information, *Prague Pravo* in Czech, March 27, 2003.

218. See Olga Gyárfášová and Marek Stastny, "Priorities and Sources of Security Policies—Slovakia," in *"Easternization" of Europe's Security Policy*, edited by Tomáš Valášek and Olga Gyárfášová (Bratislava: Institute for Public Affairs, 2004), 13.

219. *BBC Monitoring International Reports*, "Slovak Opposition Party Increases Lead—Poll," January 16, 2006.

220. Jane's Intelligence Review, "Slovakia's NATO Credentials Wane," May 1, 1996.

221. Olga Gyárfášová, "Perception of the United States in Central Europe—The Slovak Case," p. 184.

Chapter Five

Baltic Bonds

Estonia, Latvia, and Lithuania

Estonia, Latvia, and Lithuania, situated along the CEE region's northern tier, regained their statehood and independence in 1991. The three nations, with a combined population of approximately 7.2 million inhabitants, are collectively known as the Baltic states. Historical experience, as opposed to language, religion, or culture, is the uniting force of Baltic identity. The foreign policies of the three countries have a specific commonality: each state feels particularly vulnerable to Russian political and economic pressures and views the United States as their chief protector against Moscow's overtures. Hence, balancing their security postures vis-à-vis the United States and the European Union, the most effective political and security deterrents against Russia, figure prominently in their decisions.

The forced incorporation of the Baltic states into the Soviet Union in 1940 and the subsequent deportations, sovietization, and russification left indelible imprints on these peoples.[1] Regaining their freedom and independence guided the political transitions of all three states.[2] One key principle of transformation was the "rejection of all things Soviet," which still drives cooperative policies among the Balts in their pursuit of security and guides their debates within international institutions. All three countries remain grateful to the United States and other Western countries for not recognizing their annexation by the Soviet Union.

The Soviet occupation left sizable Russian-speaking settlers in all three countries, especially in Latvia and Estonia. Twenty-nine percent of Latvia's population is Russian-speaking.[3] A nonindigenous Russian and Sovietized population accounts for 25.6 percent of Estonia's populace, and a smaller 6.3 percent resides in Lithuania.[4] Moscow has frequently manipulated the issue of minority rights as a political tool to undermine Baltic Euro-Atlantic aspirations.

183

The Baltic states' membership in the EU and NATO has not completely eliminated insecurities over Russian policy. A complicating factor has been "a serious disconnect" in EU-Russia relations.[5] Whereas the EU strategy toward Russia has focused on "partnership and cooperation," Russia's policy toward the EU has centered upon ensuring its own national interests, including meddling in the affairs of its former satellites. Moscow endeavored to undermine the Baltic independence movements and to thwart plans by all three states to join the EU and NATO. Moscow cut energy supplies in 1990 and 1992 in retaliation for Baltic insistence that Russian troops leave the region.[6] At the opening of the EU accession process with the first group of CEE countries—Estonia, Poland, Hungary, and the Czech Republic—Russia's demands to participate in the debate illustrated its desire to derail EU membership for its former satellites.[7] Moscow's refusal to sign border treaties with the three Baltic countries was also a strategy to prevent their membership in both the EU and NATO.[8]

To blunt Moscow's aggressive strategy, the Baltic states worked cooperatively before attaining membership and later have sought to shape EU policy toward Russia within EU institutions. While the threat posed by their larger neighbor is perceived to be serious, neither Tallinn, Riga, nor Vilnius wish to be perceived as Russophobic agitators within the EU. Their efforts have not merited the full attention of the larger "appeasement-minded" West European (WE) powers and they have been cautioned against becoming one-issue countries. Nevertheless, Moscow's intent to interfere in their domestic politics will continue to dominate Baltic policies within the European Union.

Close ties between Paris, Berlin, and Moscow remain a source of concern for the Balts, especially in the way that these capitals "negotiate among themselves about matters which affect the smaller states between them."[9] The three Baltic states were initially omitted from European Community considerations for membership in the mid-1990s evidently to placate Moscow. Later on, the Community attempted to divide the republics by proposing Estonia's entry ahead of Latvia and Lithuania. When Moscow enacted plans to derail NATO membership for the three countries, for example by fomenting ethnic conflict in Latvia, the EU appeared to align itself with Moscow.[10] Baltic distrust of WE policy seemed to be further validated when the former German chancellor Gerhard Schröeder and Russian president Vladimir Putin agreed in September 2005 to construct a gas pipeline between their two countries that bypassed the Baltic states. The deal eroded confidence that EU common policies will supersede the national interests of particular countries.[11] As Russia's energy exports to the older EU member states increase, Moscow's leverage over EU decision making is also likely to grow.

Whereas France and Germany have often been viewed with mistrust, the United States is more favorably perceived in the region. The Baltic states were thankful to Washington for its nonacceptance of their incorporation into the Soviet Union. They also appreciated Washington's recognition of their restored sovereignty in the early 1990s, although the United States was not the first country to do so. By 2001, the United States was advocating simultaneous NATO accession for all three countries. In preparation for Alliance membership, several U.S.-Baltic initiatives were launched and encompassed economic and military assistance. The U.S.-Baltic Charter, signed in January 1998, underpinned U.S. support for their Euro-Atlantic integration and emphasized that no country should be omitted or discriminated against due to history or geography. Other forms of U.S.-Baltic cooperation have included the North European Initiative (NEI), launched in 1997, which focused on the enhancement of regional security by providing "space for Russia's integration into the European economic project."[12] In 2003, the enhanced Partnership in Northern Europe (e-PINE) framework featured multilateral cooperation between the Baltic and Nordic states and the United States in various areas including security and economic policy.[13] Although U.S. initiatives in the region did not accelerate until the late 1990s, Washington's commitment to the security and independence of the region has laid the foundation for strong U.S.-Baltic relations.[14]

Following the election of George W. Bush in November 2000 and the terrorist attacks of 9/11, U.S. policy toward Russia appeared to be more accommodating despite Moscow's more assertive foreign policy under the Putin presidency.[15] Cooperation in the struggle against terrorists gained in importance and this shift in priorities raised anxieties in the Baltic capitals, generating questions about Washington's lenient position toward Moscow. The April 2005 U.S. Congressional resolution asking Moscow to recognize the illegality of the Soviet occupation of the Baltic states helped to alleviate some of those fears. President Bush's visit to Riga in May 2005 also contributed to reassuring Baltic leaders that the United States strongly supported their sovereignty regardless of Russian pressures. Estonia, Latvia, and Lithuania have in turn exhibited their solidarity with Washington through their support for the U.S.-led war against terrorist groups and radical regimes in Afghanistan and Iraq.

Baltic support for U.S. policies is likely to hold steady if the national interests of the larger EU powers continue to dominate EU-Russian relations over the heads of the new member states.[16] A more assertive U.S. policy toward Russia, or at least an approach that defends the interests of the three Baltic nations, will help maintain reliable American allies in the region. There is also a perception in the Baltic capitals that if American interest in Russia diminishes, then U.S. involvement with the Baltic states could also be diluted.[17] Even as members of NATO and the EU, each Baltic state needs assurances that its alliance with the United States will endure and will be based on a common approach toward regional security.

ESTONIA

After a decade of transition Estonia, with a population of 1.4 million, was recognized as one of the most politically stable states in the CEE region. Political disputes have been limited to domestic issues, especially over economic policy. In contrast, a broad consensus exists on international affairs, especially concerning the EU, NATO, the United States, and regional relations. Estonia's foreign policy priorities have included membership in both NATO and the EU, and Tallinn's 2004 National Security Concept underlined the country's Euro-Atlantic integration as a security priority, together with a strong partnership with the United States and other allies. The document pays special attention to the changed post-9/11 security environment and concludes that this has "significantly expanded Estonia's security policy into regions in which Estonia previously had no direct interests."[18] This position underscores the strong Atlanticism of Estonia's political leaders.

European Union

Estonia was a frontrunner among candidates for the European Community, the forerunner of the European Union.[19] In December 1997, the country was invited to begin EU accession talks together with the Czech Republic, Hungary, Poland, Slovenia, and Cyprus; the discussions officially opened in 1998. Estonia received an official invitation to join the EU during the Copenhagen Summit in December 2002 and two-thirds of voters supported Estonia's membership in a public referendum held in September 2003.[20] Estonia joined the EU on May 1, 2004.

The government's European Union Strategy for 2004–2006 called for the "rapid integration" of all new member states into the EU decision-making process. Tallinn considered equal integration a priority for the "effective functioning" of the EU-25, laboring to avert the development of a two-speed Europe. The document also asserted that competitiveness should not be hindered and that the "four freedoms of the internal market" (free movement of persons, goods, services, and capital) should be granted to all EU members. These priorities illustrate Tallinn's desire for full participation in the EU and indicate its opposition to fiscal policies that may undermine economic growth as Estonia has one of the most competitive economies among the new EU members. The EU Strategy document also emphasized the need for promoting democratic reform further east.[21] Fears of a perpetually assertive Russia, together with instability on the EU's new eastern border, have contributed to guiding Tallinn's strategy within the European Union.

Estonia desires an equal voice in the EU decision-making process and the government has favored the adoption of the EU Constitutional Treaty to facilitate greater transparency and effectiveness within key institutions. The French and Dutch no votes on the treaty in May and June 2005 demonstrated the presence of isolationism and anti-foreigner sentiments in Western Europe and generated uncertainties in CEE concerning the breadth of European identity and the acceptance of new members as equal partners. At the time of the failed referenda, Estonian support for the treaty registered among 52 percent of the population. Opponents of the treaty comprised about 15 percent of the citizenry, while those with no opinion encompassed 36 percent.[22] The Estonian parliament began its ratification of the treaty in February 2006, but the process has not been completed.

Tallinn favors the development of the EU's Common Foreign and Security Policy (CFSP) and understands the potential benefits of a more coherent EU voice in foreign policy matters especially in dealing with Russia and other eastern neighbors. Despite the uncertainties surrounding the future of CFSP, 71 percent of Estonian citizens indicated their support for this initiative in late 2005.[23] However, the Estonian government is aware that it will be viewed as a one-issue country if it exclusively focuses on the Russia question. Estonia has registered some successes in its Russian agenda, including generating EU pressure to obtain Moscow's signature on the Estonia-Russia border treaty in May 2005. Nonetheless, Russia has thus far refused to ratify the bilateral pact.

NATO Involvement

Since independence, NATO membership has been a priority for all Estonian administrations. Tallinn initially participated in the North-Atlantic Cooperation Council (NACC) beginning in 1991, and after 1997 in its successor, the Euro-Atlantic Partnership Council (EAPC), the consultative body between NATO members and candidate states. Estonia joined NATO's Partnership for Peace (PfP) program in February 1994. As the republic did not possess armed forces during the Soviet occupation, Tallinn had to construct its own military capabilities basically from scratch. However, this enabled a high degree of flexibility and adaptability to the requirements of modern warfare.

Trilateral defense cooperation was a condition of Baltic NATO membership and in 1995 joint efforts were formalized through an agreement between the three defense ministers. The Baltic Battalion (BALTBAT), an infantry regiment, was initiated in 1994 to serve in international and regional peace-keeping operations. It fulfilled its objectives and was disbanded in September 2003. Continuing cooperative efforts have included BALTSEA, the Baltic Security Assistance Group in 1997; BALTRON in 1998, the joint naval squadron; BALTNET, the Baltic airspace surveillance system; and BALTDE-FCOL, the Baltic Defense College.[24]

Ahead of NATO membership, Estonia demonstrated its commitment to the Alliance through participation in various peacekeeping missions, including the Stabilization Force in Bosnia-Herzegovina (SFOR) and its successor EU-FOR (EU Force), as well as in Kosova Force (KFOR) operations. Since 2002, a mine-clearance team has been operating in Afghanistan with plans to send more soldiers by 2007 and a thirty-four-man light infantry Estonian platoon (ESTPLA) was dispatched to Iraq in June 2003.[25] Tallinn's participation in these efforts helped to secure the country's membership in NATO in March 2004 during the second round of Alliance enlargement since the end of the Cold War. Following admission, Tallinn continued to fulfill its commitments to military operations abroad. In 2005, plans to lead a NATO Provincial Reconstruction Team (PRT) in Afghanistan were initiated. Also, the mandate of ESTPLA, serving in Iraq, was renewed by parliament until the end of 2006. This platoon has been stationed at the Taji Military Training Base, north of Baghdad, and has been conducting several dangerous missions, including search-and-cordon operations, rapid reaction missions, and patrol duties. In addition, Tallinn has contributed weapons, ammunition, and funding to the Iraq Trust Fund.[26] Despite its efforts Estonia's defense spending fell short of NATO recommendations, estimated at 1.6 percent of GDP during the first year of membership.[27]

Among government officials and the larger public, NATO continues to be viewed as the country's principle security guarantee although political leaders fear that the U.S. commitment to NATO is diminishing. Tallinn does not want to see the Alliance marginalized as the EU's defense policy is developed. Divisions within the EU and NATO over the security of the continent and its evolving organizational framework is met with some trepidation in Tallinn amid growing concerns that NATO will become an irrelevant player in Europe. The fact that transatlantic divisions over the U.S.-led mission in Iraq accelerated such discussions just ahead of Estonian accession, led to increased support for NATO among Estonian political elites out of fear that the Alliance would be marginalized or dismantled in favor of EU-based security structures.

The Estonian government regularly conducts opinion polls concerning popular attitudes toward national security, including Alliance membership.

According to a June 2005 survey, 78 percent of Estonian residents supported NATO, while 14 percent were opposed. Sixty-six percent of citizens viewed NATO membership as the country's primary security guarantee. Among all residents, ethnic Estonians perceived NATO more favorably (84 percent) than non-Estonians (48 percent).[28]

U.S. Relations

In July 1922, the United States recognized an independent Estonia and a diplomatic mission representing the republic opened in Washington the same year. Under Soviet occupation, the mission continued to operate and was recognized by the United States as the legal representative of the Estonian state.[29] The ideals of freedom and democracy were heavily stressed by the United States during Soviet rule and played a prominent role in generating political and public support for U.S. policies. Estonian political leaders have sought to maintain a special relationship with Washington and the driving force behind Tallinn's insistence on U.S. engagement is national security, as NATO's Article V can only be guaranteed with U.S. involvement. Once Estonia obtained NATO membership, the country's priority was to maintain U.S. engagement in the Baltic region. Prior to the military action in the Middle East, Estonia signed the February 2003 Vilnius Group letter supporting the U.S.-UK position on Iraq and complied with the U.S. request for assistance. Following an emergency cabinet session in March 2003, the government released a statement noting that Iraq did not "take advantage of the opportunity to resolve the problem peacefully." Tallinn supported U.S. action despite indications that public opinion was less than enthusiastic. In fact, an EOS-Gallup Europe survey carried out in January 2003 showed that only twelve percent of Estonians supported U.S. action in Iraq without a UN mandate.[30]

Tallinn hoped that only minimal and short-term use of force would be necessary in Iraq.[31] The cabinet proposed the deployment of up to fifty-five troops for postwar peacekeeping and reconstruction efforts and the mission obtained parliamentary approval in May 2003.[32] A thirty-four-member light infantry platoon and four staff officers were dispatched in June to serve alongside U.S. troops. The government adhered to its decision to support U.S. efforts in spite of poor public perceptions about the war. The majority of Estonians (72 percent) thought that the United States was too eager to resort to military force overseas. Sixty percent did not believe that the outcome of the war would ensure greater peace and stability in the Middle East as was claimed by American leaders. After the Iraqi military was defeated, only 30 percent of Estonians perceived the war as having been justified, whereas a majority of 52 percent viewed it as unjust.[33]

Despite unfavorable public opinion toward the war, the government continued to support the Iraqi mission. In April 2004 parliament extended the mandate of Estonia's military contribution in Iraq until June 2005. Again in April 2005, parliament voted to renew the troop's mandate for an additional six months, until December 2005. A further parliamentary decision, by a vote of sixty-eight in favor and three against taken in December, extended the mission by one more year.[34] According to this decision, Tallinn could send up to forty members of its defense forces to serve in Iraq.[35] Although two Estonian soldiers have died and ten have been wounded during the course of the mission, Estonia's small military has valued its participation in Iraq, especially for the experience gained and the generous compensation obtained.[36]

Regional Relations and Eastern Dimension

Estonia's political leaders consider regional cooperation as the cornerstone of the country's Euro-Atlantic integration efforts and regard regional development as essential for security. Already in 1991, the Baltic Assembly, a cooperative mechanism for the parliaments of Estonia, Latvia, and Lithuania, was founded. In 1994, the Baltic Council of Ministers was established as an important initiative for intergovernmental cooperation. Joint defense projects were also launched in the 1990s with Western assistance—BALTBAT, BALTNET, and BALTDEFCOL—and now operate with Baltic resources. In June 2004, the Baltic defense ministers agreed to seek additional opportunities for trilateral military cooperation.[37]

Cooperation with the Nordic states—Sweden, Finland, Denmark, Iceland, and Norway—has also featured as a strategic priority for Tallinn. High-level government officials meet regularly in the Nordic-Baltic-Eight (NB8) format. EU eastern enlargement, the global war against terrorists, energy security, and common policy toward Russia comprise some of the major issues deliberated.[38] Following the October 2005 Nordic Council session in which Estonia, Latvia, and Lithuania participated, the Swedish prime minister emphasized the need for a coherent EU policy toward Russia, citing that France and Germany have their own particular policies, but that Brussels does not.[39] The Nordic and Baltic states share similar foreign policy priorities reflected in these cooperative efforts.

Sweden has been one of Estonia's strongest allies, with a foreign aid package established in 1990 that supported the development of regional security, a market economy, and environmental projects. Stockholm backed Estonia's membership in the EU and led efforts in all three Baltic states to provide information on EU issues. In the sphere of defense, cooperation has been evident in consultations, logistics, and training. In May 2005, Estonia signed a memorandum on the formation of an EU battle group with Sweden, Finland, and Norway, which should be operational by 2008.[40] Sweden and Estonia have established several joint projects that have encouraged training and reform in states neighboring the EU, including Moldova, Georgia, and Ukraine, and Sweden also became Estonia's largest foreign investor.[41]

Estonia has developed cooperative relations with Finland and Norway. The Wise Men Assembly established in 2002 between Helsinki and Tallinn has generated numerous joint initiatives, including public servant exchanges, protective measures for the Baltic Sea, and educational and research cooperation. Finland remains the second largest investor in Estonia. Norway was a strong supporter of Estonia's aspirations for NATO and EU membership and Oslo was the first NATO member to ratify Estonia's Protocol of Accession to NATO in April 2003.

Relations between Estonia and Russia have been strained, marked by incessant disputes during the post–Cold War era. After a decade of negotiations, a treaty demarcating common land and sea borders was signed in May 2005. However, just prior to the Estonian parliament's ratification of the document in June 2005, MPs added an amendment noting the illegal occupation of Estonia by Soviet forces. The treaty was ratified by seventy-eight votes in favor and four against with nineteen abstentions. Moscow opposed the amendment and contended that it allowed for future Estonian claims to Russian territory that had been annexed by the Russian Federation after World War II. Although the EU backed Tallinn's position, Moscow insisted on new negotiations.[42] In addition to the border dispute, Russian aircraft have violated Estonian airspace numerous times between 2004 and 2006, both before and after Tallinn joined NATO, and are a continual source of tension between the two states. Further, several Estonian government officials have been denied visas to travel to Russia. For example, Estonia's foreign minister, Urmas Paet, was refused a visa by Moscow in November 2005 with Russian authorities claiming that the refusal was a "technical error."[43]

The unsettled countries to the east of the EU border are a priority for Tallinn. Estonia has signed bilateral agreements with most other post-Soviet states and works closely with Georgia and Ukraine in training police and border guards and promoting civil-military reform. An Estonian friendship group was established in Moldova's parliament, which focuses on assistance and support for Chisinau's EU ambitions. Tallinn's main objective is to bolster the sovereignty of nations within its immediate neighborhood so they will not be politically absorbed by Russia. The EU's hesitant performance during the revolutions in both Ukraine and Georgia out of fear of provoking Moscow reinforced Tallinn's belief that Washington can better spearhead democratic efforts by utilizing combined Baltic and Polish experiences.

Cooperative efforts in this sphere would also serve to strengthen U.S.-CEE relations.

Political Options

Estonian participation in the international missions in Afghanistan and Iraq has been underpinned by a general political consensus. Parliament approved the deployment of Estonian troops in May 2003 and has extended their mandate three times since. There has been minor variation in support for the United States, the European Union, and NATO among the main political contenders, with some parties assuming more populist positions on foreign policy issues when it suited their interests. However, more pronounced differences can be found in their domestic policies, especially in fiscal strategies. Following the March 2003 parliamentary elections, three parties, Res Publica, the Reform Party, and the People's Union, formed a coalition government. Its foreign policy priorities included continued progress toward Euro-Atlantic integration in order to increase living standards and for Tallinn to have a stronger influence in international affairs.[44] In March 2005 this government dissolved following the resignation of Prime Minister Juhan Parts. A new coalition was formed by the Reform Party, Center Party, and the People's Union in April 2005, led by Reform Party leader and new prime minister Andrus Ansip.

The Center Party is largely populist and flexible, focusing primarily on changes in public opinion to register political gains. The Center Party was part of the ruling coalition with the Reform Party from January 2002 until 2003, and again after April 2005 with the Reform Party and the People's Union.[45] When out of government the party has been strongly resistant to most government decisions and divided over Euro-Atlantic integration. Although in favor of Estonia's EU accession, party leaders argued about the accession process and challenged the government's capacity to protect national interests.[46] At the same time, there was a party faction that sought to capitalize on the apathy of citizens toward the European Union. Ahead of the September 2003 referendum on membership, some Center Party members appealed to the public to vote against EU accession. This stance, coupled with other internal disputes, caused a split in the party and those who left formed a new party: the Social Liberals.[47]

Regarding support for Iraq, some members of the Center Party advocated the return of Estonian troops, submitting a resolution in March 2005 for withdrawal. The motion failed as most members of both the ruling Center Party and the People's Union approved the renewed mandate in December 2005. Nevertheless, many Centrist MPs expressed their preference for Estonian soldiers to return home. Members of the Reform Party, Pro Patria Union, and

Res Publica voted in favor of a continued Estonian presence in Iraq to underscore the country's reliability as a partner and ally of the United States and to increase Tallinn's ability to influence international affairs. MPs from the Social Democratic faction opposed the extension criticizing the government for a lack of public discussion on Iraq and emphasized the need to concentrate efforts on EU and NATO missions.[48]

Public Opinion

As a consequence of Soviet occupation, national security and the protection of sovereignty remain preeminent concerns for the Estonian population. NATO and EU membership, as well as friendly relations with Russia, are all perceived as key elements for ensuring security. In a May 2005 poll, NATO membership registered as the most important factor in assuring Estonian security at 66 percent. This was followed by membership in the EU (50 percent) and good relations with Russia (44 percent). A small 21 percent of those polled indicated that the country's armed forces were the best source of protection against foreign threats.[49] Support for the armed forces has been widespread among the population, especially as the country rebuilt its military structure after securing independence. The military's international reputation for being highly effective, despite its small size, remains a source of popular pride. The armed forces have also been a model of integration for Estonia's ethnic Russian population. Although the Iraq war precipitated a drop in military support, deployments are in high demand among soldiers who seek to gain peacekeeping experience and higher pay. The pride evident in Estonia's armed forces has helped to preserve the good standing of the United States and support for the Iraqi campaign among Estonians. Only 38 percent of citizens claimed that the war negatively impacted on their perception of the United States, whereas 51 percent stated that the U.S. military action in Iraq had no effect at all on their attitude toward America.[50] A small protest against the war by ethnic Russians took place in front of the U.S. embassy in March 2003.

Public support for the EU has been relatively volatile since the start of accession talks in 1998. The percentage of citizens defining the EU as a "good thing" remained at around 33 percent between 2001 and 2003. The adoption of EU regulations has contributed to widening the gap between rich and poor and these socioeconomic pressures have generated apathy toward the EU among the poorer sectors of society. People with higher incomes continue to form the main base of EU support.[51] Although 56 percent of Estonians perceived definite benefits from EU membership in 2005, outright support for the EU has been declining with more citizens providing neutral responses to questions about the Union. Between the spring and autumn of 2005, the percentage of citizens who viewed the EU as a "good thing" dropped seven points from 48 to 41 percent.[52] This growing neutrality has been attributed to the seemingly infinite EU regulations, the rising prices of goods since accession, and the continued restrictions imposed on Estonian citizens in the EU labor market.[53] While the country lacks overwhelming public support for the EU, at the same time, it does not have a sizable Euro-skeptic contingent.[54] Despite the findings of Eurobarometer polling, government initiated surveys have registered higher favorability ratings for the EU, between 57 and 72 percent, over the past three years.[55]

LATVIA

Latvia's security priorities in the postcommunist period have centered on ensuring the country's statehood and territorial integrity.[56] Political leaders in Riga sought integration into NATO and the EU to help ensure this objective. Although both institutions were given primacy in official policy documents, NATO membership assumed precedence. NATO has been perceived as the only security institution capable of defending the country against foreign threats. Latvian relations with the United States have been a priority for all governments in Riga due to the steady American commitment to Latvia's independence and sovereignty.[57] Under Soviet rule, the Kremlin moved large numbers of Russian emigrants into all three Baltic states in order to consolidate its power in the region. Combined with forced deportations and executions of ethnic Latvians, the ethnic balance in Latvia shifted substantially and by 1990 more than 40 percent of the population was Russian-speaking.[58] Today, this percentage is estimated at 30 percent—the largest nonindigenous Russian-speaking population among the three Baltic states.

The issue of minority rights has played a large role in Moscow's attempts to put pressure on Riga in the post-Soviet period, especially in attempting to block Latvia's inclusion in NATO. However, following Latvia's entry into the Alliance and the EU, the Russian population has increasingly viewed its future as tied to the Euro-Atlantic integration process. This development is likely to gradually undermine Moscow's ability to play the ethnic card against Riga in international politics.[59] Nevertheless, the lingering threat from Moscow, especially as it seeks to restore its influence in the broader region, has strengthened Latvia's Atlanticist posture.

European Union

The European Commission recognized the restoration of Latvian independence in 1991 and by 1993 economic cooperation and trade agreements were concluded with the country. Latvia submitted its application for EU accession in 1995, accession talks opened in 2000 and concluded at the December 2002 Copenhagen Summit. In Latvia's referendum on EU membership held in September 2003, 67.49 percent of eligible voters declared their support for accession and Latvia became a member of the EU on May 1, 2004.[60]

Among EU policies, Latvia has strongly favored participation in the development of the EU's Common Foreign and Security Policy (CFSP). Similarly to the other Baltic capitals, Riga sees the benefits of having common EU policies that allow smaller countries to play a larger role in decision making. Riga's main priorities within the CFSP are to generate a common policy toward Russia and to guide EU reform efforts toward Belarus, Ukraine, and Moldova. Seventy-three percent of the public has favored the development of CFSP.[61]

A component of CFSP, the European Security and Defense Policy (ESDP), is met with slimmer support among political leaders. The development of ESDP has been perceived as a competitor to NATO, underscoring the Franco-German desire to marginalize the Alliance. Political discussions about ESDP have divided the government into two political camps: one advocated the concentration of resources within NATO while the other promoted involvement in ESDP to make sure that the United States remained a focus of European security. In late 2005, 88 percent of Latvians actually favored the development of ESDP.[62] The notion that Russia will not only influence the development of ESDP, but will also continue to exert pressure within the Baltic states, has strongly influenced Riga's security posture. The need to actively participate in shaping the direction of ESDP also stems from differing perceptions regarding the future of security policy among EU members. For France and Belgium, their former African colonies have assumed precedence, whereas the new member states, including Latvia, want to focus ESDP eastward. During intergovernmental debates, France, Spain, and Italy blocked Riga's motion to concentrate ESDP efforts toward the former Soviet republics. The larger EU nations seek to earmark resources for former colonies and do not want to derail EU-Russian relations by focusing EU engagement eastward.[63]

French and German ties to Russia have figured prominently in public perceptions of the EU. Support for the EU dropped in 2005 from 42 to 36 percent, the lowest figure among the Baltic states. Following accession, only half of Latvians believed that the country had benefited from membership, two points below the EU-25 average. This number represented a 7 percent drop from the spring of 2005. Overall support was in steady decline during 2005 as a result of growing economic disparities among the population, perceptions of lost sovereignty as a consequence of EU regulations, and the EU budget dispute that created the potential for reduced subsidies to new members. All of these factors generated a sense of second-class status for Latvians within the European Union.[64]

Involvement in NATO

Latvia did not possess its own armed forces when its independence was restored in 1990 but steadily created its own military units. The country joined NATO's Partnership for Peace (PfP) program in 1994 and Riga's Foreign Policy Concept in 1995 emphasized membership in NATO as a key priority. In September 1996, U.S. Secretary of Defense William Perry's comment that the Baltic militaries were not prepared for Alliance membership served to strengthen the resolve of all three capitals to accelerate the process for meeting NATO requirements. Defense cooperation among the Baltic states was a prerequisite for NATO entry and all three states played an active role in such efforts. In 1994, the infantry regiment Baltic Battalion (BALTBAT) was established for international and regional peacekeeping missions.[65] Continuing cooperative efforts have included the Baltic Security Assistance Group (BALTSEA), the joint naval squadron (BALTRON), the Baltic airspace surveillance system (BALTNET), and the Baltic Defense College (BALTDEFCOL).[66]

Ahead of membership, Riga illustrated its commitment to the Alliance by participating in several NATO missions. From 1998 onward Latvia has contributed troops to the joint Baltic Battalion, which served in the Stabilization Force in Bosnia-Herzegovina (SFOR) under Danish command. The effort was later duplicated in the Kosova Force (KFOR) where Riga sustained the participation of twenty-five troops. Latvia also exhibited a strong commitment to the U.S.-led war against international terrorists. Military personnel were deployed to Afghanistan in February 2003 and 122 troops, including an explosive ordnance disposal (EOD), have served in Operation Iraqi Freedom (OIF). The country has a total military force of approximately 4,250 troops and plans to reach 5,000 by 2007.[67] After successfully accelerating its military reform program and developing specialized capabilities, Latvia joined NATO in March 2004.

The security guarantee offered by NATO membership has led to strong and stable popular support for the Alliance. In January 2003, 68.5 percent of the population backed membership, up from 66 percent in July 2002.[68] In August 2004, 74 percent of respondents were in favor and by June 2005 the figure stood at 77 percent.[69] Popular support for international military missions among the general population has also been high, especially during the country's participation in the Balkan region and Afghanistan. In August 2004, 63.7 percent approved the country's participation in international peacekeeping missions.[70]

Additionally, strong political and popular support for NATO stems from a perception that NATO can be instrumental in encouraging democratic reform further east where other international organizations have fallen short of offering solid incentives for reform. Political leaders have stressed that NATO offers a greater incentive than the EU. In addition to the Article V security guarantee, Riga believes that its NATO membership will weaken Russia's imperialist ambitions.[71] Defense spending was estimated at 1.3 percent of GDP in 2004 and Riga is due to host the next NATO summit in November 2006.[72]

U.S. Relations

Following Latvia's declaration of independence, it took the United States seventeen months to officially recognize the country. Relations began to strengthen only in 1993, with the Clinton administration's resolve to help negotiate the withdrawal of Russian troops from Latvian territory. Initial U.S. involvement generated concern that Riga would be treated as a pawn between the two big powers. However, perceptions changed after Washington successfully brokered an agreement by conditioning U.S. aid to Russia on troop withdrawal from the Baltic states. This greatly influenced Riga's foreign policy and created an unwavering Atlanticist posture. Policy makers realized the importance of maintaining U.S. engagement in the Baltic region as such involvement could help Riga accomplish other foreign policy objectives.[73] The United States recognized that the Baltic states belonged in the West and its support of their efforts to "rejoin Europe" impacted favorably upon perceptions of Washington. The U.S.-Baltic Charter of 1998 acknowledged "the intensity and importance of the U.S.-Baltic link."[74] The subsequent U.S. initiatives, the North European Initiative (NEI), and the enhanced Partnership in Northern Europe (e-PINE) also strengthened bilateral ties.

Following the terrorist attacks of September 11, 2001, Latvian Prime Minister Andris Bĕrziņs expressed his country's readiness to help America. Ahead of requests for participation in the anti-terrorist campaign, Riga's political leadership backed the U.S. position in the campaign against international terrorist networks. In January 2002, parliament amended its legislation on the participation of the country's military forces abroad to include not only peacekeeping and humanitarian missions related to NATO, but also actions of collective defense.[75] To assist Latvian efforts in Afghanistan, parliament approved with a clear majority in February 2003 the dispatch of eight military medics and staff to serve with a Dutch peacekeeping unit. The only party to vote against the deployment was the Russian minority political alliance, For Human Rights in a United Latvia (HRUL).

The Latvian government insisted that Iraq should comply with the UN Security Council resolution to disarm. In late January 2003, Riga granted its airspace to the United States for military transport flights in the event of an attack against Iraq. As the U.S.-led military mission began in March 2003, Riga offered troops to assist in postwar stabilization. And since May 2003, Riga has provided 119 troops to the multinational stabilization force in Iraq. The government's decision to back the U.S. initiative was both sincere and pragmatic. Not only did Riga feel the necessity of maintaining strong U.S.-Baltic relations, its decision was also a gesture of gratitude for U.S. support of Baltic security throughout the postcommunist period. However, the fact that Latvia's NATO membership had not yet been entirely secured also influenced Riga's backing for the U.S.-led mission.

Latvia's supportive position did not extend to all of Washington's policies. In the summer of 2003, Washington suspended military assistance to Latvia (as well as to Bulgaria, Estonia, Lithuania, and Slovakia) for Riga's refusal to exempt U.S. citizens from the International Criminal Court (ICC). The U.S. Ambassador to Riga authored a public letter as a form of apology for what may have been perceived as punitive U.S. policy in cutting back military aid to Riga.[76] In November the same year, military aid restrictions were lifted in recognition of Riga's support for the U.S. invasion of Iraq.[77] In November 2005, parliament voted to extend the mandate of Latvian troops serving in Iraq until the end of 2006, following the UN Security Council Resolution 1637 (2005) to support the interim Iraqi government's request for the extension of the Multinational Force for the same period. The decision met approval with a vote of 51 to 27 out of the 100-seat assembly.[78] Within the ruling coalition, the Greens and Farmers' Union (GFU) stood in opposition to the extension as they sought to increase their popularity ahead of the 2006 general elections. A local poll carried out one month prior, in October 2005, showed that nearly 74 percent of citizens favored the troop withdrawal. Within the Russian minority population, almost 78 percent wanted the troops to return home.[79]

Public opinion regarding the military operations in Iraq contrasted sharply with the popular support expressed for other military missions, such as Latvia's participation in peacekeeping in the Balkans. Less than 30 percent of citizens believed that the military action in Iraq was justified, with about 80 percent disapproving of the war.[80] Inadequate equipment to protect soldiers and a casualty sustained by Latvian troops contributed to popular opposition.[81] Although a majority (78 percent) of Latvian citizens perceived the United States as too eager to use military force against Iraq, those who believed that the war had not negatively impacted America's image (53 percent) outweighed those who stated that the war had unfavorably altered their perceptions of the United States (40 percent).[82]

Strong U.S.-Latvian relations are a priority for Riga. With EU and NATO membership achieved, Riga's objective has been to preserve U.S. engagement in the region and support Latvian foreign policy. High-level bilateral visits have featured prominently, including U.S. President Bush's visit to Riga in 2005 and Latvian President Vaira Vīķe-Freiberga's visit to Washington in March 2006. Foreign and security priorities continue to be underscored to maintain a viable and durable U.S.-Latvian partnership.

Regional Relations and Eastern Dimension

Most of the Nordic and Baltic states share similar perceptions of Russia, the transatlantic relationship, and economic policies, and cooperative efforts among them have steadily developed. Iceland was the first country to recognize the newly independent Latvian state, followed by Denmark and Sweden. The Nordic countries provided financial and diplomatic assistance to Riga and encouraged an Atlantic orientation in Latvia's foreign policy.[83] Regional cooperation among the three Baltic states has been visible, especially in the areas of military cooperation and EU eastern policy. However, Tallinn and Vilnius were dismayed by the unilateral decision of Latvian President Vaira Vīķe-Freiberga to participate in the sixtieth anniversary of the Soviet victory over Nazi Germany in Moscow in May 2005 without reaching consensus on the issue with her Baltic neighbors.[84]

Latvia's relations with Russia have been characterized by friction during the postcommunist period. Latvia hosts the region's largest Russian population due to the influx of Russian laborers, administrators, and military personnel and their families during the period of Soviet occupation.[85] Aside from Moscow's attempts to thwart Riga's Euro-Atlantic aspirations, difficulties have been evident in the status and rights permitted to Latvia's Russian and Sovietized population. Although legislation was strict in the early to mid-1990s with regard to citizenship requirements, over time these policies have been moderated. Other contested issues between Riga and Moscow have included the unsigned border treaty. Latvia added an explanatory declaration to the treaty in April 2005 that was perceived by Moscow as allowing for future territorial claims against Russia. Latvia's parliament passed an official demarché in May 2005 that denounced communism and urged Russia to condemn the repressions under Soviet rule. The government established a special commission in August 2005 to assess the damages incurred by the country and its population under the Soviet regime.[86]

Latvia's history of occupation has given emphasis to promoting democratic practices and freedom in other former Soviet states. Riga has engaged in substantive efforts to promote democracy to countries such as Belarus,

Ukraine, Moldova, and Georgia. It has favored both NATO and EU incentives to stimulate democratic and economic reforms in these countries and to expand regional stability. Riga has supported the creation of a Ukraine-EU free trade area and Ukrainian membership in the World Trade Organization (WTO).[87] Government policy is congruent with public opinion, where 62 percent of Latvians support further EU enlargement eastward.[88]

Political Options

Latvia has had a dozen governments since the restoration of its statehood. The high number of political parties permitted only small parliamentary gains and the formation of fragile coalition governments. Latvian politics has also been driven as much by personalities as by programs. When the transatlantic crisis erupted over U.S. policy toward Iraq, Riga's governing coalition was composed of the conservative New Era Party, the Greens and Farmers' Union (GFU), For Fatherland and Freedom (FFF), and the First Party of Latvia (FPL). The ruling coalition, together with the opposition People's Party (PP), supported a parliamentary decision in March 2003 to allow Latvian troops to participate as part of the international coalition to disarm Iraq. They cited the implementation of the UN Security Council resolution for disarmament should diplomatic efforts in Iraq fail. This decision was approved by a parliamentary vote of seventy-three in favor and twenty-four against. The MPs who voted against the decision argued that the text adopted by parliament implied that Latvia was joining a war effort and contended that economic interests were primarily behind U.S. policy.[89]

In December 2003, parliament was faced with the decision to renew the mandate of its peacekeeping operations in Iraq. The major parties exhibited internal divisions regarding whether to continue the country's support of U.S. policy or to terminate Latvia's participation. The MPs in favor of maintaining a troop presence in Iraq viewed this as a component of the country's obligations as a member of NATO. Those against argued that the United States had concealed its true intentions for invading Iraq. The decision to extend the mandate until October 2004 was approved by fifty-eight votes in favor and twenty-one against.[90]

The government coalition collapsed in January 2004 and by March 2004 a new administration was formed, led by the GFU, and included the FPL and the People's Party (PP). The coalition held only forty-six seats, but the National Harmony Party (NHP) also lent its support to the government. In September 2004, parliament approved the renewal of the country's military mission in Iraq by a vote of seventy-five to twenty, extending the mandate until June 2005.[91]

Although Latvia's parliament has continued to support the Iraqi operation, debates concerning the country's participation have repeatedly featured the same concerns. Although the GFU was initially supportive, the failure to locate weapons of mass destruction left party leaders feeling let down by Washington. Additional complaints have been linked with the lack of reconstruction contracts in Iraq for Latvian companies, as well as restrictive U.S. visa policies. Political leaders opposing the extension of the Iraq mission have gained in prominence as the general public has been consistently against the war effort.

In November 2005, parliament again approved the extension of Latvia's military participation in Iraq. The decision passed by fifty-one votes to twenty-seven.[92] Parties belonging to the ruling coalition backed the decision; however, some members of the GFU did not lend their support.[93] A publicized discussion about the war in Iraq took place among select members of parliament following the November 2005 parliamentary decision. Juris Dalbins of the People's Party asserted that Latvian soldiers had been instrumental in meeting their security objectives and their participation in missions abroad helped to secure Latvia's NATO membership. The recently appointed Minister of Defense, Linda Murniece, from the New Era Party, argued that Latvian participation in Iraq had served national interests.[94]

The only party to vote outright against Latvian troop deployments was the minority political alliance, For Human Rights in a United Latvia (HRUL), comprised of the Socialist Party, the National Harmony Party, and the Equal Rights movement. The HRUL came in second place with 18.9 percent of the votes and took twenty-four seats in the October 2002 parliamentary elections. The party's electoral base was Russian-speaking and its policies have been both anti-NATO and anti-EU. In addition, Socialist Party head Alfred Rubiks was the communist leader in Latvia during Soviet rule has made frequent calls for closer economic, social, and political ties to Russia. The HRUL alliance has opposed the U.S.-led war in Iraq and has attempted to block Riga's participation.[95] The next parliamentary election is scheduled for October 2006.

Public Opinion

Public support for Latvian participation in military missions has traditionally been high, as the newly created armed forces have been a source of popular pride. In June 2005, 77 percent of citizens favorably viewed Latvia's membership in the NATO Alliance.[96] However, analysts and policy makers alike see public support for the military to be in decline since the onset of the Iraq war as between 70 and 80 percent of the public have been opposed to the mission.[97] Opponents have viewed the war as driven primarily by economic interests rather than the threat of terrorism and WMD proliferation. During the military campaign, several anti-war groups formed, including the "All for Latvia" and "I'm for Peace" initiatives. In addition to small protests in Riga, an anti-war campaign was conducted through the local media. Anti-Americanism has also featured in some television programs, particularly in commentaries broadcast from Russia aimed primarily at the Russian-speaking minority. Efforts to counter such campaigns by alternative international sources have not been forthcoming.[98]

Public support for the EU among Latvians has been among the lowest in the CEE region. In 2001, a third of citizens viewed the EU as beneficial. This number climbed to 35 percent in 2002 and reached 37 percent by 2003.[99] Latvian support for the EU was recorded at 36 percent in the fall of 2005, down six percentage points from the spring, on a par with countries such as Finland (38 percent) and the United Kingdom (34 percent).[100]

LITHUANIA

Lithuania was the first Baltic state to declare the restoration of its statehood in March 1990. The Soviet attempt to destroy the independence movement in January 1991 resulted in the loss of fourteen lives, but failed to avert the disintegration of the USSR.

Upon gaining independence Lithuania's political parties forged consensus on the country's structural transformation and international institutional integration. Both NATO and EU membership, together with stronger U.S.-Lithuanian relations, were emphasized as key goals by Vilnius. Compared to its Baltic neighbors, Lithuania experienced the fewest problems with Moscow as the country hosted the smallest Russian minority and was largely free of inter-ethnic disputes. The small size of the Russian minority, estimated at 8 percent in 1991, prevented the exploitation of ethnicity by radical local leaders and by Moscow. In addition, more than 90 percent of the country's minorities acquired Lithuanian citizenship soon after statehood was restored.[101] Political agreements with provisions for minority rights were also concluded and ratified by Vilnius with Russia, Belarus, Ukraine, and Poland.[102] Representatives from Russian and Polish minority political organizations have been elected both to parliament and to local government.[103] The absence of internal ethnic tensions improved conditions for Lithuania's political and economic transformation.

As a member of both the EU and NATO since 2004, Vilnius has sought the development of a strong Europe with close U.S. engagement.[104] The protection of national security, the promotion of democracy eastward, and a strengthened transatlantic relationship form the core of Vilnius' foreign policy, and were approved by all political parties in a formal agreement for the 2004–2008 period.[105] The document emphasized the need to foster close relations between the EU, NATO, and the United States and to strengthen Lithuania's position within all international institutions. The parties committed Lithuania's participation in NATO-led operations, as well as in other international missions "undertaken to support peace, protect human rights and guarantee adherence to other international norms."[106]

European Union

In August 1991, the European Community (EC) recognized Lithuania's independence and diplomatic relations between Vilnius and all EC member states were established. In December 1995, Lithuania submitted its official application for EU membership. By February 2000 accession talks were formally initiated and the country was incorporated into the EU's Northern Dimension initiative in June 2000. The accession process was concluded at the EU Copenhagen Summit in December 2002. The EU allocated aid for specific projects, including expenditures for closing the Ignalina nuclear power plant and subsidies for transit from Russia to its Kaliningrad exclave on the Baltic coast.[107] The May 2003 referendum registered 91 percent support for EU accession, the highest among the Baltic states, and Lithuania became an EU member on May 1, 2004.

Vilnius sought explicit economic and security objectives within the EU, including influencing European policy toward Russia. These objectives have generated enthusiasm for EU integration, including support for common institutions and Lithuania was the first EU member to ratify the Constitutional Treaty. Support for the constitution largely stemmed from the document's protection of economic competitiveness and its references to European security.[108] In addition to upholding common institutions, Vilnius has backed the European Security and Defense Policy (ESDP) to facilitate conflict prevention and crisis management. Vilnius has indicated its preparedness to contribute troops and equipment to the EU Rapid Reaction Force (RRF), while pushing to safeguard the transatlantic dimension in EU defense policy.[109] The development of ESDP has essentially been viewed as complementary to NATO.[110] In reaction to the Belgian initiative to create a European Defense Union outside of NATO in late 2003, Lithuanian Defense Minister Linas Linkevicius stated that, "the outcome of the ESDP project must not in any way compromise the role of NATO as the cornerstone of Euro-Atlantic security but must strengthen it."[111] Aside from concerns that EU leaders will endeavor to marginalize NATO's importance in Europe through their support for ESDP, there is also trepidation that the EU will engage in crisis areas outside of Europe where Lithuania has little interest or experience. Support for ESDP registered at 84 percent among the population at the end of 2005.[112]

Lithuania has also backed the EU's Common Foreign and Security Policy (CFSP), seeking to participate in guiding EU decision making. Within CFSP, Vilnius has advocated cooperation between the EU and the new border states, especially Belarus and Ukraine. Promoting and advancing democratic reform and increasing engagement with these eastern neighbors can assist Vilnius in combating transnational threats, such as organized crime and human trafficking. Although Vilnius, together with Warsaw, was able to rally a common EU stance toward Ukraine's Orange Revolution at the end of 2004, a relative success in shaping EU foreign policy, Lithuania's desired impact on CFSP has proved restricted. Seventy-two percent of the Lithuanian population favored the development of CFSP in late 2005.[113] Since Lithuania's 2003 referendum on EU membership, public support for the Union has been the highest among the three Baltic countries. A small drop in favorable ratings was witnessed in late 2005 due to the EU budget negotiations that reduced payments to the new member states. Nevertheless, public perceptions of the EU have remained positive with a pronounced view that membership has benefited the country. In late 2005, 70 percent of citizens recorded their satisfaction, the third highest percentage among the EU-25. In sum, Lithuanians trust EU institutions more than their Baltic neighbors.

NATO Involvement

In December 1991, NATO formed the North Atlantic Cooperation Council (NACC), which included the Alliance members and nine CEE states, including the three Baltic countries. NACC constituted the launching pad for Lithuania's evolving relations with NATO and the country's readiness for accession was recognized by Alliance leaders. Lithuania formally applied for NATO membership in January 1994. In addition to adopting democratic rule and a market economy, Vilnius ensured full civilian control over the armed forces to meet Alliance requirements.[114] In May 2001, the parliamentary parties signed a Defence Policy Agreement covering the 2002–2004 period. They expressed their support for NATO integration and committed Lithuania to defense spending at two percent of GDP. There was overall political consensus on strengthening the country's military capabilities in order to be prepared for collective defense and participation in both NATO and EU operations, as well as in crisis management and conflict prevention. Estimated defense spending was recorded at 1.4 percent of GDP in 2004.[115]

Lithuania joined NATO's Partnership for Peace (PfP) program in 1994 and in 1998 the Ministry of Defense outlined a ten-year military modernization and procurement program approved by parliament in 2000. Consecutive governments consistently met the political and technical requirements for Alliance membership. Vilnius gave priority to NATO interoperability and contributions to peace-support operations, crisis management, humanitarian relief, and collective defense.[116] The country's Zokniai airbase was selected as a key infrastructure site for the Alliance and both Vilnius and NATO have allocated funds to modernize its infrastructure and communications. Together with its two Baltic neighbors, Lithuania acceded to NATO in March 2004.

Lithuanian military personnel have received training in Western institutions, which aided the country's Alliance integration. Personnel and troops have participated in the NATO-led Stabilization Force (SFOR) in Bosnia-Herzegovina where approximately 700 troops have served since 1996. Some 230 soldiers have taken part in NATO's Kosova Force (KFOR) mission since 1999. Medical personnel and military observers have also fulfilled various missions in Kosova with their Danish, Czech, and Slovak counterparts.[117] From November 2002 to November 2004, forty-five Lithuanian troops served under the U.S.-led Operation Enduring Freedom in Afghanistan. Since June 2005, Lithuania has led a Provincial Reconstruction Team (PRT) in the Ghor province of western Afghanistan as part of the NATO-led International Security Assistance Force (ISAF) mission. Over 100 Lithuanian troops have participated in the PRT and have helped to stabilize the area, allowing for parliamentary and municipal elections in September 2005.[118]

In the spring of 2005, 65 percent of Lithuanians indicated support for the country's NATO membership, whereas this figure stood at 62 percent at the time of accession. Only 21 percent of citizens disapproved of the Alliance.[119] NATO is viewed as the principal guarantor of Lithuania's security and the renewal and consolidation of the organization forms a key component of Vilnius's foreign policy objectives. This position has secured wide political acceptance and was included in the government's new foreign policy concept for 2004–2008.

U.S. Relations

U.S.-Lithuanian diplomatic relations were established in 1922 and the mass emigration of Lithuanian refugees to America following the Soviet takeover of Lithuania in 1940 and again after the Second World War, buttressed political ties. During the years of occupation, the United States became a source of inspiration, as Washington did not recognize Lithuania's incorporation into the Soviet Union. When Lithuania restored its statehood in 1991, diplomatic relations with the United States were reestablished and Washington helped to negotiate the withdrawal of Russian troops from Lithuanian territory during 1993. Bilateral relations with Washington were enhanced through various initiatives to promote economic and political reform and foster regional stability, including the Baltic Action Plan (BAP) in 1996, the Northern European Initiative (NEI) in 1997, and the U.S.-Baltic Partnership Charter in 1998. In October 2003, e-PINE (enhanced Partnership in Northern Europe) was launched to reinforce security and economic cooperation and replace the previous initiatives. Overall, multilateral projects between Washington, Vilnius, Riga, and Tallinn have been valued by all three Baltic capitals as indicative of the strong commitment by the United States to Baltic Euro-Atlantic integration. In addition, U.S.-Baltic military cooperation has been fostered through the Baltic Security Assistance Group (BALTSEA) framework, which has contributed to joint Baltic military projects, including the naval squadron (BALTRON), the Baltic Peacekeeping Battalion (BALTBAT), the Baltic airspace surveillance system (BALTNET), and the Baltic Defense College (BALTDEFCOL). Joint military exercises helped prepare Lithuania for NATO membership and strengthened Vilnius's ties to Washington.[120]

Between 1997 and 2002, the United States provided approximately $50 million to Lithuania through assistance programs such as the Foreign Armed Forces Funding and International Troops Training. The funds were used for training sessions, the development of the Baltic air space observation system, and the Baltic peacekeeping battalion. In the summer of 2003, Washington suspended $12 million in military assistance to Lithuania for Vilnius's refusal to sign a bilateral agreement exempting U.S. citizens from prosecution at the International Criminal Court (ICC). In November 2003, the U.S. president rescinded a portion of these restrictions on military aid as a sign of gratitude for Lithuanian support for the Iraqi mission.[121]

Vilnius accepted Washington's request to participate in Iraqi stabilization and reconstruction. The first Lithuanian military personnel dispatched in April 2003 were eight cargo-handling specialists and four medical personnel. The military medics were integrated into a Spanish humanitarian unit that withdrew in June 2003. The cargo-handling team completed its Talil airbase humanitarian mission in November 2003. In addition to these small missions, Lithuania maintained a presence of approximately one hundred troops in Iraq: the fifty-troop peacekeeping unit, LITDET (Lithuanian Detachment), has served under Polish command in the province of Babylon, and the fifty-strong mission LITCON (Lithuanian Contingent) has served in the British-controlled sector under Danish command. Connected to the 2005 Polish decision to gradually reduce its forces in Iraq, the Lithuanian Ministry of Defense announced that LITDET would withdraw in January 2006. Following the decision, Vilnius supplied three military instructors to the Polish-led multinational division to train Iraqi troops.[122]

At the end of the initial coalition attack in Iraq, 42 percent of Lithuanians surveyed perceived the military action as unjustified, whereas 37 percent believed that it was warranted. Fifty-nine percent viewed the United States as too eager to exert military force abroad, whereas 26 percent disagreed with this sentiment. Fifty-nine percent said that the Iraq war had no effect on their attitude toward America, whereas smaller percentages indicated a negative impact (30 percent) and a positive impact (10 percent). Fifty-four percent of respondents answered that American foreign policy has had no effect on Lithuania; 22 percent claimed a positive effect, and an equal percentage claimed a negative effect.[123]

Regional Relations and Eastern Dimension

Lithuanian-Polish relations have been governed through various bilateral initiatives, including the Consultative Committee of the Presidents of Lithuania and Poland, the Assembly of the Members of the Lithuanian and Polish parliaments, and the Lithuanian and Polish governmental Cooperation Council. Warsaw was a main supporter of Lithuania's accession to both NATO and the EU and a protocol on defense cooperation was signed in July 2000. A military unit for international security and peacekeeping, LITPOLBAT, was the most significant bilateral project, as it joined Lithuania with a NATO member prior to Alliance accession.[124] In addition, the respective minority populations in both states enjoy substantial rights in preserving their language, culture, and education.

Diplomatic relations between Lithuania and the Russian Federation were established in July 1991 leading to signatures on several major agreements and high-level official bilateral meetings have featured regularly. Russia's relations with Lithuania have been less strained over minority issues than with Estonia or Latvia. Lithuania hosts a small Russian minority population and its citizenship law passed in 1989 included most current residents. Lithuania's border treaty with Russia was ratified by the Russian parliament in 2003, six years after it was signed by the countries' presidents. Nevertheless, relations between the two capitals have not been trouble-free. Since Lithuania's admission to NATO, Russian aircraft have repeatedly violated Lithuanian airspace, leading to official protests and suppositions that Moscow was intent on intimidating its smaller neighbors. Despite initial controversies, disputes have subsided over transit between Russia and its Kaliningrad region via Lithuania since the EU became more closely involved in resolving the issue.

Lithuania has continued to push for the augmentation of the EU's eastern policy, advocating democratic change and economic reform in neighboring states, particularly in Belarus and Ukraine. Lithuania, together with other CEE states, has experienced the shortcomings of EU policy and a secure eastern border and the stability of its neighbors remains a critical foreign policy and security priority. Vilnius also views the eastern dimension as an area of cooperation in which the U.S.-Lithuanian partnership can be further strengthened.

Vilnius has been actively engaged in promoting democratic reform and offering assistance to its eastern neighbors in order to prepare the countries for eventual NATO and EU accession. Officials and NGOs have been involved in numerous projects aimed at promoting democracy and strengthening civil society in Belarus, including training and seminars for Belarusian journalists and the democratic opposition. At the same time, Vilnius has encouraged Minsk to implement the recommendations of international organizations for ensuring human rights.[125] Vilnius welcomed U.S. Secretary of State Condoleezza Rice's strong message to Belarusian president Lukashenka during her visit to Lithuania in April 2005 as it reassured political leaders of Washington's commitment to democracy in the neighborhood.

In addition to active engagement in Belarus, Ukraine has also been a foreign policy priority for Vilnius. Lithuania played an instrumental role under Poland's initiative for a western diplomatic intervention in the 2004 postelection crisis in Kyiv. Where Russian interference in support of one presidential candidate was blatant, and the EU Commission was largely silent in the early stages of Ukraine's election crisis, Warsaw and Vilnius helped to mediate the standoff between Ukraine's two political blocs. Lithuania has also established cooperative projects to promote reform in Georgia, Moldova, and Armenia. Bilateral relations with Armenia were established in 2005 with the objective of increasing trade and economic cooperation. Vilnius has also backed Moldova's goal to join NATO.[126]

Political Options

Support for Lithuania's participation in the missions in Iraq and Afghanistan was comprehensive across the political spectrum. During parliamentary debates on Iraq, the New Democracy party voiced concern that Lithuania was giving too much to Washington and not enough to the core EU powers. The fear that the country would not be viewed as a reliable EU member was expressed by other smaller political formations.[127] In September 2005, the Liberal Democratic Party, led by the impeached former president Rolandas Paksas advocated the termination of Lithuania's military participation due to the threat of terrorist actions in Lithuania. A party statement advocated that Vilnius should align its policies regarding Iraq with the larger EU member states. It further emphasized that Vilnius should be sympathetic to Iraqi resistance against a foreign presence due to Lithuania's own history of occupation. The Liberal Democratic Party holds nine seats in the 141-member parliament. The smaller People's Progress Party and the Lithuanian People's Union for a Just Lithuania have also opposed the country's military involvement in Iraq. By December 2005, following the announcement of a gradual Polish withdrawal from Iraq, political debate intensified over the country's engagement. However, parliament voted against a resolution on troop withdrawal in December 2005 and instead approved an extension of its peacekeeping missions in the Persian Gulf, the Balkans, and Central Asia until the end of 2007.[128]

Public Opinion

Among the three Baltic states, Lithuania has registered the highest public support for the EU. A November 2005 poll showed that employment opportunities (48 percent) and increased exports (48 percent) were two principal benefits stemming from EU membership. Economic development (31 percent) and enhanced national security (29 percent) were also cited by respondents as positively correlated with the European Union. Future problems associated with EU membership included price increases (76 percent) and a potential brain drain (62 percent). Almost 40 percent of Lithuanians fear that the EU will be "dictatorial," with the potential to undermine the country's sovereignty.[129] However, enlargement is favored by 69 percent of citizens.[130]

Support for NATO has also been high among Lithuanian citizens. Ahead of accession, between 61 and 68 percent of residents viewed the Alliance with favor according to surveys conducted between 1998 and 2002. Between 2004 and 2005, these figures remained around 60 percent, while 21 percent of inhabitants were opposed to the Alliance.[131] NATO membership has been considered not only as a guarantee of the country's security, but also as a means for economic growth by improving conditions for increased foreign investment. Although the majority of Lithuanians do not perceive external threats to the country, many have felt that the country's security is most vulnerable to international organized crime and official corruption.

NOTES

1. Toomas Ilves, quoted in Mikko Lagerspetz, "How Many Nordic Countries? Possibilities and Limits of Geopolitical Identity Construction," *Journal of Cooperation and Conflict: Journal of the Nordic International Studies Association* 38, no. 1: 53.

2. For the ethnic breakdown of Latvia's population, see the Latvian Statistical Office at www.csb.lv/lteksts.cfm?tem_kods=dem&datums=%7Bts%20'2005-06-29% 2013:00:00'%7D (accessed March 10, 2006). According to the Latvian law on citizenship adopted in 1995 and amended in 1997 and 1998, persons who were Latvian citizens on June 17, 1940, and their descendents, were granted automatic citizenship. See the Council of Europe, Legal Affairs, at www.coe.int/T/E/Legal_Affairs/Legal_ co-operation/Foreigners_and_citizens/Nationality/Documents/National_legislation/ Latvia-Law%20on%20citizenship.asp (accessed March 7, 2006).

Estonia similarly granted automatic citizenship to individuals and their descendents since the interwar period (1918–1940). See Human Rights Watch at www.hrw .org/reports/1994/WR94/Helsinki-08.htm (accessed March 9, 2006).

Lithuania was the first Baltic state to have a law on citizenship in 1989, which granted citizenship to those persons who could prove that they were permanent residents and legally employed for the past ten years. See Human Rights Watch, "Estonia, Latvia, and Lithuania," at www.hrw.org/reports/1992/WR92/HSW-03.htm#P206_ 57306 (accessed March 9, 2006).

3. Population data taken from the CIA World Factbook, January 2006.

4. Erik Männik, "Estonia and the European Defence Policy: A Realist View," in *The Estonian Foreign Policy Yearbook 2005,* ed. Andres Kasekamp (Tallinn: The Estonian Foreign Policy Institute, 2005): 76–77.

5. Keith C. Smith, "Current Implications of Russian Energy Policies," *CSIS Europe Program Issue Brief* (Washington, D.C.: Center for Strategic and International Studies, January 2006).

6. Toomas Hendrik Ilves, "The Pleiades Join the Stars: Trans-Atlanticism and Eastern Enlargement," *Cambridge Review of International Affairs* 18, no. 2 (July 2005): 10.

7. A border treaty was signed between Russia and Lithuania in 1997. A treaty demarcating borders was signed with Estonia in May 2005, but Moscow withdrew its signature in June over what it called an "untruthful preamble" drafted by Tallinn, which included the terms "aggression by the Soviet Union" and "illegal incorporation" of Estonia by the Soviet Union. Latvia was due to sign a border treaty with Russia in May 2005, but Moscow refused to sign the pact after Riga appended a declaration saying that Latvia had been occupied by the Soviet Union.

8. Kristi Raik and Teemu Palosaari, *It's the Taking Part that Counts: The New Member States Adapt to EU Foreign and Security Policy,* FIIA Report (Finnish Institute of International Affairs, 2004): 30.

9. In March 1998, approximately 1,000 elderly Latvians protested price increases in front of the Riga City Council. The protest was not authorized by permits while several newspapers had advertised the demonstration. Police broke up the protest. Moscow criticized Riga over its human rights' policies and many in Latvia looked toward Russia as the instigator of the event in an effort to destabilize and discredit the country. See Andrejs Plakans, "Twelve Months on a Roller Coaster," *Transitions Online,* January 26, 1999.

10. Vladimir Socor, *Eurasia Daily Monitor* 2, no. 169 (September 13, 2005) The Jamestown Foundation.

11. Christopher Browning, "Complementarities and Differences in EU and U.S. Policies in Northern Europe," *Journal of International Relations and Development* 6, no. 1 (March 2003): 23–50.

12. Estonian Ministry of Foreign Affairs, "Estonia and the U.S.," February 15, 2005, at www.vm.ee/eng/kat_176/aken_prindi/412.html (accessed June 10, 2005).

13. White House Summary on U.S.-Baltic Charter, January 16, 1998, at www.fas .org/man/nato/national/98011609_wpo.html (accessed September 12, 2005).

14. For a summary of the high and low points of U.S.-Russian relations in the past decade see Vahur Made, "Estonian-Russian Relations in the Context of the International System," in *The Estonian Foreign Policy Yearbook 2005*, ed. Andres Kasekamp (Tallinn: The Estonian Foreign Policy Institute, 2005).

15. See Ilves, "The Pleiades Join the Stars."

16. Authors' interviews with foreign affairs representatives and officials in Vilnius, Tallinn, and Riga, May/June 2005.

17. National Security Concept of the Republic of Estonia (Tallinn, 2004).

18. Estonia was the best prepared of the Baltic countries to enter into talks for EU accession and its pre-negotiation questionnaire was the most complete of the three Baltic states. In addition, opening talks with Estonia sent a clear message to Moscow that the Baltic states would eventually join the Union.

19. *AFX European Focus*, "Estonia Votes to Join EU," September 15, 2003.

20. The Estonian Government's European Union Policy, 2004–2006, April 22, 2004 at www.riigikantselei.ee/failid/The_Government_s_European_Policy_for_ 2004_2006_FINAL.pdf (accessed June 15, 2005).

21. Eurobarometer 64: Public Opinion in the European Union (December 2005).

22. Ibid.

23. Estonian Ministry of Foreign Affairs, "Regional Cooperation: Baltic States," www.vm.ee/eng/kat_176/ (accessed January 30, 2006).

24. *Financial Times Information*, "Small Nation Helps Build Democracy in Iraq, Afghanistan," February 1, 2006.

25. Estonian Ministry of Defense, "Estonian Participation in International Operations," July 1, 2005, at www.mod.gov.ee/?op=body&id=249 (accessed November 1, 2005). *Global Security*, "Iraq Coalition Troops," at www.globalsecurity.org/military/ ops/iraq_orbat_coalition.htm (accessed January 14, 2006). See also, *Financial Times Information*, "Small Nation Helps Build Democracy in Iraq, Afghanistan," February 1, 2006.

26. NATO International Staff, "NATO-Russia Compendium of Financial and Economic Data Relating to Defence," June 9, 2005, p. 7, www.nato.int/docu/pr/ 2005/p050609.pdf (accessed January 13, 2006). In each Baltic state, 2 percent of GDP has been budgeted annually for defense spending. However, various factors, ranging from higher-than-expected GDP growth, shortfalls in tax collection and reallocation of resources, have created the illusion that commitments were not met.

27. Ministry of Foreign Affairs, "Support for NATO Membership," July 12, 2005, at www.vm.ee/eng/nato/kat_359/1007.html (accessed July 29, 2005).

28. Estonian Ministry of Foreign Affairs, "Estonia and the U.S.," February 15, 2005, at www.vm.ee/eng/kat_176/aken_prindi/412.html (accessed July 1, 2005).

29. John Springford, "'Old' and 'New' Europeans United: Public Attitudes Towards the Iraq War and US Foreign Policy," *Background Brief* (London: Centre for European Reform, 2003).

30. *Radio Free Europe/Radio Liberty Newsline*, March 22, 2003.

31. *Radio Free Europe/Radio Liberty Newsline*, March 26, 2003.

32. Gallup International, "Post War Iraq 2003 Poll," www.gallup-international .com/download/Post%20war%20Iraq%202003%20Results%20update%2013 .05%20-%20Rest%20of%20the%20World.pdf (accessed June 15, 2005).

33. Baltic News Service, "Estonian Parlt Extends Defense Forces Mission in Iraq," April 20, 2005.

34. Baltic News Service, "Estonian Parliament Extends Defense Forces Mission in Iraq," December 7, 2005.

35. Rory Carroll, "Estonian Troops Relish Iraqi Patrols," *The Guardian* (London), September 3, 2005.

36. "Report to the Baltic Assembly: Fulfillment of the 2004 Working Plan of the Baltic Council of Ministers." Tenth Baltic Council in Riga, December 17–19, 2004.

37. The Nordic-Baltic-Eight is comprised of Sweden, Finland, Norway, Iceland, Denmark, Estonia, Latvia, and Lithuania. See Aksel Kirch, "Quick Pace Leaves Some Struggling," *Transitions Online*, April 4, 2003.

38. Lisbeth Kirk, "Northern Europe Demands a Clear Russia Policy," *EUObserver*, October 25, 2005.

39. Estonian Ministry of Foreign Affairs, "Estonia Signed Memorandum of Understanding on EU Battle Group," at www.vm.ee/eng/nato/kat_332/5459.html (accessed June 7, 2005).

40. Estonian Ministry of Foreign Affairs, "Estonia: Regional Relations, Bilateral Relations," at www.vm.ee/eng/kat_176/ (accessed February 8, 2006).

41. Tallinn Eesti Paevaleht, "Estonian Foreign Minister Finds EU Colleagues' Stand on Border Issue Supportive," July 18, 2005. ITAR-TASS, "Russia Relieves Itself of Obligations under Estonian Treaties," August 16, 2005. See also, Interfax News Agency, "Estonia's Position over Border Treaties Unchanged," August 16, 2005.

42. Agence France Presse, "Estonian FM May Meet Russian Counterpart After Visa Dispute," November 15, 2005. See also ITAR-TASS, June 20, 2005.

43. Aleksei Gunter, "Estonia's New Government Ready," *The Baltic Times*, April 10, 2003.

44. Wikipedia, "Politics of Estonia," at en.wikipedia.org/wiki/Politics_of_Estonia (accessed March 9, 2006).

45. Authors' interview with Baltic analyst in Washington, D.C., February 2006.

46. BBC Monitoring, "Estonian Opposition Split, Government Going Strong—Newspaper," December 31, 2004.

47. Baltic News Service, "Estonian Parlt Extends Defense Forces Mission in Iraq," December 7, 2005.

48. Albert Maloveryan, "Estonians Pin Hope for Security on NATO, EU, Good Ties with Russia," ITAR-TASS News Agency, July 1, 2005.

49. Gallup International, "Post War Iraq 2003 Poll."

50. Aksel Kirch, "Quick Pace Leaves Some Struggling," *Transitions Online*, April 4, 2003.

51. Eurobarometer 64: Public Opinion in the European Union (December 2005).

52. Authors' interviews with Baltic analysts in Washington, D.C., February 2006.

53. There was no robust pro-EU campaign in Estonia prior to membership. As Estonia's economy has developed the fastest within the European Union, coupled with the fact that Estonia is one the most economically liberal countries, citizens see the EU's regulations as inhibiting Estonia's future growth. See Mel Huang, "What the EU Brings to Estonia," *Central Europe Review*, May 31, 1999, at /www .ce-review.org/authorarchives/amber_archive/amber36old.html (accessed March 11, 2006).

54. Estonian Ministry of Foreign Affairs, "Public Opinion on the European Union," February 6, 2006, at www.vm.ee/eng/euro/kat_315/2973.html (accessed February 14, 2006).

55. Foreign Minister Sandra Kalniete, "Latvia's Foreign Policy at the Crossroads of Change," *Yearbook of Politics: Latvia 2004* (Riga: Zināte Publishers, 2005), 20–33.

56. Edjis Boš, "Understanding Baltic Atlanticism: Latvia 1988-2003" (M.Phil. diss., University of Cambridge, July 2004).

57. For an overview of Baltic-Russian relations see Keith C. Smith, "Baltic-Russian Relations: Implications for European Security" (Washington, D.C.: Center for Strategic and International Studies, February 2002).

58. See F. Stephen Larabee, "The Baltic States and NATO Membership," Testimony presented to the United States Senate Committee on Foreign Relations, April 3, 2003. Available online at http://www.rand.org/pubs/testimonies/2005/CT204.pdf (accessed March 7, 2006).

59. See International Foundation for Election Systems (IFES) Election Guide at http://www.electionguide.org/results.php?ID=379 (accessed February 10, 2006).

60. Eurobarometer 64 (December 2005).

61. Ibid.

62. Authors' interviews with defense officials in Riga, May 2005.

63. Eurobarometer 64 (December 2005).

64. BALTBAT fulfilled its objectives and was disbanded in September 2003.

65. Estonian Ministry of Foreign Affairs, "Regional Cooperation: Baltic States," www.vm.ee/eng/kat_176/ (accessed January 30, 2006).

66. Jeffrey Simon, *NATO Expeditionary Operations: Impacts upon New Members and Partners*, Occasional Paper no. 1 (Washington, D.C.: National Defense University Press, Institute for National Strategic Studies, March 2005).

67. *Baltic Caucus Update*, vol. 3, no. 1, Baltic American Freedom League, January 2003.

68. "Attitude Towards Membership of Latvia in NATO," at www.am.gov/lv/en/nato/news/4455/?pg=6031 (accessed December 5, 2005).

69. Agence France Presse, "Latvian Support for International Peacekeeping Missions Soars: Poll," September 14, 2005.

70. Authors' interviews with defense officials in Riga, May 2005.

71. *NATO International Staff*, "NATO-Russia Compendium of Financial and Economic Data Relating to Defence," June 9, 2005, 7, www.nato.int/docu/pr/2005/p050609.pdf (accessed January 13, 2006).

72. For an overview of U.S. policy making and the Baltic states during the mid-1990s, see Ronald Asmus, "A Baltic Challenge," *Lithuanian Foreign Policy Review*, 2003/1–2 (11–12): 26–37. See also Edjis Boš, "Understanding Baltic Atlanticism: Latvia 1988–2003." Iceland was the first country to recognize the newly independent Latvian state, followed by Denmark and Sweden. The Nordic states provided financial and diplomatic assistance to Riga and at the same time encouraged the Atlanticist orientation of Latvia's foreign policy.

73. Boš, "Understanding Baltic Atlanticism."

74. Ria Novosti, "Latvia's Army Can Participate in NATO Military Operations," January 31, 2002.

75. Boš, "Understanding Baltic Atlanticism," 63–64.

76. Baltic News Service, "U.S. President Unfreezes Military Assistance Programs to Lithuania, 5 Central European Countries," November 24, 2003.

77. Agence France Presse, "Latvia Extends Mission of its Peacekeepers in Iraq," November 10, 2005.

78. See the Latvian Ministry of Foreign Affairs at www.am.gov.lv/en/nato/4455/?pg=6814 (last accessed December 5, 2005).

79. John Springford, "'Old' and 'New' Europeans United: Public Attitudes Towards the Iraq War and US Foreign Policy," Background Brief, Centre for European Reform, 2003.

80. Simon, *NATO Expeditionary Operations*, 28. Also, authors' interviews with defense officials in Riga, May 2005.

81. Springford, "'Old' and 'New' Europeans United."

82. Boš, "Understanding Baltic Atlanticism."

83. BBC Monitoring International Reports, "Latvian President Criticized and Praised for Decision to Visit Moscow on 9 May," January 14, 2005.

84. See Wikipedia, "History of Latvia," at en.wikipedia.org/wiki/Latvia (accessed March 1, 2006).

85. Interfax News Agency, "Russian Diplomat Slams Riga for 'Raking-Up' Soviet Past," August 13, 2005.

86. Speech by Prime Minister Indulis Emsis at the Bureau of European Commission, Berlin, July 9, 2004, "European Union Policy Toward the New Neighbors: The View of Latvia," in the *Commission of Strategic Analysis, Yearbook of Politics: Latvia 2004* (Zināte, 2005): 14–19.

87. Eurobarometer 64 (December 2005).

88. Baltic News Service, "Parliament Supports Latvia's Participation in Operations Disarming Iraq," March 20, 2003.

89. Baltic News Service, "Latvian Parliament Extends Mandate of Peacekeepers in Iraq," December 4, 2003.

90. Agence France Presse, "Latvian Soldiers to Remain in Iraq Until June 2005," September 9, 2004.

91. Agence France Presse, "Latvia Extends Mission of its Peacekeepers in Iraq," November 10, 2005.

92. BBC Monitoring, "One Year On, Latvian Governing Coalition Seen as Stable but Complex," December 1, 2005.

93. BBC Monitoring, "Latvian MPs Debate Military Presence in Iraq," December 1, 2005.

94. Baltic News Service, "Latvian Socialist Leader Calls for Stronger Ties with Russia, Referendum on NATO," December 8, 2001.

95. "Attitude Towards Membership of Latvia in NATO," at www.am.gov/lv/en/nato/news/4455/?pg=6031 (accessed December 5, 2005).

96. Authors' interviews with NGO representatives in Riga, May 2005.

97. Ibid.

98. See Candidate Countries Eurobarometer (CCEB) 2001 (Autumn 2001), CCEB 2002 (Autumn 2002), and CCEB 2003.2 (Spring 2003).

99. Eurobarometer 64 (December 2005), 13–14.

100. Minorities at Risk Project (MAR), "Chronology for Russians in Lithuania," (University of Maryland, 2004) at www.cidcm.umd.edu/inscr/mar/chronology.asp?groupId=36802 (accessed March 1, 2006).

101. For a comprehensive list of bilateral treaties signed between CEE states on good neighborly relations and minority protection before 1999, see Kinga Gál, "Bilateral Agreements in Central and Eastern Europe: A New Inter-State Framework for Minority Protection?" ECMI Working Paper 4 (Flensburg: European Centre for Minority Issues, May 1999).

102. *Lithuania's Security and Foreign Policy Strategy*, Center for Strategic and International Studies and the Institute of International Relations and Political Science, (Washington, D.C.: CSIS, 2002).

103. Authors' interviews with officials and NGO representatives in Vilnius, May 2005.

104. Ministry of Foreign Affairs of the Republic of Lithuania, "Agreement between Political Parties of the Republic of Lithuania on the Main Foreign Policy Goals and Objectives for 2004-2008" at http://www.urm.lt/popup2.php?item_id=255 (accessed February 12, 2006).

105. Ibid.

106. *Baltic Caucus Update*, vol. 3, no. 1 (Baltic American Freedom League, January 2003).

107. See Kestutis Jankauskas, "NATO, ESDP, and Relations with the USA," in *Third Baltic-German Dialogue* (Berlin: Stiftung Wissenschaft und Politik, August 2004), 34–35.

108. Ibid., 35.

109. Dovile Budryte, "The Dilemma of 'Dual Loyalty': Lithuania and Transatlantic Tensions," in *Old Europe, New Europe and the U.S.*, edited by Tom Landford and Blagovest Tashev (London: Ashgate, 2005), 160.

110. Quoted in Budryte, "The Dilemma of 'Dual Loyalty,'" 161.

111. Eurobarometer 64 (December 2005).

112. Ibid.

113. *Lithuania's Security and Foreign Policy Strategy*, Center for Strategic and International Studies and the Institute of International Relations and Political Science (Washington, D.C.: CSIS, 2002).

114. NATO International Staff, "NATO-Russia Compendium of Financial and Economic Data Relating to Defence," June 9, 2005, p. 7, www.nato.int/docu/pr/2005/p050609.pdf (accessed January 13, 2006).

115. *Lithuania's Security and Foreign Policy Strategy*, Center for Strategic and International Studies and the Institute of International Relations and Political Science (Washington, D.C.: CSIS, 2002).

116. Lithuanian National Ministry of Defense, www.lrv.lt (accessed January 10, 2006).

117. Baltic News Service, "Lithuania-Led Mission in Afghanistan May Get Considerable EU Financial Assistance," January 4, 2006.

118. Agence France Presse, "Year After Joining NATO, Even More Lithuanians Support Membership: Poll," April 20, 2005.

119. *Lithuania's Security and Foreign Policy Strategy*, Center for Strategic and International Studies and the Institute of International Relations and Political Science (Washington, D.C.: CSIS, 2002).

120. Baltic News Service, "U.S. President Unfreezes Military Assistance Programs to Lithuania, 5 Central European Countries," November 24, 2003.

121. Lithuanian National Ministry of Defense. See also Baltic News Service, "Lithuanian Reducing Number of Its Troops in Iraq," November 25, 2005.

122. Gallup International, "Post War Iraq 2003 Poll."

123. *Lithuania's Security and Foreign Policy Strategy*, Center for Strategic and International Studies and the Institute of International Relations and Political Science (Washington, D.C.: CSIS, 2002).

124. Ibid. See also Vygaudas Ušackas, "Strengthening the U.S.-Lithuania Partnership: Lithuanian Perspective," *Lithuanian Foreign Policy Review* 2003/1–2 (11–12) at http://www.lfpr.lt/latest.phtml

125. BBC Monitoring, "Lithuania to Assist Armenia in European Integration," Public Television of Armenia, Yerevan, June 30, 2005.

126. Budryte, "The Dilemma of 'Dual Loyalty,'" 158.

127. Agence France Presse, "Lithuanian Parliament Rejects Call to Withdraw Troops from Iraq," December 15, 2005. See also, Baltic News Service, "Lithuanian Parliament Chair Sees Lack of Strategy on Future Presence of Troops in Iraq," December 16, 2005.

128. BBC Monitoring, "Lithuanian Opinion Poll Shows Positive, Negative Opinions on EU Accession," January 8, 2006.

129. Eurobarometer 64 (December 2005).

130. Agence France Presse, "Year After Joining NATO, Even More Lithuanians Support Membership: Poll," April 20, 2005.

Chapter Six

Balkan Partners

Romania and Bulgaria

Bucharest and Sofia exhibit some differences in their approaches to the United States, the European Union, and NATO. Romania has sought to position itself as the main U.S. partner and key player in the Balkan region, effectively capitalizing on its geostrategic location and as a valuable jumping off point for U.S. military operations in the Middle East. Bucharest places strong emphasis on its bilateral relations with Washington, as it sees U.S. involvement in the Black Sea region as crucial for its security and economic interests and as a counterforce to Russian influence. Furthermore, Romania has actively advocated American commitment to resolving the "frozen conflicts" close to its borders, especially in neighboring Moldova. Bulgaria, also occupying a strategically valuable location, has focused on strengthening its partnership with the United States as well. However, Sofia has at times taken a more cautious approach, more in tune with eroding public support for U.S. military missions overseas. Bulgaria has not aspired to assume a stronger leadership position in the Black Sea region and instead views its responsibilities defined under the auspices of NATO membership. In many respects Sofia sees multilateralism, especially its role in NATO, the EU, and the UN, as a preferred mechanism for upholding its national interests.

Romania and Bulgaria are the region's late reformers, taking six and seven years, respectively, to complete a thorough transformation from the makeshift policies of the postcommunist Socialist administrations that dominated politics during much of the 1990s. It was Romania's Constantinescu government from 1996 to 2000 and Bulgaria's Kostov government between 1997 and 2001 that initiated the shift toward Western institutions and commenced comprehensive economic, political, social, and military restructuring. Since then, there has been a notable consistency in the foreign and security policies of both states. As a result, Bucharest and Sofia became full-fledged NATO members in 2004 and are scheduled to join the European Union in 2007.

ROMANIA

Democracy took root slowly in Romania, the largest country in the CEE region, with a population of 22.3 million. The secong political coalition, which took over power after Nicolae Ceauşescu's execution on Christmas Day in 1989, was an integral part of the Communist state apparatus. The political leadership, divided between communist reformers and quasi-democrats, embraced reform gradually while the democratic political opposition was too weak to challenge the new regime. The lack of a genuine reformist wing within the Communist Party, coupled with the absence of a strong dissident movement, undermined Romania's development throughout much of the early 1990s.[1]

Only by 1996 did reformists gain sufficient strength to form a viable opposition. However, since 1996, Romania's governments have displayed a determination to more resolutely tackle social and economic problems, embrace democratic values, and join NATO and the EU. Although still lagging behind with regard to key economic indicators, Romania has received recognition of its reformist endeavors and its commitment to regional security.

Bucharest's foreign policy and security agenda, especially in the post-9/11 context, has enabled the country to raise its international profile. Romania has become a stalwart U.S. ally in the war against international terrorists, having contributed troops to missions in Afghanistan and Iraq, as well as supplying peacekeeping troops to Bosnia-Herzegovina and Kosova. In early January 2003, ahead of the operations in Iraq, Prime Minister Adrian Năstase stated that "Romania has its own interests and partners with which it wants to further collaborate, both within NATO and within the EU."[2] Although most CEE states have been accused by critics of favoring America ahead of the European Union, Romania has been reproached particularly vehemently. Romania was the first European country to sign a bilateral immunity agreement with Washington, exempting U.S. citizens from the International Criminal Court (ICC), thus contradicting overall EU policy. Regarding the EU request that Bucharest halt international child adoptions following reports of abuse and trafficking in children, Romania vacillated under alleged U.S. pressure to allow such adoptions to continue.

With regard to its commitments to foreign missions, Bucharest has been assertive and unwavering. Although military operations pose a significant fiscal burden for the country, the government has been consistent in supporting the efforts in Iraq and Afghanistan and has benefited from overwhelming political consensus. With the exception of the ultranationalist Greater Romania Party (GRP), parties across the spectrum view a strong partnership with the United States as essential for elevating the country's stature, raising foreign direct investment, and increasing its overall security. In July 2005, when many other states had set timetables for troop withdrawal, President Traian Basescu stated that the "U.S. may count on Romania's further contributions to the fight against terrorism. Our country will comply with all its engagements taken in Iraq and Afghanistan, as long as it takes."[3]

In late 2005, in recognition of the U.S-Romanian partnership, Washington and Bucharest signed an agreement to station U.S. military bases on Romanian territory. Although the bases are not expected to bring substantial direct economic benefits to Romania, the U.S. presence is likely to increase investor confidence.

Romania perceives itself as an essential player in consolidating the transatlantic relationship and, despite occasional policy clashes with Brussels, Romania has also worked hard to implement reforms necessary for EU entry. Bucharest managed to close all chapters of the EU's *acquis communautaire*, and on April 25, 2005, together with Sofia, it signed the treaty on EU accession. If Romania maintains rigor in implementing the reforms, and if the process is not delayed by internal EU problems, Bucharest should be on track for EU accession in January 2007.

Romania's desire to act as a catalyst in consolidating transatlantic relations is particularly visible in its regional policies. Bucharest views the Black Sea zone as an area where the interests of Brussels and Washington converge, especially regarding energy, terrorism, and transnational crime. Romania thus aims to be a key actor in the region and a generator of stability for the wider neighborhood.

The European Union

During communist rule, Romania's foreign policy was the most independent of the Soviet satellite states; the country was the first in the CEE region to establish official relations with the European Community through its inclusion in 1974 in the Community's Generalized System of Preferences. Diplomatic relations were established in 1990 after the ouster of Ceauşescu. On June 22, 1995 Bucharest formally submitted its application for EU membership and in 2000 accession talks began. The Copenhagen Summit in December 2002 cited 2007 as a possible entry date for Romania and Bulgaria. Both countries lagged behind the other CEE states due to the lingering influence of former communists, which thwarted the transition process and contributed to "political clientelism, criminalization of the economy and society, and partisan control of the administration and the judiciary."[4] Bucharest and Sofia initially disliked being paired for EU entry but their shared sense of competition helped to push both capitals forward with tough reforms.

Support for EU membership has extended beyond the political elite and the Union has consistently been perceived positively among the Romanian population. Public support for the EU registered at 75 percent in the fall of 2004 and 66 percent in the spring of 2005 with 70 percent of the population believing that membership will bring advantages to the country.[5] The high public backing stems from the popular expectation that Union entry will raise living standards and ease the movement of goods and people. Support for the EU is also a consequence of the belief that Romania rightfully belongs within the European family and not at its periphery.

After the EU Accession Treaty was signed in April 2005, it was presented for ratification in the parliaments of the twenty-five member states. Twelve countries, including the Netherlands, Greece, Latvia, Estonia, Italy, Spain, Cyprus, Slovakia, Slovenia, Hungary, the Czech Republic, and Malta, had endorsed the treaty by February 2006.[6] However, problems related to the EU constitution, budgetary adjustments, institutional restructuring, and labor movement have eroded popular support for further Union enlargement among EU citizens. The new EU members are more supportive of Romania's membership bid than are the EU-15 countries: out of the ten new member states 53 percent of those surveyed favored Romania's entry into the Union compared to 43 percent of citizens from the EU-15.[7]

Romania is scheduled to accede to the EU in 2007 together with Bulgaria. However the Accession Treaty includes a provision that allows the Commission to delay both countries' entry date by one year, should the states fail to meet the necessary requirements. EU admission will be a consequence of Romania's determination to execute domestic reforms, especially in the judicial and administrative systems. Although Romanians support EU entry and enlargement, they do not view the country's EU membership as a substitute for partnership with Washington. Domestic polls in October 2005 showed only 16 percent of citizens advocated a unified Europe that contests the power of the United States, while 52 percent believed that EU and the United States should be equal partners.[8] Seventy-five percent of the public supports a common defense and security policy according to a December 2005 Eurobarometer poll, up five percentage points from surveys conducted in mid-2005.[9] Although support for NATO membership has remained slightly lower than that for the EU, hovering at around 60 percent, most Romanian politicians believe that the continent can be secured only through a combined EU-NATO effort.

Once Romania joins the Union, it will be the seventh largest state in population. Older EU members have expressed concern over the impact of Romania on EU policy given Bucharest's strongly pro-U.S. orientation and alleged disregard for its traditional allies, such as France. French president Jacques Chirac's harsh rejoinder to Romania and Bulgaria's signatures on the February 2003 Vilnius 10 declaration was in part a reaction to Bucharest's purported snub of the historical relationship with Paris. Romania's positions on disputed issues such as the ICC and international adoptions were eventually reconciled with EU policies ahead of the country's EU accession. However, critics have alleged that after membership is finalized, Romania could become a "Trojan horse" of the United States in Europe as Bucharest may disregard any common EU foreign and security policy.

NATO Involvement

Early public support for Romania's NATO entry was a result of the security gap left by the dissolution of the Warsaw Pact. This vacuum became increasingly evident during the wars in the former Yugoslavia in the early to mid-1990s. In October 1991, President Ion Iliescu expressed his country's interest in a partner relationship with NATO and in January 1994 Romania became the first postcommunist state to join the Partnership for Peace (PfP) program. By the end of 1995, Romania and NATO signed an agreement permitting the transit of NATO noncombat aircraft through Romanian territory. Bucharest's desire for membership was reiterated in February 1997 by newly elected President Emil Constantinescu at a meeting of the NATO Council in Brussels. However, at the July 1997 Madrid Summit, Romania was deprived of an invitation to the Alliance. Despite this disappointment, in October 1998 parliament conceded to NATO's request for airspace in the event of military action against Serbia. During the March 1999 intervention over Kosova, Bucharest granted several NATO requests despite prevailing public sentiments toward Belgrade. Some media commentaries viewed the NATO intervention as the first step toward Kosova's eventual independence, which could allegedly set a precedent for potential Hungarian separatism in Transylvania. Bucharest, similar to Sofia, denied over-flight rights to Russia during the crisis and helped enable NATO to occupy Kosova at the end of the war.

Similar to other CEE states, Romania's political leaders perceive NATO as necessary for stability and security, while at the same time Bucharest feels less directly threatened by historical adversaries. Although Moscow attempted to dissuade Bucharest from joining NATO, the threat of Russian domination was not as strong an incentive for pursuing membership as it was for the Baltic republics or Poland. Lingering Russian influence is more visible in the breakaway Transnistria region of neighboring Moldova.

At the Washington Summit in April 1999, Romania was officially recognized, together with six other CEE states, as a candidate for future NATO membership. But Romanian officials remained frustrated that no precise date for accession was given.[10] Nevertheless, the government continued to support NATO operations. The armed forces participated in peacekeeping missions in Bosnia-Herzegovina and Kosova in the late 1990s. Since January 2002, Bucharest has also committed approximately 550 troops to NATO's International Security Assistance Force (ISAF) in Afghanistan and has participated in numerous missions initiated by the United States. In order to fulfill NATO requirements, Romania increased civilian control over the military, downsized and modernized the armed forces, and improved transparency in defense-related matters.[11] Romania was invited to join NATO at the November 2002 Prague Summit, where allied leaders agreed to transform the Alliance to meet contemporary threats according to the Prague Capabilities Commitment (PCC). Romania vowed to continue its military reform and restructuring, to offer forces within the PCC and to allocate between 2.5 and 2.8 percent of its GDP to defense.[12] Parliament ratified the treaty for joining NATO in February 2004 and the official ceremony for Alliance induction was held in March 2004.

Romania has worked hard to prove itself as a reliable NATO ally and U.S. partner. In April 2004, Bucharest donated 1,500 AK-47 assault rifles, rocket launchers, and over 200 light machine guns to the Afghan National Army. In August 2005, it augmented its forces with an additional 400 soldiers under NATO command. In 2005, Romania contributed 13.5 million euros to NATO's common resources, equal to 1.14 percent of Alliance spending.[13] Bucharest's defense budget in 2005 reached 1.5 billion euros, and is earmarked to increase to 2.025 billion euros in 2006.[14] In line with NATO requirements, Romania achieved the full professionalization of its navy and air force by the end of 2005 and hoped to complete the same process for the army by the end of 2006.

Despite the fact that three Romanian soldiers were killed between 2003 and 2005 in military missions overseas, the general population remains supportive of NATO. An October 2005 survey showed that 64 percent of the population favored NATO membership. Forty-seven percent believed that membership brought advantages to the country, whereas only 13 percent viewed the relationship as disadvantageous. Twenty-seven percent perceived neither benefits nor drawbacks, and 13 percent held no opinion on the matter.[15] The main benefits of Romania's membership in the Alliance includes security guarantees, political recognition, and the transfer of military and technical knowledge. NATO also opened new opportunities for the country's defense industry. Bucharest has improved cooperation with NATO agencies such as NAMSA

(NATO Maintenance and Supply Agency) and NC3A (the NATO Consultation, Command and Control Agency). As a result, NAMSA has added eleven Romanian companies to its database of possible equipment providers, while one Romanian company signed a basic ordering agreement with NC3A, allowing it to participate in the agency's international bids.[16]

For Bucharest, NATO accession signaled one of its most significant foreign policy achievements and provided recognition of Romania's progress in implementing reform. NATO's future role in global security remains vital for Romania as the country provides one of the largest military contributions to the Alliance among the new members. Romanians see NATO not only as a political and military alliance, but also as a system of values to which they adhere, while a weakened NATO is seen as undermining transatlantic relations. The next NATO summit in Riga in November 2006 will be focused on broadening the Alliance mandate both regionally and operationally. Romania will likely seek to ensure a NATO-operational footprint along Europe's eastern border and will use its experience to address the unstable areas in the CIS (Commonwealth of Independent States), along the Black Sea littoral, and in the Western Balkans.

U.S. Relations

U.S.-Romanian relations started to thaw as President Ceauşescu began to distance Romania from Soviet foreign policy, and scientific, educational, and cultural exchanges between the two countries were cultivated much earlier than in the rest of the CEE region. Improving official contacts throughout the 1960s and 1970s led to the visit of U.S. president Richard Nixon to Bucharest in 1969 and culminated in the granting of Most Favored Nation (MFN) trading status by Washington to Romania in 1975. However, the deterioration of human rights during the 1980s led the U.S. Congress to revoke Romania's MFN status. Following the fall of Communism, Washington encouraged and assisted Romania's political, economic, and social transformation. By 1997, the election of the reformist government under the leadership of President Emil Constantinescu visibly improved relations.[17]

Since September 11, 2001, two governing coalitions have been highly supportive of U.S. policy. In 2001, the Party of Social Democracy of Romania-Social Democratic Party (PSDR-SDP), led by Ion Iliescu, formed the government with an official agreement of cooperation with the Hungarian Democratic Federation of Romania (HDFR). Both government and parliament denounced the 9/11 attacks and appealed to all democratic states to combat terrorism.[18] Parliament voted to grant the use of its airspace, territorial waters, and land to NATO in the war against transnational terrorists.[19]

In August 2002, Romania signed a bilateral agreement with Washington, invoking Article 98 of the International Criminal Court (ICC) treaty exempting U.S. citizens from prosecution. Romania was the first European state to do so, and was second overall following Israel. Its signature generated harsh criticism from the EU for ignoring a common European position. Bucharest calculated that it had more to gain at that time from its alliance with Washington than with Brussels. One immediate benefit was realized when the United States strongly backed Romania's membership in NATO. Some analysts attribute such assertive decision making by Bucharest as a keen ability to calculate risks and benefits. Nevertheless, critics charge that the government has a limited policy-planning staff and undertakes *ad hoc* decisions. Bucharest subsequently postponed the ratification of the ICC agreement in order to appease the EU ahead of the country's accession, scheduled for 2007.

Romania signed the Vilnius 10 declaration in February 2003, which stated that "the United States presented compelling evidence to the United Nations Security Council detailing Iraq's weapons of mass destruction programs, its active efforts to deceive UN inspectors, and its links to international terrorism." The move prompted strong criticism by French President Jacques Chirac for Bucharest's pro-American stance, especially in view of Romania's traditionally close ties with France. To clarify its position, Bucharest released an official statement, asserting that it understood the dangers posed by the regime in Baghdad and believed that the international community should act in solidarity against the dangers posed by weapons of mass destruction.[20] President Iliescu also addressed a letter to President George W. Bush in early February 2003 in which he guaranteed Romania's resolute commitment to the international struggle against terrorists.[21] Iliescu repeatedly stated that Romania would stand with Washington, but frequently added that the country did not possess sufficient military capabilities. In March 2003, surveys showed that 86.6 percent of Romanians did not support Romania's participation in Iraq without a UN mandate.[22]

On February 10, 2003, the Romanian Supreme Defense Council (CSAT), a body that included the president, the prime minister, the minister of national defense, the minister of interior, and the minister of foreign affairs, allowed the United States to use the country's airspace and infrastructure in case of a military attack against Iraq. Parliament approved this decision. The Council also agreed that the country could deploy 149 engineers, 25 military police, four liaison officers, 30 medics, and a decontamination unit of 70 personnel.[23] Parliament approved the deployment with 351 votes in favor and 74 abstentions. However, after the arrival of U.S. troops in Romania in late February 2003, Romanian defense minister Ioan Mircea Paşcu and foreign minister Mircea Dan Geoană contended that the country's military bases were being used by Washington solely for staging and transport purposes and not for a military offensive against Iraq. Romania allowed the United States to use its military bases and ports to compensate for the loss of logistical support in Turkey when Ankara refused to permit Washington the use of its ground facilities for launching an attack on Iraq. On March 10, 2003, the U.S. Commerce Department granted Romania the status of a "functional market economy," which some analysts interpreted as Washington's acknowledgment of Bucharest's allegiance.

Romania had its own security stake in the Iraqi mission. In May 2003 Romanian Intelligence Service (RIS) divulged that prior to the war, the RIS had thwarted an Iraqi plan to launch terrorist attacks against Western and Israeli targets in Romania. The plan was to be carried out with AG-7 grenade launchers provided to terrorists by a member of the Iraqi Embassy in Bucharest who was the head of Iraqi spying operations in Romania.[24] Due to this intelligence, Bucharest expelled ten Iraqi diplomats and thirty-one other Iraqi citizens from Romania in March 2003. These reports were confirmed by U.S. sources later that year.

During the Iraqi operation, Romanian political leaders viewed their position as one of bridging transatlantic divisions. They concentrated their efforts on highlighting mutual values and interests.[25] Iliescu referred to Romania as an integral part of Europe due to its history and refused to accept U.S. secretary of defense Donald Rumsfeld's delineation of "old and new Europe." Romania campaigned for transatlantic unity, stressing that any rift damaged the effectiveness of the West's stance in the anti-terrorist war.[26] In May 2003, parliament approved additional deployments to Iraq and by July 2003 Bucharest had fully committed its armed forces to Operation Iraqi Freedom. Parliament approved an additional supplement of fifty-six military and civilian staff to its military mission in October 2003. By December 2005, the country's presence in Iraq numbered 863 troops, including de-mining experts, infantry, military intelligence, military police, medics, and UN guards. Troops and personnel have been active in the Multinational Division Center South under Polish command, in the Multinational Division South-East under British command, in the U.S. hospital at Abu Ghraib, in the Multinational Force Command, and the Coalition Provisional Authority in Baghdad, as well as in the UN Assistance Mission for Iraq (UNAMI) in Basra. Romania's military contribution in Iraq has been the eighth largest among coalition partners.

Meanwhile, through its role as a nonpermanent member of the UN Security Council from January 1, 2004 to December 31, 2005, Romania endeavored to align other nations behind the democratization and stabilization efforts in Iraq. The country was a cosponsor of Resolution 1546, which paved the way for the restoration of Iraq's sovereignty, as well as supporting a resolution on counterterrorism.

Bucharest has consistently stated that it will remain engaged in Iraq regardless of international and domestic pressures. Romania withstood West European pressures following Spain's withdrawal from Iraq in 2004. The government also remained firm in its stance when in March 2005 three Romanian journalists were kidnapped in Iraq.[27] Bucharest refused to concede to terrorist demands in spite of growing public opposition to the war. At the time of the abduction, 55 percent of the Romanian public was against the country's military presence in Iraq, whereas 36 percent was in favor.[28]

In December 2005, an agreement was signed between U.S. secretary of state Condoleezza Rice and Romanian foreign minister Mihai-Răzvan Ungureanu allowing the United States to establish joint military bases on Romanian territory. An East European Task Force (EETAF) was agreed to be established at the Mihail Kogălniceanu airbase in Constanta on the Black Sea, together with three other sites for U.S. forces: the training ranges Smârdan, Babadag, and Cincu.[29] The U.S. presence will be in the form of forward operating sites, "small installations that can be rapidly built up," and cooperative security locations, or "host-nation facilities with little U.S. personnel but with equipment and logistical capabilities."[30]

The public has been supportive of the basing agreement, viewing it as a means to guarantee stability, secure foreign investment, and raise living standards. In late 2005, 59 percent believed that the U.S. military bases would increase foreign investment overall, 58 percent perceived that the country's national security would be augmented, and 51 percent stated that the bases would help improve Romania's image abroad. However, in addition to material gains, 61 percent of Romanians feared an increased danger of terrorist attacks stemming from the basing agreement.[31] The Romanian leadership must conduct informational campaigns to ensure that the population understands that security and stability is likely to improve as a result of the U.S. military presence within the country, rather than increasing its vulnerability to terrorist threats.

Anti-Americanism barely features in Romanian politics or in public opinion. When U.S. president Bill Clinton visited Bucharest in July 1997, tens of thousands of Romanian citizens gathered to greet him. The general population did not display resentment toward the United States for delaying Romania's NATO membership, but appeared to understand that the country's reform process had not been completed in line with NATO requirements.[32] Despite their positive views of the United States, a 2005 survey showed that only 9 percent of Romanians believed that the United States should remain the sole world superpower. About 43 percent of Romanians perceived Washington as responsible for tensions in the world, followed by the Arab countries at 28 percent, Israel at 6 percent, and Russia at 1 percent.[33] At the same time, there was significant support among the Romanian public for a complementary U.S.-EU relationship that can help stabilize and develop the Black Sea and western Balkan regions.

Regional Relations and Eastern Dimension

Romania has endeavored to assert itself as a significant player in the Black Sea region since the demise of the Soviet Union. Membership of NATO has enhanced such aspirations, as has the strategic partnership with the United States. Approximately 50 percent of European energy imports pass through the Black Sea, and it is projected that by 2020 the amount will increase to 70 percent. The region is viewed as strategically important in linking the Caspian basin resources with Europe. Bucharest has highlighted its location and its democratic progress as a potential model for the region. President Basescu stated that the government's primary interest is to consolidate its position in the Black Sea region.[34]

Due to a shared history, culture, language, and religion, officials in Bucharest consider relations with Moldova as a foreign policy priority. Much of Moldova belonged to Romania before the Second World War. After Chisinau gained independence from the Soviet Union in 1991, Bucharest was the first to recognize the new state. Romania has been the main supporter of the Moldovan government during the Transnistrian crisis provoked by pro-Moscow separatists in that enclave, and has demonstrated its strong support for an integrated Moldova. Bucharest has backed economic and political reform in Moldova, as well as Chisinau's eventual membership in NATO and the EU. Although in the early 1990s Moldovan officials were reticent concerning Romanian objectives for reunification, Bucharest's renouncement of any territorial ambitions has helped to strengthen relations between the two countries.

Romania's relations with its larger eastern neighbor, Ukraine, have improved in recent years, but disputes over border demarcations have not yet been fully resolved. Both sides claim rights to Snake Island in the Black Sea and both have conflicting views on the Ukrainian canal project in the Danube delta. Romania contends that the Ukrainian construction project will have a negative ecological effect and has filed a lawsuit against Kyiv at the International Court of Justice (ICJ) in The Hague. Both Kyiv and Bucharest also have differing approaches toward Moldova, as Kyiv is more circumspect regarding Moldova's westward direction and more protective of the Ukrainian minority in the Transnistrian region.

Romania has had a turbulent history with its western neighbor, Hungary, partly due to the 1.5 million-strong Hungarian minority living in western Romania or Transylvania since the close of World War I. Consecutive Hungarian governments during the interwar period sought to reclaim former Hungarian lands and northern Transylvania seceded to Hungary in August 1940. Following World War II, the territory was returned to Romania by the Allied powers. Comprising approximately 6.6 percent of the population, Hungarians were often considered by Romanian nationalists as a destabilizing factor in Romanian politics. Several attacks on the Hungarian cultural and historical heritage by ultranationalists complicated reconciliation.

However, the goals of NATO and EU membership have helped to foster cooperation between Budapest and Bucharest on a political level. A basic bilateral treaty, renouncing territorial claims and recognizing minority rights, was signed and ratified in 1996. In 2001 Hungary's proposed Status Law reopened debate on the conditions and rights of Hungarian minorities in neighboring states. The Hungarian government's approach to provide cultural, economic, and social support to Hungarian minorities clashed with the views of the Romanian authorities. However, subsequent negotiations dissipated the conflict. Hungary has been one of the strongest supporters of Romania's EU integration, cultural and economic ties have developed, and military cooperation has been exemplary. Hungary's parliament ratified Romania's EU Accession Treaty in October 2005. Nonetheless, Budapest has raised concerns that the environmental protection standards for Romania have not been as stringent as those for the 2004 accession countries following three hazardous spills into the Szamos and Tisza rivers over the past five years.

Political Options

The Social Democratic Party (SDP) has undergone various transformations since it was inaugurated in the early 1990s as the National Salvation Front. The SDP controlled the government between 1992 and 1996 and again from 2000 to 2004. The party was led by former president Ion Iliescu until April 2005 when former foreign minister Mircea Dan Geoană garnered more votes than Iliescu at the party's Congress.

The SDP has been a strong supporter of the United States and has assisted Washington in its security missions. Officials maintained a high profile in the international arena, emphasizing Romania's strategic location and U.S. partnership and making a strong case for the country's accession to NATO and the EU. Ahead of the November 2004 general elections, Geoană underscored that NATO was the most important strategic organization and that stronger collaboration should be developed between NATO and the UN. The SDP has supported further NATO and EU enlargement eastward, especially the integration of Ukraine and Moldova.[35]

The Romanian Humanist Party (RHP) ran in coalition with the Social Democratic Party during the November 2004 elections. Following the defeat of SDP candidate Adrian Năstase and the victory of Traian Basescu for the presidency, the RHP switched sides to join the Justice and Truth Alliance, forming part of the current ruling coalition. Within the coalition, the RHP was the sole voice of dissent regarding Romania's participation in Iraq. Following the abduction of four Romanian citizens by terrorist groups, the party called on its coalition partners to withdraw its military units from Iraq. The RHP's small size, combined with its need to remain in the government, effectively diminished its ability to persuade the major coalition partner to alter its foreign and security policy.[36]

The Greater Romania Party (GRP) is the country's most visible ultranationalist political grouping. In existence since 1991, the GRP has been widely viewed as the country's most extremist, chauvinistic, and anti-Semitic party, and has registered relatively strong results in parliamentary and presidential elections. In the November 2004 ballot, the party gained 13.63 percent of the vote and twenty-one seats. When the United States asked Bucharest to participate in a possible war against Iraq, the GRP abstained from the parliamentary vote on the grounds that the United Nations had not approved the military intervention. The GRP is opposed to Romania's engagement in overseas military missions, but its estrangement from other political forces has sidelined its position to the periphery of national decision making.

Public Opinion

Support for both the EU and NATO have consistently remained high in Romania. In 2002, both the EU and NATO were viewed approvingly at 78 and 75 percent respectively.[37] In 2003, 74 percent of the public favored EU membership and 77 percent placed their trust in the Union.[38] By 2005, 64 percent of Romanians viewed the EU positively, 20 percentage points ahead of the EU-25 average, and 64 percent held a favorable impression of NATO.[39] Fifty-eight percent believed that European security should be guaranteed by a combination of NATO and the European Union.[40]

The general public is divided on the issue of whether Romania should participate in military missions abroad with 49 percent in favor, 42 percent against, and 9 percent holding no opinion. For example, 50 percent of Romanians did not agree with a military presence in Bosnia-Herzegovina, whereas 42 percent supported involvement. Fifty percent were against the Romanian presence in Kosova and 41 percent were in favor. Out of those who supported foreign missions, 81 percent favored providing humanitarian aid to war victims. Only 35 percent supported military action to remove a dictator who had violated human rights.[41] Public opinion concerning the Iraqi mission has leaned slightly toward opposition to the country's participation. Polls in October 2005 indicated that 52 percent disagreed with the country's involvement whereas 41 percent agreed. The greatest number of respondents (38 percent) believed that Bucharest's participation in Iraq was undertaken specifically "to please the United States." Only 24 percent perceived that Romanian troops could genuinely assist in Iraq's stabilization. Twenty-two percent deemed that the country's participation was the result of allied involvement and 14 percent did not know. Regarding Afghanistan, public opinion is comparable: 52 percent disagree with the country's military presence, whereas 42 percent are in favor of participation.[42]

Only two small protests against the war in Iraq were held in Bucharest. On March 15, 2003, several hundred young people marched in Bucharest calling for the exit of U.S. troops stationed in the country, in opposition to the Năstase government's pro-American position in the Iraq conflict. Extremist parties attracted approximately one hundred protestors in a demonstration at the end of March 2003. Despite their stated opposition to the mission, Romanians have not engaged in mass street protests.

With regard to the EU, the Romanian population overwhelmingly aspires to membership. However, there has been increasing fear that integration could be delayed unless tougher judicial and anti-corruption reforms are instituted by Bucharest. Some of the public is also suspicious that the Union may seek to delay Romania's entry in order to appease EU publics that are opposed to further enlargement. Despite frustrations with Brussels over stern EU requirements and potential delays in membership, many Romanians see the accession process as the main driving force behind ensuring good governance in their country.

BULGARIA

Bulgaria is nestled in the eastern Balkans on the Black Sea coast with a population of almost eight million. With a geopolitical location at the crossroads of three continents, Bulgaria has been at the center of clashing interests by larger neighboring powers. Bulgarian leaders have come to understand that attempts to protect national sovereignty and assert the country's interests can best be accomplished within a wider European framework. In the seventeen years since the fall of the Iron Curtain, Bulgaria has successfully conducted two historic transformations: from a centrally controlled communist system to a pluralistic, market-oriented democracy and from the closest ally of the Soviet Union in the former Warsaw Pact to a full member of NATO. This dual transformation was neither consistent nor predictable. Politically Bulgaria was divided between pro-western and pro-eastern camps, which stifled the country's development for the first seven years of postcommunism. For much of the early and mid 1990s, the Bulgarian Socialists resisted full-blown capitalism and a close alliance with the West largely in an effort to preserve their political and economic positions and maintain their traditional ties with Moscow.

The severe economic and financial crisis of 1996 necessitated new national priorities. A sharp decline in GDP growth, a collapse of the banking sector, high unemployment, and hyperinflation provoked public protests, forcing the Socialist government of Zhan Videnov to resign. The 1997 election of a reformist government accelerated the development of democratic institutions and a market economy. The introduction of an IMF currency board system, extensive privatization, trade liberalization, and energy sector restructuring induced lower inflation, improved investor confidence, and sustained economic growth. The government also sought to battle rampant corruption through reforms of the state administration by expelling individuals tied to Russian criminal networks who had taken advantage of weak governments and an ineffective judicial system by using Bulgaria as a base of operations for their illicit activities.

Bulgaria's foreign, security, and defense policies also experienced a fundamental redefinition. In the late 1990s, the major political parties reached a consensus that only a Euro-Atlantic orientation could guarantee Bulgaria's security. This consensus resulted from the realization that in a post–Cold War environment "security" was no longer defined solely in military terms, but also in terms of social stability and economic development.

The United Democratic Forces (UDF) government of 1997–2001 was the first postcommunist cabinet to serve a full term. Similar to other postcommunist transitions, the short-term pain of the reform process outweighed the long-term advantages for average citizens and the UDF gradually lost popular support. Matters were made worse by a number of corruption scandals involving UDF party members and cabinet officials. Russian interests might also have been involved in de-legitimizing the Kostov government following the expulsion of Russian businessmen seeking to assert economic influence in Bulgaria.

In April 2001, Simeon Saxecoburgotski, Bulgaria's former monarch, returned to the country with political ambitions. He formed the National Movement Simeon II (NMS) party, which promised to improve living standards and combat corruption. His populist platform and the population's disillusionment with various governments resulted in an overwhelming victory for the NMS in the June 2001 parliamentary elections. Saxecoburgotski became prime minister and pressed forward with the reforms initiated by the UDF. He maintained consistency in Sofia's security and foreign policy and during his tenure Bulgaria's partnership with the United States became the closest in the country's history.

The Bulgarian Socialist Party (BSP), spending eight years in opposition, had the opportunity to regroup and revise its agenda. The BSP's electorate had traditionally consisted of pensioners, blue-collar workers, and rural populations. However with the aim of attracting the younger generation, the party assumed a more pro-Western stance. It strongly supported EU membership and was no longer critical of NATO and the United States. Emphasizing the principal goal of defending the country's national interests, the BSP managed to gain wider public support. The party garnered the highest number of votes in the June 2005 elections, but not enough for an absolute majority in parliament. Lengthy political negotiations followed, which threatened to derail Bulgaria's timetable for EU accession. In the interest of political stability, the BSP formed a coalition government with the center-right NMS and the Movement for Rights and Freedoms (MRF), the party of the Turkish minority. Although fragile, the coalition achieved a level of effectiveness in speeding up the implementation of reforms necessary to qualify for EU entry. The country still confronts low living standards, crime, and corruption. Nevertheless Sofia has achieved major successes in its two main foreign policy priorities. Bulgaria became a member of NATO in 2004 and the country expects to join the EU in 2007. Although Bulgaria's western orientation is irreversible, Sofia will need to devise a long-term security strategy in balancing its NATO and EU obligations and its close relations with the United States.[43]

The European Union

Since the fall of communism, the issue of EU membership has been less controversial than relations with NATO and Washington, and Union accession enjoyed wide support across the political spectrum. Bulgaria established diplomatic relations with the European Community (EC) in 1989. A free trade zone was established and financial and technical assistance was provided by the EC under the 1993 Europe Agreement. The Copenhagen European Council in 1993 and the Madrid European Council in 1995 spelled out the political and economic requirements for EU membership to the CEE states and Sofia submitted its formal application for accession in December 1995. In December 1999, Bulgaria was invited to start membership talks and in March 2000 the process began. By mid 2004 the government had successfully completed all chapters of the EU's *acquis communautaire*, and in December 2004, accession talks were formally closed. In April 2005, the Accession Treaty with Bulgaria was signed and passed to the parliaments of the twenty-five member states for ratification in 2006.

The European Commission's progress report for Bulgaria issued in October 2005 cited shortcomings in the fields of justice, internal affairs, and the integration of the Roma minority. The slow implementation of reforms was partly attributed to the impasse following the June 2005 parliamentary elections and the subsequent political bargaining. Consequently, Sofia took swift measures to fulfill EC recommendations with regard to combating organized crime.[44] The Commission stated that Bulgaria's unpreparedness to meet membership requirements in the areas of the judiciary, fighting corruption and human trafficking, and the equal integration of Roma may result in the postponement of Bulgaria's accession by one year.[45] The EC was due to give a final verdict in October 2006 in issuing progress reports for both Bulgaria and Romania.

As the accession date loomed closer, pro-EU sentiments have been in decline in Bulgaria. The level of public support for EU entry registered at 59 percent in August 2004 and dropped to 54 percent in September 2005.[46] The fall in support could be attributed to fears over the complexities of the EU and how membership would affect the lives of ordinary citizens. The public also worried about the influences that Euro-assimilation could have on their culture, traditions, and language. A poll conducted in March 2005 showed that half of those surveyed described their knowledge of the EU as "rather poor" or "very poor," while 25 percent expressed fear that EU accession would result in a loss of national identity.[47] As the crisis over the EU constitution unfolded in the summer of 2005, concerns grew whether Bulgaria's leadership could succeed in ensuring EU entry while protecting national interests.

Sofia supports a European Security and Defense Policy (ESDP), as long as it does not counter or duplicate NATO's operations. In late 2005, 78 percent of Bulgarians registered support for ESDP, one point higher than the EU-25 average. Support for a Common Security and Foreign Policy (CFSP) registered less support, at 70 percent, but still two percentage points higher than the EU average.[48] According to government officials, Sofia supports CFSP, but it will also remain close to Washington in order to defend its security interests; should new disputes between Europe and the United States occur, Sofia should aim to facilitate dialogue rather than choosing sides.[49]

EU accession will close an important chapter in Bulgaria's post–Cold War history, signaling that the country successfully completed its transformation from a communist dictatorship to a capitalist democracy. However, EU entry could also bring some turbulence in Bulgarian-American relations at a time when transatlantic divisions on a number of issues have become pronounced. Although Sofia and other CEE capitals are looking to strengthen the transatlantic link within the EU, at the same time, they will be subject to increasing pressures from Brussels and various West European capitals to coordinate their policies with the EU's emerging security and foreign policy even if the latter is sometimes at odds with Washington.

NATO Involvement

The first free elections in Bulgaria in the spring of 1990 resulted in victory for the Bulgarian Socialist Party (BSP), the successor of the Communist Party. The former communists still enjoyed public support not so much for ideological reasons, but because the nascent pro-democratic formations were poorly organized particularly at the local level. However, mass protests and civil disobedience forced the Socialist government to resign and the Union of Democratic Forces (UDF), the country's anti-communist coalition, assumed power after elections in November 1991. UDF leaders immediately designated the evolving NATO alliance as a pact that could guarantee national security in the face of changing security threats. The UDF government was voted out of office in October 1992, followed by a period of political instability and caretaker cabinets. Nevertheless, aspirations to develop a closer partnership with NATO did not subside and in 1994 Bulgaria became one of the first countries from the former communist bloc to join NATO's Partnership for Peace (PfP) program.

In December 1994, the BSP again won a majority in the parliament. The party's victory was due to the previous political instability and economic crisis that made many Bulgarians nostalgic for the assured standard of living under the Communist system. The BSP did not view NATO as a necessary component of the country's security and Alliance membership was not considered a foreign policy priority. The BSP's 1995 National Security Concept confirmed that "Bulgaria may seek NATO membership only after the Alliance [has] transformed itself into one of the elements of a pan-European security framework in which Russia would have a major role." Relations with NATO were subsequently placed on hold and by 1996 the BSP declared that it did not want to pursue Alliance membership.[50]

In February 1997, the caretaker government of Stefan Sofianski officially submitted Bulgaria's application for NATO membership. By March, an Intergovernmental Committee on NATO Integration was established and the UDF government of 1997–2001 commenced far-reaching military reforms. Substantial progress was registered in restructuring the armed forces into a modern and combat-ready military tailored to NATO needs. The April 1997 victory of the UDF continued the country's orientation westward. The government of Prime Minister Ivan Kostov outlined continued democratic and economic development and admission into NATO and the EU as essential to the country's security and prosperity in its 1998 National Security Concept. Priority areas included curbing regional stability threats, most notably organized crime and official corruption, that could derail Sofia's reform efforts.[51]

In 1999, when NATO intervened to stop the atrocities perpetuated by the Serbian regime in Kosova, the Kostov government granted over-flight rights to the Alliance and provided logistical support to NATO's Kosova Force (KFOR) with parliamentary approval. Both Prime Minister Kostov and President Peter Stoyanov urged Belgrade to end the war and imposed sanctions on Serbia. Bulgaria also played an important role in avoiding a possible crisis in relations between NATO and Russia by denying Russian forces over-flight rights during the later stages of the crisis.[52]

Sofia's delayed pro-Western shift and its limited participation in international peacekeeping missions had left the country with less experience than other CEE states and at a disadvantage in its interoperability with NATO.[53] The bulk of Bulgaria's post–Cold War peacekeeping experience comes from missions under UN auspices, such as in Cambodia (1992), Angola (1995–1999), Tajikistan (1995–2001), Ethiopia and Eritrea (2000–2001), Bosnia-Herzegovina (1997–2002), and Kosova (2000–present). Nonetheless, Sofia worked hard to fulfill NATO requirements, participate in joint exercises, and fund personnel training.

On March 18, 2004, parliament ratified the North Atlantic Treaty with 226 members voting in favor and four against. Eleven days later, Prime Minister Saxecoburgotski attended the inauguration ceremony in Washington for NATO's newest members. Political and public backing for NATO has been present despite the country's financial constraints and the unemployment it generated due to the required downsizing of the armed forces. The extent of support for NATO membership rose between 1999 and 2001, from 52.9 percent to 64 percent.[54] This support was mainly a result of the perception that NATO accession would result in tangible benefits. However, public opinion has been influenced by persistent questions regarding the financial burdens of membership, the future of the Alliance, and relations between NATO and Russia, although a majority of citizens continued to support membership.

Since its formal accession in 2004, Bulgaria has proven to be a committed ally. It is one of only seven member states, including France, Greece, Romania, Turkey, the UK, and the United States, that has met defense spending requirements. Bulgaria's defense expenditures were estimated at 2.4 percent of GDP in 2004.[55] Sofia also demonstrated dedication to participating in NATO's Rapid Reaction Force (RRF). In April 2005 it sent a platoon of nuclear, chemical, and biological protection specialists to the RRF and intended to broaden its role by 2007 once the planned goals of force restructuring were achieved. Bulgaria has hosted a number of Alliance exercises, most notably Cooperative Key in the summer of 2005, involving 1,500 personnel and 68 aircraft. Since January 2006, the multinational Southeastern Europe Brigade (SEEBRIG), performing within the framework of the NATO-led International Security Assistance Force (ISAF) in Afghanistan has been under Bulgarian command. The brigade has been tasked with maintaining security in Kabul and adjoining areas.[56]

Sofia also seeks a more active role in the debate on the future of NATO. Bulgaria hosted the informal NATO Foreign Ministers meeting at end of April 2006 to prepare the agenda for NATO's November 2006 summit in Riga. According to Bulgarian officials, Sofia wants to push for more active NATO involvement in the Balkans to combat terrorist and criminal networks. Cooperative and stable relations among its Balkan neighbors has been a long-standing priority for Bulgaria and NATO is viewed as a vehicle through which long-term regional stability can be achieved.

U.S. Relations

The U.S. role in the fall of communism resulted in growing pro-American attitude among the Bulgarian public. Ensuring Washington's involvement in the CEE region was also identified by a sector of Bulgaria's leadership as a way of limiting Russian ambitions. The United States provided a viable model of governance due to its high living standards, freedom of speech, and strong democratic values. The United States was more trusted than the West European powers who were seen as having betrayed Bulgaria and other CEE states at the close of the Second World War in acquiescing to Soviet domination. Despite positive public sentiments toward the United States, official policy evolved along a different path, neither overtly pro- nor anti-American. Relations remained restricted as the Socialist governments of 1989–1991 and 1995–1997 maintained close relations with Moscow, insisting that Russia would remain Bulgaria's closest political, economic, and cultural ally. Although the Socialists subsequently supported NATO membership, some of their leaders have maintained close links with the Russian authorities, which have sought to diminish America's global role.

Cooperation increased between Bulgaria and the United States following the country's Euro-Atlantic shift in 1997. The 1998 Working Plan established bilateral groups in the areas of economy, military, and law enforcement. The U.S. Congress in November 2001 passed the Gerald Solomon Freedom Consolidation Act granting military assistance worth $10 million, but later blocked it in July 2003 when Sofia refused to sign a bilateral agreement with the United States exempting American citizens from prosecution by the International Criminal Court (ICC). Sofia had signed the ICC statute in 1999 and ratified it in 2002. Bulgaria, a non-permanent member of the UN Security Council at the time, had even cosponsored a resolution permitting the exemption of U.S. peacekeepers serving in Bosnia-Herzegovina from the ICC, but later abstained from voting on it. Sofia was pressured by both Washington and Brussels to align with their respective positions on the ICC, as well as by domestic political actors to protect national interests. Bulgaria chose to resist U.S. demands and Washington eventually lifted the restrictions in November 2003 to reward Sofia's contribution for the war in Iraq.[57]

Bulgaria has been a partner and ally of the United States in the anti-terrorist campaign. Sofia has contributed to U.S.-led operations enabling air, land, and sea transit to coalition forces in the Middle East and Central Asia, and permitting the operation of U.S. aircraft for refueling and cargo-lifting purposes in both the Afghani and Iraqi missions. Sofia has allocated military units to the International Security Assistance Force (ISAF) in Afghanistan and dispatched an anti-nuclear, biological, and chemical (NBC) unit to a country neighboring Iraq. Bulgaria consistently supported the U.S. position toward the Iraqi question during its tenure as a non-permanent member of the UN Security Council between 2002 and 2003.[58] In February 2003, parliament authorized the use of airspace and bases for U.S operational flights. There was limited political consensus on the Iraqi conflict and members of the BSP and five independent parliamentarians abstained from voting. The president and the BSP opposed the war and the country's participation in postwar reconstruction without a UN mandate. However, with international authorization they indicated their willingness to approve the mission.

On the eve of the war in Iraq, the public was split on the issue. Forty-eight percent believed that military conflict with Iraq was unjustified, 26 percent believed that the actions were warranted, while 26 percent held no opinion on the matter.[59] The decision to send troops to Iraq was political and it was not opened to a public debate or subjected to a thorough assessment of Bulgarian capabilities. Despite a favorable public attitude toward the United States, its solidarity with the oppressed Iraqi people, and a broad sense of shared values with the Euro-Atlantic democracies, Bulgaria's resolution to engage was mostly a top-down process. The government desired to break with the unsustainable policy of neutrality, which dominated during the early and mid-1990s. Although Bulgaria lacked interventionist traditions, evolving security threats necessitated participation in counterterrorist and peacekeeping operations.

Among the pragmatic reasons for joining the "coalition of the willing" were the perceived benefits of a stronger partnership with the United States, including military aid, reconstruction contracts, and U.S. bases on Bulgarian territory. Sofia also nurtured hopes that a $2 billion dollar debt that the Saddam regime owed Bulgaria could be repaid. Furthermore, many anticipated that the mission would be completed quickly and decisively with limited collateral damage. Bulgaria was the largest creditor vis-à-vis Iraq in proportion to its GDP: Iraq's debt was equal to one tenth of Bulgaria's annual GDP. Of the $1.7 billion debt, about $1 billion represented the principle accrued before the 1991 Gulf War. Other CEE states were in a comparable situation.

Recognition for Bulgaria's position as a strategic U.S. ally came with the announcement in November 2003 that Washington was looking to Sofia and Bucharest for improving its global military posture. The U.S. aim was to build small, forward operating bases in proximity to conflict regions close to the Black Sea. At the beginning of 2004, negotiations commenced and on December 19, 2005, parliament overwhelmingly approved a resolution granting the United States and NATO the right to use military bases on Bulgarian territory. A formal agreement was signed between Sofia and Washington in April 2006.

While only a small percentage of the Bulgarian public supported the war in Iraq, open opposition was initially meager and sporadic. However, as the course of events in Iraq became more adverse and unpredictable, the expected material benefits failed to materialize, and Bulgarian casualties mounted, skepticism toward the United States and its policy in Iraq strengthened. In late December 2003, five Bulgarian soldiers died and twenty-six were injured during an attack on their base in Karbala and in April 2004 three Bulgarian soldiers were killed during an ambush. Although public criticism and opposition grew, official policy remained unchanged. In July 2004, two Bulgarian truck drivers were taken hostage with the demand that the United States free all Iraqi prisoners. A special taskforce was formed in Sofia to deal with the crisis. Although President Georgi Parvanov was more skeptical about Bulgaria's involvement in the war, the government refused to submit to blackmail and with substantial political backing it vowed to remain in the U.S.-led coalition. Foreign Minister Solomon Passy emphasized the humanitarian dimension of Bulgaria's participation in Iraq and its compliance with UN Security Council Resolutions. The parliamentary committee for foreign affairs affirmed the continuation of Bulgaria's military presence in Iraq, supported by broad political consensus within parliament.[60]

The desire to protect Bulgarian nationals, as well as the need to remain strong in the face of terrorist threats was evident in public discourse. Newspaper editorials highlighted the need for steadfastness against terrorism, supporting the government's position not to bow to pressure from the kidnappers. But some condescending attitudes also appeared that mocked the political leadership and their perceived need for support among their external allies rather than their own citizens. During the height of tensions over the two Bulgarian hostages, frequent mention was made in the press of the Philippine government's decision to pull its troops from Iraq under a similar threat, as well as Spain's withdrawal following the terrorist attacks in Madrid in March 2004. Although the Bulgarian hostages were murdered, opinion polls indicated that close to 90 percent of the public supported the government's position during the crisis.[61] The multinational forces in Iraq denounced the kidnapping and slaughter of innocent civilians, stating their resolve not to give in to terrorist threats. They also stated that their presence in Iraq was in accordance with UNSC Resolution 1546. Foreign Minister Passy proposed a more unified international policy for similar crises, which Washington praised as the "first step towards an international code against terrorism."[62]

In March 2005, another Bulgarian casualty generated stronger anti-coalition feelings among the general public. Junior-Sergeant Gardi Gardev was killed by friendly fire due to a lack of communication between his patrol and the U.S. command. Washington accepted responsibility for Gardev's death following an investigation. A poll conducted the same month showed that 30 percent of Bulgarian respondents placed responsibility with the Bulgarian command, while 39.2 percent blamed the United States for the incident. Some 30 percent called for the resignation of the defense minister. The same survey demonstrated that opposition to Bulgaria's presence in Iraq grew from 62 percent in January 2005 to 72 percent in March during the same year.[63]

The BSP called for the evacuation of troops from Iraq and hoped that the issue would be a deciding factor in the June 2005 elections. The incumbent NMS government feared that the Iraq question would cost them the elections, and agreed in May 2005 to withdraw troops by the end of the year. In May 2005, the outgoing parliament voted to reduce the number of Bulgarian troops from 470 to 400 by June 2005 and to withdraw them completely by the end of 2005. The parliamentary vote passed with 110 in favor, 53 against, and 45 abstentions. This was a consequence of pre-election pressures and the country's pending EU membership.[64] Nevertheless, the Iraq issue was not a primary concern for the public during the election campaign. Disillusionment with the NMS administration was due to domestic economic problems and transparency issues surrounding various privatization deals and military contracts. As a result, the BSP emerged as a winner in the balloting, but failed to secure a majority in parliament. The election results necessitated the formation of a coalition government between the Socialists, the NMS, and the Movement for Rights and Freedoms.

The new government, which took office in August 2005, was the first left-right coalition in the region. Differences between the parties' priorities made Bulgarian support for future U.S.-led initiatives uncertain, especially as the BSP had traditionally upheld stronger ties with Russia. With tough U.S. visa regulations and the lack of pronounced U.S. involvement in reviving NATO, support for Washington could become even more tenuous. Even if the new government does not reverse Bulgaria's Euro-Atlantic orientation, the lack of an explicit effort to react to rising anti-Americanism could lead to stronger opposition to U.S. policies.[65] Although an agreement was signed in April 2006 on U.S. basing in Bulgaria, public opposition has outweighed support. Opponents have feared property loss, a new form of political clientelism, and threats of terrorist attacks against American and Bulgarian targets. Polls in March 2005 indicated that 64 percent of citizens were against foreign military bases and only 17.8 percent were in favor.[66] In line with an earlier parliamentary vote, Bulgaria withdrew its forces from Iraq at the end of December 2005. By the time of the withdrawal, Sofia's participation in the mission cost the lives of thirteen soldiers and six civilians. However, mindful of maintaining good relations with the United States, in December 2005 parliament approved the deployment of a 120-strong noncombatant unit on a humanitarian mission to a refugee camp north of Baghdad.[67]

Bulgaria has the potential to become a durable and reliable partner for the United States, but the relationship also requires a stronger commitment from Washington. The United States must establish a more visible and positive presence in the country that is not only linked to the military, but is also economic and cultural. While political forces in Bulgaria are divided between pro-U.S. and U.S.-skeptic camps, the public is weary of any international power imposing its will on the country. Washington needs to demonstrate that the relationship is beneficial to both partners and to their citizens.

Regional Relations and Eastern Dimension

Bulgaria maintains good relations with all of its neighbors and has no outstanding disputes. It has played a leading role in a number of cooperative regional formats, including the multinational South East European Peacekeeping Force (SEEBRIG) and the regional security initiative SEEDM (South East Europe Defense Ministerial). Bulgaria has played a constructive role vis-à-vis Macedonia and was the first country to recognize Macedonia's independence in 1992. It has also contributed to democratic developments in Serbia following the ouster of Slobodan Milošević in October 2000.

Sofia has also developed good relations with Greece and Turkey, seeking to balance its ties with the two Balkan neighbors. Sofia has supported Turkey's bid for EU membership and relations between the two countries have flourished in various areas, including trade and investment.[68]

The government in Sofia has been active in developing regional initiatives to enhance security and cooperation across Balkan borders. In July 1999, finance ministers from Bulgaria, Macedonia, and Albania negotiated a common approach to infrastructural projects for the region. At a trilateral meeting of the Bulgarian, Albanian, and Macedonian foreign ministers, Sofia proposed establishing a Center for Democracy in Bulgaria, which would promote civil societies in neighboring states. In December 2003, the ministers of energy from Albania, Bosnia-Herzegovina, Bulgaria, Croatia, Greece, Italy, Macedonia, Romania, Serbia, Montenegro, and Turkey, and the Special Representative and Head of the United Nations Interim Administration for Kosova (UNMIK) signed a memorandum for a regional energy market in Southeast Europe. The idea was to create a liberalized market for energy resources and to stimulate several trans-European energy projects. In addition, Bulgaria's highly active NGO sector engages in cooperative cross-regional policies and advocates that Sofia should be more active in the stabilization process by sharing its EU and NATO experiences with aspiring candidates to both organizations.

For Sofia, the eastern dimension of its security and foreign policy has slowly evolved beyond its relations with Russia. For much of the 1990s Bulgaria's Socialists remained closely linked to Moscow and when the BSP returned to power in December 1994, Russia's influence in Bulgaria increased. During a visit to Sofia in March 1996, Yeltsin mentioned Bulgaria as the only East European country that could become a member of the Russian-dominated Commonwealth of Independent States (CIS). By contrast, the oppositionist UDF was perceived as a dangerous formation by the Kremlin that would move the country closer to NATO. The UDF's election victory in April 1997 was seen by Moscow as a setback, as the new Bulgarian administration embraced the prospect of NATO entry. The Russian authorities endeavored to divide the UDF by seeking to corrupt officials with "lucrative business propositions" and by investing "large amounts of money to undermine the government between 1997 and 2001." Resources were designated for "the mass media and several political parties to discredit the UDF and to promote the more trusted Socialists." Within the BSP, pro-Russian lobbying groups "canvassed on behalf of Moscow's economic interests and against Bulgaria's NATO membership."[69]

Bulgaria's center-right NMS did not oppose maintaining good relations with Russia but articulated anxiety that Moscow was intent on influencing Bulgarian foreign policy to the detriment of its relations with the United States. During President Vladimir Putin's visit to Bulgaria in March 2003, analysts contended that Putin attempted to influence Sofia's position on Iraq and worsen relations with Washington. To counterbalance the center-right government, Putin cultivated ties with Socialist President Georgi Parvanov.[70]

Under the new government coalition, which included both the NMS and the BSP, Sofia sought more equal and pragmatic ties with Russia, but achieving such a balance has proved difficult. Bulgaria depends on Russian energy resources for almost 90 percent of its needs and any open confrontation with

Moscow could have adverse effects on the country's economy. In January 2006, Bulgaria and Russia had an open dispute over energy issues as Moscow threatened to cut gas deliveries unless Sofia renegotiated an existing contract and agreed to increased prices. The Bulgarian government initially maintained its strong position, but eventually succumbed to pressures to review some aspects of the deal.

Historically close ties to Russia and the country's energy dependence have prevented Sofia from openly advocating EU and NATO integration for Ukraine, Belarus, Moldova, and Georgia. Following the popular revolutions in Ukraine and Georgia, Bulgaria remained less involved than its CEE neighbors in helping to move the CIS states away from the Russian orbit. Sofia issued congratulatory notes for the triumph of democratic leaders, but carefully worded any statements on Kyiv's and Tbilisi's relations with Moscow. Furthermore, unlike Romania, Bulgaria has not clearly defined its position in the evolving geopolitics of the Black Sea region. In view of the engaging Balkans-Central Asia energy corridor, Sofia needs to establish itself as a vital link for transport of Caspian resources to Western Europe. Bulgaria can help diversify its energy supplies and attract stronger political and economic commitment from Washington, which has a high stake in European energy security, while curtailing its dependence on an increasingly assertive Russia.

Political Options

The Bulgarian Socialist Party (BSP) benefited from its superior organization and resources to maintain a hold on power for much of the 1990s. The election victory of the Union of Democratic Forces (UDF) in 1997 diminished Socialist influence in policy making. The UDF was responsible for aligning Bulgaria with a Euro-Atlantic orientation. Between 1997 and 2001, the government viewed EU and NATO membership as a legitimation for its reformist efforts and as a fundamental strategic reorientation. The UDF disintegrated after the 2001 election because of internal fractures and public disillusionment with the impact of macroeconomic reforms. In the June 2005 elections the party only received 7.68 percent of the vote and 20 parliamentary seats. Although the UDF initiated Bulgaria's path to the EU and NATO, as well as closer links with Washington, during its five years in opposition since 2001 the party frequently criticized the administration for not upholding national interests during the EU accession process.[71] UDF leaders also expressed doubts that the ruling coalition would be transparent in administrating EU funds. Such criticism has often been interpreted as a form of growing EU- and Atlanto-skepticism, but it is more accurately a reflection of domestic political skirmishes, which have not diminished the party's Euro-Atlantic orientation.

Until its return to power in 2005, BSP policies were less clear and the party remained skeptical of NATO's purpose. The BSP also asserted that Russia should be one of Bulgaria's main partners. The Socialists expressed support for EU integration but initially viewed European integration as a leftist project, in which West European socialist and social-democratic forces dominated.[72] BSP rhetoric changed shortly before NATO's Prague summit in November 2002. Socialist leaders began to indicate support for Euro-Atlantic integration; however, they continued to stress that the protection of national interests outweighed any strategic partnerships with NATO or the United States. Upon NATO accession in 2004, the Socialists were reluctant to accept U.S. leadership and advocated a more active dialogue with Moscow within the framework of the NATO-Russia Council and a stronger EU-wide defense policy. In the midst of mounting opposition to the war in Iraq, the BSP criticized Sofia's support for U.S. policies, but did not call for an immediate troop withdrawal. After the BSP won a majority in the June 2005 parliamentary elections and became part of the coalition government, it scaled back its opposition to Bulgaria's presence in Iraq, because it no longer needed to exploit the issue for political purposes. Since September 2005, the Socialists have rarely questioned Sofia's commitment to Iraqi stabilization, but have distanced themselves from alleged U.S. unilateralism. Instead they define Bulgaria's continued involvement under the auspices of NATO and the UN.

A new political party emerged two months prior to the June 2005 elections, the ultranationalist *Ataka*. The party surprisingly achieved fourth place in the ballot obtaining 8.14 percent of the votes and twenty-one seats in the parliament. The party's anti-NATO, anti-U.S., and anti-Iraq war positions appealed to a stratum of voters. *Ataka* leaders harshly criticized the government's posture toward EU entry, but did not entirely oppose EU membership for Bulgaria. The party's relative election success is mostly attributed to its nationalist and populist appeals of allegedly protecting the country from various ethnic minorities and outside threats.

Bulgaria finds itself in a peculiar position: the BSP-NMS-MRF coalition is considered to be unstable, but there is no viable alternative in parliament. *Ataka*'s radical rhetoric softened after it entered parliament and its influence has since been marginalized. The UDF changed its leadership, but continues to struggle with internal crises. The Bulgarian Popular Union (BPU) and Democrats for a Strong Bulgaria (DSB), both enjoy single-digit public support and are difficult to define politically, since they offer little by way of platform beyond their criticism of government policies. Across most of the political spectrum politicians realize that good relations with the United States remain necessary for Bulgaria. While the center-right considers the partnership with Washington to be a key objective primarily for security reasons, the left generally believes that relations with the United States should not be given precedence over other international alliances.

Public Opinion

Public criticisms of Washington and Brussels have become more vocal in recent years, but they do not signal a shift away from basic transatlantic interests. Instead, the public wants Bulgaria to become more assertive in expressing its national priorities in dealing with the EU and the United States. As a result of the mission in Iraq, America's popular image has been tarnished. According to a Gallup poll in 2003, 35 percent of Bulgarians indicated that the U.S. military action negatively impacted on their feelings toward America.[73] The same poll also showed that a majority of respondents portrayed the United States as too keen on using military power. Cynicism toward U.S. foreign policy has continued to grow and it represents a glaring departure from the idealistic view of America that dominated during much of the 1990s.

Despite mounting opposition to the Iraqi mission and a distrust of Washington's global agenda, no major anti-war or anti-U.S. protests have been staged in Bulgaria. Two small anti-war organizations were formed—the Citizens of Bulgaria for Bulgaria and the Citizens Against War—following the murders of two civilian hostages in Iraq. They issued a joint request demanding the withdrawal of Bulgarian troops.[74] However the government was not subject to any significant pressure to alter its policy on Iraq. The prominent analyst Ivan Krastev has defined anti-Americanism in Bulgaria as "lite," referring to mixed feelings toward the United States politically, socially, and economically, but not seeking America's destruction.[75]

Some political forces may seek to use anti-Americanism in an attempt to unite the electorate. Since the beginning of the Iraqi mission, the two highest-circulation left-leaning newspapers have featured anti-American propaganda, while the pro-Atlanticist media has been slow to respond and counter this phenomenon. Leaders in Washington can help shape Bulgarian public opinion by dispelling the perception of an unstable asymmetry in bilateral relations and demonstrating that Bulgaria has become a long-term strategic partner. According to a Bulgarian foreign ministry spokesperson, leaders in Sofia also have the capacity to guide public opinion in a positive direction, much like the government did during NATO's Kosova campaign in 1999.[76]

Bulgarians are generally pragmatic and seek a competent political leadership that will protect the country's foreign interests. Although a U.S. presence and close bilateral relations are regarded as positive developments, there are still lingering fears that weak domestic leadership could subject Bulgaria to an unequal relationship as happened during the Soviet period. In this context, most analysts advocate a more assertive foreign and security policy agenda to enable the country to have a louder voice in world affairs.

NOTES

1. Aurelian Craiutu, "Romania: The Difficult Apprenticeship of Liberty (1989–2004)," *Woodrow Wilson International Center for Scholars*, Meeting Report 298 (2004).

2. BBC Monitoring, "Romanian Premier Says U.S. Minister's Statement 'Greatly Honours' Eastern Europe," *Rompres News Agency*, January 24, 2003.

3. BBC Monitoring Europe, "President: U.S. Can Count on Romania's Contribution in Fight Against Terror," July 11, 2005.

4. Victor D. Bojkov, "Neither Here, Not There: Bulgaria and Romania in Current European Politics," *Communist and Post-Communist Studies* 37, no. 4 (December 2004).

5. Eurobarometer 63: Public Opinion in the European Union (published September 2005), 98, 101.

6. *Sofia Echo*, "Netherlands Ratifies Bulgaria's EU Accession Treaty," February 8, 2006.

7. Eurobarometer 64 (December 2005), 34.

8. Institute for Public Policy, "Public Perceptions on Foreign Affairs in Romania," (Bucharest, October 2005).

9. See Eurobarometer 63 (September 2005), 64. See also Eurobarometer 64 (December 2005), 36.

10. See Joseph F. Harrington, *American-Romanian Relations, 1989–2004: From Pariah to Partner* (New York: Columbia University Press, 2004), 115.

11. See NATO International Staff, "NATO-Russia Compendium of Financial and Economic Data Relating to Defense," June 9, 2005, p. 7, www.nato.int/docu/pr/2005/p050609.pdf (accessed December 5, 2005).

12. Mihail E. Ionescu, "Romania's Position Towards the Evolution of the Transatlantic Link," in *Old Europe, New Europe and the US: Renegotiating Transatlantic Security in the Post 9/11 Era*, edited by Tom Lansford and Blagovest Tashev (Aldershot, UK: Ashgate, 2005), 275.

13. BBC Monitoring, "Romania Contributes 13.3 Million Euros to NATO Common Resources," *Rompres News Agency*, February 24, 2005.

14. *Defense News*, "Interview with Romanian Defense Minister Teodor Atanasiu," January 23, 2006.

15. Institute for Public Policy, "Public Perceptions on Foreign Affairs in Romania," (Bucharest, October 2005), 22.

16. *Defense News*, "Interview with Romanian Defense Minister Teodor Atanasiu," January 23, 2006.

17. See U.S. Department of State, Bureau of European and Eurasian Affairs, "Romania Profile," December 2005, www.state.gov/r/pa/ei/bgn/35722.htm#defense (accessed January 5, 2006). For a comprehensive overview of the Constantinescu government, see

Joseph F. Harrington, *American-Romanian Relations, 1989–2004: From Pariah to Partner*, 107–37.

18. Radio Free Europe/Radio Liberty Newsline, September 14, 2001.

19. Adrian Năstase, *NATO Enlargement: Romania and the Southern Dimension of the Alliance*. See also Radio Free Europe/Radio Liberty Newsline, September 20, 2001.

20. Bucharest Mediafax, "Romania's Government Sees Proof Presented by U.S. Powell as 'Convincing,'" February 6, 2003.

21. Rompres News Agency, "Romania to Offer USA 'Solidarity and Coherence' in Event of Iraq War," February 6, 2003.

22. BBC Monitoring, "Survey: Majority of Romanians Against War in Iraq," *Rompres News Agency*, March 26, 2003.

23. BBC Monitoring, "Defense Ministry Presents Romania's Offer of Forces to NATO for Iraq War," *Rompres News Agency*, February 11, 2003.

24. Radio Free Europe/Radio Liberty Newsline, May 16, 2003.

25. Mihail E. Ionescu, "Romania's Position Towards the Evolution of the Transatlantic Link," 273–74.

26. Ibid.

27. Romanian Ministry of National Defense, english.mapn.ro/operations/index .php (accessed December 13, 2005), and Radio Free Europe/Radio Liberty Newsline, April 19, 2004.

28. Polia Alexandrova, "Bulgaria and Iraq: Withdrawal Methods," *Transitions Online*, May 3–9, 2005, and BBC Monitoring, "Romania/Iraq: Authorities Take Measures to Find Journalists Kidnapped in Iraq," *Romanian Pro TV*, March 29, 2005.

29. *Yahoo News*, "U.S. Signs Deal for First Permanent Military Base in Ex-Soviet Bloc," December 6, 2005.

30. Alexander Cooley, "Base Politics," *Foreign Affairs* 84, no. 6 (November/December 2005).

31. Institute for Public Policy, "Public Perceptions on Foreign Affairs in Romania," 24.

32. John F. Harris and Michael Dobbs, "Clinton Discovers All is Forgiven in Romania; 1st U.S. Leader to Visit Since Fall of Communism is Hailed Despite Stalling NATO Bid," *The Washington Post*, July 12, 1997.

33. Institute for Public Policy, "Public Perceptions on Foreign Affairs in Romania," 43.

34. Power and Interest News Report, "Bulgaria, Romania and the Changing Structure of the Black Sea's Geopolitics," www.pinr.com/report.php?ac=view_report& report_id=302&language_id=1 (accessed January 2, 2006) and Templetonthorp, www.templetonthorp.com/pl/news886 (accessed January 2, 2006).

35. BBC Monitoring, "Romanian Should Rethink 'Strategic Profile' as NATO, EU Member—Minister," September 14, 2004.

36. BBC Monitoring, April 24, 2005.

37. Eurobarometer CC-EB 2003.2: Public Opinion in the Candidate Countries (June 2003), 7. See also, BBC Monitoring, "Romanians Like NATO But Do Not Want Foreign Troops, Bases—Poll," November 18, 2002.

38. Eurobarometer CC-EB 2003.2, 7.

39. Eurobarometer 64 (December 2005), 18; and Institute for Public Policy, "Public Perceptions on Foreign Affairs in Romania," 11.

40. Institute for Public Policy, "Public Perceptions on Foreign Affairs in Romania," 23.

41. Ibid, 25.

42. Ibid, 26.

43. Interview with officials, Sofia, Bulgaria, August 2005.

44. Bulgaria Interior Ministry, "Results of the Activity of the Minister of Interior Against Organized Crime" (meeting at the Center for Strategic and International Studies, Washington, D.C., February 17, 2006).

45. See European Commission, "Bulgaria: 2005 Comprehensive Monitoring Report," SEC (2005) 1352, Brussels, October 25, 2005.

46. Boyko Pangelov, "Is it Time for a U-Turn on Iraq," *Sofia Trud*, July 28, 2004; ed. Ognyan Minchev, Valeri Ratchev, and Marin Lessenski, *Bulgaria for NATO 2002*, (Sofia: Institute for Regional and International Studies, 2002), 360. See also Eurobarometer 63: Public Opinion in the European Union (September 2005), 98.

47. BBC Worldwide Montoring, "Poll shows nearly 70 percent of Bulgarians support EU entry," *BTA, Sofia*, March 31, 2005.

48. Eurobarometer 64 (December 2005), 38.

49. Interview with government official, Sofia, Bulgaria, August 2005.

50. Blagovest Tashev, "In Search of Security: Bulgaria's Security Policy in Transition," in *Old Europe, New Europe and the US: Renegotiating Transatlantic Security in the Post 9/11 Era*, edited by Tom Lansford and Blagovest Tashev (Aldershot, UK: Ashgate, 2005), 127–50.

51. Ibid, 133.

52. See Janusz Bugajski, "The Future of NATO: Do Bulgaria and Romania Qualify?" Testimony before the U.S. Senate Committee on Foreign Relations, April 3, 2003, www.senate.gov/~foreign/testimony/2003/BugajskiTestimony030403.pdf (accessed May 1, 2005).

53. See Jeff Simon, "Bulgaria and NATO: 7 Lost Years," *Strategic Forum* 142 (May 1998), www.ndu.edu/inss/strforum/SF142/forum142.html (accessed October 1, 2005).

54. Ed. Ognyan Minchev, Valeri Ratchev, and Marin Lessenski, *Bulgaria for NATO 2002*, 371.

55. NATO International Staff, *NATO-Russia Compendium of Financial and Economic Data Relating to Defence*, June 9, 2005, 7.

56. BBC Monitoring, "Bulgarian Commander to Lead NATO Mission in Afghanistan," January 12, 2006.

57. Radio Free Europe/Radio Liberty, "U.S. Unblocks Military Aid to ICC Dissenters," November 23, 2003. U.S. president Bill Clinton had signed the ICC treaty during his final days in office. When the George W. Bush administration came to power, the government "unsigned" the treaty in May 2002 fearing politically motivated prosecution of American citizens and soldiers during a period of American predominance on the international stage.

58. Janusz Bugajski, "The Future of NATO: Do Bulgaria and Romania Qualify?" 3.

59. Gallup International, "Post War Iraq 2003 Poll," www.gallup-international.com/download/Post%20war%20Iraq%202003%20Results%20update%2013.05%20-%20Rest%20of%20the%20World.pdf (accessed June 15, 2005).

60. Veselin Toshkov, "Bulgarian Troops to Remain in Iraq, Parliamentary Committee Decides," April 23, 2004.

61. See Agence France Presse, "Bulgarian Court Rejects Claim Minister Hid Facts in Iraqi Hostage Crisis," May 19, 2005. See also Lilia Dimitrova, "Bulgaria Wants to Help Iraqis, Pleads FM Amid Hostage Crisis," *Paris AFP*, July 10, 2004. See Polia Alexandrova, "Bulgaria: Coalition of the Desperate?" *Transitions Online*, July 13–19, 2004.

62. Todor Tokin, "Mum is the Word," *Sofia Trud*, August 7, 2004.

63. BBC Monitoring, "Polls Show Majority of Bulgarians Oppose Mission in Iraq, Foreign Bases," *BTA news agency*, March 17, 2005.

64. Polia Alexandrova, "Bulgaria and Iraq: Withdrawal Methods."

65. Interview with analysts and officials (Sofia, Bulgaria, August 2005).

66. BBC Monitoring, March 17, 2005.

67. *The Sofia Echo*, "New Bulgarian Mission to Iraq," December 26, 2005.

68. BBC, July 7, 2004.

69. Janusz Bugajski, *Cold Peace: Russia's New Imperialism* (London: Praeger, 2004), 213.

70. Ibid, 213.

71. *Media Pool*, "Interview with former Prime Minister Ivan Kostov," June 20, 2005, www.mediapool.bg/show/?storyid=106172&srcpos=2 (accessed September 12, 2005).

72. Ognyan Minchev, "Limping Toward Europe: How Does the Formula EU or BSP Look Today," *Politiki*, June 23, 2005.

73. Gallup International, "Post War Iraq 2003 Poll."

74. Albena Shkodrova, "Chorus Grows for Bulgarians to Quit Iraq," *Institute for War & Peace Reporting*, August 13, 2004.

75. See Ivan Krastev, "The Anti-American Century?" *Journal of Democracy* 15, no. 2 (April 2004).

76. Interview with government official, Sofia, Bulgaria, January 2005.

Chapter Seven

Conclusions and Recommendations

This book does not seek to convince the CEE states to support the foreign policy of the United States or to persuade the United States to stand consistently with Europe and its new allies. The purpose is to better inform policy makers of the causes and consequences of either a stronger or a weaker transatlantic link and the role America's new allies from central and eastern Europe can play in this process. Recommendations in this concluding chapter focus on particular areas of cooperation that can better enable both Washington and the CEE capitals to make sound decisions to promote their national interests.

These conclusions extrapolate from the preceding analysis and offer several pertinent recommendations for U.S. and CEE policy makers. Implementation of these policy options can help ensure that Washington's newest partners become more dependable long-term allies who will continue to calculate that it is in their national interests to maintain a close relationship with the United States. At the same time, the U.S. administration should calculate that it is in the U.S. national interest to ensure sufficient strategic benefits for its new allies in order to guarantee their commitment to the transatlantic relationship.

The most beneficial result of EU enlargement and integration for the United States and for the CEE countries would be the emergence of a coherent set of new EU states that are determined to remain strong Atlanticists. The CEE countries can simultaneously become good Europeans by helping transform the European Union into a politically cohesive, economically competitive, and strategically vital region that can complement and work together with Washington to resolve numerous common challenges at the start of the twenty-first century.

IMPLICATIONS FOR U.S. POLICY

The European Union remains a work in progress and its final shape and structure cannot be easily predicted. In the interim, the union's future is contingent upon the political aftermath of the failure to approve and ratify the EU constitutional treaty. Some analysts speculate that rejection of the treaty will turn the union inward, forestall any further enlargement, and prevent the emergence of an effective EU security and foreign policy.[1] Whether such a scenario would weaken or strengthen transatlantic relations is a matter of debate. Some U.S. policy makers would prefer to deal with a more fractured EU and focus on stronger bilateral relations with individual EU capitals, but others believe that this would make each member state less effective in supporting or complementing U.S. policy and prone to disputes with their European partners.

For the CEE states that have entered the EU, the union has grown in importance in numerous domains—trade, foreign direct investment, social contacts, and cultural and educational interchanges. Although the process of integration seems unavoidable, it can also seriously erode transatlantic relations if it develops at the expense of CEE-U.S. ties. Washington needs to invest significant political capital to develop its new alliances and remodel its relations with the EU as a whole.

In recent years, U.S. policy analysts have concentrated on the deteriorating U.S. ties with traditional EU powers, especially France and Germany, although analysts have not yet systematically and comparatively assessed relations between the United States and the new NATO and EU members from central and eastern Europe. Policy makers have not sufficiently explored scenarios for the evolution of the EU itself following its enlargement eastward. It is insufficient merely to highlight the foreign policy dilemmas of the CEE states as they seek to balance their relations with the EU and the United States. Many commentators emphasize what is now common knowledge— CEE countries do not wish to make stark choices between the United States and the EU but instead are pursuing transatlantic complementarity in security questions. Such analyses lack a longer-term perspective on political orientations and public trends within individual CEE states, distinctive foreign policy priorities, and bilateral relations that are developing with Washington and the major EU capitals.

Surveys of CEE public opinion published in the United States and western Europe do not cover the range of questions on U.S.-CEE relations that need to be answered in the context of foreign policy directions since September 11, 2001. In addition, analyses of anti-Americanism throughout Europe do not delve deeply into the changing political and public landscape in CEE countries. Some essays focus on specific bilateral relations and assess a particular policy decision, such as the impact of the Iraq War, but they do not consider U.S.-CEE relations in a comparative context or their long-term impact on the NATO alliance.

A wealth of official and unofficial documentation—policy statements, policy papers, official interviews, independent analyses, and expert commentaries—is available on the subject of evolving transatlantic relations in each of the CEE states. Policy makers, in order to competently monitor a fast-changing Europe and assess the impact of enlargement on long-range U.S. foreign policy, need to thoroughly examine these rich sources of information. Moreover, the expertise of CEE policy makers and analysts needs to be fully appreciated and used in order to help influence the constructive evolution of the U.S.-EU relationship.

While the EU is struggling to find its identity, scope, and long-term mission, the NATO alliance is also in a prolonged period of flux as it seeks to find its own identity and mission in a post–Cold War world. NATO's security agenda and the agendas of its individual members have become more "diffuse, multifaceted, and complex as clear 'threats' to national and alliance security give way to more ambiguous and imprecise 'risks and challenges.'"[2] Clearly, the anti-terrorist campaign or any other contemporary international crisis does not have the same transatlantic adhesive force as the struggle against communism and Soviet expansion once did. Various NATO members exhibit contrasting national priorities and a variable willingness to contribute to NATO missions. Moreover, some western European capitals are emphasizing the EU's emerging security policy and even de-emphasizing their commitments to NATO. These trends have important implications for the new allies.

It is in the U.S. interest to ensure that it has dependable and predictable partners within the EU and areas of commonality with the new allies sufficient to avoid strategic divergence on essential security issues. Such a situation would help forestall the EU from developing into a potentially hostile bloc that might seek to oppose or neutralize U.S. policies on numerous foreign security and policy questions. Policy makers in the United States must accurately gauge political developments in each country because of their important impact on the reliability of both old and new allies. Much of central and eastern Europe senses that the United States is steadily withdrawing from the region, whether politically or economically, and Washington views the region as a secondary concern or through the prism of selected EU members. CEE countries perceive the U.S. diplomatic and business presence as shallow and shrinking compared with the growing western European role.

It is in the U.S. national interest to have a coherent and united European ally that can cooperate and complement the U.S. projection of political authority, economic strength, and military power. Conversely, a more Atlanticist EU may encourage a more multilateralist U.S. policy, at least on issues of primary concern on both sides of the Atlantic. In the best-case scenario, CEE inclusion in the EU will buttress the union's security capabilities and reinforce the transatlantic connection. In an alternative favorable scenario for Washington, the EU will prove unable to develop a coherent foreign policy that could challenge U.S. interests, but the majority of key European states will continue to maintain close ties with the United States. Regardless of the degree of European unity, the significance of any new ally would then be measured by that ally's contribution to transatlantic relations.

In a third scenario, favored by some U.S. policy analysts, the United States would actively try to disaggregate the EU through a modern-day version of divide and rule. The United States would work selectively with European partners, favor some states over others, promote political disputes between the European allies, reward the most loyal capitals, and undercut any emerging common EU foreign and security policy. Such an approach assumes that Washington would intensify its unilateralist approach. Dangers of such a policy include the possibility of increasing Euro-Gaullist trends in the EU, limiting the number and effectiveness of U.S. partners, and severely weakening an institution that could complement U.S. strategy around the globe.

A fuller comprehension of the motives, objectives, and capabilities of the new CEE allies will be essential for devising a durable U.S. strategy toward each country, the wider region, and the EU as a whole. Significant questions remain for the U.S. administration in the ongoing global campaign against unconventional insecurities, including the durability of the current U.S. coalition with the CEE states. Policy making is often based on short-term calculations of mutual goals rather than on long-term analysis of strategic interests and the enduring capabilities of various partners. The United States has been most attentive to the instrumentality of its recently formed alliances with central and eastern Europe in the context of NATO expansion and its campaigns against terrorists and rogue states. An analysis of the NATO alliance in the context of the evolution of both the EU and NATO can enhance understanding of Washington's support base in central and eastern Europe and the impact that European enlargement will have on transatlantic relations. Such an assessment can help provide a more solid foundation for the development of an effective and long-range U.S. policy that can enhance both U.S. and allied security.

In this equation, the Bush administration needs to reinforce ties with its new CEE allies as well as with more traditional partners. Political support for CEE priority issues—whether toward Russia, the East European neighbors, the Black Sea region, or the western Balkans—together with appropriate economic and business benefits may help guarantee more durable CEE commitments to the transatlantic relationship. Simultaneously, the challenge for the new allies is not simply balancing U.S. and EU interests but making these interests compatible, complementary, implementable, effective, and durable. The challenge for Washington is to transform the EU into a partner that complements U.S. strategic goals and does not obstruct or divert them.

The White House can reinvigorate the U.S. approach through more effective and active relations based on concrete political and economic commitments. For example, Washington can more resolutely support Warsaw's inclusionist eastern strategy and help implement lasting solutions to the "frozen conflicts" in Moldova and Georgia. U.S. military basing in central and eastern Europe could be tied to the development of major infrastructural projects that could benefit wider sectors of the population. The antiterrorist pact should involve a host of U.S. assistance programs such as civil emergency training, technical modernization for border guards, and the development of intelligence capabilities. U.S. defense companies that have shown a renewed interest in central and eastern Europe's military sector as the modernization process intensifies should be offered incentives to invest. Above all, a regular consultative process between Washington and the CEE states can be developed in which all sides can pinpoint their priorities and decide on the possibilities for coordinated action.

Such measures can help promote Washington's newest European partners as long-term allies that will calculate that their national interests call for maintaining a close relationship with the United States. At the same time, the U.S. administration will need to understand that it is in the U.S. national interest to ensure sufficient strategic and economic benefits for the CEE states in order to guarantee their commitment to the transatlantic relationship.

It is incumbent on the CEE capitals to define appropriate programs for developing bilateral links with the United States. However, public expectations of material benefits should not be raised too high in the CEE countries as they were before the Iraq War or in the midst of negotiations over the emplacement of U.S. military bases. Equally necessary is a U.S. strategic vision toward central and eastern Europe and the EU as a whole that will outlast any particular administration and outlive any specific policy. In sum, Washington needs to ensure that it will have a majority of dependable partners within the enlarging EU in order to avoid divergence on essential issues that could further undermine international security. Such a constructive strategy will require commitment and determination on both sides of the Atlantic, and Europe's new democracies can play an instrumental role.

RECOMMENDATIONS FOR U.S.-CEE RELATIONS

Countries on both sides of the Atlantic should reexamine and recalibrate their policies to reaffirm, reform, and strengthen transatlantic relations in light of the CEE countries' entry into both NATO and the European Union. The following steps could serve as the foundation for such a long-term strategy.

Political Investment

Washington needs to define clearly the purpose of its partnership with its new allies in central and eastern Europe and make long-term political investments to meet its goals. With the diminishing importance of the factors that brought the United States and central and eastern Europe closer together, including NATO membership and the Iraq War, U.S. leaders will have to look to future challenges and goals to rebuild the transatlantic relationship. They will need to ask some fundamental questions about the future of these relations: What does the United States need central and eastern Europe for? How important is this relationship? What kind of goals are envisaged in these partnerships? What are U.S. national interests in strengthening relations with the new European democracies? The CEE capitals must also soberly consider why they need the United States, how this relationship benefits their national interests, and how it can be strengthened.

Official declarations are insufficient to address these questions. A constructive and durable strategic dialogue needs to be developed not only between state and government leaders in the United States and central and eastern Europe but also among wider sectors of the political establishment, including parliamentarians and policy analysts. Bilateral and multilateral mechanisms need to be developed for purposes of regular consultations and with broad agendas on issues of common concern to all the parties. The United States and Poland have launched periodic bilateral consultations at the subministerial level, but this is insufficient. Annual consultative meetings could involve the U.S. secretary of state and CEE prime ministers or foreign ministers. More regular meetings could be held in response to a particular crisis and could include lower-ranking officials and specialist agencies.

The United States and its NATO and EU partners need to underscore that their alliance is vital for the national interests of all capitals. If the transatlantic partnership is to be renewed, the United States and the CEE states that are members of the EU will need to agree on two key issues: common priorities and joint strategies. The two sides may indeed share values and even long-term interests, but they need to agree on priorities and strategies before they can achieve specific foreign and security policy targets. Although they should prioritize the most important outstanding issues, they must address at the outset the less contentious questions, not the most problematic ones. Democracy building and security promotion have become vital components of the common agenda, and both sides can contribute in their own ways on specific issues.

The further removed an issue is from the immediate focus of national security, the more conditional the CEE-U.S. relationship is likely to be. In areas of common threats—combating international terrorist networks, WMD proliferation, dealing with regional trouble spots—the United States and CEE countries can devise durable joint strategies. CEE countries can help define joint priorities and capabilities as they work more closely with older EU members and with the United States. CEE countries may be prepared to have a Pax Americana with a strong U.S. superpower, but they need to understand what role they would play and how they would benefit from any U.S. grand strategy. Also needed is a broad dialogue on redefining the West in terms of identity, interests and objectives.[3] Some analysts argue that the designation "the West" has little practical relevance, but a dialogue on its meaning would help policy makers better understand the significance of transatlantic relations.

Refocusing NATO

For the CEE capitals, NATO remains the main structure of European security and political partnership with the United States. Hence, CEE countries oppose transforming NATO into a military toolbox or only a format for technical and operational consultation. To prevent the toolbox from quickly emptying, Washington will need to reinforce the NATO link by redefining and clarifying NATO's evolving role, achieving consensus on the organization's new challenges and its members' obligations, and making the alliance relevant and capable in a rapidly changing security environment. Disbanding NATO would be seen in central and eastern Europe as a U.S. withdrawal from Europe, as a strategic victory for Russia, and as the dawn of a new era of regional insecurity. Furthermore, the demise of NATO would be counterproductive for Europe because it would mean diminished security at greater cost to the European Union.

Berlin, Paris, and several other western European capitals believe that NATO is no longer the center of gravity in the transatlantic relationship, and they contend that the United States should not channel all of its policy instruments toward Europe through NATO. CEE capitals, however, exhibit little faith that the EU can fill the vacuum or become a credible security player in the near future. CEE governments do not welcome the weakening of NATO as an institution without a commensurate strengthening of the security functions of the EU with the active participation of CEE countries.

CEE states, as new members of NATO, will need to define their specific roles within a pact that is currently searching for its raison d'être. Steps can be taken to foster greater military cohesion and improve NATO's joint operations. Some even suggest forging a new Atlantic Charter to detail common security interests and agreed strategies to promote those interests, which would entail broadening NATO's 1999 Strategic Concept, redefining NATO's relations with other multinational institutions, and concretizing such concepts as prevention and preemption. However, U.S. leaders must be careful not to breed resentments among some EU partners that any new NATO initiative is intended to reassert U.S. dominance and undermine the EU's emerging security and foreign policy initiatives.

NATO can focus more intensively on transatlantic military coordination and coalition building in planning for expeditionary and special force warfare. To accomplish this, the United States must work closely with its new allies together with its traditional allies in raising public support for meeting future security challenges and backing NATO participation in distant missions.[4] Simply working with ad hoc coalitions of the willing on specific missions with partners possessing limited capabilities will prove insufficient for meeting future challenges. The reinforcement of the North Atlantic Council in the fall of 2005, with the involvement of senior policy personnel at the subministerial level, is a positive step in reviving the NATO alliance. Furthermore, the NATO summit scheduled for Riga, Latvia in November 2006 presents a valuable opportunity to redefine NATO's strategic mission and give the organization both direction and vitality.

A refocused NATO would also entail various forms of practical and technical support to CEE militaries for counterinsurgency and counterterrorism measures, closer coordination between defense ministries and interior ministries in combating unconventional threats, and a new system of financing international military operations, particularly for new allies that remain financially constrained. Eventually, each NATO member should be able to deploy up to half its forces abroad with up to ten percent actually deployed at any given time. Reaching this goal will be arduous but necessary, especially for CEE states that are either reducing and modernizing their forces or building completely new military organizations.

America's new allies are developing their own policies, particularly regarding their eastern frontiers and the western Balkans, where ensuring stability and security is of utmost importance. Washington should be more keenly attuned to the security threats emanating from those regions. Trafficking of drugs, weapons, and people as well as the potential for future civil or ethnic unrest and Russian intervention can be handled more effectively through closer U.S.-CEE cooperation and by benefiting from the NATO structure.

Despite EU endeavors to form a common European security and foreign policy independent of Washington, the contours of such a policy remain in dispute, with little prospect for agreement anytime soon. NATO remains the only viable organization that can buttress transatlantic security. Rather than bypassing NATO in dealing with crisis situations, Washington could aim to strengthen Alliance effectiveness. NATO's future role will be to prevent military conflict and a destabilizing crisis not simply within Europe, but along Europe's periphery. Security challenges posed by conflicts in the Caucasus, the Black Sea region, Central Asia, and the Middle East can be better managed through a more concerted transatlantic strategy in which the roles of NATO and the EU are more precisely defined. The next NATO summit will be a valuable opportunity to define and strengthen this relationship and provide a framework for joint actions.

At the operational level, the proposed 20,000-strong NRF should be fully activated as planned and reinforced as it develops. It can serve as a practical vehicle for NATO cooperation and integration in crisis response situations, including counterterrorism, military deterrence, peacekeeping, embargo enforcement, and humanitarian response.[5] Above all, the NRF could promote the transformation of European forces to meet the requirements of flexible warfare, rapid response, effective deployment, logistical support, and long-term sustainability. Its competence will also help improve mutual perceptions of actual capabilities across the Atlantic.

U.S.-EU Complementarity

The United States should not present the CEE governments with either/or choices: either the EU or NATO; either Europe or the United States. Regardless of their status with the EU, the CEE countries are intent on upholding their relations with the United States. Indeed, their close relations with Washington can help strengthen their position in the EU, while their increasing number and influence within the EU can help promote U.S. security interests. Hence, Washington should view the evolving EU as a complementary international entity that needs to be creatively and constructively nurtured and its unity and strength consistently supported. An enlarged and integrated EU can be politically, strategically, economically, and commercially beneficial for the United States. CEE officials closely monitor Washington's reactions to EU developments, including the EU constitutional crisis. White House support for a strong Europe has been well received among the new allies as it reinforces their own position in the union.

Because the EU is vitally important to both the old and new allies of the United States, the EU should also be important for the United States. The good relations between the older and newer EU member states should not be seen as threatening U.S. interests but as a valuable element in reinforcing the transatlantic relationship. Countries that resent the EU or are in conflict with other member states are unlikely to be reliable U.S. partners because they may swing in an isolationist direction or become too dependent on Washington to have any significant influence within the European Union. Moreover, a weak and internally divided EU will not be a stable or reliable diplomatic, economic, or security partner for the United States and could bring to the forefront those EU countries that would sideline the pro-Atlanticist states.

Continuing apprehensions about Russia's regional ambitions, the remaining echoes of the western Balkan conflicts, including unresolved status questions, the need for assistance in combating and curtailing cross-border crime and corruption, and the potential for more substantial business investment ensure that the CEE capitals will seek to maintain U.S. involvement in European affairs. At the same time, EU enlargement may alter the political balance within European institutions as any common EU policy is less likely to be dominated by the largest states but will instead be determined by compromises between diverse but often overlapping national interests in which the new allies will be represented.

Washington should take advantage of the Atlanticist commitment of the EU's newest members and make sure that it endures. Such a task will not be easy. Popular attitudes among residents of CEE countries, even in the most pro-U.S. countries, are moving closer to much of Western Europe on a range of issues. Most of the new EU entrants are dependant on the union's structural funds, and infrastructural projects under the EU umbrella are vital for these developing economies. As the EU's foreign and security policy evolves, new entrants may be inclined to better tune their policies with Brussels, depending on the issue. In addition, the generation of pro-U.S. elites in central and eastern Europe is gradually being replaced by younger people whose careers are increasingly tied to the EU. More citizens may therefore question why their country should remain closely tied to the United States.

To reverse the transatlantic rift, the United States needs to understand the evolution of EU decision making. Although ad hoc military and political coalitions were possible a few years ago, EU accession may cause CEE states to become more restricted and less flexible in their policy options. If America's new allies are given tangible incentives and concrete results, however, the process of European unification may actually benefit the United States as it could embed strong Atlanticist states in the expanding union. Washington will have little to fear from a militarily capable EU, especially an EU that maintains a close link with NATO, is not dominated by any specific powers, can defend European security, and is able to act as a more effective partner for the United States in various regional crisis zones.

At the end of 2005, NATO had twenty-six members and the EU had twenty-five, but only nineteen countries belonged to both organizations. As the EU becomes more involved in security issues and military operations and as NATO garners experience in modern combat operations and postconflict peacekeeping, the long-term relationship between NATO and the EU will need to be clarified. One important component of this process would be to specify that all EU members could ultimately become NATO members and that all NATO allies can accede to the European Union.[6] This would help forestall unnecessary duplication and even conflict between the two organizations, eliminate confusion over the roles and goals of both entities, and enable a more effective complementary security role.

Washington can also encourage a more independent EU political and military capability as long as this remains within a broader NATO framework.[7] Washington can thereby enhance coordinated security assistance to central and eastern Europe with the EU, especially as most of America's new allies are EU members. Washington must also acknowledge the constructive role played by the EU in spreading democracy and stability within a wider Europe by comprehensively supporting EU policies that promote these goals. Indeed, the prospect of EU membership has been one of the most important incentives for the CEE states as they pursue structural reforms and meet democratic standards. Hence, an enlarging EU is of direct national interest for the United States, and the European Union's effectiveness in managing security and stability both within the EU and along its expansive border will be a measure of its success and value to Washington.

Although the United States must broaden its consultation with Brussels and with individual EU members through existing U.S.-EU mechanisms and various institutions such as NATO, Washington must be careful in forging any bilateral agreements with the EU as an institution that may have several unintended and negative consequences.[8] First, such arrangements could bypass and weaken the NATO alliance and provide ammunition to EU capitals that prefer to sideline NATO. Second, such arrangements could promote the centralization of EU decision making and shift more power to France and Germany to the detriment of the CEE members and other strongly pro-U.S. European countries. Instead of a bilateral partnership, Washington should focus on pragmatic and effective multilateral arrangements that concentrate on specific common threats and problems and avoid conflicts that encourage anti-U.S. forces within the EU.

Pursuing Freedom and Democracy

The U.S. administration must better communicate its stated commitment to expanding human rights and democracy; this would help garner international support and reduce anti-American trends in public opinion. Both the EU and the United States seek to expand the democratic world, but their methods often differ as they work toward such an objective. In addition to advancing a more coordinated U.S.-EU response that can enhance the strengths of both partners, Washington should look more closely at what the CEE states can bring into this process. CEE officials point out that the region's experience with far-reaching political and economic transformations can serve as lessons for other aspiring democracies and help U.S. interests in promoting pluralistic systems in unstable regions. Washington should consider helping to fund a regional institute of democracy in a CEE capital, where foreign policy experts and parliamentary advisers could be trained and democracy practitioners could share their experiences with activists from newly democratized states.

In pursuit of freedom, democracy, and durable security on a global scale, the United States must work with its partners in the EU to develop a coherent, coordinated, and effective policy toward an increasingly authoritarian and imperialistically ambitious Russia, which may also face major internal instabilities in the years ahead. Above all, the NATO allies need to be clear that Moscow's attempts to prevent or reverse democratic changes among its neighbors will not be accepted but will be countered with effective U.S.-EU support for democratic forces along NATO's and the EU's eastern borders. Closer coordination of policy would also prevent the Kremlin from trying to drive a wedge between Europe and the United States. Even if the EU and NATO cannot offer an imminent prospect of membership to a particular East European state, they can enhance programs and links with such countries and send strong political messages that Europe is not complete until all of its countries become members of the continent's principal institutions.[9]

Rewarding New Allies

Iraq has been the most contentious issue in U.S.-CEE relations. The partisan dispute in the United States during the 2004 elections over the timing and justification for the war resonated in the CEE region, and the people of central and eastern Europe have increasingly questioned the rationale for their own commitment. The United States welcomed the initial eagerness of CEE states to contribute to the missions in Iraq and Afghanistan but thus far has fallen short in adequately rewarding their sacrifice. It is important for policy makers in Washington to distinguish between the way CEE states view their commitments in Iraq and elsewhere and the way the United States thinks they view their commitments. It is arrogant and dismissive to refer to coalition members as coerced partners, as some anti-Bush commentators have done, but it is also naive to conclude that they joined the effort purely out of pro-

U.S. sentiment. A certain level of pragmatism guided the policies of the CEE capitals even when they held doubts about the feasibility of "exporting democracy" to authoritarian Middle Eastern states.

Washington did not come to grips with two issues affecting CEE participation in Iraq: Iraqi debts and reconstruction contracts. Many CEE leaders were expecting U.S. help in recovering some of the Iraqi debt accumulated during the 1980s. Immediately after President Bush announced the end of major combat in Iraq in the summer of 2003, U.S. diplomats visited leaders of many of the CEE capitals and pressured them to forgive Iraq's debt. The new allies were unwilling to forgive the entire sums of their loans and, thus, have also sought to negotiate repayments in crude oil or discounts on oil deliveries. A portion of the debts could also be settled by signing postwar reconstruction contracts with CEE companies.

CEE specialists have significant reconstruction experience throughout the Middle East because they have been performing services in the region for more than twenty years. Their expertise is most notable in health care and construction. Despite hopes that CEE companies would participate in reconstruction in Iraq, so far very few contracts have been awarded to the new allies. Although U.S. embassies in the CEE region held numerous workshops introducing contracting regulations, central Europeans have questioned the process that in the future should be more transparent, competitive, and rewarding for loyal U.S. allies.

Economic, Social, and Cultural Interchange

Although the CEE region is not a major trading bloc and investment destination for the United States, it is certainly not marginal. Without greater economic interchange in trade and investment, U.S. interests and influences are likely to shrink and transatlantic ties will gradually weaken. In the economic arena, CEE officials and experts stress that U.S. investors and exporters could benefit from the increased opportunities that an expanded EU market could provide if U.S. firms boost their investments in high technology and computerization in CEE states. A more stable macroeconomic investment climate will also be created by the integration of the CEE countries in the euro zone.[10] U.S. business will thereby benefit from the uniformity of regulations in an enlarged EU, which can become an even more valuable economic partner and a stronger ally.

Cultural, social, academic, and educational contacts can also be enhanced as a consequence of CEE inclusion in the visa waiver program. Only a small sector of the CEE elite, including younger parliamentarians and executive branch officials, are familiar with the United States; and most citizens have had little

exposure to the breadth of U.S. culture and social life other than the stereotypes generated in cinema and music videos. The United States is less of a
tourist destination than it once was; the total number of visitors to the United
States from all the CEE countries in 2003 was only 434,000 out of a total number of EU visitors of more than 10.2 million. The number of students at U.S.
universities from CEE countries has been steadily declining; it dropped from
more than 20,000 in 2001 to a little more than 18,500 in 2003.[11] College students as well as young and well-qualified professionals from the CEE region
increasingly prefer western European locations instead of the United States.

Thus, the EU has become more attractive because of the absence of visa restrictions and more employment opportunities, and U.S.-CEE contacts among
educated elites as well as ordinary citizens have been undermined. Although
some of this is an inevitable result of EU enlargement and the elimination of
strict border regimes, U.S. policy has contributed to dissuading many CEE
citizens from traveling, working, or emigrating to the United States. Talented
CEE workers with great potential would benefit the United States, particularly in the field of applied research. Bilateral exchange programs should be
increased beginning at the high school level and greatly expanded at the university level; this would promote personal contacts and help build a new elite
knowledgeable about the United States. CEE states also need to display more
initiative in promoting such programs. Each CEE state, with budgetary inputs
from both the public and private sectors, can develop its long-term strategy
for consistently increasing economic, social, cultural, and educational interchange with the United States.

Military Basing

Many CEE officials are concerned about declining military assistance from
Washington. To counteract such a trend, CEE capitals have displayed a high
level of support for hosting U.S. military bases. Meanwhile, new security
challenges have prompted the United States to rethink its global military posture and focus on smaller, mobile, and rapidly deployable units that will require access to a network of staging posts for fuel and supplies. This realign-
ment is the major factor determining U.S. base relocations. Bulgaria, Poland,
and Romania—out of political, economic, and security considerations—announced their eagerness to host a permanent U.S. military presence, but the
slow pace and secrecy of the process has caused some enthusiasm to fade.

Washington announced plans for base reshuffling without providing a concrete strategy and timetable for CEE countries. Because the Washington announcement coincided with U.S. efforts to consolidate a coalition for intervention in Iraq as well as with disputes over the ICC, public opinion among

the new allies increasingly assumed that CEE countries were falsely lured by the promise of a U.S. military presence. Much needed are tangible guarantees for U.S. basing plans, a timetable, a plan of action, and an assessment of the bases' economic and security impact. The formal agreement with Romania in December 2005 and with Bulgaria in April 2006 to establish U.S. bases in these two countries helped to address some but not all of these issues. A U.S. military presence could also be an important exercise in public diplomacy because it would demonstrate a clear U.S. commitment to the security of CEE countries. Some CEE officials would welcome closer military-to-military relations with the United States, whether in the form of relations between special forces or other specialized units, more regular joint exercises and training missions, or the transfer of modern weapons technology.

In the longer term, Washington can better assist CEE states by supplying more tangible military aid and helping restructure their military budgets so they can participate effectively in U.S.-led operations.[12] Several CEE capitals would also welcome participation in the U.S. missile defense program as both a strategic defense and a source of military and economic development. Washington should closely evaluate the suitability of CEE countries as it positions elements of its anti-missile shield over the coming years.

Regular elections in all the CEE countries may encourage public expression of opposition to participating in U.S.-led overseas military or reconstruction missions. Unless voters in CEE countries believe the United States is rewarding them for their support despite generally negative public opinion toward Washington within the wider EU, the United States runs the risk of undermining its political leverage in the CEE region. CEE states did not enlist in the war against international terrorist networks and in the mission in Iraq because they felt directly threatened by Al Qaeda or Saddam Hussein, but as a result of their participation they now feel more exposed and vulnerable. Their close ties with Washington may have ensured they are now prime terrorist targets. Hence, the positive results of their ties with the United States need to be promoted and highlighted in order to ensure the durability of these relations.

Public Diplomacy

Washington needs a more effective public relations campaign that explains the importance of the U.S.-CEE relationship in both historical and contemporary perspectives. Political communication needs to be enhanced through better contacts with journalists, students, intellectuals, politicians, and NGOs and through more accurate and timely information about U.S. policy.[13] Part of the existing problem is that the CEE publics primarily understand the economic and security self-interests behind U.S. actions rather than the mutual benefits accruing from common goals and joint actions. The citizens of CEE countries also need a permanent reminder of the U.S. role in their liberation from Moscow and from communism, which could be accomplished by erecting monuments of remembrance in the CEE capitals and other commemorative and informational displays.

Washington must avoid placing its new allies in the unwelcome position of choosing between Europe and the United States. Assertive U.S. leadership in a unipolar world should not be presented and perceived as arrogance and unilateralism. The EU for its part must understand that an exclusive focus on diplomacy, international organizations, and soft power in dealing with pressing crises will further estrange Washington from Brussels and highlight to U.S. policy makers that the EU is not a serious security player. The principal partners should aim to consult closely during a crisis and avoid inflammatory rhetoric that ultimately assists anti-Western forces. CEE states can be useful in this endeavor because they support both hard and soft power and have major stakes in both their European and U.S. connections.

The United States can capitalize on the historical foundations of pro-Americanism, but it should not take these for granted. Decades of Radio Free Europe (RFE) and Voice of America (VOA) broadcasts, Fulbright scholarships, and educational exchanges produced a local elite that admired the U.S. political model. But the mission of public diplomacy is never complete, especially in a fast-changing world with numerous security challenges and a new generation that may be more pragmatic and even skeptical than their pro-U.S. predecessors. RFE unfortunately has discontinued its broadcasts in the region and VOA has a limited audience in many of these states. The United States needs a more attractive international television channel—for news, culture (both high culture and mass culture), education, entertainment, and sports—that appeals to all generations in central and eastern Europe.

CEE countries have graduated from U.S. Agency for International Development programs, and the spotlight for educational exchanges has moved to other regions of the world. This shift in U.S. active public diplomacy is unsettling and counterproductive. Washington must act to prevent the spread of anti-Americanism and should continue to sponsor informational, educational, academic, scientific, and cultural programs to strengthen bonds with an emerging generation of leaders and opinion makers. It must also answer not just domestic sources of anti-Americanism but also the anti-U.S. stance persistently promulgated by the Russian media in several CEE countries. Media from EU countries also often exhibit an anti-U.S. slant.

Public diplomacy in itself is unlikely to sway public opinion if wide-scale opposition to a particular U.S. policy already exists.[14] Instead, Washington must focus on regaining legitimacy for U.S. objectives and strategies through a combination of clear and persuasive argumentation, the development of bilateral partnerships, and efforts to work within the general parameters of international law and multinational institutions. Washington also needs to better highlight the shortcomings of international bodies in dealing with serious global threats. The first requirement for explaining the U.S. position toward various trouble spots is to have in place a prominent and proactive U.S. presence in each CEE country.

Defusing Controversies

U.S. public diplomacy will receive a boost if visa issues with the CEE countries are resolved. Citizens of CEE countries have traveled to western Europe without visas for at least half a decade, but they remain subject to fees, frustrating checks, and delays when they try to enter the United States. Including the new democracies that are members of both NATO and EU in the U.S. Visa Waiver Program would go far to advance U.S.-CEE relations. Inclusion would boost public diplomacy in a practical way and demonstrate that CEE citizens suffer no discrimination compared with the western European countries, many of which did not assist Washington in either Afghanistan or Iraq. The United States has no valid reason to fear mass immigration from CEE countries; according to regular opinion polls, the overwhelming majority of citizens in the region do not intend to leave their countries permanently, and those who do invariably possess the education, energy, and entrepreneurial skills that would make them into productive Americans.

The CEE states reject a U.S. approach that ties U.S. engagement with the new allies to the allies' uncritical support for U.S. foreign policy. Moreover, the description of the NATO alliance as a toolbox both denigrates the identity of the new allies and creates the image of the United States as an opportunistic power that will abandon its allies when they are no longer useful. Divisive and derisive terminology from the U.S. side feeds perceptions of U.S. politicking and could erode the U.S.-CEE relationship and lead to greater rifts in the future. Public opposition to U.S. policy or resistance to involvement in U.S.-led missions could also increase the specter of anti-Americanism.

Engaging Emerging Allies

Pressing regional questions of direct concern to the CEE countries will necessitate greater U.S. engagement, U.S.-EU complementarity, and closer policy coordination among the CEE capitals. In particular, the eastern region between central and eastern Europe and Russia remains unstable and uncertain. America's new allies seek greater clarity in U.S. policy toward Russia and the wider region and more resolute support for Russian democratization and the curtailment of Moscow's regional neoimperialist ambitions. A long-term commitment to democracy and security in these states would add substance to President Bush's global initiative on behalf of spreading freedom and democracy.

It is in the direct national interest of the United States to intensify U.S. engagement with the eastern European states that currently remain outside the EU and NATO structures. Their inclusion in both organizations and the creation of a more stable and wider Europe would help expand and consolidate democratic systems, open up new markets, stabilize Washington's new allies, and increase the number of potential U.S. partners.

To underscore its more activist and transformational approach, the United States should remove the label "Eurasia" from all U.S. government institutions. Just as the three Baltic states were never officially recognized by the United States as part of the Soviet Union, the eastern European states bordering Russia today should not be defined as part of a grand Eurasian or post-Soviet space in which Russia predominates. Such labeling is inaccurate and insulting to the citizens of diverse countries with divergent aspirations. Labelling affects perception and creates a strong impression that Washington and Brussels will keep these states at a distance and accept the premise that some eastern European states should remain subservient to Russia's national interests.

Alongside such political redefinitions, the eastern European countries should be consistently and constructively involved in the process of their transformation into stable democracies and credible aspirants for the EU and NATO. CEE capitals support a concerted U.S.-EU approach in dealing with neighboring countries and regions; however, where the EU seems to be failing, Washington must take the lead and spearhead the "eastern dimension."

- The Bush administration has called for greater involvement by Poland, Lithuania, and other nearby CEE states in the democratic transformation of Belarus. Washington, Brussels, and the EU member states need to give this approach more substance in terms of political and financial support for opposition activists and even some disillusioned government officials as they become engaged in the prolonged struggle for democratic change after the March 2006 presidential elections.
- Southeastern Europe overlaps with the Black Sea region; hence, Romania and Bulgaria are keenly interested in promoting greater involvement with Ukraine, Moldova, Georgia, Armenia, and Azerbaijan in a broader regional format. Washington needs to seek a more durable engagement in the three Caucasian states by working with its new allies in central and eastern Europe and by offering each the prospect of security protection and eventual membership in NATO.

- The stability and territorial integrity of Moldova are of grave concern to Romania and other nearby CEE states. Washington can pursue a more active policy in reintegrating the divided state, discouraging Russian interference, promoting democratization, combating the criminal networks in Transnistria, and extending to Moldovans the prospect of a closer partnership with the United States.

- Ukraine must still evolve into a stable pro-Western state. Although Russia views Ukraine as the main prize in a strategic tug-of-war between the Atlantic and Eurasian-Russian options, many Western states seem unwilling to damage relations with Moscow by more resolutely helping to prepare Ukraine for NATO and EU membership. The United States can provide the democratically elected Ukrainian government, whatever its composition, with an attractive counteroption to Moscow's dominance, including membership in NATO and better defense cooperation, if Kyiv undertakes a sustained effort at structural reform. Currently Ukraine has only restricted relations with NATO, which reinforces the perception that Ukraine is a peripheral state and not a genuine partner.

- In the Western Balkans, unresolved political disputes between Kosova and Serbia are of direct concern to neighboring new allies, especially Hungary, Romania, Bulgaria, and Slovenia. Moreover, Washington and Brussels need to make greater progress in securing NATO and EU membership for the three European signatories of the U.S.-Adriatic Charter—Albania, Croatia, and Macedonia—and include Montenegro in the process. The region will require firmer U.S. leadership alongside the EU in moving each of these countries, together with Bosnia-Herzegovina, Serbia, and Kosova toward institutional stability, structural reform, economic development, regional cooperation, and eventual international integration. A priority should be the development of effective and sustainable statehood for all western Balkan countries. The EU will play a major role in the western Balkans because of its approximately 30,000 troops in the region and its peacekeeping responsibilities in Bosnia-Herzegovina. The European Union has also established and deployed to Macedonia a 5,000-strong EU police force. Nevertheless, a prominent U.S. role in ensuring an international political status for each West Balkan state remains essential for durable security in the region.

NOTES

1. Charles Grant, "A British No Would Destroy More Than the Treaty," *Financial Times*, March 16, 2005.

2. Adrian Hyde-Price, "Continental Drift? Transatlantic Relations in the Twenty-First Century," 5.

3. German foreign policy officials, discussions with the authors, Berlin and Munich, June 2005.

4. Simon, *NATO Expeditionary Operations*, 3, 33–34.

5. Michael Mihalka, "NATO Response Force: Rapid? Responsive? A Force?" 67–79.

6. Simon Serfaty, ed., *Visions of the Atlantic Alliance: The United States, the European Union, and NATO* (Washington, D.C.: CSIS, 2005).

7. Peter W. Rodman, "Drifting Apart? Trends in US-European Relations," vi.

8. Van Oudenaren, "Containing Europe," 57–64.

9. Some analysts have also proposed partial EU membership, including a "variable geometry" in which countries could participate in selected EU structures and policies and opt out of others, that might help maintain the momentum of enlargement without alienating the West European states. See Charles Grant, "Can Variable Geometry Save EU Enlargement?" *Centre for European Reform Bulletin* October/November 2005, no. 44, www.cer.org.uk/articles/44_grant.html. Such arrangements will be opposed, however, by both western European federalists and CEE countries that oppose the emergence of an avant-garde that could potentially sideline the interests of new EU members.

10. Michael Baun, "The Implications of EU Enlargement for the United States," *Perspectives* 21 (Winter 2003/2004): 28.

11. U.S. Department of Homeland Security, "Yearbook of Immigration Statistics," 2004, http://uscis.gov/graphics/shared/statistics/yearbook/index.htm.

12. Radek Sikorski, "Defense Reform in Europe: The Case of Poland," *European Outlook* (July–August 2005), www.aei.org/publications/pubID.22985/pub_detail.asp.

13. For valuable recommendations on how to enhance U.S. public diplomacy on a global scale, see Stephen Johnson, Helle C. Dale, and Patrick Cronin, "Strengthening U.S. Public Diplomacy Requires Organization, Coordination, and Strategy," *Heritage Foundation Backgrounder*, no. 1875 (August 5, 2005), www.heritage.org/Research/NationalSecurity/bg1875.cfm.

14. Robert W. Tucker, "The Sources of American Legitimacy," *Foreign Affairs* 83, no. 6 (November/December 2004).

Selected Refrences

Ágh, Attila. "Smaller and Bigger States in the EU25: The Eastern Enlargement and Decision-Making in the EU," *Perspectives* 21 (Winter 2003/2004).

Ash, Timothy Garton. *Free World: America, Europe, and the Surprising Future of the West* (New York: Random House, 2004).

Asmus, Ronald D., and Alexandr Vondra. "The Origins of Atlanticism in Central and Eastern Europe," *Cambridge Review of International Affairs* 18, no. 2 (July 2005).

Barany, Zoltan. "Hungary: An Outpost on the Troubled Periphery," in *America's New Allies: Poland, Hungary, and the Czech Republic in NATO*, ed. Andrew A. Michta (Seattle: University of Washington Press, 1999).

Bilcik, Vladimir. "Slovakia," in *Bigger EU, Wider CFSP, Stronger ESDP? The View From Central Europe*, ed. Antonio Missiroli (Paris: The European Union Institute for Security Studies, Occasional Papers No. 34, April 2002).

Blinken, Anthony. "The False Crisis over the Atlantic," *Foreign Affairs* 80, no. 3 (May/June 2001).

Bojkov, Victor D. "Neither Here, Not There: Bulgaria and Romania in Current European Politics," *Communist and Post-Communist Studies* 37, no. 4 (December 2004).

Browning, Christopher. "Complementarities and Differences in EU and US Policies in Northern Europe," *Journal of International Relations and Development* 6, no. 1 (March 2003).

Browning, Christopher S., and Pertti Joenniemi. "The European Union's Two Dimensions: The Eastern and the Northern," *Security Dialogue* 34, no. 4 (December 2003).

Brzezinski, Zbigniew. *The Choice: Global Domination or Global Leadership* (New York: Basic Books, 2004).

Budryte, Dovile. "The Dilemma of 'Dual Loyalty': Lithuania and Transatlantic Tensions," in *Old Europe, New Europe and the U.S.*, edited by Tom Lansford and Blagovest Tashev (London: Ashgate, 2005).

Bugajski, Janusz. *Cold Peace: Russia's New Imperialism* (Westport, CT: Praeger/CSIS, 2004).

Cimbalo, Jeffrey L. "Saving NATO From Europe," *Foreign Affairs* 83, no. 6 (November/December 2004).

Cimoszewicz, Wlodzimierz. "Poland in the European Union: What Foreign Policy?" Public address given at the Polish Institute of International Affairs, May 22, 2003, *The Polish Foreign Affairs Digest* 3, no. 3 (8) (2003).

Cooley, Alexander. "Base Politics," *Foreign Affairs* 84, no. 6 (November/December 2005).

CsergŒ, Zsuzsa, and James M. Goldgeier. "Nationalist Strategies and European Integration," *Perspectives on Politics* 2, no. 1 (March 2004).

Debeljak, Ales. *The Hidden Handshake: National Identity and Europe in the Post-Communist World* (Lanham, MD: Rowman & Littlefield, 2004).

Dunay, Pál. "The Half-Hearted Transformation of the Hungarian Military," *European Security* 14, no. 1 (March 2005).

Falkowski, Mateusz. "Attitudes of the Poles Towards the United States of America and Transatlantic Relations," in *Bridges Across the Atlantic? Attitudes of Poles, Czechs and Slovaks Toward the United States*, edited by Lena Kolarska-Bobinska, Jacek Kucharczyk, and Piotr Maciej Kaczynski (Warsaw: Instytut Spraw Publicznych, 2005).

Gajewski, Jacek. "Visegrad Cooperation," in *Yearbook of Polish Foreign Policy, 2004*, ed. Barbara Wizimirska (Warsaw: Polish Ministry of Foreign Affairs, 2005).

Gogolewska, Agnieszka. "Public Images of Security, Defense, and the Military in Poland," in *The Public Image of Defense and the Military in Central and Eastern Europe*, ed. Marie Vlachova (Geneva: Geneva Centre for the Democratic Control of Armed Forces [DCAF], 2003).

Gnesotto, Nicole. "Introduction, ESDP: Results and Prospects," in *EU Security and Defence Policy: The First Five Years (1999–2004)* (Paris: European Union, Institute for Security Studies, 2004).

Grabbe, Heather. "Poland: The EU's New Awkward Partner," *CER Bulletin*, no. 34 (February/March 2004).

Gyárfášová, Olga. "Perception of the United States in Central Europe—The Slovak Case," in *Bridges Across the Atlantic? Attitudes of Poles, Czechs and Slovaks Towards the United States*, edited by Lena Kolarska-Bobinska, Jacek Kucharczyk, Piotr Maciej Kaczynski (Warsaw: Institute of Public Affairs, 2005).

Gyárfášová, Olga, and Marek Stastny, "Priorities and Sources of Security Policies—Slovakia," in *"Easternization" of Europe's Security Policy,* edited by Tomáš Valášek and Olga Gyárfášová (Bratislava: Institute for Public Affairs, 2004).

Halper, Stefan, and Jonathan Clarke. *America Alone: The Neo-Conservatives and the Global Order* (New York: Cambridge University Press, 2004).

Hanley, Sean. "From Neo-Liberalism to National Interests: Ideology, Strategy, and Party Development in the Euroscepticism of the Czech Right," *East European Politics and Societies* 18, no. 3 (2004).

Harrington, Joseph F. *American-Romanian Relations, 1989–2004: From Pariah to Partner* (New York: Columbia University Press, 2004).

Hunter, Robert E. "A Forward-Looking Partnership: NATO and the Future of Alliances," *Foreign Affairs* 85, no. 5 (September/October 2004).

Hyde-Price, Adrian. "Continental Drift? Transatlantic Relations in the Twenty-First Century," *Defense Studies* 2, no. 2 (Summer 2002).

Ilves, Toomas Hendrik. "The Pleiades Join the Stars: Transatlanticism and Eastern Enlargement," *Cambridge Review of International Affairs* 18, no. 2 (July 2005).

Ionescu, Mihail E. "Romania's Position Towards the Evolution of the Transatlantic Link," in *Old Europe, New Europe and the U.S.: Renegotiating Transatlantic Security in the Post 9/11 Era*, edited by Tom Lansford and Blagovest Tashev (Aldershot, UK: Ashgate, 2005).

Kapiszewski, Andrzej, and Chris Davis. "Poland's Security and Transatlantic Relations," in *Old Europe, New Europe, and the U.S.: Renegotiating Transatlantic Security in the Post 9/11 Era,* edited by Tom Lansford and Blagovest Tashev (Aldershot, UK: Ashgate, 2005).

Knowles, Vanda. "Security and Defence in the New Europe: Franco-Polish Relations—Victim of Neglect?" *Defence Studies* 2, no. 2 (2002).

Kolodziej, Edward A. "Introduction: NATO and the Longue Duree," in *Almost NATO: Partners and Players in Central and Eastern European Security*, ed. Charles Krupnick (Lanham, MD: Rowman & Littlefield, 2003).

Kostadinova, Tatiana."East European Public Support for NATO Membership Fears and Aspirations," *Journal of Peace Research* 37, no. 2 (2000).

Krastev, Ivan. "The Anti-American Century?" *Journal of Democracy* 15, no. 2 (April 2004).

Kuzniar, Roman, and Andrzej Szeptycki. "The Role of the United States in the Foreign Policy of the Third Republic of Poland," in *Bridges Across the Atlantic? Attitudes of Poles, Czechs and Slovaks Toward the United States*, edited by Lena Kolarska-Bobinska, Jacek Kucharczyk, and Piotr Maciej Kaczynski (Warsaw: Instytut Spraw Publicznych, 2005), 139.

Lagerspetz, Mikko. "How Many Nordic Countries? Possibilities and Limits of Geopolitical Identity Construction," *Journal of Cooperation and Conflict: Journal of the Nordic International Studies Association* 38, no. 1.

Lang, Kai-Olaf. "The German-Polish Security Partnership Within the Transatlantic Context—Convergence or Divergence?" *Defense Studies* 2, no. 2 (2002).

———. "Populism in Central and Eastern Europe: A Threat to Democracy or Just Political Folklore?" *Slovak Foreign Policy Affairs* 6, no. 1 (Spring 2005).

Marusiak, Juraj. "Poland as Regional Power and Polish-Slovak Relations," *Slovak Foreign Policy Affairs* 1 (2001).

Maull, Hanns W. "Europe and the New Balance of Global Order," *International Affairs* 81, no. 4 (July 2005).

Mead, Walter Russell. "Goodbye to Berlin? Germany Looks Askance at Red State America," *National Interest* (Spring 2004).

Meszerics, Tamás. "The Security Policy of Hungary," in *"Easternization" of Europe's Security Policy,* edited by Tomáš Valášek and Olga Gyárfášová (Bratislava: Institute for Public Affairs, 2004).

Michalowski, Stanislaw. "Poland's Relations With Germany," in *Yearbook of Polish Foreign Policy, 2004*, ed. Barbara Wizimirska (Warsaw: Polish Ministry of Foreign Affairs, 2005).

Michnik, Adam. "What Europe Means for Poland," *Journal of Democracy* 14, no. 4 (4 October 2003).

Mihalka, Michael. "NATO Response Force: Rapid? Responsive? A Force?" *Connections: The Quarterly Journal* 4, no. 2 (Summer 2005).

Minchev, Ognyan, Valeri Ratchev, and Marin Lessenski. *Bulgaria for NATO 2002* (Sofia: Institute for Regional and International Studies, 2002).

Missiroli, Antonio. "Central Europe between the EU and NATO," *Survival* 46, no.4 (Winter 2004–2005).

Moisi, Dominique. "Whither the West?" *Foreign Affairs* 82, no. 6 (November/December 2003).

Moravcsik, Andrew. "Striking a New Transatlantic Bargain: Back on Track," *Foreign Affairs* 82, no. 4 (July/August 2004).

Nicolaidis, Kalypso. "We, the Peoples of Europe...," *Foreign Affairs* 83, no. 6 (November/December 2004).

Onyszkiewicz, Janusz. "The Central Issue for NATO," *Baltic Defence Review* 1, no. 11 (2004).

Osica, Olaf. "In Search of a New Role: Poland in Euro-Atlantic Relations," *Defense Studies* 2, no. 2 (Summer 2002).

———. "Poland: A New European Atlanticist at a Crossroads?" *European Security* 13, no. 4 (2004).

Paszewski, Tomasz. "Przyszlosc CFSP/ESDP A Stosunki Transatlantyckie: Punkt Widzenia Polski i Francji," [The Future of the CSFD/ESDP and Transatlantic Relations: The Point of View of Poland and France] (Center For International Relations, Warsaw, April 24, 2004).

Pelczynska-Nalecz, Katarzyna. "The Enlarged European Union and its Eastern Neighbors: Problems and Solutions," (Center for Eastern Studies, Warsaw, October 2003).

Piatas, Czeslaw. "Poland's Military Contribution to Transatlantic Security Policy," *Military Technology* (Monch Publishing Group, Bonn, Germany) 24, no. 8 (August 2000).

Rhodes, Matthew. "Whose Trojan Horses?" *International Affairs* 57, no. 4 (Autumn 2002).

———. "Central Europe and Iraq: Balance, Bandwagon, or Bridge?" *Orbis* 48, no. 3 (Summer 2004).

Rubin, Barry, and Judith Colp Rubin. *Hating America: A History* (Oxford: Oxford University Press, 2004).

Samson, Ivo. "Slovakia," in *Old Europe, New Europe and the US: Renegotiating Transatlantic Security in the Post 9/11 Era*, edited by Tom Lansford and Blagovest Tashev (Burlington: Ashgate, 2005).

Schmitt, Burkard. "European Capabilities: How Many Divisions?" in *EU Security and Defence Policy: The First Five Years (1999–2004)*, ed. Nicole Gnesotto (Paris: European Union, Institute for Security Studies, 2004).

Sedivy, Jiri, and Marcin Zaborowski. "Old Europe, New Europe and Transatlantic Relations," *European Security* 13, no. 3 (Autumn 2004).

Simon, Jeffrey. *NATO Expeditionary Operations: Impacts upon New Members and Partners*, Occasional Paper no. 1 (Washington, D.C.: National Defense University Press, Institute for National Strategic Studies, March 2005).

Smith, Karen E. *The Making of EU Foreign Policy: The Case of Eastern Europe*, 2nd ed. (New York: Palgrave Macmillan, 2004).

————."The Outsiders: The European Neighborhood Policy," *International Affairs* 81, no. 4 (July 2005).

Smith, Michael E. *Europe's Foreign and Security Policy: The Institutionalization of Cooperation* (Cambridge: Cambridge University Press, 2004).

Stachura, Jadwiga. "Poland in Transatlantic Relations," in *Yearbook of Polish Foreign Policy, 2004*, ed. Barbara Wizimirska (Warsaw: Polish Ministry of Foreign Affairs, 2005), 125.

Szayna, Thomas S. "The Czech Republic: A Small Contributor or a 'Free Rider'?" in *America's New Allies*, ed. Andrew Michta (Seattle and London: University of Washington Press, 1999).

Szayna, Tomasz. *NATO Enlargement 2000–2015, Determinants and Implications for Defense Planning and Shaping* (Santa Monica, CA: RAND, 2003).

Tashev, Blagovest. "In Search of Security: Bulgaria's Security Policy in Transition," in *Old Europe, New Europe and the US: Renegotiating Transatlantic Security in the Post 9/11 Era*, edited by Tom Lansford and Blagovest Tashev (Aldershot, UK: Ashgate, 2005).

Tucker, Robert W. "The Sources of American Legitimacy," *Foreign Affairs* 83, no. 6 (November/December 2004).

Vachudova, Milada Anna. *Europe Undivided: Democracy, Leverage, and Integration after Communism* (Oxford: Oxford University Press, 2005).

Valašek, Tomas. "New EU Members in Europe's Security Policy," *Cambridge Review of International Affairs* 18, no. 2 (July 2005).

Valki, László. "Hungary," in *Old Europe, New Europe and the US: Renegotiating Transatlantic Security in the Post 9/11 Era*, edited by Tom Landsford and Blagovest Tashev (Burlington, VT: Ashgate Publishing Company, 2005).

Van Oudenaren, John. Uniting Europe: *An Introduction to the European Union*, 2nd ed. (Lanham, MD: Rowman & Littlefield, 2005).

————. Containing Europe," *National Interest* (Summer 2005).

Vancura, Petr. "Czech Republic's Role with Regard to the Trans-Atlantic Security Challenges," in *Old Europe, New Europe and the US: Renegotiating Transatlantic Security in the Post 9/11 Era,* edited by Tom Lansford and Blagovest Tashev (Burlington: Ashgate, 2005).

Wagrowska, Maria. "Polish Participation in the Armed Intervention and Stabilization Mission in Iraq," *Reports & Analyses* (Center for International Relations, Warsaw), May 2005, 08/04.

Wisniewski, Dariusz. "Relations Between Poland and the United States," in *Yearbook of Polish Foreign Policy, 2004*, ed. Barbara Wizimirska (Warsaw: Polish Ministry of Foreign Affairs, 2005).

Zaborowski, Marcin. *From America's Protégé to Constructive European: Poland's Security Policy in the 21st Century*, Occasional Paper no. 56 (European Union: Institute for Security Studies, December 2004).

————. "Between Power and Weakness: Poland—A New Actor in the Transatlantic Security," *Reports & Analyses* (Center for International Relations, Warsaw), September 2003, 4/03/A: 4.

Zarycki, Tomasz. "Uses of Russia: The Role of Russia in the Modern Polish National Identity," *East European Politics and Societies* 18, no. 4 (Fall 2004).

Index

About the Authors

Janusz Bugajski is the director of the New European Democracies Project and senior fellow at the Center for Strategic & International Studies. He chairs the South Central Europe (Balkans) Area Studies program for U.S. Foreign Service Officers at the Foreign Service Institute, U.S. Department of State. His books include *Cold Peace: Russia's New Imperialism* (2004), *Political Parties of Eastern Europe: A Guide to Politics in the Post-Communist Era* (2002), and *Toward an Understanding of Russia: New European Perspectives* (2002).

Ilona Teleki is the deputy director of the New European Democracies Project and a fellow at the Center for Strategic & International Studies.